Praise for Susan Kepner's biography on M.L. Boonlua Debyasuvarn,
A Civilized Woman

"An intimate view of an extraordinary life. M.L. Boonlua's passage from precocious child of an aristocratic lineage under the absolute monarchy to fiery debater in the liberal explosion after 1973 cuts across the social upheavals of twentieth-century Thailand. Susan Kepner succeeds in conveying the sheer complexity of her life, resulting in not only a fine biography and literary appreciation but also a unique essay in social history."

—Chris Baker, historian and writer, co-translator of *Khun Chang Khun Phaen*

"When Boonlua Kunchon was born to one of her father's many consorts in 1911, he was the official in charge of the Siamese king's elephants and the impresario of all Grand Palace entertainments, and she was his thirty-second child. By the time she died in 1982, Boonlua was one of Thailand's most prominent novelists, educators, and literary historians. Susan Kepner's biography is an authoritative and highly readable account of a fascinating woman whose life encompassed much of Thailand's turbulent twentieth century."

—Alan Elms, Emeritus Professor of Psychology, University of California, Davis

"This is not only an excellent biography of a unique Siamese lady, but it is also a wonderful social history of Siam from the reign of Rama VI to the end of the twentieth century. Anyone who wants to understand the subtleties of Thai culture and the delicacies of personal interaction should not fail to read this book."

—S. Sivaraksa, a Thai public intellectual

"Susan Kepner stands out among observers of Thailand in pairing her familiarity with its twentieth-century social elite with an unsentimental perspective on that elite's place in Thai history and society. Her deeply affecting biography of M.L. Boonlua Debyasuvarn reveals the inadequacy of standard invocations of Thai 'culture' and 'tradition' by turning to Thai intellectual, social, and literary history to offer a challenging and invaluable understanding of the continuities between the Thailand of 1910–20 and that of the 1980s and beyond."

—Michael J. Montesano, Visiting Research Fellow, ˆSoutheast Asian Studies, Singapore

"The author succeeds brilliantly in making M.L. Boonlua come alive as a real human being, bringing out both her virtues and her shortcomings. M.L. Boonlua's illustrious career, breaking trail while navigating sexism and prejudice in postwar Thailand, holds poignant and illuminating lessons for a country seeking to reinvent itself in contemporary times. Her historically informed yet thoroughly modern worldview, her understanding of the inevitability of change, and her struggle for balance within that context, all point to an exceptionally learned mind, and yes, a civilized one too! Her enduring wisdom, life-long contributions, and unassuming repartee in a male-dominated world will ensure her place in the pantheon of modern Thai intellectuals."

—Ambhorn Meesook, President, Foundation for Life-long Education

"Susan Kepner has produced a wonderfully balanced and perceptive account of the life and work of the complex and often 'difficult' M.L. Boonlua, which draws on her extensive and revealing interviews with M.L. Boonlua's family members, colleagues, and former students."

—David Smyth, Senior Lecturer in Thai, SOAS, University of London

"The exceptional Boonlua Debyasuvarn comes to life with all her piercing intelligence, wit, and eccentricity in Susan Kepner's biography, *A Civilized Woman*. From her privileged early childhood, to her grief-stricken teenage years, through an adulthood intricately linked with Thailand's tumultuous politics, to recognition as one of Thailand's top intellectuals and finding true love—this is the intriguing life story of a woman born before her time, a bridge between old Siam's feudal past and Thailand's modernity."

—Sanitsuda Ekachai, Editorial Pages Editor, *Bangkok Post*

"With elegant prose and occasional humor, Susan Kepner documents the difficult life of the uncomely but brilliant royal, M.L. Boonlua, a complicated liberal traditionalist whose educational ideal for Thailand—to balance *oprom* with *sueksa*—holds currency today. By situating the biography in a social history covering four tumultuous reigns, Kepner dramatizes both the biological fragility of monarchies and the limitations of reformers in a continuing quest for lasting democracy."

—John Hartmann, Board of Trustees,
Northern Illinois University

A CIVILIZED WOMAN

A CIVILIZED WOMAN

M.L. Boonlua Debyasuvarn and the Thai Twentieth Century

SUSAN FULOP KEPNER

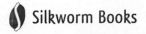

Silkworm Books

ISBN: 978-616-215-061-6

Published in 2013 by

Silkworm Books
6 Sukkasem Road, T. Suthep
Chiang Mai 50200 Thailand
info@silkwormbooks.com
http://www.silkwormbooks.com

Cover design by COVERKITCHEN

Typeset in Minion Pro 10 pt. by Silk Type
Printed in Thailand by O. S. Printing House, Bangkok

5 4 3 2 1

For my husband, Dr. Charles H. Kepner, whose belief that I must do what I was meant to do in the world has been unwavering, and whose steadfast love has sustained me in the work of making that happen

CONTENTS

FOREWORD

Susan Kepner should be commended for this biography of M.L. Boonlua Debyasuvarn, *A Civilized Woman: M.L. Boonlua Debyasuvarn and the Thai Twentieth Century*. If M.L. Boonlua were alive, she would have approved of this portrayal of her as she really was.

Based on a number of written sources including correspondences, conversations, and interviews, Kepner weaves a candid and vivid picture of M.L. Boonlua against the social, political, and cultural background of Thailand's twentieth century. She was first seen as an outspoken child prodigy whose father was of royal lineage and who held many high positions in the royal court of King Rama V. Her early education was at home, where basic knowledge of Thai language and Buddhism were gradually instilled in her, and music and dance were part of her daily life. Due to her father's modern outlook, she was sent to Catholic convent schools both in Penang and in Thailand. Having been exposed to two cultures at a young age, she emerged as an independent thinker with intercultural perspective and understanding. Kepner clearly shows how these exceptional qualities of Boonlua served as guiding principles that led her through the turbulent years of rapid change in the twentieth century.

After reading this biography, one cannot but agree that M.L. Boonlua was indeed a "civilized woman." All through her life she had been a bridge linking the old era and the new, the East and the West.

The year 2012 commemorated the centenary of Boonlua's birth. This biography can be considered a grand finale. It serves as a perfect tribute to Boonlua, in remembrance and celebration of her life.

Ms. Nitaya Masavisut
Vice President
M.L. Boonlua Debyasuvarn Fund

ACKNOWLEDGMENTS

First, I wish to thank my friend Anong Lertrakskul, who contributed so much to this biography. I treasure our conversations and correspondence concerning the writings and lives of Thai writers over many years.

Many people generously shared their memories of M.L. Boonlua with me and their thoughts concerning her life and work. In particular, I would like to thank Khunying Ambhorn Meesook; Emeritus Professor Chetana Nagavajara of Silpakorn University, Bangkok; and Professor M.L. Pattaratorn Chiraprawat of California State University at Sacramento.

Professor Nitaya Masavisut, a friend of many decades who also was a colleague and friend of M.L. Boonlua, provided insights into the depth and meaning of Boonlua's contributions to Thai literary criticism and to the teaching of Thai literature. She also shared poignant and sometimes humorous stories about Boonlua's great gifts as a friend and mentor. I am grateful to D. Michael Bear, M.D., for his advice, suggestions, and informed opinions in regard to health issues in the lives of M.L. Boonlua and her sister M.L. Buppha Kunchon Nimmanhemin; and to Dr. Larry Smith, former Director of the East-West Center at the University of Hawaii, Manoa, who shared years of correspondence between himself and M.L. Boonlua.

Professor Herbert P. Phillips contributed so very much to this biography, and I am particularly indebted to him for sharing the taped interviews he conducted with M.L. Boonlua during the late 1960s. The sound of her voice has been an incalculable gift.

To my wise and encouraging publisher, Trasvin Jittidecharak, and my excellent editor at Silkworm Books, Susan Offner, your patience and faith have sustained me as I labored to put at least some of M.L. Boonlua's extraordinary life between covers.

I am grateful for the support of the M.L. Boonlua Debyasuvarn Fund in Bangkok, and the Faculty of Arts at Silpakorn University, Nakhon Pathom, which M.L. Boonlua founded in 1968 and to which she donated her personal library. There, I found friendship, advice, and the astute observations of Professors Wibha Kongkanan, Khunying Vinita Diteeyont, and other members of the Department of Thai Language and Literature.

Finally, I wish to thank my dear husband, Dr. Charles H. Kepner, for his constant, good-natured support of all things that have interested me, including this biography.

INTRODUCTION

Boonlua Kunchon Debyasuvarn was born in 1911, the first and only child of her mother, a classical Thai dancer, and the thirty-second child of her father, a high-ranking nobleman named Chao Phraya Thewet. There are people who seem to have been born to play an important role in the great events of their nation, and Boonlua was such a person. Not only did she live through the overthrow of the absolute monarchy in 1932, the curious and difficult years of the Second World War, and the frequent episodes of social and political turmoil and chaos following the war; she also played a significant public role in all of these events.

For a girl born in the Siam of 1911, whether into the Bangkok aristocracy or a rural village family, expectations about adult life were limited to marriage and motherhood. Not all women married, but those who did not spent their life within their father's home or lived with other relatives. Because of unprecedented social and political changes, Boonlua was educated far beyond the dreams of both her mother and her grandmother. She became an influential educator, civil servant, essayist, and novelist. She traveled the world, representing Thailand at conferences and international meetings on the subjects of education and intercultural communication. She did not marry until she was nearly fifty years old, and while she never became a mother herself, she was a devoted aunt and beloved teacher as well as a champion of opportunities beyond the home, for women who wanted such challenges.

The culture in which we are raised profoundly affects how we understand and react to all that we see, hear, and feel of the world and of the people in it. Those of us raised beyond Southeast Asia will find it fascinating and perhaps challenging to understand Boonlua as a daughter, the youngest of her siblings. Her mother died when she was four, her father when she was eleven. Her relationships with her many siblings and "stepmothers," as she called the many women in the household, were complex, to say the least. She was a child prodigy and her father's favorite, delighting him and his friends with her fantastic memory and irrepressible ways. Predictably, her siblings were less taken with her gifts.

Boonlua's ideas about the realities of life were grounded in Theravada Buddhist teachings, according to which there are no accidents of birth. All human beings arrive in this life in circumstances determined by their behavior during many previous lives. Kings and beggars, scholars and farmers all have earned, for better or for worse, the place in which they take their first breath in this life, be it a palace, a hovel in an urban slum, or a thatch-roofed house on stilts at the edge of a rice field. Boonlua always knew that she was born the daughter of a nobleman and the great-great-granddaughter of a king, not by chance but because of her own karma—the collective balance of volitional actions, bad and good, in her previous lives. But she also knew that with privilege comes responsibility. She was born to serve her family and the kingdom. The purpose of her life was to improve her karmic balance through her own actions and by doing so she would positively affect the lives of those around her. Boonlua learned her Buddhism at her father's knee but was formally educated first by Catholic nuns in convent schools, then at a Thai university in which some of the professors were Western, and finally at the University of Minnesota. Like many educated Thai of her generation, she grew up quite literally in two worlds. Unlike many of her friends and relatives, she tried to avoid compartmentalizing Thai and Western ways of thinking and behaving and sought to synthesize them instead. Sometimes these carefully created syntheses led to great results, as in the teaching of Thai and English literature; but sometimes they did not, as when, during meetings at the Ministry of Education, she was unable to resist making funny and scathing comments on policies she disapproved. Then, colleagues would privately agree that Boonlua had gone too far once again, that her behavior was "too *farang*," (*farang* means "Western foreigner"), or "too *siwilai*," (*siwilai* is the Thai pronunciation of "civilized").

The actual Thai word for "civilization," *ariyatham*, is a Sanskrit-based term reflecting largely Indian concepts about society and suggesting the arts, music, and literature of great civilizations such as India or China. The term *siwilai* was coined by King Mongkut (1851–68). At the time, France and England were busily dividing Southeast Asia between themselves. The king was determined to appear civilized in ways that these grasping colonial nations would respect, so he began the modernization and westernization of Thai society. For example, punishments for criminal behavior that Westerners had deemed "barbaric" were changed. Monogamy was emulated if not practiced, as noblemen began taking their major wives to social events with foreigners, leaving all the minor wives at home. But in some ways, the materialist trappings of *siwilai* were even more important. In general, to become personally *siwilai* in terms of dress, education, and manners and to make use of inventions such as electric lights, motorcars, and anesthesia, were approved. However, to become excessively *siwilai*, overstepping the boundaries of basic, traditional Thai mores such as concealing one's feelings (*kep khwam rusuek*) could jeopardize the progress of one's career in the Thai bureaucracy, both before and after the overthrow of the absolute monarchy in 1932—and this has changed remarkably little in the twenty-first century. Socially, Boonlua could not be "cut" because of her royal background, but advancement in the Thai bureaucracy was another matter because she was, as one of her superiors remarked, "too *siwilai*." She spoke her mind, and she was inarguably an "individual." She could be excessively, inappropriately *siwilai*, and she saw no reason to change her ways.

Most biographies of Thais appear in cremation volumes, which are distributed at the funeral ceremony. This tradition began late in the reign of King Chulalongkorn (1868–1910), when printing presses became numerous enough to allow wealthy people to use them for this purpose. The basic format of a cremation volume remains the same today. A favorite poem of the departed loved one, or an excerpt from a classical literary work or religious text, is included, along with a brief biography, photographs, letters, and essays containing the fond memories of relatives and friends. Accomplishments and good qualities of the departed are extolled and unbecoming qualities or incidents are never included. A Thai friend once said, "If you want to read the biggest lies in Thailand, read the cremation volumes." I am indebted to my subject herself for witty and characteristically scathing comments about the state of biography in Thailand. She deplored the practice of hagiography and said so. She greatly admired a biography of her sister Buppha, the famous novelist who wrote under the pen name Dokmai Sot. This biography gives a faithful account of Buppha's depression, her hypochondria, and the insomnia that led her to spend her nights in a gazebo in the garden of Wang Ban Mo (Ban Mo Palace), the family home, smoking cigarettes and writing novels that would become famous and that are read to this day. Boonlua called it "the first real biography of a Thai." And so, I have tried to be faithful in conveying what I think she would have wanted in her own biography.

Boonlua suffered feelings of abandonment during her childhood that she never conquered and suffered under the weight of bitter disappointments and periods of depression throughout her life. She was often ill but worked straight through her most difficult years, even when her hands were too weak to type and she had to dictate parts of her novels. She celebrated the value of the devoted wife and good mother and was suspicious of the term "feminist"; yet the simple justice of equal social and career opportunity for males and females was of great importance to her and she shared this belief as a teacher and as a novelist. She was unswervingly loyal to the king and to others of the Chakri dynasty—all of whom were, after all, her relatives. Although she was an unapologetic royalist, in general she disliked ideologies, partly because she was contemptuous of unthinking partisanship and partly because from early childhood she had been a dedicated contrarian. Like other members of her immediate family she was contemptuous about the *form* of democracy that followed the absolute monarchy in Siam but admired Western democracies that had retained their monarchy while constructing a fully participative polity.

There is necessarily a good deal of history in this biography, which I have tried to condense as much as possible without over-simplifying important events, people, and ideas. In order to understand Boonlua's life story, it is necessary to understand some basic facts about the absolute monarchy before its overthrow, about the rise of guided democracy under military rule during the 1930s, and about Thailand's experience of World War II, during which the nation was allied with the Japanese and bombed by the British and the Americans. It is also important to understand Thailand's position in the Indochina War of 1954–75 when the nation allied itself with the United States and became a base of operations for air attacks on Vietnam, Laos, and Cambodia, and to understand as well the triumph and eventual defeat of a student-led revolution that brought down the military dictatorship in 1973, only to be crushed in 1976. The years that followed were quiet and introspective, for Boonlua and for her nation, until her death in 1982.

I met Boonlua once, we talked for hours, and I continued to think about her. After our meeting, I read one of the novels she had written in Thai and knew exactly what she had meant when she said that "history books do not tell us what people's emotions were—that is the work of novels." I taught her work and her words to my students at the University of California, Berkeley, for many years. Gradually I came to believe that not only was her life immensely interesting, but also that it reflected and demonstrated virtually all of the important social transformations and major political events and developments of the Thai twentieth century. It is, of course, a view from the top of Thai society—but what a tremendous view it is, from the perspective of a brilliant and creative mind. In the late 1990s I came across some tape recordings of interviews with Boonlua, and as I listened to her wistful, often hilarious stories about her own life, as well as her witty remarks about other interesting people, always

M.L. Boonlua (Kunchon) Debyasuvarn

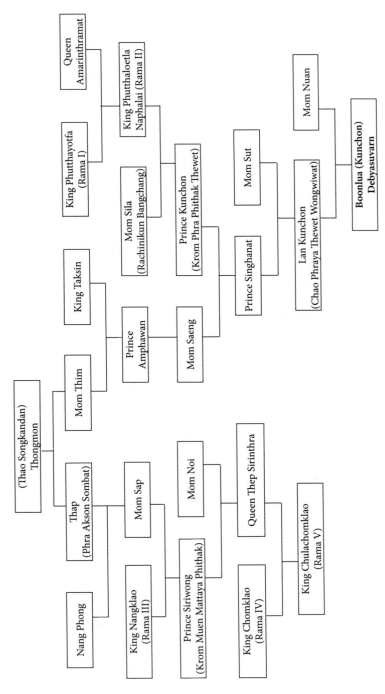

SOURCE: *Ton chabap saisakunwong sueng chat tham doi Khun Nattada Itsarasena na Ayutthaya*;
Debsirin Alumni Association, http://www.debsirinalumni.org/history.php?id_his=1&page=1&group=3

followed by an amusing, somewhat apologetic chuckle, I knew that the
time had come to begin this biography. I could not know that I would
finish it on the one hundredth anniversary of Mom Luang Boonlua
Kunchon Debyasuvarn's birth.

Berkeley, California
June 2011

I

IN HER FATHER'S HOUSE

In the photograph, we see a distinguished older Siamese aristocrat and two young women sitting in small, graceful European chairs. It is the year 1914—or, according to the Siamese calendar, the year 2457 of the Buddhist Era—in the fourth year of the reign of King Vajiravudh, Rama VI, sixth king of the Chakri dynasty. The gentleman in the photograph is Chao Phraya Thewet, a high official in the Royal Palace of Siam, and a great-grandson of the second king of the dynasty.[1] The small girl standing within the circle of Chao Phraya Thewet's arm is his youngest child, three-year-old Boonlua, born on December 13, 1911. Another of his thirty-two children, a boy of about twelve, stands just behind him.

The women in the photograph are wearing nearly identical costumes: long-sleeved, lacy blouses of Western design and, from the waist down, traditional silk *chongkraben*, voluminous skirts drawn back between the legs and tucked in at the back of the waist. The resulting pantaloons reach mid-calf, so that the women's silk stockings are visible, as well as their dainty leather European shoes with modest high heels and bows.

Chao Phraya Thewet rests one elbow on a delicate square tea table. He is wearing an impeccably tailored white jacket buttoned high at the throat. His lower garment is similar to those the women are wearing, as are his white silk stockings, but his shoes are polished leather oxfords.

The girl is dressed in a small replica of the women's attire, but instead of their traditional short, stiff hairstyle her uncut hair is wound into the charming topknot worn by pre-adolescent Siamese children of both sexes, encircled by a ring of jasmine blossoms.[2]

Her father had given her the name "Boonlua," meaning "merit remaining." The merit remaining was his, proven by the delightful surprise of her birth when he was nearly sixty. Her birth, six years after the birth of the child born before her, proved that he must have accrued more merit in his present and previous lives than he had thought. Everyone agreed that Boonlua was not only a prodigy, but *duang chai pho* as well—"her father's heart," the apple of his eye. She was not a pretty child. Her ears were too prominent, her skin was too dark to meet Siamese standards of beauty, and she showed no sign of developing the sweet submissiveness of a truly beautiful girl. On the contrary, she was often stubborn and occasionally petulant, yet her unusual gifts outweighed these faults, at least in her father's eyes. She had already learned the 64-letter Thai alphabet and could read quite well. She delighted in reciting lengthy Buddhist prayers and poetry that she had memorized and reading the newspaper aloud to her siblings, who were less charmed than their father. If he had named her, it was they who would provide a nickname: *lot thanong*, "[she who] leaps with pride."

The photograph of Chao Phraya Thewet and family members was staged in imitation of portraits of elite European families of the era. The backdrop, dainty chairs, tea table, draperies, and "oriental" carpet were *de rigeur*. The setting is determinedly *siwilai*, "civilized." By the time of this photograph, the connotations of *siwilai* would be understood by everyone in the extended royal family, which included Chao Phraya Thewet's household. Betel-stained teeth meticulously polished to a fashionable red and black glow were beginning to look distinctly un-*siwilai*. Within a decade, they would mark one as woefully behind the times. A woman who wanted to appear fashionably modern would give up betel nut chewing and tooth polishing, whiten her teeth by various means, and, if her commitment to the project was serious, she might take up smoking—or at least lighting—cigarettes.

This carefully staged photograph reflects almost none of the realities of the family's life. There were between twenty and thirty children living at the time it was taken, by almost as many mothers. The clothing in the photograph, if not outright costumery, is not what the women, at least, customarily wore. Their home looked nothing like the small corner of European gentility provided by the photographer. Any dwelling in which a royally connected Siamese family lived was referred to as a *wang* (palace) or *tamnak* (royal residence), regardless of its appearance. This family's home was called Wang Thewet but was more commonly known as Wang Ban Mo after the Ban Mo market that stood beside it, an important feature of the neighborhood even before the eighteenth-century residence was constructed. Because Boonlua almost always referred to it as Wang Ban Mo in her remarks and writings, it is the name I shall generally use.

Until wealthy Thai began imitating the imposing colonial villas built by the French in Indochina, the British in Burma and Malaya, and the Dutch in Java, virtually all buildings in Siam, with the exception of important Buddhist temples, were made of teakwood, as was Wang Ban Mo. Like other noble houses built in a traditional Thai style, it is large, dark, and plain. The great hall is of simple design and splendid proportions. Old, beautiful chests are set against the walls at intervals, with family portraits hanging above them. The most prized and often the most materially valuable objects in the homes of the Siamese elite never have been on display in public rooms. These are the family's Buddha images, kept in the *hong phra*, or "Buddha room," along with receptacles containing ancestors' ashes. Before modern times, jewelry and other valuable items were kept in locked trunks in rooms that also were locked, or they were hidden elsewhere.

For the most part, life in Siamese society traditionally has been conducted at floor level, whatever one's class. People slept on mats that were rolled up and stored during the day. Only the king, princes, and aristocratic males slept on a Chinese or Western bed, a matter more of status than of comfort.[3] Meals were served on trays on the floor or on tables no more than eighteen inches high. Dishes and bowls, glasses and cups, however costly, rarely graced a dining table. The main difference between great houses and the homes of ordinary people lay in their size, not their style or method of construction, and in the value of a family's possessions. For example, wealthy people such as Chao Phraya Thewet and his family used bowls and dishes made of precious metals and porcelain, often imported, while the poor used pottery, with containers of bamboo, leaves, and various kinds of shells for serving food and liquids. Western flatware had been introduced in the late nineteenth century, but Thai food traditionally was eaten by dipping a ball of rice into small dishes of food. If chairs were in sight in a noble house, they had been put there in the interest of the *siwilai* project and used when Western foreigners visited. They were seldom used by family members on ordinary occasions. If we think of the floor of a Thai home as a dining table, we understand why floors were cleaned and polished every morning and why shoes were never worn indoors. To this day, the floors in a Thai home are meticulously cared for and never sullied by shoes.

Kunchon, Boonlua's surname, is a Sanskrit word meaning elephant, reflecting one of her father's royal responsibilities: he oversaw the care of the king's elephants, as his father and grandfather had before him.[4] This was a position of great responsibility and high status before the overthrow of the absolute monarchy in 1932. His royal civil service title and the name attached to that title were "Chao Phraya," the highest rank, and "Thewet," another family name. Until 1909 when he retired, Chao Phraya Thewet also managed all theatrical performances in the Royal Palace, most famously the Thai classical dance troupe of the inner palace which was comprised only of women. All of these women, including Boonlua's mother, Nuan, lived at one of Chao Phraya Thewet's two residences in Bangkok, and most of them gave birth to at least one of his children. After his official retirement in 1909, daily life in these households changed little. Few women left, choosing instead to go on with their lives as before, complete with rehearsals of dance dramas and occasional performances.

The subject of Thai names is complicated, sometimes even for Thai. Although the given name of Boonlua's father was Lan and his surname was Kunchon, very few people would address or think of him as Lan Kunchon or even Mom Rachawong Lan Kunchon, the title that indicates his position in the extended royal family as differentiated from his title at the palace. A *mom rachawong* is the great-grandchild of a king; *mom luang*, Boonlua's own royal title, is for great-great grandchildren; and the children of a *mom luang* are officially commoners, although everyone will be keenly aware of the identity of their father, their grandfather, and the king from whom they are descended. When he was a boy, Lan Kunchon was often at the Royal Palace with his grandfather, and so everyone there called him Lan, which means simply "grandson," and no other name supplanted it. By the time he was thirty, he had become a man of several names, like other men of his class and era.

THE OLDEST NOBLE HOUSE

The main building and most of the other buildings in the Wang Ban Mo compound were constructed during the reign of King Phra Nangklao (Rama III, 1824–51). At the time of this writing, it is the oldest noble house standing in Bangkok, continues to be occupied by members of the Kunchon family, and is preserved under the care of the Royal Fine Arts Department. Boonlua lived there most of her life, but during her earliest years she lived at the other main family residence in Bangkok, Wang Khlong Toei (a *khlong* is a canal), so named because of its location near Khlong Toei Port, the main port of Bangkok. In general, it was the younger faction of women and their children who lived at Wang Khlong Toei, with visits to the main residence, Wang Ban Mo. After Chao Phraya Thewet's death, all of the family gradually converged upon Wang Ban Mo. Both residences were located near the Chao Phraya River, which was still the major travel route in Bangkok when Boonlua was a child. *Khlong* crisscrossed the city, giving boats access to all neighborhoods.

When responding to questions about her childhood, Boonlua often began with the words, "I was, raised by men, you see . . ." This assertion did not exactly reflect the truth, but her reasons for clinging to the belief that it was, are understandable. She was always keenly aware of what would impress her father, who was the most, and arguably the only, important person in the household. To be one of his favorites was everything. What would impress him? Chao Phraya Thewet was dedicated to the *siwilai* ideas and actions encouraged by King Chulalongkorn. Like his king, he disapproved of old superstitions as relics of pre-Buddhist, animist, *boran* (ancient) ways of thinking. He saw no contradiction, however, between Buddhist beliefs and modern living. For example, memories of former lives were evidence of Buddhist truths, and stories based upon them thus were not only acceptable but admired—a fact of which Boonlua was well aware, as demonstrated in this recollection by one of her relatives.

> When she was only three or four, Phi Lua[5] was taken by her father to a temple in Ayutthaya, and she pointed out two women she had never met and told him that they had been her nursemaids in a former life. She called them "Auntie Chueam" and "Auntie Seng." Thai [Buddhist] people believe that small children are still close to their former life and lose those memories as they grow up.[6]

If this story was welcomed, stories about ghosts and the spirit world were not. Chao Phraya Thewet particularly disliked and discouraged the telling of ghost stories, which have nothing to do with the basic teachings of the Buddha, although the "popular Buddhism" of Thailand encompasses them. He wanted his children to be afraid of nothing, not even ghosts, an almost universal fear then and now.[7] "In this," Boonlua wrote in her autobiography *Successes and Failures*, "My father failed, and I failed, for I listened avidly to ghost stories throughout my childhood, and I have never lost my fear."[8]

Boonlua's position in Thai society, beginning with her descent from "the poet king," Phra Phutthaloetla (Rama II, 1809–24), is a case study of social change and social mobility in modernizing Siam. This second king of the Chakri dynasty had the daunting task of recreating the kingdom's literature and fine arts, devastated in 1767 by the Burmese sack of Ayutthaya, which had been the capital of Siam since the fifteenth century. Three of the outstanding novelists of the early twentieth century are his direct descendants: Boonlua, her sister Buppha, and M.R. Kukrit Pramoj.[9]

Prince Phra Phithak Thewet was the great-grandfather of Boonlua and twenty-second of the seventy-one children of King Phra Phutthaloetla. He began his career by serving in the cavalry, leading troops in the famous suppression of the Lao Prince Anuwong's rebellion in Laos and northeast Siam in 1827.[10] Unlike some other members of the nobility, Prince Phithak Thewet was able to steer a safe and honorable course between factions at court that were divided in their support of one or the other of two sons of King Phra Phutthaloetla by different mothers: Prince Nangklao and Prince Mongkut. Prince Nangklao, who was older and much more experienced in matters of governance, came to the throne upon their father's death and reigned from 1824 to 1851 (Rama III). His younger half-brother, Prince Mongkut, was the son of a queen with higher royal antecedents, for which reason the "pro-Mongkut" faction believed that he should have followed his father on the throne, despite his youth and inexperience. Nevertheless, Mongkut spent the next twenty-seven years as an influential and active Buddhist monk and scholar, and it was only upon his brother's death in 1851 that he ascended the throne (Rama IV).[11]

Prince Phithak Thewet managed to serve his king loyally while also treating the king's younger half-brother with respect and kindness. When Mongkut became king, the king showed his gratitude to the prince by elevating him to the status of "royal brother," and when the prince died the king not only sponsored the cremation ceremony, but also ordered the construction of a special *monthop*, the traditional urn used for royal Thai cremations, because he was too large to fit into any existing *monthop*.[12]

Prince Phithak Thewet had a concubine named Khun Saeng, who became the mother of Prince Singhanat, Boonlua's grandfather. Khun Saeng was the granddaughter of King Taksin, a Thai general of Chinese descent who occupied the Siamese throne during the brief Thonburi period (1767–82) between the fall of Ayutthaya in 1767 and the establishment of the Chakri dynasty in Bangkok in 1782, thus giving Boonlua's family the unusual distinction of descent from two dynasties— albeit Taksin was the only king of the Thonburi era and thus no real "dynasty" had time to develop.[13] Prince Singhanat followed in his father's footsteps as a valued servant of the crown, teaching horsemanship and many other skills to King Mongkut's heir, Crown Prince Chulalongkorn, who ascended the throne in 1868 (Rama V) and lived until 1910, the year before Boonlua was born.

Among Prince Singhanat's wives was Mom Sut, a daughter of Khun Pat Hong, a wealthy Chinese merchant who owned the Ban Mo market. *Mom* was a flexible term, conferring honor on those female commoners who were allied with a titled male. Marriages between the children of titled Siamese and wealthy Chinese immigrants or their descendants were common, and these unions have had an incalculable impact on the social and economic development of the nation. Mom Sut, who was said to be greatly loved by everyone in her husband's family and who was called "Middle Hall Mother," bore Prince Singhanat a son, and this child, M.R. Lan Kunchon, was Boonlua's father. Mom Sut's children were titled, regardless of the fact that she was the daughter of a Chinese merchant, for children bore the title appropriate to the father's lineage. Thus, a Thai whose great-grandparents or even grandparents on his or her mother's side had been poor farmers might be born into the extended royal family. This would not be the case, however, if a titled woman were to "marry down," a very unlikely event.

Lan Kunchon was born in 1852, the second year of the reign of King Mongkut and one year after the birth of Prince Chulalongkorn. The boys grew up together, playing together like brothers within and beyond the palace, and King Mongkut himself sponsored two very important events: Lan's topknot-cutting ceremony, which signaled the end of childhood, and his ordination as a Buddhist monk at the age of twenty.[14]

When King Mongkut died in 1868 and Chulalongkorn ascended the throne, he was fifteen years old and Lan Kunchon was fourteen. The teenaged king frequently would appear at Wang Thewet in the middle of the night, accompanied by palace bodyguards, who also were friends. Dressed in ordinary clothes, he and Lan and the rest would go off to a noodle shop downtown, where owner and customers would (perhaps) mistake their king for a commoner. Boonlua delighted in telling these stories. "My father and the king loved to go out for those crispy fried noodles—you know, *mi krop*—and then they would go back in a rickshaw to Wang Ban Mo."[15]

There are many stories of this kind about King Chulalongkorn's endearing "common touch," although there is certainly no equivalent for this term in Thai. He was somehow even *more* elevated, *more* kingly as the result of such youthful escapades as slipping out of the palace in the middle of the night to visit noodle shops with his friends. His subjects would have held him in supreme respect in any event, but because of the way he interacted with people at every level of his society, they loved him.

It was during King Chulalongkorn's reign that young princes and noblemen were first sent abroad in numbers to study at European universities. Chao Phraya Thewet made one trip to Europe with a group of Siamese officials, but he did not know any European language and so could not converse with any of the Westerners he met. It was a discouraging experience, this trip that he had so anticipated. After his return he began referring to himself as an antiquated man (*khon boran*). He resolved to send all of his children, even the girls, to the European and American Christian missionary schools then flourishing in Bangkok so that they would be prepared, as he now sadly realized he never could be, for a future in which the ability to converse with and understand Western foreigners, the *farang*, would be essential.

Leading poets and artists of the reign of King Rama II (1809–24), some of them born in the eighteenth century, were still alive when Chao Phraya Thewet was a young man during the 1860s and 1870s. His attitude toward them was worshipful, and he passed this reverence for his elders to his children. Thus, the most influential person in Boonlua's young life was a man who was most comfortable with people whose primary social identity was moored in the late eighteenth century, the dawning years of the Chakri dynasty. This curious circumstance was of great importance to her development. It would shape her worldview, and that of others of her generation who also were the younger children of older aristocratic fathers. They would grow up in modernizing Siam, many of them would study in Europe and the United States, but they

IN HER FATHER'S HOUSE

would never entirely lose the attitudes, the aesthetics, and some of the obsessions of earlier centuries.

Fear of the European colonial powers that already had overtaken Burma, the Malay Peninsula, Laos, Cambodia, and Vietnam was great, but fear was not the sole factor underlying the extension and improvement of education and the conditions of life in Siam in the decades preceding and following Boonlua's birth. Pride was another factor of great importance, as the regime worked to demonstrate that not only was the kingdom of Siam exceptional in terms of its glorious history and culture; it was also inestimably superior to failed neighboring kingdoms in terms of its ability to rule itself and deal with other nations in the modern world. The colonial powers' insistence that they were motivated not by greed or ambition but by the imperatives of their civilizing mission was not lost on King Chulalongkorn. He showed the world that Siam could create at least the beginnings of a national infrastructure for development; invite, pay, and efficiently use the services of Western advisors; and send Siamese princes to be educated abroad so that they could return home and replace these advisors. Siam did not require and would not tolerate interference in its affairs, much less its governance.

The revered king died in 1910, the year before Boonlua's birth. In 1909, her father had resigned from his posts at the Royal Palace, never to return. Her half-brother, Mom Luang Wara Kunchon, nineteen years her elder, was given the title of "Phraya Thewet" under the new regime of King Vajiravudh (Rama VI). Not only was Chao Phraya Thewet officially retired, he had begun to look back and to make remarks to the effect that the apogee of Siamese intellectual and artistic accomplishments had passed. The Siamese royal court had been his world, but that world had changed drastically with the ascension of King Vajiravudh, who had lived in England during his entire adolescence and had been educated first at Oxford and then at Sandhurst. The new court was not a place where Chao Phraya Thewet felt comfortable, as he had always felt during the previous reign. He had been all for change while Chulalongkorn was on the throne. Now, momentous changes had occurred, but too many of them had left him embittered and sad.

IN A GARDEN OF WOMEN

Wang Ban Mo had been a household of talented and spirited women for several generations. Despite his other duties and offices, Chao Phraya Thewet's personal as well as professional life had revolved around the royal dance troupe. He was the equal of any impresario of his lineage and a proficient singer with a large repertoire that he had learned by heart. The classical dance drama or *lakhon* was until the reign of the new king Vajiravudh performed either by all males (*lakhon nok*, outside the palace) or all women (*lakhon nai*, within the inner palace where no men were allowed).[16] The dramas most commonly performed included *Inao*, an adaptation of a Javanese tale, and excerpts from the *Ramakian*, the Thai version of the *Ramayana*, the Indian epic that Southeast Asians have performed, transformed, and made their own over many centuries. Boonlua and her siblings learned the most popular parts of these dance dramas as children, and she was able to sing them all her life.

In her writing and interviews Boonlua rarely mentioned her siblings by name, with a few exceptions. She did speak of her elder brother, Phraya Thewet. After becoming the family patriarch, he also became the arbiter of the fates of his many sisters—at least, he tried. Occasionally, Boonlua would remark on an event shared with "some of my sisters" or "one of my stepmothers," as she referred to all of the women who shared her mother's status. Later in life, she frequently spoke and wrote about her sister Buppha, especially after Buppha's death. This sister, six years older than Boonlua and the second-youngest child in the family, would become a very popular novelist under the pen name Dokmai Sot, "fresh flower." Various siblings and other relatives would appear thinly disguised both in Buppha's novels and in the novels Boonlua began writing shortly before her sister's death, but only a few readers of their own class, familiar with the real cast of characters, would recognize them. Another older sister named Chalaem also played a significant role in Boonlua's life.

The lives of Boonlua and the two half-sisters with whom she lived most of her life represent three distinct life paths for elite Thai women of their generation. Although she was the youngest, Boonlua received the most education, both in Siam and abroad. After the overthrow of the absolute monarchy in 1932, the year in which she turned twenty-one, she would eagerly accept the opportunity to join the first group of women to attend Chulalongkorn University, and upon graduation she would begin a career in teaching and in public service. These were choices that no Thai women before her generation could have imagined.

Buppha, the sister who would become the novelist, was educated first in the inner Royal Palace, where she lived with her aunt, Princess Chom, one of Chao Phraya Thewet's sisters, and subsequently at St. Joseph Convent School, where her sisters were already studying. Always sickly and delicate, Buppha was not considered strong enough to venture far from home, nor did she wish to do so. Despite her success as a writer, she would live and write her novels at Wang Ban Mo until her marriage at the age of forty-nine, after which her associations would continue to be restricted to upper-class friends and relatives and a few Western acquaintances.[17]

Chalaem, who like Buppha was beautiful and possessed of charming manners, would become the spinster dowager of the Kunchon family, living in Wang Ban Mo her entire life. A young relative remembered Chalaem in middle age telling the young women of the family, "When you go out [beyond the walls of Wang Ban Mo], say to yourself, 'This land is *ours*'—then, you will always feel confident." Chalaem's world was narrow, comfortable, and certain. During her adolescence, she became the confidante and closest companion of her half-brother, Phraya Thewet, and remained so as long as they lived. He would marry; she would not.

Boonlua was told that her mother, Mom Nuan, then about twenty years old, wept when she learned that she was pregnant because she did not expect her child to know many years of a father's love and care, and because the fate of a minor wife's children was uncertain—as the plots of many early modern Thai novels attest. Ironically, it was Mom Nuan who would die first, seven years before Chao Phraya Thewet.

When Buppha, the second youngest child of the family, was five years old, her mother, Mom Malai, shocked the family by announcing that she was going to leave the household and start her own classical dance school. But this was nothing compared to the further declaration that she was going to marry a Western foreigner who was demanding a bill of divorcement from Chao Phraya Thewet before there could be a wedding. This request was emphatically declined on the grounds that since they had never been "married" in the way that Western people were, he could hardly give her a piece of paper announcing that they were now "divorced." In the end, he agreed to give Malai a letter declaring that no marriage currently existed between them, which was undeniable. Until this unprecedented event, Chao Phraya had rather doted on Buppha, but years later she would tell friends that "following my mother's defection, I was my father's least favorite child."

Men of that era did not give up their children. Mom Malai might go, but Buppha must stay in her father's home. The price of custody was that the girl was a constant, visible, and vexing reminder of Malai's ungrateful and immoral behavior. Fortunately, the problem was solved by her aunt, the childless Princess Chom, a minor consort of King Chulalongkorn who for years had been begging her brother for a daughter to raise. He had always refused, preferring to keep all of his daughters at home and send them as day students to the Catholic nuns at St. Joseph Convent, where they would learn English and French, and a fair understanding of the essentials of scientific Western subjects.

Now, however, Princess Chom's offer was gratefully accepted and five-year-old Buppha was packed off to the Royal Palace. Traditionally, ladies in the palace had educated girls of the aristocracy for the tasks of managing a great household. Many little girls like Buppha were sent off to live with an aunt or a cousin in the palace where she would spend years learning how to dress properly and artfully, arrange flowers, prepare complicated palace cuisine, and converse easily with royalty using *rachasap*, the "royal language," a form of Thai that incorporates a great many Khmer and Sanskrit-based terms.[18] Such girls were raised to be *chao wang*, "palace ladies," with training that would greatly increase their chances of making an excellent marriage, which most of them did. During past reigns, a fortunate few of these girls had attracted the king's notice and became consorts. The most fortunate had become the mother of a prince or princess, ensuring their family's permanent place at the top of the Thai social hierarchy.

Buppha stayed at the Royal Palace until she was thirteen years old, with brief visits home to Wang Khlong Toei, where Boonlua also lived. After she returned home to live, she joined her sisters at St. Joseph Convent School and soon developed a life-long passion for French language and literature, which she taught after her graduation. She also studied English but was always more comfortable in French. Her years in the palace formed Buppha in ways that made her different from her half-sisters. When she arrived in the inner palace as a five-year-old, it was still a thriving walled city at the height of its splendor. And then King Chulalongkorn died. Sooner than anyone could have imagined, the Royal Palace would begin to decline, for the new king, Chulalongkorn's son Vajiravudh, would choose not to live there, and it would never recover its former glory. For Buppha, however, life in the palace as she had known and lived it, and the attitudes and behaviors of those who lived there, would always symbolize the finest and truest expressions of Siamese culture. While she would be the first Thai woman author to write modern novels with modern heroines, none of which were set in the palace, the worldview that she had acquired there would be at the core of every novel she wrote.

Boonlua's view of her sister Buppha during their childhood appears in remarks she made to Somphop Chantaraprapha, a younger relative who was devoted to her and became her biographer.

> Buppha was always clean and tidy, and of course she was dressed beautifully. I thought she was the ultimate "palace lady." Her shining hair was combed meticulously, her face looked so smooth and soft, and she wore embroidered slippers. How different from her brothers and sisters at Khlong Toei [where Boonlua lived and Buppha had lived]! We were like a pack of upcountry urchins, our sunburned faces smeared with dirt, running and jumping about like ordinary children.[19]

Boonlua would always be ambivalent about this sister who was beautiful and became so famous. During interviews with the American anthropologist Herbert P. Phillips in 1966 when she was fifty-four years old, Boonlua spoke of Buppha, who had died during the previous year, with a poignant combination of sadness, envy, and love. Here, she answers a question about her own childhood goal of becoming a novelist.

When I came back [from the convent school in Penang] at seventeen, I found the sister right next to me [in age] writing, and I just saw no reason for my taking up writing. . . .

Which child was this?

Dokmai Sot. Very, very . . . the novelist, you know . . .

Were you particularly close to her?

I suppose so. Well . . . I don't know whether she has influenced me more than I have influenced her. I—I don't know. But—she made me sensitive to a lot of things that I would probably have overlooked because of—you know, she was brought up in the Royal Palace . . . and I think she was sensitive to a lot of things that . . . I was not. For example—hmm—admiration. I was a spoiled child, I never cared about whether people talked about what I said. I just said it. She sort of—oh, I'm afraid she was very sorry to have such a sister. She always said she loved me so much because I was her only younger sister and she sort of tried to make me more . . . feminine. I don't think she succeeded. [laughter][20]

Boonlua always claimed that, as a child, she preferred the company of her brothers to that of her sisters. She and the boys "ran wild," she said, under the more or less watchful eyes of a great number of servants. "We had a big estate, twenty-five rai [10 acres]. I had no mother. I just more or less roamed the place with the boys. I learned all kinds of secrets of life which I found later to be all wrong."[21]

The fact that Boonlua played with boys was not unusual. Until puberty, boys and girls in all social classes played together. In Lady Siphroma's memoirs of her life in the Royal Palace during a slightly earlier period, she wrote, "The girls . . . were as naughty as the boys. His Royal Highness Prince Chainat Narenthon, when he saw me in Russia and Germany, said that I was the naughtiest one . . . [B]ut in fact some were naughtier than I."²² Lady Siphroma went on to recount how she and other boys and girls in the palace spent their days in reckless bicycle riding, playing with fireworks, and bedeviling their elders in countless ways. It was not until their topknots were cut at puberty that boys and girls were separated—but after that the separation became absolute until the girls were safely married.

Boonlua's preferred version of her childhood—knocking about with the boys, always up to mischief, and ignoring her sisters whenever possible—is misleading. Although she insisted that girls bored her and that she found their pursuits and interests to be very silly, there is considerable evidence that her childhood relationships with women— sisters, aunts, nieces who were of her own generation, stepmothers, grandmothers, other female relatives, and servants—were closer, often more painful, and certainly more complex than she chose to reveal. Her early years, when she learned to navigate frequently stormy weather in this sea of women, would affect her relationships with others, especially elders and peers, throughout her life. Relationships with younger people, and especially with her students, would be much easier and far more rewarding for her and for them.

Home was a competitive environment. Anuwong Kunchon, the daughter of Boonlua's oldest brother, Phraya Thewet, was only six months younger than her Aunt Boonlua. They grew up together, were boarding students at the Convent of the Holy Infant Jesus in Penang at the same time, and saw each other frequently throughout their lives. Yet, not once is Anuwong mentioned in Boonlua's own memoir, *Successes and Failures*, an omission that is given weight by references to "the unkindness of other Thai girls" in Penang.

Mom Anuwong's reminiscences about their childhood reveal an enmity between the two that would last until Boonlua's death.

We girls were constantly being compared with each other. You were told, "Too bad you aren't as clever as your sister"—or if you *were* clever then someone would remind you that another girl was *much* prettier. You could never "measure up," you see, because there was always something about you . . . Well, that's how they raised children, in those days.

When we were children, my grandfather [Chao Phraya Thewet] offered each child four baht to learn to say a long prayer from memory. And Boonlua got the four baht when she was very young—and I *never* got that four baht! I could *never* remember the whole prayer.[23] Boonlua was so smart, and she was always acting smart, and she was always trying to teach everybody, even when she was a little girl. She wanted everyone else to agree with her. She never changed, you know. Don't think that she *became* a teacher. Oh, no—that was just the way she *was*. We would be walking out of the house when we were all girls, and she would be preaching at everyone, you know, trying to get everyone to agree with her, and I would think, "Oh, Boonlua's in her pulpit again." But she was very good at telling stories. We would lie awake in the dark, and she would make up very good stories.

Do you know that she was my grandfather's favorite? Always the favorite. When we had dance practice, all the other girls would have their fingers bent back, except for her. Nobody dared to bend her fingers back.[24] And she thought that she was not only smarter than everyone, but beautiful, too—oh yes, she definitely did! You seem to think that she knew she was plain, but that is not so—no, she thought she was beautiful. When we left the convent school, some of the nuns teased us, saying that I would be the first to marry. And then Boonlua laughed, and said that *she* would be the first to marry. *She* would be first! Well, by the time *she* got married, you know, I had grandchildren.[25]

A photograph of Chao Phraya Thewet taken a year before his death shows him sitting in a chair in his garden, surrounded by nine of his daughters, including Boonlua, Buppha, and Chalaem. He looks vigorous and content and all of the girls are strikingly beautiful—except for Boonlua. Buppha, apparently welcome at home again, is seated on the grass at her father's left. She is about sixteen years old, with a perfect oval face, lovely eyes, and delicate features. She leans on her right hand, her legs gracefully folded to the left, her left hand resting on her lap. A large pale hyacinth over her right ear appears to hold back a shining wave of hair that hangs over her shoulder in what everyone called "the English fashion." Her clothes represent the fastidious and fashionable combination of European and Thai styles: above, a loose, Western-style blouse with puffy "Gibson Girl" sleeves to the elbow; below, a Thai skirt.

Chalaem sits on the grass at her father's right. She also is very pretty, with a sweet, winsome expression. Her hair is parted in the center and pulled back neatly, and she is wearing an English blouse with lace collar and cuffs.

Seated on the grass between Buppha and Chalaem, in the center of the picture and therefore directly in front of her father, is Boonlua—ten years old, plain as a pot, and scowling. She wears a rumpled Western-style schoolgirl's dress, and her hair is parted in the center, with a fat pigtail on either side of her face. She leans on her left arm, grasping her elbow with her right hand, which pitches her slightly forward toward the camera. Her expression seems to say, "You may be able to make me sit here, but nothing you can do will make me smile."

One "Thai value" that was hardly mentioned in an otherwise quite comprehensive study of Thai values published by the National Institute of Development Administration in 1990 was the importance of aesthetics in Thai life.[26] This would include such seeming minutiae as the most pleasing (and *correct*) way to string a flower lei, or the most appetizing and graceful way to peel and carve a particular kind of fruit. Such attention to aesthetic details remains of great importance in Thai life, as is a nearly obsessive concern with how people look, move, stand, walk, sit, dress, and groom themselves. In the photograph of Chao Phraya Thewet and his daughters, Boonlua is not only a plain child but also the least attractive daughter in a family that prized female beauty and endlessly discussed the details of perfect or imperfect nose shapes and complexions (with dozens of terms to describe gradations of skin color); the shapes of fingers, noses, and chins, the dimensions of earlobes and eyebrows; the characteristics of desirable hair; and on and on.

Prince Narit, a son of King Mongkut, who was a close friend of Chao Phraya Thewet and also an expert on the classical dance drama, left meticulous notes on applying makeup to the dancers in the troupe.

These included methods of correcting facial flaws in order to bring each dancer's appearance as close as possible to ideal standards of beauty. Boonlua's mother, Nuan, is included in these notes. Her facial flaws are listed as a too-narrow mouth (from side to side) with thick lips, too-full cheeks that are somewhat pendulous, and a receding chin— all of which describe Boonlua's own appearance as a young woman. Prince Narit notes that Nuan's too-full lips should be corrected with makeup, and the corners "lifted" with lip color; the cheeks and chin should be shaded to give the illusion of more regular and pleasing proportions.

There are few photographs of Boonlua smiling at any age, and if she did smile, she was careful to keep her lips firmly closed over slightly prominent upper teeth. Although it is true that a full smile would have been considered undignified, it is likely that she made an effort to keep her lips closed, even when she appeared to be amused, in order to hide an overbite. How much it mattered to her that she was plain in a house of beautiful women is uncertain. Some of her friends felt that she suffered throughout her life from feelings of inadequacy because of her looks.

Boonlua often said that she possessed one quality for which her siblings, stepmothers, and others in the household admired her without reservation, an assertion borne out by the observations of many of the friends she made as an adult. She heard and remembered everything that went on about her—but she never, ever carried tales, and so was able to maintain a precarious but generally amicable relationship with all factions in the family.[27] This quality, which no doubt helped her survive emotionally in the household after her mother's death, became a fixed part of her personality, so that decades later she still declined to carry tales and had no use for those who did. All her life she was a person who could be (and often was) trusted with secrets, including secret sorrows.

I went from one section of the house to another and I noticed that people criticized each other a great deal, but I knew by some instinct or something that I was never to carry tales. I knew that if I did that, I would lose all of my advantages. I could enter any room, get cakes, anything I wanted from anybody, and I suppose that influenced my life quite a lot. There were many kinds of people living in my house, like our immediate servants, my sisters' maids, my stepmothers' maids. How many? Probably a hundred something.[28]

Boonlua's mother and the women she called stepmothers did not form one large harem but succeeded each other in the two residences over a period of fifty years, in groups. At the time Boonlua was born, Chao Phraya Thewet had a relationship with nine or ten women in the household, most of whom had been dancers in the troupe.

Intrigues and jealousies among the stepmothers and between the Wang Ban Mo contingent and the smaller household of Wang Khlong Toei were rife, abetted by an abundance of theatrical temperament. Almost all of the stepmothers were talented dancers—well-trained, disciplined, highly skilled, and highly competitive.

Ordinarily, in an elite household there would be one "major wife" of good family. This would be a match arranged by their families, a careful blending of lineages and of fortunes. The major wife would manage the household and everyone in it. As the years went by, she might well have a hand in choosing her husband's minor wives—if only to the extent of finding young women whom she believed would remain cognizant of their debt to her and placing them where her husband would notice them. Not one of the stepmothers in Chao Phraya Thewet's households was ever officially elevated above the others, which was unusual. None of the stepmothers ever accompanied him to social or official occasions. Of course, the children often went about town with their father, which was quite another matter. If their mothers did not appear in public with him, they enjoyed relatively high status in society by reason of their place in a noble household. Boonlua chose to interpret this state of affairs as proof of a "democratic" tendency on her father's part to avoid jealousy among the women, a view that her sister Buppha shared.[29] In 1966 Boonlua gave a rare glimpse into her relationships with her siblings:

With my family, my sisters, of course we have family ties and then we have those ties that involve singing and dance and drama and this sort of thing, which to us is our life and soul—because we were brought up with these things. All of my—my mother and all but five or six of my stepmothers were dancers in the troupe. . . . In such a troupe, you [the male leader] took the women as a matter of course. It was expected of you. You made them your wives. You had children with them. And they were treated not like the minor wives or concubines of other households. They had their own status. . . . They were . . . it's difficult to . . . well, these women were professional people, and they were proud of their status. And also more rebellious than many other women. My father had a lot of trouble with my stepmothers. They quarreled more and—two stepmothers, you know, on one occasion they were in a dance drama where they had to fight each other, and they wouldn't stop fighting. [Boonlua laughs heartily.] They went right on fighting even though they were supposed to stop, you know, this sort of thing. They had plenty of temperament, and temper. . . .[30]

In traditional Thai society, no connection was made between a man's domestic arrangements and his "character." A devout Buddhist, Chao Phraya Thewet was respected for his belief that the tenets of Buddhism ought to be applied to human relations in the family and also in the work environment, and was admired for putting these beliefs into practice throughout his life. In all of Boonlua's reminiscences, the traditional roles of men and women in Thai society are presented as morally acceptable, and she describes polygyny as preferable to monogamy, under some circumstances. For example, in one essay she asserted that if a woman became ill and thus unable to perform all of her wifely duties, she would be much better off welcoming a minor wife into the household than facing divorce.[31]

Not only Boonlua but also her sister Buppha, whose mother had so wounded her father's pride, always spoke of their father with reverence and great respect. They also regarded their brother, Phraya Thewet, with affection and respect, and Buppha claimed that he was the model for the leading male character in what is perhaps her best novel, *People of Quality* (*Phu di*, approximately, "good people, people of good family"). As far as the reader knows, the male character in the novel is monogamous, devoted and faithful to his wife throughout her slow death from tuberculosis. Phraya Thewet maintained quite a different kind of family life, though it was typical for his era and class. He married and had children by one publicly recognized wife, but according to people who knew them well, his close relationship with his half-sister Chalaem, who had no known children, was the most important relationship of his life, and he left his estate to her. He also had children by other women, including another half-sister, according to members of the family. It seems reasonable to compare such relationships between children of different mothers but the same father in a polygynous household to the relationships of cousins in a society of nuclear families.

Despite what they may have said, there is compelling evidence that both Boonlua and Buppha felt more critical of the traditional polygynous model of marriage than they admitted. Nearly all of the heroes in their stories are monogamous and generally behave in a far more "Western" way (as Boonlua and Buppha perceived Western ways) than did Chao Phraya Thewet, his son, or any of the brothers, cousins, and other men who surrounded them in real life.

Even if the classical dancers who bore Chao Phraya Thewet's children were not completely pleased with the circumstances of their lives, it should not be assumed that they regretted their decision to enter his household. There were but two avenues to high social status for Thai women until relatively late in the twentieth century: a woman was either born into the nobility, or she formed an alliance with a man of high birth and bore his children. Young women and their parents made the best choices they could given the realities of their lives and their era.

Another factor that must be considered in understanding the polygynous, elite Siamese household is the reality that many women died young, usually of the complications of childbirth or tuberculosis. Boonlua's mother Nuan was typical: she married young, bore one child, and died of tuberculosis four years later.

Women could and did leave marriages in which they were unhappy, as Buppha's mother Mom Malai had left Chao Phraya Thewet, but it was an unusual event at this level of society. Adolescence, for the daughters of aristocrats in Boonlua's time, comprised a Thai version of the pursuit of "good matches" that fill the pages of Victorian novels. In Sri Burapha's 1937 novel *Behind the Painting (Khang lang phap)*, a woman from an aristocratic family whose "good match" had provided no joy pours out her heart to a young friend of the family:

> I beg you to understand what it is *to live as women do. We are born to decorate the world and to pander to it.* . . . When a young bird grows into its wings, it forsakes its nest and flies off into the great world. But a human being who is a female must remain in her cage. I had remained in mine and longed for that great world, craving change. . . . Only one thing would enable me to realize these dreams: *marriage.*[32]

Boonlua did not call her mother *mae*, the ordinary Thai word for mother, but *nai*, a pronoun prefix that denotes respect.[33] Today, the term *nai* is seldom used in speaking to or about women, but during Boonlua's childhood and within her social class, one respectfully addressed a lady as either *nai sao*, if she was single, or *nai ying*, if she was married or otherwise attached to a man.

Only a few memories of her mother appear in Boonlua's untranslated autobiography, *Successes and Failures*, but they are significant. Boonlua remembered her as being ill all the time, probably because of her illness and death from tuberculosis.

Whatever the state of her health, Nuan was a strict mother and teacher, and she began teaching Boonlua to read as soon as she could speak. "No matter how sick she was," Boonlua recalled, "my mother was never too sick to reach out and pinch me!"[34] This memory is significant, for there are no recorded memories to offset the image of Nuan as a strong and even punishing mother, no recollections of her mother taking her into her lap or indulging her as she was indulged by her father.

Even at three, Boonlua understood that to her mother, reading was of great importance. Chao Phraya Thewet described himself as illiterate. This was not quite the truth, for he had studied Thai in order to read prayers and sutras during his obligatory monkhood at twenty. Nuan's education is unknown, although she could read very well indeed, and we can only speculate as to what she hoped literacy might do for her only child. Given the opportunities for women at the time, her determination would seem to represent a blind faith in her child's future. While Boonlua always insisted that it was her father who was the great intellectual influence in her childhood, the fact remains that it was her mother who taught her to read and insisted that she do it well. This literate and demanding young woman, avid reader and classical dancer, was almost certainly more intellectually gifted than Boonlua realized, or gave her credit for.

THE DEATH OF BOONLUA'S MOTHER

By far the most important memory Boonlua had of her mother was the funeral, as described in her autobiography, *Successes and Failures*:

> I saw Father standing near the funeral pyre, and I ran to him. Perhaps he thought that I wanted to see my mother—well, I don't know what he thought—but he nodded to me, as if to say, "Yes, all right," and then he extended his arms as he said, "Here, Papa will lift you." I was amazed, thrilled actually, for Father had never to my memory lifted me in his arms, and before I could understand his intention, he was holding me up to see my mother's burning body. She had been embalmed. In those days they used only wood for cremations, and an embalmed body burned very slowly. I was aware that it was smoldering red, but I didn't note its exact appearance because I didn't want to see it, and so I have only a blurred memory of Mama looking like a roasted duck. However, I have never on that account had an aversion to roast duck, which is in fact one of my favorite foods, nor have I felt any unusual reaction to the color red. The colors I hate are green, yellow, and gray, mixed together.[35]

Boonlua's insistence that her mother's appearance during her cremation had no effect on her—not even on her future appreciation of roast duck—is characteristic. It is a preemptive strike against the possibility of other people's assumptions about her feelings or her behavior—or worse, their pity. It is also an example of her delight in shocking people, a behavior invariably mentioned by those who knew her.

After Nuan's death, Chao Phraya Thewet gave Boonlua into the daily care of a half-sister named Mom Wong. After Mom Wong's marriage to Prince Sukprarop Komalat, Boonlua's care was shifted to another half-sister, Mom Lamai (not to be confused with Buppha's mother, named Malai), and although Boonlua wrote that Mom Lamai was "like a mother to her," she never elaborated upon this statement.[36] Throughout her life, she would claim that the most "maternal" care she received as a child came from the Catholic nuns in the convent schools. Yet, when the adult Boonlua was asked about her relationships with her siblings, mother, stepmothers, or others in the household, she would gently steer the conversation away from them and toward a discussion of her father and of his famous friend, Prince Narit.

PRINCE NARIT: THE IDEAL SIAMESE MAN

Prince Narit (Narisara Nuvativongse) was Chao Phraya Thewet's closest friend. A man of superb intellect and creativity, one of the noted "Renaissance men" of the Chulalongkorn era as Thai invariably describe them, he was considered to be the leading expert on classical Thai music and on classical dance drama. He also was a superb architect and the designer of the internationally admired Wat Benchamabophit (the Marble Temple) in Bangkok, which has stained-glass windows and other features of churches and cathedrals he had admired on trips to Europe. Prince Narit built a house beside Chao Phraya Thewet's Khlong Toei residence, where Boonlua was born, and chose to live there much of the time for his health. It was then considered a remote, quiet location by comparison with Wang Ban Mo, which was nearer to the busy "downtown" area of Bangkok. Boonlua always insisted that, aside from her father, Prince Narit was the single most influential person in her childhood.[37]

After her mother's death, where could the four-year-old Boonlua turn for emotional sustenance? Half-sisters and stepmothers may have been recruited to care for her, but before Boonlua's fifth birthday, she felt safe and comfortable in the company of her father and Prince Narit. Boonlua recalled being "with my father or Prince Narit most of the time." If this remark was a considerable exaggeration, it also underlines their importance to her. These two elderly men (as men in their fifties were considered to be in that era) may be fairly compared with doting grandfathers in whose eyes the beloved grandchild can do no wrong.

> I heard such a lot of arguments between Prince Narit and my father, some things that my father did that Prince Narit disapproved of. And my father didn't admire Prince Narit very much but respected him a great deal. Because my father was a man of the world, he had a lot of wives, he did things that men of his time did—but he always went a little *over* . . . a little over the border. He had more wives than most of his colleagues, probably only fewer than King Chulalongkorn.
>
> But Prince Narit was an entirely different sort of man. My father could recite a lot of verse, and he could compose, but he wasn't a *poet*. He just did things because it was the fashion to do them. But not Prince Narit. He was a real poet and he lived his whole life for poetry—he was an artist. . . . Certain things my father did, Prince Narit just couldn't stand and disapproved of very strongly. He never practiced polygamy— he had only one wife. And he was very economical, he never wore extravagant clothes, and my father was awfully extravagant. But Prince Narit was very fond of all of his friends' children and he sort of took an objective interest—he loved them but he took an objective interest in their character, he studied them as if they were characters in a book. He encouraged us children, who were only *mom luang*, not of a very high rank in the royal hierarchy, but he encouraged us to behave as if we were very important, as if the princes had no more importance than us. And he encouraged us to be very fearless.[38]

Chao Phraya Thewet and Prince Narit delighted in Boonlua's questions and laughed at her bold assertions. But Prince Narit's influence was more than intellectual. He involved himself in the small details of

life and provided some of the warmth, acceptance, and understanding
that the child craved.

> I think he spoiled me entirely. For example, I can remember going
> into his room when he got up and he was still dressing. I would go
> and do all kinds of things and I don't ever remember being chased
> out, which was a very unusual thing for Thai children in those days.[39]

Prince Narit's interest in Chao Phraya's children's lives extended to
many ordinary details of life that Boonlua believed most men of his
class might fail (or not care) to notice.

> I remember in those days all girls had their earlobes pierced for
> wearing earrings, but my sisters were never allowed to do that because
> we were told that Prince Narit didn't like it. . . . He said, "There are
> so many places for ornaments on the body that it is unnecessary to
> go through pain in order to wear ornaments." When my father died,
> [my sisters] went straight to a quack, and he pierced their earlobes
> for them, and they suffered from infections, and one of them had to
> have almost all of her earlobes cut away because they were infected
> and there were some queer growths on them, too. I thought it was
> very funny. [Hearty laughter.][40]
>
> [Prince Narit] encouraged me to say things that Thai children don't
> say. I grew up to be a very unpleasant adolescent. People just couldn't
> stand me. My brother [Phraya Thewet] and especially his wife—she
> couldn't stand me *at all*—well, *lots* of older people couldn't stand me. I
> would ask questions while grown-ups were talking, discussing things
> together. My eldest brother [Phraya Thewet] was already quite a high
> government official by then and he would express dissatisfaction with
> the government, and I would . . . well, I would say things I felt, that
> sort of thing—oh my, they couldn't stand me.
>
> But you see, that was the sort of thing I was encouraged to do by
> my father and Prince Narit. If they were talking [with others], they
> were much higher [in status] than my brothers or my brothers in law

and *they* would always answer my questions. I would make a remark, and they would say, "Hm! Very good!" That sort of thing.[41]

Unfortunately, this uncritical admiration did Boonlua a disservice. It prepared her poorly for life. None of the attitudes or behaviors that charmed the two old noblemen would be admired by others, especially after she reached adolescence, when girls were admired most for being beautiful, graceful, and silent. She would cling to the belief that "speaking one's mind," as they had allowed and encouraged her to do since the age of eight or nine, to their delighted laughter and praise, comprised "traditional Thai" behavior. It did not, at least not in the case of females. Had she remained in their care through her adolescence, she might well have discovered that behavior they had found charming in a little girl they would not find charming at all in a young woman.

Decades later, in meetings at the Ministry of Education and elsewhere, Boonlua's forthright comments and especially her air of "entitlement" would infuriate and alienate some whose good opinion she would have liked to have—and could have used. That she was unable to understand how inappropriate her straightforward behavior seemed to others may fairly be blamed on her early indulgence by Chao Phraya Thewet and Prince Narit.

Had she remained in the household instead of being sent off to a convent school in Penang at the age of eleven, she might have been forced to temper her behavior and to act more "feminine." Instead, she went from the doting grandfathers straight to the European nuns in Penang. They were strong women who taught her how to think and how to behave and express herself in an academic (and Western) setting. But the nuns could not teach her how to comport herself in Thai society in ways that would be seen as becoming or appropriate.

Boonlua's father frequently took her with him when he went to the temple to visit with monks and make merit.[42] Often as not, she would fall asleep while he conversed with the learned monks, but Chao Phraya Thewet did not consider this any reason to stop taking her along, for he was confident that she would gain merit and absorb both knowledge and piety whether she was awake or asleep.

ALONE

When she was eleven years old, Boonlua's father died and her world collapsed. Her version of the events that followed was that the brother and sister-in-law who "couldn't stand" the "very unpleasant adolescent" decided to send her to the Convent of the Holy Infant Jesus in Penang, then a popular school for Thai and other Southeast Asian girls, to get rid of her. She never got over feeling betrayed by them.

> My sisters didn't like me to stay at home because I was such an unpleasant character and my sister-in-law [Phraya Thewet's wife, Anuwong's mother] just couldn't stand me. . . . She was of the type of older generation [women who] liked to keep people down. It's difficult to explain in English and—you would not understand the little shades of meaning.[43]

In fact, Boonlua was not, as she claimed she was, the only girl in the family who was sent to the convent in Penang. By the time Boonlua was sent there, Anuwong, Phraya Thewet's own child, had already been there for four years. When Boonlua left Bangkok for Penang in 1922, Buppha and Chalaem were already too old to be sent abroad, and apparently no one had thought of sending them earlier. Sending children away to be raised by relatives or good friends, or to be educated, was a common occurrence at all levels of Thai society at the time, and it still is quite common. In the memoir of a Thai woman named Lady Siphroma, she recalls that her father sent her away to be educated, which made her mother very sad:

> He wanted his child to have an education and to see the world. . . . [My mother] was sad and missed me so much that she became crazy and ran away to the woods. [My father] had to console her: "Don't be so sad. Those who are religious can give away their children and gain merit like Phra Wetsandon when he gave [away his children] Kanha and Chali . . ."[44]

There is no doubt that Boonlua's older siblings found her difficult to manage and occasionally exasperating, but the most important aspect of this event, in terms of Boonlua's own emotional development, is that she believed her family had rejected and betrayed her. She blamed herself for it and she blamed them. She was confused and angry and grieved during all the years in Penang for the lost paradise of her childhood.

She discounted the influence of Nuan, the literacy-minded mother who had produced a prodigy, and the examples of "stepmothers" who were talented, creative, and physically and mentally strong. All of the women in the household were relegated to insignificant roles in Boonlua's own version of her early years.

By the age of eleven, Boonlua had absorbed pride of family and learned to believe in her own ability to achieve difficult goals. Her self-esteem had been nurtured by Chao Phraya Thewet and Prince Narit and threatened by the critical and competitive behavior of her sisters and stepmothers. She found it difficult to love the one sister who tried to love her, Buppha, because she was so envious of the older girl's beauty and lovely manners. These feelings would only deepen and become more complex when Buppha became a famous novelist.

What did Boonlua know by the time she left home at eleven bound for the convent school in Penang? She knew that she was a Siamese girl of exceptional family, with responsibilities toward kingdom and king. She knew that she had been loved dearly by her father but that otherwise her family could not be trusted. Her memories of her mother were vague and not very satisfactory. She knew, as a young but serious Buddhist, that life led inexorably to suffering and death, teachings that even her own few years of life had proved to be sadly true. Her father had stressed the Buddhist teaching that ultimately a human being is responsible for his or her own life.

"Work out your own salvation with diligence," the Buddha had taught. "Be a lamp unto yourself."

Boonlua understood very well that she would have to light her own lamp and learn how to keep it burning.

2

FROM THE PALACE TO THE NUNS

Chetana Nagavajara, a literature professor and lifelong friend of Boonlua, remarked that Boonlua's personality "may be understood best if you remember that she went from the palace straight to the nuns."[1]

Boonlua's earliest years were regulated by the largely unspoken but endless rules of an elite household, to which were added the practices and disciplines of a Thai classical dance troupe. From age four to eleven, Boonlua attended St. Joseph Convent School in Bangkok as a day student. There she took readily to the pleasures of English and French language and literature and the particular joys of school plays. She was happy spending her days in the culture of the convent school and equally happy to return home each afternoon. To the bright, inquisitive, drama-loving little girl, the daily journey "from the palace to the nuns" and back again was not confusing. On the contrary, it was nearly ideal.

THAI DEFINITIONS OF EDUCATION

The first pages of Boonlua's autobiography are devoted to an explanation of the difference between the terms *oprom* (to rear, bring up, cultivate, nurture) and *sueksa* (to study and acquire knowledge, generally from written sources). Thais often use the two words as a pair, *oprom-sueksa,* to describe the education of children in general, but it was important to Boonlua that her readers appreciate the differences between knowledge that was *bestowed*—*oprom*—and knowledge that was *sought*—*sueksa*. She explained that in her own early life, the most valuable *oprom* had come from her father, from Prince Narit, and from others at home. *Sueksa*, on the other hand, referred to education one received in school, such as language and literature, arithmetic, and science—subjects she and her sisters and friends studied at the convent schools. Although she did not draw a strict line between Thai *oprom* and Western *sueksa*, the summation of her lengthy explanation of these terms is that she was a Thai, in terms of culture, with a Western education—but a Thai, first and foremost. Yet, when we look at her early education, we find that elements of *oprom* and *sueksa* were present and important both at home and in the convent schools.

Boonlua conflated the great event of her eleventh year, "the exile to Penang," with her nation's exile from Ayutthaya in 1767. During the Burmese sack of Ayutthaya virtually the entire canon of the nation's classical literature had been destroyed—whole libraries—in the fires that consumed most of the famed capital. The people were driven away, leaving all that was precious behind them. The voice and soul of Thai literature would have to be painstakingly re-created along with so much else. During the first reign of the Chakri dynasty in Bangkok (1782–1809), the major tasks were necessarily the restoration of governance and the establishment of order, but during the reign of the second king, Boonlua's great-great grandfather Phra Phutthaloetla (1809–24), the immense project of resurrecting the arts and literature of Siam began.

The Siamese had learned from bitter experience that what was written could be destroyed, but what was remembered and shared, generation after generation, could not. Nothing was equal to the sheer power of memory after precious manuscripts had vanished in the ashes of Ayutthaya.

Professor Chetana, in many essays and lectures, has spoken to the power of memory.

It may be no exaggeration to claim that without orality and memory, we would never have been the literary nation that we are today. . . . [L]earned men of the early Bangkok era. . . . were commonly engaged in two types of activities: first, rehashing from available written and oral sources, and secondly, recomposition of commonly known stories and tales. . . . [O]rality played a significant role in both categories, and memory was instrumental in these restorative endeavours.[2]

Like all of Boonlua's older relatives, Chetana's grandmother had a great gift for storytelling. Chetana writes:

My grandmother. . . . was endowed with extraordinary memory—which was common among her contemporaries—and possessed a very large repertoire of literary works that she could recite. It was perfectly natural for her to recite, say, *Phra Aphai Mani* [by Sunthon Phu, the famous poet of the late 18th and early 19th century] for a continuous period of a few hours. . . . To be able to recite effectively, one has to be a "performer" of some kind, and I still recall how my grandmother chanted and sang her favorite pieces and how she would manipulate her voice to suit the emotional contents of the respective texts. It goes without saying that I myself and some of my contemporaries had been exposed to literature long before we could read, and that would not have been possible without orality and memory.[3]

Thai poetry (and, therefore, Thai classical drama, which is written in poetic form) had to be composed in such a way that it could be remembered and recited by a great many people who could not read. Although poems and stories were written down, usually by scribes, storytelling in Siam always was essentially a performing art in a performative culture. The oral mode of dissemination must be "propped by its capacity to delight," in Chetana's words, and the words chosen to tell the story must be "delectable" in order to be preserved.[4] If a Thai poem or poetic drama must be aurally *delectable*, it must also be perceived as *sanuk*, an essentially untranslatable Thai word that is usually translated as "fun" but encompasses a great deal more than fun.

An event or activity that is *sanuk* provides pleasure, satisfaction, and excitement or fascination. If it fails to provide even one of these, it will be avoided, if possible.

In Boonlua's youth, and even today, classical and modern literature are described using distinct terms. *Wannakhadi* refers to classical, poetic works representing the "literary arts," while *wannakam* is used for modern fiction. The most respected genre continues to be poetry, and because of this the oral tradition in Thailand is not yet a historical artifact. Nor, despite the fact that poetry enjoys greater status than prose, is poetry the exclusive property of the elite. Thomas Hudak has written:

> While the more formal poetic compositions generally remained the domain of the upper classes and literary circles, the lower classes exhibited a great interest and enjoyment in a simple, folk type of poetry. . . . [F]armers engaged in word play and in rhyming song contests which included bouts between two groups of people, each group having a leader ready to lead members in attempts to defeat the other group with a contest marked by "a ready wit, a good thrust at an opponent . . . smart repartee, a pretty compliment, or persuasive arguments."[5]

For girls of Boonlua's generation and class, poetry and clever repartee in the form of suggestive rural love songs were not (supposed) to be thought of. But she was always fond of this kind of music, which appealed to the earthy streak in her nature. It was emphatically *sanuk*.

Boonlua was hardly alone in being sent to study abroad at a young age. In that era, traveling to a foreign land to study was a fact of life for many children of the Siamese elite. Girls and young women rarely went very far from home. The Convent of the Holy Infant Jesus (Convent Light Street) in Penang, where Boonlua was sent, was as far as most people would send a daughter. It was not until after World War II that young women went off to universities abroad, usually in the United States. Since then, almost as many women as men have become *nakrian nok*, literally, "students [who have studied] outside [the country]."

Throughout the late nineteenth and early twentieth centuries, education was a cornerstone of the effort to maintain Siamese sovereignty while adopting Western technology and methods of governance. The tacit subtext in acceptance of the missionary schools was, "Send us your teachers to educate our children. Send us your science and your advisors but not your philosophy, much less your religion." By the second decade of the twentieth century, studying abroad had become common, at least for children of the extended royal family and of the wealthy business class.

Acceptance of and respect for Western education, whether that meant girls going to Catholic convent schools or boys going abroad to Oxford or Cambridge, never interfered with absolute faith in the primacy of Siamese culture, religion, arts, or literature. Because Siam escaped direct colonization by a European power, it also escaped the effects of a conquering culture continually demonstrating its declared superiorities and making explicit and implicit demands that train colonized subjects to perceive their own cultural and artistic products as primitive, backward, and minor. Not only did the independent Siamese remain proud of their own language and literature; never having been given cause to doubt the quality or value of these things they remained in exclusive control of their uses, dissemination, and appreciation. When Thai began to compose short stories and novels from about 1880 on, they did so as an amusing pastime, but these byproducts of Western education were hardly to be considered alongside Siam's traditional poetic and dramatic compositions. Thai writers never felt compelled to either adapt or reject foreign literary influences as an affirmation of artistic excellence.[6] In short, they adapted certain European literary forms and techniques, and used them because they were *sanuk*—just as they used convenient and pleasant aspects of Western technology, such as electric lighting in their homes. They fastened the sconces to the walls, turned on the lights and saw, with great satisfaction, that everything that was illuminated was theirs and would remain theirs.

Many of the political developments in late nineteenth-century and early twentieth-century Siam have been labeled "internal colonialism," with the monarchy and the Siamese elite, including Boonlua's family, taking the hegemonic role of a foreign power—for example, using natural and human resources largely to their own benefit.

Less widely reported or speculated upon was the rarely admitted, nagging suspicion that although neighboring countries had lost their independence to categorical colonialism, they had nevertheless gained certain benefits of Western civilization, including superior education, at least for native elites. If independence was worth any price, the fact remained that there *was* a price. It was vexing for Thais to consider the Vietnamese elite speaking excellent French, reading Victor Hugo, and sending their children to schools where they learned the perplexing yet impressive exploits and traditions of "*nos ancestres les Gauls.*" As for the Malay elite, not only were they speaking English and reading Shakespeare, Arthur Conan Doyle, and old editions of the *Times*, they had also achieved a level of bureaucratic orderliness that Siam was able to achieve and maintain only by the careful, constant importation of advisors and civil servants from a number of Western nations, particularly England, Denmark, Germany, and the United States. If it is true that Siam was never colonized by a European power, it is also true that the Royal Government of Siam supported a permanent and privileged stable of Western economic, engineering, and other advisors during the late nineteenth and early twentieth centuries.

Official objectives in sending the young Siamese elite class abroad to study, whether in addition to missionary schools in Siam or in place of them altogether, were pragmatic and strategic. The overriding long-range objective was the assurance of Siam's continuing sovereignty. King Chulalongkorn, in this excerpt from a letter to his sons studying in Europe, makes that objective perfectly clear.

> I would at this point impress upon you the fact that in sending you abroad for a European education, it is not my object to have you useful solely through your knowledge of foreign languages and European methods of work. Your own language and literature must be ever in constant use. . . . Knowledge of a foreign language is merely the means of acquiring further learning.[7]

The following excerpt from another letter is even more blunt.

If after acquiring proficiency in foreign languages you cannot turn what you have learned into Siamese, little advantage will have been gained, *for we can employ as many foreigners as we need.* What will be required of you is an ability to turn a European language into Siamese, and Siamese into a European language. You would be useful then.[8]

These objectives, then articulated by King Chulalongkorn, would change very little during the twentieth century, even after the overthrow of the absolute monarchy in 1932. One went abroad to study for the benefit of the nation, and this invariably prepared one for a career chosen by officials in the administration. A boy's own preferences were of little consequence. A retired Thai general recalls the decisions that shaped his own education in England during the 1960s, six decades after King Chulalongkorn began sending young men abroad:

I wanted to be a doctor. But just before I was to begin my medical studies abroad, my family received a message from the Ministry of Education that I was the only boy in that year who was qualified to enter Sandhurst, because of my studies at Eton, the examinations I had passed, and so forth. And they needed a boy for Sandhurst that year; and so, of course, I went to Sandhurst.[9]

Foreign-educated, substantially "Westernized" Thais have held many if not most of the positions of greatest influence and power in their nation for the past century. During the 1920s, when the increasingly liberal policies of the government gave not only aristocrats but also commoners with uncommon scholarly gifts the privilege of studying abroad, the results of Western education would begin to have effects on the future of Siam that King Chulalongkorn could not possibly have anticipated.

A WESTERN EDUCATION BEGINS

Boonlua's introduction to formal education began in 1915 when her father lifted her from his carriage, took her by the hand, walked her to the door of St. Joseph Convent School, and presented her to the nuns. A girl was supposed to be six years old to enter St. Joseph, but Chao Phraya Thewet never doubted that his four-year-old prodigy would be equal to the challenge. He whispered to her that she must keep her true age to herself, signed the enrollment forms, and left her with Sister Margaret.

Boonlua's late mother had taught her to read Thai and she could write a little. But English and French were the languages of St. Joseph, and for months she floated through her school days in a cloud of confusion, unable to understand anything that was said, or any of the papers that were distributed to the girls in her class, regardless of whether they could read them or not. A Sister would place a mysterious piece of paper before them, and if they could make nothing of the writing on the paper, they waited politely until the Sister returned and, without comment, removed it. Gradually, Boonlua came to understand that the cloud of confusion was in fact divided into discrete subjects such as geography and French, that girls were tested on what they had learned, and that some people placed first, or second, or even failed. That part, she quickly understood.

There is no evidence of an organized effort on the part of the nuns to wean the girls gradually from the Thai language to English and French. This was language education by immersion with a vengeance, and any infraction of the "no Thai speaking" rule was promptly punished. It was a system that worked. The Sisters believed that they were imparting civilized languages to their charges, for which the girls should be very grateful, and while the girls' parents did not consider their own language to be inferior, they invariably backed up the Sisters. Several times during her first year at St. Joseph, Boonlua was made to stand in the corner for some misbehavior, but she never learned what she had done wrong or how to avoid committing the same offense in the future. By the second year, she had learned what was expected of her and how to produce the desired behaviors. The processes of a proper education had ceased to be a mystery and she quickly rose to the rank of third or fourth student in her class.

For all the discipline they meted out, the Sisters convinced the girls that they truly loved them and had their best interests at heart, and that this love must be returned in the form of good deeds and, more important, in the avoidance of misdeeds, which caused the Sisters to be hurt deeply. Laziness, in particular, was a misdeed—a sin in fact—and it caused the Sisters immense pain and grief. Boonlua's sister Buppha, who was also a student at St. Joseph (and later studied at the St. Francis Xavier Convent School), remembered that she and her classmates became "stars at weeping, kneeling together in a line, sobbing and begging Sister Margaret to forgive us for causing her such anguish. One girl carried a small onion hidden in her fist, just in case it might be needed."[10]

Boonlua was impressed with the spotless, gleaming tile floors at St. Joseph and the smooth polished surfaces of the teakwood double desks. A girl never knew when a Sister, voluminous black cape fluttering behind her, would come swooping down the aisle to demand that a desktop be opened, and woe unto the girl whose books were heaped in an untidy pile, or—worst of all—dirty. For the rest of her life, Boonlua would wrap the books she owned in tidy covers.

Another view of life at St. Joseph appears in the autobiography of Princess Rudivoravan (as told to Ruth Adams Knight), who like Boonlua was born in the year 1911. For a time, she was a boarding student at St. Joseph, unlike Boonlua, who returned home every afternoon.

The teachers at St. Joseph were Sisters of a French order and very gentle and sweet. . . . We students wore uniforms, black-and-white-checked ones, and whenever I wanted a clean one I had to get it from Madame Terese. The school routine was very monotonous. We had long prayers in the morning and again in the evening. They were not in Thai, so I did not understand them. I . . . was only beginning to learn French—to study it was one of the reasons I was sent to the convent. I was not even sure what the religious faith there was; later I realized, of course, it must have been Roman Catholic. . . . I remember . . . a dining room where we had for breakfast a piece of bread and a banana; for lunch, curry; for tea, a piece of bread put in our hand. Dinner was a good meal; we ate it late and hurried to bed. We had to rise early, and I liked to wake before we were called, for then I could peek at the Sister in charge, combing her hair. I thought most of the Sisters looked like angels and their hair was long and lovely. I never saw hair more beautiful than theirs.[11]

Rote memory and recitation were the pillars of pedagogy at St. Joseph, which posed no problem for a child who had been learning prayers, songs, and poems by heart from her infancy. Although they were comprised of prose and not poetry, Boonlua still was able to memorize whole chapters of history and geography, reeling them off promptly and perfectly upon command. Lessons had to be written first into an ordinary copybook, and then, after the Sisters had corrected them, rewritten on clean paper. As the finishing touch, the student would pen a fine, modest design on the cover, or at the head of the page, using purple ink.

It was not simply a lack of innovation that caused both Thai and European school teachers of the early twentieth century to continue to depend upon rote memory and recitation. Books were great luxuries in both Europe and Thailand. This scarcity would plague Thai schools throughout Boonlua's career, and she would campaign tirelessly for buying books first before allocating meager resources to implement experimental educational programs. Nevertheless, according to Thai tradition, the best pupil was the child who could recite a piece *exactly*. Even after books became more available, this attitude prevailed—and it prevails to this day. A gift for memorization and precise recitation still earns high praise and high marks.

Boonlua always valued her early years at St. Joseph for teaching her the importance of meticulous attention to every task. The nuns were insistent, and the girls, already socialized to comply with the wishes of elders, complied. Habits learned became habits for life. "Convent girls," at six, sixteen, and sixty, were notorious for the rigid standards to which they held not only themselves but also those around them. It was said, not quite in jest, that the husbands of St. Joseph graduates "consoled each other all their lives with the thought that one can do nothing to change a convent girl, and that it is best not to try."[12]

The girls referred to the Sisters as *mae dam* (literally, "black mothers") because of their dress.[13] Chief among the reasons families of the elite class were comfortable with sending their daughters to convent schools was the knowledge that the nuns' ideas about how young ladies ought to behave were as rigid as their own. Privacy was unknown. The girls studied together, played together, ate together, and went to the latrine and the shower together. And whatever they did, wherever they went, they were never out of sight of a Sister. Fun, for convent girls, consisted of momentarily escaping the sight of a Sister in order to perpetrate some minute infraction of the endless rules.

Once or twice a year, the girls put on a play. Boonlua was always chosen for a leading role for two reasons: first, because she was the daughter of the famous Chao Phraya Thewet, leading authority on Thai classical dance drama, and second, because she was demonstrably the inheritor of that genius. These plays were the crowning joy of her days at St. Joseph.

During these years, Boonlua read her lessons, wrote compositions, and devoured all the fiction she was allowed to read. The Sisters approved the elevating novels of M. Delly and Sir Walter Scott. According to many reports, these were the favorite authors of convent nuns in all of Southeast Asia. The girls were often reminded that fiction was, at best, a pastime to be enjoyed when there were no better tasks to be done, such as schoolwork.

At home, no one ever read stories from books. Stories were sung, or chanted, and children listened until they were capable of joining in. But if the worlds of home and school were distinct in most ways, there were significant intersections. For example, there was the matter of Bible stories. Boonlua once brought home a picture book about Moses to ask her father's opinion of the stories. She showed him pictures of Moses and the Jews barely escaping from the Red Sea and God sending the waters crashing down upon the pursuing Egyptian soldiers. When she had finished recounting the story, she asked her father whether such a thing was really possible. Chao Phraya Thewet was not familiar with

Moses, but he knew a great many stories about gods and goddesses who had magical powers and who surely could part a sea if they wanted to. After frowning at the picture for a few moments he declared, "This is not much of a God. He helps only the people on his side and murders everybody on the other side."[14]

Boonlua explained that the story was from the Bible, and that the Christians believed that it was a sin not to believe Bible stories. He told her not to worry; someday, when she was older, she would understand about religions. The story about Moses and the Jews and their God who drowned their enemies in the sea reminded him of Indra and other Hindu celestial beings who were forever interfering in the lives of mortals and causing all sorts of trouble. It seemed to him that the Christian God was very much like those gods—temperamental, holding grudges like any mortal, and playing favorites. Buddhists, he explained, had learned from their great teacher and from what they saw with their own eyes that we humans, not gods, are responsible for our own lives and our futures. Those who do good, receive good, while those who do evil, receive evil—if not in this life then in the next. The Buddha had known this, and therefore had looked upon all people with compassion.[15]

"After the Moses incident," Boonlua wrote, "what we call critical thinking blossomed in my young mind, a faculty that would lead me to some of my successes in life—and not a few of my failures." Although she credited her father with teaching her "critical thinking," it is apparent that the daily shuttle between the worlds of St. Joseph and home caused her to contemplate the subject of *how* one ought to think about questions before trying to construct answers. She decided for herself that in the matter of Bible stories and certain other puzzling matters, neither her father nor the Sisters were entirely right or entirely wrong.

I think that being a Buddhist in a Catholic environment was very interesting. Because you had to keep comparing and making decisions all the time.[16]

THE THEATER OF HOME

After Chao Phraya Thewet's retirement in 1909, the dance troupe no longer performed at the Royal Palace. Nevertheless, dancing, rehearsing, and performing went on at home, just as before. The stepmothers and the older sisters taught the younger girls how to sing and dance, and from the age of six to eleven Boonlua was pleased to be given some of the better roles in the informal, sometimes impromptu performances that were such an important feature of their family life. She remembered being rehearsed in a male role, and she was thrilled with Prince Narit's delighted laughter at her performance although she astutely surmised that he did not appear to be overwhelmed by her talent.[17]

These juvenile performances were based on the *lakhon duekdamban*, a simplified form of classical dance drama that Chao Phraya Thewet and Prince Narit had created in response to King Chulalongkorn's request for works that Western guests at court would find enjoyable. Requirements for the new style of dance drama included a length of no more than two hours, singing by both men and women, plenty of action, and no need to be familiar with the story. Court officials were aware that Westerners, when invited to attend, clearly considered the slow, immensely long Siamese dance dramas to be feats of audience endurance. On his only visit to Europe in 1891, Chao Phraya Thewet had greatly enjoyed visits to the opera (as had Prince Narit, on several trips), and these experiences with "Western *lakhon*" influenced their thinking about how the Thai dance drama could be reimagined and reformed.

Few Thais today realize that what they themselves think of as "classical" Thai dance drama reflects the substantial abridgments made by Prince Narit in the early twentieth century. However one might regard them, after about 1890 the all-night performances of *lakhon* were relegated to history. The first public performances of *lakhon duekdamban* took place in 1899 and were highly successful. Chao Phraya Thewet opened a new theater on Atsadang Road directly in front of Wang Thewet and called it the "*rong* [theater of] *lakhon duekdamban*." This theater remained popular until 1909, when Chao Phraya Thewet resigned his positions at the Royal Palace, and for over a decade the theater stood empty. In 1924, some of the plays were resurrected and published under the auspices of King Vajiravudh and distributed on the occasion of the seventieth birthday of an aristocrat named Chao Khun Prayunwong.[18]

Later, when films became popular, Boonlua's brother, Phraya Thewet, would turn the theater into one of the first movie houses in Bangkok, a decision that was financially very successful although everyone in the household complained of the noise that lasted well into the night, every night.

After they had been at St. Joseph for a few years, Boonlua and her sisters began to bring home some of the plays they had read in school, translate them into Thai, and put on performances. In 1981, Boonlua recalled these productions:

> We barely understood the stories—we were very young, you know. We begged the servants to sew costumes and the gardeners to help us with scenery. I have to laugh, thinking what Shakespeare might have made of our productions. Of course, King Vajiravudh had already translated some of Shakespeare's plays—but we didn't know anything about that.[19]

Decades later, Boonlua and her sisters still occasionally sang together, exchanging lengthy passages of the Thai poetic dramas and songs they had learned as children. She worried that the correct singing of the music would die with the next generation. In 1966, she told an interviewer,

> It is very sad, I think. Prince Narit's music—it is going to be lost, you know. My sisters, they sing quite well. Or they used to. I have been telling them for over ten years, "You know, if we don't record what we sing it's going to be lost. We will become too old, and we will not be able to sing like now. Now they're over sixty [Boonlua was fifty-five at the time of this interview] and one of them is sick and so on, and most of the singing that they've been doing is not going to be remembered—the *style*, especially. The melody will go on, but the *style* will be lost. The next generation of singers will not hear it, and it's a particular style that is not heard outside of our own circle. But

nobody who is in a position to record this singing takes the trouble to do it.[20]

Far from suffering ill effects, Boonlua apparently thrived on being shuttled between "the palace and the nuns," during her St. Joseph Convent years. The cultural, religious, and social diversity she experienced was exciting and opened her eager mind to a wealth of possibilities. The difficulties she would soon encounter would have little to do with any disorientation between oral and literate traditions or a cultural gap between East and West. They would have everything to do with the events of her early childhood and with her own nature, which by all accounts changed little with the decades. In the extremely competitive environment of her family, beauty, brains, and talent represented both weapons and targets of intrigue. Boonlua struggled in vain to win from siblings and stepmothers the recognition of her talents and the unqualified acceptance of her value as a human being that her father had given unconditionally. She was willful, outspoken, and easily tempted by the sin of pride, a serious failing in the eyes of both her relatives at home and the nuns at school.

We know little of the last year of Chao Phraya Thewet's life from his youngest daughter. Given the fact that in her memoir, Boonlua wrote in some detail about the events surrounding her mother's death and cremation, it seems likely that she was kept at a distance from her father during his final illness. If she was heartbroken, she was not surprised when older siblings who "couldn't stand her" would immediately use her father's death as an excuse to exile her from her own home.

Boonlua left Bangkok for Penang as a grieving and lonely girl, and it would be six years before she would see her home, or her homeland, again. They would be difficult years, both physically and emotionally. She had by her own probably exaggerated account "run with the boys" on the family estate in Bangkok, getting into all manner of mischief—during the hours when she was not under the stern eyes of the Sisters at St. Joseph—but she would become a far different girl in Penang. She would experience panic attacks, dizziness, incapacitating weakness, and vague "syndromes," including heart arrhythmias that required hospitalization followed by lengthy periods of recovery, and ever-increasing amounts of medication.

LIFE IN CONVENT LIGHT STREET

The Convent of the Holy Infant Jesus in Penang, Malaya, commonly known as Convent Light Street, operated under the authority of the British government in the persons of His Majesty's inspectors, who occasionally visited and observed. In practice, however, the Sisters were given a great deal of freedom in running the school and in their teaching methods, and they took full advantage of this freedom to create a progressive learning environment for girls who came to them from a number of Southeast Asian countries. Years later, when Boonlua herself was an education inspector in Thailand, she would dismiss some of the "new" teaching methods she was invited to observe abroad during her travels in Europe and North America as having been commonplace at Convent Light Street when she was a girl.[21]

Situated near the harbor, a block from the E & O (European and Oriental) Hotel, the convent faced the sea, with a spacious lawn and rows of well-tended palm trees stretched between graceful colonial buildings and the shore. The setting was beautiful, but at first Boonlua was aware only that she felt lost and homesick, especially for her father. Boonlua's niece Anuwong, six months Boonlua's junior, had been a student at the school for several years when Boonlua arrived, but the niece and aunt had had a troubled relationship during their early childhood.[22] There were other girls from Siam in her class, including Khunying Sunetra Khomsiri, who remembered Boonlua as "often sick, and in the infirmary."[23]

Despite the number of years she spent there, Boonlua developed no close or lasting friendships among the girls who were her classmates. At first she was confused by differences between this school and St. Joseph. For example, in her first school the Sister in charge of a classroom had sat behind a large desk on a raised platform. When a student needed to approach her, the girl would crawl onto the platform on hands and knees as gracefully as possible, then rise up on her knees, place her palms together before her nose, and wait in silence until the Sister recognized her. The first time Boonlua crawled respectfully toward one of the Sisters in Penang, she was told sharply to get up off her knees, with the somewhat ironic implication that the sort of groveling she may have been used to in Siam would not do here in a British colony.

After ten days at the school, she was moved up a level, and by the end of term she was at the top of her class. In her memoir, Boonlua gives a rare glimpse of the ambiguity that elite Thais of her generation felt about the lives of their neighbors under colonial rule:

> In those days Thailand assumed that it was not so developed as its neighboring countries, which were colonies of the farang. Then why wasn't the convent school at Penang in any way lovely? The desks were made of coarse wood, oiled with some black stuff, and the chairs were poorly built. The floors in the schoolroom were covered with red clay tiles that were always dusty. They had to sweep water over them to keep the dust from billowing everywhere.[24]

Classwork was never a problem, and Boonlua soon learned how to comport herself to win the approval of the Sisters. But her fellow students—the Thai girls in particular—were another matter. Nothing she did could win them over.

> All the other Thai girls laughed when I sang Thai songs. And everything to do with [my ideas about] the *lakhon*—they saw that as funny, too. In fact, when I offered my opinion about anything, they thought it was quite comical. I felt such grief and resentment.[25]

A passionate interest in matters of style in Thai classical dance did not commend Boonlua to the girls she hoped would be her new friends. Everything she cared about and tried to share, everything that she hoped would impress them only made her appear ridiculous. They laughed at the strange girl's absurdly high opinion of her ridiculous self. This was not Bangkok and nobody was impressed by her dead father. The girls were sarcastic and cruel, they imitated her mannerisms and made fun of her appearance—her serious expression, her protruding teeth, her proud walk. In short, they behaved like a clique of young adolescent girls who have found the perfect target for their less than admirable impulses. Boonlua interpreted their reactions to her as proof that she, like her father before her, would live a life caught between generations, and perhaps even between centuries:

> Gradually I realized that my ideas about the *lakhon* had come from the Fourth Reign [1851–68], but I lived with people born in the Sixth Reign [1910–25]. . . .
>
> At first I tried to show my true personality to them, but it was no use. It was better to hide my real self. Fortunately, I was successful in my studies and gave a good name to the Thai students. . . . In almost every class in which there were Thai girls, the first place went to a Thai. [Her niece and rival from home, Anuwong, was one of these Thai girls who won prizes.] And so, my teachers came to love me and altogether, I survived.[26]

Perhaps worst of all was the bewildering discovery that she would not automatically be given good parts in school plays, a circumstance she had come to regard as her right at St. Joseph. In Penang she was never chosen. This awful realization that she would be cut out of the activity she loved most she chose to interpret as due to her English being tainted with a French accent, because French had been the first language of most of the Sisters at St. Joseph; perhaps she had learned to speak English with a French accent and that was the reason. But this was not a convincing argument because it did not explain why other girls who had been at St. Joseph were chosen, time after time, while she never was. One explanation of the unkindness of some of her Thai classmates may be that many of them were daughters of wealthy Chinese-Thai businessmen in southern Thailand. It seems reasonable that these girls would find her aristocratic bearing and manners affected, conceited, and perplexing. Certainly, Boonlua lacked the charm and sprightly gaiety that made Anuwong popular with everyone, although Anuwong too came from an exalted background. It was in Penang that the rift that had always existed between the two girls became a chasm.

The Sisters, who at first found Boonlua to be a strange and sullen child, came to respect her not only for her academic gifts but also for her character. For example, a great and continuing effort was made to convince the girls that Christianity in the form of Roman Catholicism was the one true religion and their only hope of salvation and eternal life. But in this matter Boonlua was politely stubborn. One of the Sisters told her, "The fact that one does not easily accept the religion of another people is not a bad thing. The girls who accept (Christianity) most easily are the quickest to lose it when they go home." But another Sister was of a different opinion, expressing sorrow at the fact that God apparently had taken no interest in Boonlua so far and advised her to pray nightly, "asking Jesus to enter my heart." Boonlua obeyed, and prayed nightly for this event, until at last she decided that the prayers were to no avail, Jesus did not want to enter her heart, and she might as well give it up.[27]

[To please the Sisters] I memorized the whole of the Gospel of St. Matthew and St. Mark, the Douet version. And I memorized the whole of "The Merchant of Venice" and Milton's sonnets. But you were not given high marks in this school for simply remembering things. You had to answer questions on what you remembered.[28]

Few if any Thai women converted to Catholicism as the result of going to a convent school, although Boonlua and many other convent school graduates have made it clear that the nuns did their best. This was also true for Thai boys who attended missionary schools. Why was conversion to Christianity so very rare? My own attempts to locate a single former convent school girl who had converted to Roman Catholicism were unsuccessful. I believe that the girls' parents, particularly the fathers, prevented this possibility by the way in which they spoke to their children about the religion they would be urged to embrace. Boonlua's father had told his children that no matter how absurd they might find the stories they heard (the matter of the Red Sea parting, and so forth), they were strictly forbidden to utter a word of criticism or disagreement with their teachers. No child of his must ever show disdain for the religion of his or her teacher. The teachers and the schools were offering great gifts of modern knowledge, teaching them the sorts of things that Western foreigners were very good at and that Thais needed to know. These gifts were to be accepted with gratitude and in a civilized manner. The result was that by instilling in his children the importance of not condescending to what they could only infer was an inferior faith, he managed to defeat the missionaries with irreproachable *politesse*. This was the attitude the Thai kings of the colonial era had projected, and that the cousins, nephews, and great-grandchildren of the kings faithfully continued to project. King Mongkut had delighted in civilized debates over religion with missionaries during the mid-nineteenth century, and his grandsons, King Vajiravudh and King Prajadhipok, would make their way through Eton, Oxford, and Sandhurst (in Vajiravudh's case), sitting politely and patiently beside their British classmates during Anglican church services, their Thai Buddhism intact.

There was another, perhaps more important reason why there was no possibility of the Sisters making religious headway with Boonlua. Thai Buddhism could never be separated, in her mind or her heart, from her most precious memories: the wonderful visits to Buddhist temples with her father, first sitting beside him in the carriage, then napping on the temple floor beside him as he talked with the monks; or her joy when she mastered the "four-baht prayer," not to mention a certain satisfaction at the envy of siblings who probably never would. Boonlua's Buddhism was not only the religion of her childhood, it was a gift from her beloved father, a great element in her traditional upbringing, the *oprom* of her early years, to be cherished and nurtured all her life. To open her heart to another religion, even to please the kindly nuns who taught and nursed her, would have been to let go of the lifeline of memory that sustained her in the cruel exile from a childhood that was coming to seem utopian by comparison with her present life.

Within a year of her arrival at Convent Light Street, Boonlua experienced her first menstrual period. She suffered violent nausea and vomiting, painful cramps, and weakness so debilitating that she was forced to stay in bed in the infirmary for nearly a full week. This affliction, and its treatment, recurred monthly for the entire six years in Penang. Boonlua went into some detail on the subject in her autobiography, although she offered no conjecture as to the reasons for such unusually severe symptoms—or for the fact that she was "much better" after she graduated and returned to Siam. Would most Thai women of her generation choose to include adolescent menstrual problems in an autobiography? They would not. But Boonlua often said that prudishness about bodies and their functions was affected and unnecessary. In any event, menstruation was unmistakable proof that she was growing up and becoming a woman, hardly a cheering thought for a girl who had convinced herself that she was raised by men and thus different from other girls. Or it may be that the cause of her severe menstrual symptoms was primarily physical, perhaps caused by endometriosis, for example. In any event, the treatment for her monthly indisposition, aside from a blessed week in the infirmary and the loving ministrations of the nuns, temporarily liberated her from the company of her classmates. She even got to eat special and delicious foods that the Sisters prepared for her on the advice of a doctor.

> I might say that the Sisters cared for me better than the people in my own family. . . . When I had a fever, even in the middle of the night, the Sisters would change my perspiration-soaked nightgowns, and dry my damp hair. The next morning, they would bring delicacies to tempt my appetite, and my teacher would ask whether I had any problem with my schoolwork because of my illness.[29]

Boonlua never missed a test because of illness—a great piece of luck, to her mind. Writing about these years a half-century later, she never speculated that psychological factors might have played any role in ensuring that the behavior for which she was most rewarded—achieving high score on tests—was never compromised. Nor did she even begin to examine the relationship between the loving care she received from the Sisters when she was ill and the significant presence of illness in her adult life.

Lying in bed in the infirmary, Boonlua would finish her lessons and then spend the long, quiet afternoons reading novels and listening to the music of waves rhythmically surging against the beach, and the faint sound of palm fronds clacking against each other in the breeze.

The years at Convent Light Street laid the groundwork for a lifetime of intellectual and career successes, punctuated by recurring bouts of illness and depression. Usually, these followed experiences that she considered to be personal failures—failure to impose her standards, or her greater expertise, on colleagues and superiors; failure to be understood and appreciated. Even in Penang as an adolescent, she saw her life in terms of successes and failures with very little in between.

If she prized meticulous habits and self-discipline as the most beneficial results of her years at St. Joseph, Boonlua credited the Sisters of Convent Light Street with the training of her intellect. This was not merely a place where the daughters of elite Southeast Asian families could learn to speak admirable English and French and gain a reasonable smattering of other subjects—which was Boonlua's final assessment of St. Joseph. The Sisters in Penang were enthusiastic about education. They gave their charges a real love of literature, teaching them *how* to read the novels of Austen and Brontë, Dickens and Trollope. These tales of good families, wise virgins, and just rewards for honorable behavior fascinated the girls without challenging the values they had absorbed at home.

The Sisters encouraged their charges to ask questions and even to give their opinions in class. The nuns' objectives, attitudes, and teaching techniques would become the cornerstone of Boonlua's own teaching philosophy: a student's *own* thoughts about what he or she was learning were of value, and the ability to analyze and interpret literature was far more important than the ability to memorize and recite.

When Boonlua, Anuwong, and the other Thai girls returned home from Penang, their families were proud of their fluency in English and French, the most important and useful of the *farang* languages, and pleased with their nice manners, but showed little if any interest in their academic achievements. After all, a superior education was hardly going to lead to a position in government, as it would for a young man. For a young woman, too much education might even get in the way of her marriage prospects. Young men were rarely attracted to overly clever young ladies, much less opinionated ones.

> People at that time considered education to be a matter of "training for life," but not a matter of academic competition for entrance to a high-level school, or a path to a career, or fame. [Upper-class women] of the time generally didn't have to go out to work. . . . In a family such as mine, the kind of training girls received was intended to make them courageous, proud of their ancestors, and incapable of bringing shame to the family. The Catholic schools contributed nicely to these objectives.[30]

One thing the girls learned that was impressive to their mothers was the ability to do fine handwork, such as embroidery and knitting. Boonlua, otherwise little interested in the homely arts, found these skills to be pleasurable and useful in a variety of ways. Many years later, she would knit her way through committee meetings, her eyes fastened to her work, the click-clack of her needles increasing to a staccato pace when she was annoyed.

For all that she gained from her years at Convent Light Street far from home, there was one thing that she missed: the upbringing of an adolescent female in a noble Thai household. Had she stayed home as her sisters Buppha and Chalaem did, it is more likely that she would have been "polished," made attractive to people in her own society, whether they be suitable marriage partners or people in society in general. They would have taught her how a lady behaves with and defers to men—at least, gentlemen of her own class. She would have learned to regret the boastful and frequently out-of-bounds behaviors of her early childhood, such as interrupting her elders and voicing her own opinion when no one had asked for it. What took the place of the training she would have received during adolescence, training that prepared girls who stayed home for lives as admirable matrons, was an environment in which she was expected to behave like a lady, but also expected to develop and refine her own ideas and opinions.

Mom Anuwong would return to Bangkok to marry an aristocrat and live in high society, traveling and sometimes living abroad, and maintaining her reputation as a lady of great charm and beauty. Her childhood appears, on the surface, to have been quite similar to Boonlua's, and they were very close in age. But her role in the extended family was very different. Anuwong was always a charming girl, and beautiful, whereas Boonlua was a willful and sulky child, possessed of a brilliant mind and spoiled by a proud father who gave little thought to the effects of his indulgence. As these girls had left their family home for the convent school in Penang, so they returned to it. Anuwong slipped easily into her role as a lovely lady who also was competent in the things that mattered most for a woman. Boonlua returned home with no idea as to what her role in life might be, or could be.

Between the age of seventeen, when she returned to Bangkok, and twenty-seven, Boonlua would re-create herself. She would be among the first women to be accepted to Chulalongkorn University. There, she would acquire the specific skills she needed in order to pursue a career in education. But her degree from Chulalongkorn would be only the capstone of her education. Although Boonlua always said, "I was raised by men," the truth was that she had been encouraged and inspired by men when she was a precocious and amusing little girl, but her teachers had been women: the worried young mother who had taught her to read at three and pinched her when she was naughty; the stepmothers and older sisters who taught her to dance, sing, perform, and compete; and the Catholic nuns of St. Joseph Convent School in Bangkok and Convent Light Street in Penang. It was these nuns who prepared her for the life she would lead, although she could not realize it at the time. They gave her superior work habits, the love and understanding of literature, and one final, great gift: the Sisters saw her exactly as she was—a lonely orphan whose world had collapsed and who could not see her way, and they gave her the unconditional love for which she was famished. They were great teachers, and she would follow them.

Boonlua's precious memories of her home and homeland gave her strength during her difficult adolescent years in Penang. She thought a great deal about Siam, about its culture and literature, and about the role that her own family had played in its history. None of these memories, thoughts, or ideas could prepare her for the monumental political and social changes that would soon occur in the homeland she thought she knew.

3

RETURN AND REVOLUTION

Everybody, everyone of my father's generation was expecting some kind of a revolution, because it was in the days when there were such a lot of revolutions . . .

—Boonlua

RETURN

In 1928, Boonlua returned to Siam, thrilled to be home at last and proud of her Cambridge University Certificate awarded "with honors." It may have sounded grander than it was—the equivalent of a secondary education diploma—but if her certificate paled in comparison to her male relatives' diplomas from universities in England, France, or Germany, it placed her well ahead of most young women of her age and class, in their view and certainly in hers. In 1928, it was enough to give her the status of a "foreign-educated" person—a *nakrian nok*, the term that is still used.

At seventeen, Boonlua moved with grace and confidence. She was pleasant looking, with a sardonic sense of humor and a quick wit—sometimes too quick. The former prodigy was now a clever and remarkably well-read young lady who spoke English and French with a more than passable accent. Whether these attributes would work for or against her in making a good match remained to be seen.

Boonlua bore an uncanny resemblance to a woman she admired: Eleanor Roosevelt, First Lady of the United States and a respected social activist. Besides the physical resemblance, which would increase as the decades passed, the two women had several things in common.[1] Like Boonlua, Eleanor was born into a socially prominent family. She was born a Roosevelt, one of the quasi-royal families of American society and politics, and she would marry her cousin Franklin D. Roosevelt. Her mother, Anna Hall, represented a family that produced famously beautiful women, and Eleanor was made aware from her earliest years that she was unlikely to become one of them. Also like Boonlua, she was adored and admired by her father, whom she adored in return, but received more discipline than affection from her mother.

> Although [Eleanor] was an appealing child with regular features and positively lovely blue eyes, a full mouth that was not yet marked by protruding teeth, . . . her mother saw only that she was not beautiful in the Hall tradition. . . . After careful scrutiny, Anna told her daughter, "You have no looks, so see to it that you have manners."[2]

Both girls felt rejected and abandoned when they were sent abroad to be educated, but for Eleanor boarding school turned out to be positive in every respect. She was sent to Allenswood, in Wimbledon, England, a famously progressive school under the leadership of Marie Souvestre. In many ways, Allenswood was different from, and far in advance of, Convent Light Street in Penang, as "a collegiate environment that took the education of women seriously, at a time when they were denied access to the great halls of learning."[3] Nevertheless, both Eleanor and Boonlua were taught, cared for, appreciated, and inspired by compassionate, intelligent, progressive women.[4]

Eleanor Roosevelt was twenty-seven years older than Boonlua, but both were examples of "the new woman," in the parlance of the early twentieth century. Unlike their mothers and grandmothers, both would grow up to live, work, and make significant contributions in the public sphere, far beyond the small world of elite society.

For the first few years after her return to Siam, Boonlua lived among sisters, nieces, nephews, stepmothers, and servants, all under the watchful eye of her eldest brother, Phraya Thewet, the family patriarch who was a full generation older than his youngest siblings. If life in the Kunchon household was in some ways not very different from what Boonlua remembered, in other ways it was dramatically different.

The Kunchons might be descendants of kings, owners of land, and premier examples of the old aristocracy—the *phu di kao*, literally the "old good people"—but they never had been rich, certainly not in the way the new commercial class of the 1920s was rich. By 1928, Phraya Thewet had retired from government service with a nominal pension and there were few other sources of income. The novels that Boonlua's sister Buppha was beginning to write as Dokmai Sot were popular, but then as now the profits from fiction writing were minimal, and Buppha earned just enough from her writing to keep up appearances and to help her nieces from time to time, a traditional duty of maiden aunts that Boonlua also would take seriously. All unmarried ladies in the family, even those breaking with precedent by earning some money of their own, continued to receive an allowance of fifty baht per month, a sum that once had seemed munificent but no longer did.

Fortunately for all of them, Phraya Thewet came up with a brilliant idea for supplementing the family's income, one that would succeed despite the looming Great Depression. He opened the Ban Mo movie theater in 1927, and within a year it had developed into a lucrative enterprise. He made room for the theater by tearing down an old three-story building where Buppha and Chalaem had formerly had their rooms. They moved to a small annex that stood to the east of the main hall beneath an old ilang-ilang tree, and when Boonlua returned from Penang she joined them there.

The Ban Mo theater was an impressive structure for its time, even if it was covered with a tin roof rather than tiles, like the much older structures in the compound. The lower-priced seats were benches on the first floor, but comfortable wicker chairs filled the balcony. Outside on the terrace there were lawn chairs, great porcelain jars filled with ferns, and a bar at which theater patrons could order drinks. Inside, an elaborately carved proscenium arch was installed, made to Phraya Thewet's own design, depicting Rahu, the god of darkness, and the moon.[5]

The theater opened at eight o'clock every evening and closed at eleven. Just before eight, a brass band would begin to play on the street in front of the theater, following the crowd inside when it was time for the first feature to begin. If it was one of the audience's favorites—a Hoot Gibson or a Tom Mix—the crowd would cheer the band on, urging it to play ever louder and more exciting music. Both the music and the noise of the crowd could be heard for a mile.

Boonlua, Buppha, and Chalaem's new quarters were situated less than thirty feet from the theater and occupied no more than forty square feet, a space almost entirely filled by their three beds. They would share this small, crowded dwelling until Buppha and Boonlua, as middle-aged women of nearly fifty, married and moved away.

During the day, Buppha could write in the theater if she wished, for it was as quiet then as it would be clamorous at night, but she kept a very different schedule, writing after midnight in the *sala*, a teakwood gazebo that stood in the front garden facing the main hall of Wang Ban Mo. There, the slender, reserved young novelist could be alone, sipping tea and chain-smoking in the lamp-lit darkness, writing stories about well-born young women who quietly persevered despite trying circumstances. Buppha's *sala* was, and remains to this day, a charming structure, open to the breeze and covered with flowering vines.

Boonlua never wrote about and seldom spoke of the great changes she found at Wang Ban Mo upon her return from Penang. There can be little doubt that she was less than pleased to find the home she had missed so much and idealized as the center of the Thai classical performing arts for over two centuries, resounding with the cacophony of American cowboy movies accompanied by a brass band. Within a few years, when other grander movie theaters were built, the Ban Mo movie theater would become a music hall, and in its last days a *like* theater featuring the popular folk versions of classical dramas. But in its earliest years, from

1927 to 1930, it was Bangkok's first and most famous movie theater, so popular that Phraya Thewet decided to move the entire household to a more peaceful location, the new Kunchon residence in Phetchaburi.

Boonlua recorded in her autobiography that she spent most of her time, in her first years back home, with Buppha and Chalaem in Phetchaburi—and that both sisters strongly supported her desire for further education. A few years earlier, Buppha had approached Phraya Thewet with the same request. She too felt the need for more education. When he flatly rejected the idea, she gave up, but on her younger sister Boonlua's behalf, she would not give up.

REVOLUTION

In 1932, the year Boonlua turned twenty-one, she saw the world she had known shaken to its royal foundations. Immense political and social changes had been occurring in Siam since her birth in 1911 and the country was now on the brink of revolution. Mid-year, the absolute monarchy was overthrown by a small group of commoners demanding constitutional democracy and comprehensive social reforms. They called themselves the "People's Party" and were generally referred to as the "Promoters."[6] Their actions changed the future of the entire nation, but for Boonlua, the results of political change were quite personally significant. She and her family, along with nearly all members of the extended royal family, deplored the overthrow and despised the Promoters. Nevertheless, Boonlua's university education, her career, and her achievements in Thai society would have been impossible were it not for their actions.

There was no general uprising of the populace, or even of a considerable faction, class, or geographic or ethnic segment of the population. It was a stripping of the monarchy's power and prerogatives by a very small group, followed by the bestowal of a new form of government upon an amazed, even bewildered, populace. The Promoters called the result of their actions a "change in the form of government" rather than a "revolution."[7] There is a significant reason why they insisted upon this

unwieldy phrase, which is used to this day. There was no Thai term for
"revolution" that was not pejorative. The common term for "revolution"
or "rebellion" is *kabot*—but this word implies shameful disloyalty and
treason. A failed rebellion may be termed *kabot* by a leadership that has
prevailed despite the challenge; a successful intervention in the affairs
of state, a coup d'état that works, constitutes "change." To the victors
belong the semantics.

The Promoters wanted to reorganize and modernize Thai society
along lines reflecting ideas they had learned and admired while attending
European universities during the 1920s. Yet, although some aspects of
Thai political and social life did change, Thai political culture changed
very little.[8] In the words of Thai anthropologist Yos Santasombat, "While
the overt forms of democracy can be achieved overnight, as was the
case of the 1932 coup d'état in Thailand, the cultural and psychological
changes necessary to sustain it cannot."[9]

The Promoters were middle-class scholarship students who had
been sent abroad to study for essentially the same reasons King
Chulalongkorn had sent the princes abroad decades before: to acquire
Western education and to learn to work with Westerners, all in the
interests of Siam's continued sovereignty and development. But when
the soon-to-be Promoters returned to Siam in the late 1920s, they found
that the highest places in their government and in Siamese society at
large continued to be reserved for princes and their progeny. It was clear
that, short of a complete replacement of the system of rule in Siam, the
political, social, and economic reforms in which they believed could
never come to pass.[10] Moreover, their own stars seemed unlikely to rise
very high—unlike, say, the star of Boonlua's brother, M.L. (Colonel)
Khap Kunchon, who, like them, was a member of this generation of
foreign-educated men—but, unlike them, also was the son of a Chao
Phraya and a descendant of kings. His career prospects in the Royal
Siamese Army looked bright indeed.[11]

Prince Vajiravudh and his brother Prince Prajadhipok followed their
father King Chulalongkorn on the throne, reigning 1910–25 and 1925–
35 respectively. They were well-meaning, well educated, and intelligent.
However, they lacked the talents, temperament, and charisma that had

made their father revered, loved, and successful as king. Prajadhipok was also forced to deal with the worldwide Great Depression. By 1932, it would be no great feat for the Promoters to seize power from a regime that was much diminished from what it had been three decades earlier and enforce their own version of governance.

The idea of such a relatively radical change was not new. A constitution and some form of representative government had been considered since the reign of King Chulalongkorn, but consideration had never moved ahead to the stage of discussion, much less implementation. Senior princes and other advisors who served King Prajadhipok during the late 1920s and up to 1932, including several Europeans and Americans, strongly discouraged the king from pursuing his quite sincere desire to grant his people a constitution and some measure of participation in government.[12] It is sadly ironic that King Prajadhipok, the king who looked most favorably on the ideas of constitutional monarchy and representative government, would not only become the last absolute monarch of Siam but would be vilified, at least at the outset of the coup d'état, as a ruler who was "eating rice on the backs of the poor."

Because King Chulalongkorn had fathered many sons, no one could imagine that the issue of succession would present a problem. While various estimates of the number of women in Chulalongkorn's inner palace have ranged from hundreds to thousands, the most likely estimate seems to be that of his grandson, Prince Chula Chakrabongse: the king had ninety-two wives and seventy-six children, including thirty-two sons and forty-four daughters (a seventy-seventh child died before birth when his mother drowned). Only thirty-six of the ninety-two wives bore children. Two of these wives, namely Queen Saowapha (with nine offspring) and Queen Sawang Watthana (with eight), had more than four children; three of the other wives had four children, four had three children, nine had two children, and eighteen bore only one child each.[13]

If a young woman was presented to the king by her family and accepted, it was assumed and expected that the king would have sexual relations with her at least once. The family's hope was that even if the king did not care to form a permanent attachment, the woman might become pregnant and give birth, causing a most significant change in her status, from *chao chom* (consort) to *chao chom manda* (consort and also the mother of a king's child), in which case great and immediate benefits would accrue not only to her but also to her family. Moreover, since her child would be born a royal prince or princess, his or her descendants would hold royal titles for several generations—as did Boonlua, a *mom luang* by virtue of the fact of her descent from King Phra Phutthaloetla. This being said, the chances of a thirtieth son by a thirtieth consort ever becoming king were extremely remote. A Thai king's eldest son by his senior queen was expected to succeed him, barring any unusual complications.

Three of King Chulalongkorn's major queens, his half-sisters, were full sisters to each other: Sawang Watthana, Saowapha, and Sunantha, daughters of King Mongkut by Queen Piam.[14] Queen Sawang Watthana gave birth to Prince Vajirunhis, by all accounts a boy of great charm who was greatly loved not only by his father the king, who designated him crown prince in 1886, but also by members of the court at large.

Boonlua's father, Chao Phraya Thewet, was Vajirunhis's mentor in the ways of the palace. He taught the young prince to ride and was devoted to him. When Prince Vajirunhis died unexpectedly at the age of seventeen, it was a devastating loss.[15] Prince Vajiravudh, son of Queen Sawang Watthana's sister, Queen Saowapha, was then named crown prince. According to Nigel Brailey, this act opened the way "for the promotion of Vajiravudh's mother, Queen Saowapha, to the status of chief consort to which she had long aspired."[16]

VAJIRAVUDH, THE IMAGINATIVE KING

The death of Crown Prince Vajirunhis, who for nine years had been expected to succeed his father, and the subsequent elevation of his half-brother Vajiravudh, set in motion a chain of events that was to have momentous consequences for the future of Siam. Unlike Vajirunhis, who was kept in Siam to be trained for his future role as king, Prince Vajiravudh was sent to England at the age of twelve, in 1893, to be educated along with a number of other princes, and he stayed in England for the next nine years.[17] After working with tutors, he received special military training at Sandhurst and then served with several British infantry and artillery units. In 1900 he went to Oxford to study history and law. Although he never graduated from either Sandhurst or Oxford, he did well in his studies.

There was a good deal of discontent among members of the royal family as well as palace officials over King Chulalongkorn's naming Vajiravudh as crown prince. It was said that Chao Phraya Thewet himself pleaded with the king to name another of his many male heirs.[18] To be sure, Chao Phraya Thewet had been greatly attached to Prince Vajirunhis, and once a man had formed such an attachment to a leader—especially to a child destined for leadership—that attachment would seldom be transferred, even after death. But there was another aspect to Chao Phraya Thewet's distress. It was common knowledge that Vajiravudh had not produced any children so far. All of the other kings had fathered children during their adolescence. It was also common knowledge that the prince preferred the company of men to that of women. This in itself would not be a fatal flaw, provide that as king, he would be willing to meet his dynastic obligations by taking at least a few wives (or even one, although that would be considered odd) and provide heirs to the throne.[19] However, the fears of those who opposed his selection were to be more than realized: he would refuse to compromise, and the conduct of his court, which he staffed with his personal favorites, would have far-reaching effects upon the kingdom and upon the institution of the monarchy itself.

When twenty-two-year-old Crown Prince Vajiravudh returned to Siam in 1903, the majority of Thais were proud to welcome their young, Oxford-educated king, who spoke, read, and wrote English very well and was a man of outstanding literary gifts. This was a quality that always had been admired in Siam; the first and second kings of the Chakri dynasty had been fine poets.

The crown prince was made inspector general of the army and commander of the Royal Guards. He accompanied his father to meetings of the Council of Ministers, was made familiar with all-important matters of state, and served as acting king during King Chulalongkorn's second trip to Europe in 1907. Yet, his activities were considerably more limited than his several official posts would suggest. He chafed under the requirement to work under his elders in the Regency Council and the Council of Ministers. He would never be comfortable with these men, who undoubtedly made it plain, in infuriatingly polite ways, that he would never have been their first choice as a successor to his father.

It is well known that writing about anyone in the extended Thai royal family from an objective or nuanced perspective is problematical, and it has become increasingly so in recent decades. Only remarks that depict a member of the royal family (especially, the current or any former king) in an entirely positive light are considered appropriate or patriotic. Sympathy regarding troubled events in a royal life is no more acceptable than criticism would be, for an expression of sympathy is seen as a suggestion of weakness, or some kind of disability, and therefore disrespectful—and therefore illegal.[20] Nevertheless, only a nuanced and sympathetic portrayal of King Vajiravudh can enable us to appreciate his noble and heartfelt dreams for Siam. He was very shy but prone to occasional displays of arrogance, pique, and temper. His aesthetic sense was highly developed and he loved beautiful clothes, jewels, and decorations. He was painfully aware of his physical appearance; he was small as a boy, and grew up to be a short, balding, overweight man who communicated with difficulty, stuttering and often using awkward gestures. Dr. Malcolm Smith, a physician who attended the king's mother, Queen Saowapha, wrote:

> King Vajiravudh was in many ways a gifted man, particularly in literature and the arts. But he suffered all his life from an unconquerable shyness. It was particularly evident in his association with Europeans, and some of his meetings with them were distressing to witness. . . . When he returned to Siam he gathered round him a band of young men as his associates. Some were princes of the third rank, others the sons of noblemen. . . .[21] When he came to the throne he maintained that circle; his brothers who were to help him, his uncles who had had long experience in State affairs were hardly taken into consideration. . . . Envy and hatred of his clique lasted throughout

his reign and made him unpopular with a large class of his subjects. A real head [of state] he never was, for he lacked the gift of leadership.[22]

Far more critical than Dr. Smith—a foreigner—was Phra Sarasas, a Thai critic of royalty who snidely described Vajiravudh as "a king who was fat and bald and a bachelor, who spent his time in writing plays and poems. . . . His mind was so absorbed in his intellectual pursuits, that it seemed to be in a state of unwonted intellectual confusion. . . . [S]ometimes he would show naivety beyond comprehension, sometimes brilliant, volatile intelligence. At times his mind would run to fantasy, with a vivid dash of irrationality . . ."[23]

As crown prince, Vajiravudh was determined to be respected, but the actions he took to earn respect were sometimes ill-conceived, and occasionally his judgment was disastrous. A seemingly minor incident that was to have repercussions throughout his reign and beyond occurred during the year before he ascended the throne. A small group of regular army soldiers got into a heated argument with a group of the crown prince's pages. The soldiers, armed with sticks, finally chased the pages into the safety of Vajiravudh's palace. Enraged, the crown prince went to his father the king and demanded that these soldiers be sentenced to a severe lashing with a rattan whip. Not only did the king resist this request; so did Prince Rabi, the minister of justice, on the grounds of Siam's new Westernized penal code. He was afraid that such an "uncivilized" sentence, if known abroad, would jeopardize Siam's efforts to remove treaty restrictions on its juridical sovereignty.[24] But in this instance the crown prince, usually excessively hypersensitive concerning the opinion of Europeans, hysterically insisted that his wishes be obeyed. The king relented, the lashings were administered, and the incident would not be forgiven by the men involved or by their families. Twenty years later, the Promoters would turn to them as they sought allies to help them carry out their overthrow of the absolute monarchy.

On the positive side, as crown prince and as king, Vajiravudh made immense contributions to Thai literature, writing an astonishing number of original plays, poetry, and essays, and somehow found time to translate Shakespeare's *Merchant of Venice, As You Like It, Romeo and*

Juliet, and *Othello*; Sheridan's *School for Scandal*, Molière's *Le Médicin malgré lui*, and several other works.[25] He acted in plays he wrote, which scandalized the elite, and he insisted that women act the female parts, which further scandalized them.[26] Heretofore, dramas had been performed by casts that were either all female or exclusively male, and it was unthinkable that a king would appear upon the stage like a common actor. But appear he did, with male and female actors, and invitations to these performances could hardly be ignored. Vajiravudh tried his hand at nearly every Western fiction genre, including detective mysteries, starring the intrepid "Nai In," a Siamized Sherlock Holmes, and he also wrote several fine travel accounts.

Echoing both the words and the views of his grandfather King Mongkut, who had been distressed at the thought that European visitors would be offended by such breeches of *siwilai* behavior as the failure to wear a shirt to court, Vajiravudh wrote, "[S]ince Siam is a [*siwilai*] country and understands [*siwilai*] ways, we should not cling to the ancient ways of our forefathers *who were forest people*."[27]

The king feared that his subjects would fail to keep up with the West and thus appear backward; simultaneously, he feared that they would destroy their heritage because of their infatuation with Western ways. He tried to address both concerns with plans to make expanded and improved education one of the chief accomplishments of his reign. In 1892, King Chulalongkorn had established a school for the royal pages. King Vajiravudh reorganized this school as Chulalongkorn University, a memorial to his father. (Only after the overthrow of the absolute monarchy in 1932 would women, including Boonlua, be admitted to the university.)

In 1921 the government announced compulsory primary education, requiring children to attend school until age fourteen. At first, only 45 percent of the kingdom's students were affected. But the effort continued and was quite successful. Significantly, the percentage of girls in school rose from 7 percent in 1921 to 29 percent in 1922, and to 38 percent in 1925.[28]

Vajiravudh took specific steps to change women's lives. Vella wrote that "Vajiravudh looked on Thai women with Western eyes."[29]

For example, he was determined that betel-stained black teeth, the traditional short, "brush" hairstyle of Thai women, and the wearing of *chongkraben*, the voluminous pantaloon-skirt style that had long been popular, must be abandoned.[30] After his adolescence in England, he was embarrassed by these things, although his expressed reasoning for discouraging them was that traditional Thai fashions "could be explained only as deliberate devices fostered by Thai men to keep their women in bondage. Thai men . . . wanted to keep their women unattractive so that they could hold them back better."[31]

The king's pronouncements about women were characterized by the same curious fusion of traditional Thai customs and European modern culture as other aspects of his overall program of social reform. One of the strangest examples was his revival of the "Heavenly Food Ceremony," which was recalled by Princess Rudivoravan. Her sister had become the first consort of King Vajiravudh, a relationship that was annulled. Apparently, the ceremony of which she writes was held after the annulment.

> The ceremony was traditionally connected with the selection of a royal bride. That *did* sound as if he thought of [another] marriage. . . . The test appalled me. If, while the young princesses stirred the mixture known as the Sacred or Heavenly Food [consisting of, among other ingredients, coconut, bananas, and sugar], a fly alighted on a girl's hand, or a bit of crumpled leaf fell on her veil, she stood condemned. To make such a test of a woman's virtue seemed absolutely ridiculous, yet for centuries it had been used on the groups of young girls from which the kings chose their wives.
>
> It had been a long time now since the ceremony had been performed in public.[32]

Despite what she undoubtedly knew of her sister's brief experience as consort, an entire chapter of Princess Rudivoravan's autobiography is devoted to the Heavenly Food Ceremony and speculation as to King Vajiravudh's choice of a new consort.

KING-CENTERED NATIONALISM

Vajiravudh was engrossed throughout his reign in devising a version of nationalism focused completely upon his absolute, paternalistic rule. He wrote stirring essays for his public on the subject of the "Thai nation."[33] He rejected both socialism and democracy as unsuitable for Siam and published a remarkable statement on the subject of "class."

> In Thailand, there are only two classes: the king—to whom the people give their rights and powers because they do not have enough time and individual ability to acquire and keep power; and the ordinary Thai people.[34]

The king worried about the possibility of revolution, and was particularly moved by the plight of the Romanov dynasty in 1917. Several members of the Thai royal family had lived in Russia and developed lasting ties to the Russian royal family.[35] The king was frustrated by many situations that he was unable to control or to change. For example, he wanted to free Siam of foreign economic control, yet he was and had to remain dependent upon European and American economic advisors. He wanted to curb Chinese domination of the domestic economy, but he was unable to convince ethnic Thais that they should be interested in commerce. He was angered by the fact that many of the recent Chinese immigrants—*not* long-established immigrant families whose intermarried descendants were Thais, for all practical purposes— sent part of their considerable profits from commerce in Siam back to China. He was very disturbed when, during a visit to Chinatown in San Francisco in 1902, he saw street signs bearing Chinese characters, and store windows too. The king began to view Chinese emigration as a conspiratorial diaspora that could—as he had seen with his own eyes in San Francisco—establish Chinese outposts even in a huge and powerful country such as the United States. He wrote a pamphlet entitled "The Jews of Asia," modeled on British, anti-Zionist rhetoric of the era that he had seen during his years at Oxford.[36]

When World War I loomed, Siam promptly joined the allies, largely because of the nation's—and Vajiravudh's—strong ties to England. Some prominent army officers who had been trained in Germany were very disappointed in their king's decision. Kanpirom suggests, however, that the king's personal grudge against Germany played a role. He had visited the country as a young prince on holiday from his studies in England and was outraged to discover that the decoration the German government awarded him on that occasion was inferior to one that had recently been given to the crown prince of Japan. He never forgot the slight.[37]

King Vajiravudh developed and promoted the slogan "nation, religion, king" (*chat satsana phramahakasat*) as a sacred triad.[38] To be a Thai, the king declared and wrote, is to feel and to demonstrate intense loyalty to the *nation*, to the *religion*—only Buddhism, according to his original conception, but since modified to encompass other religions—and to the *king*, the father and leader of his people. This is the definition of patriotism and "Thai-ness" that Thai children continue to learn in the first grade.

Vajiravudh chose quite purposefully to identify himself less with his revered father and grandfather, and more with the distant and dramatic kings of the Sukhothai and Ayutthaya periods, especially Ramkamhaeng (1279?–98) and Naresuan (1590–1605).[39] In identifying himself and his reign with the glories of an abstract Siamese past, Vajiravudh would set the stage for the nationalism of the 1930s and 1940s, which also emphasized the heroism of the Sukhothai and Ayutthaya eras, rather than reminding the people of the great and far more recent achievements of the Chakri dynasty.

The king thought that the names of the Chakri monarchs, including his own, were too difficult for foreigners, and decided to give the appellation "Rama" to all of them, retroactively. General Chakri, the first king of the dynasty, whose kingly name was Phra Phutthayotfa, became "Rama I"; the second king, Phra Phutthaloetla, became "Rama II," and so on.

The adoption of surnames by the Thai citizenry was another of the king's initiatives. Like many of his social projects, it had its inception in the king's exposure to British customs, manners, and mores during his years as a student. In 1913, he ordered the creation of a department to provide appropriate surnames for all Thai people. Certain people were honored by receiving their surname directly from the king himself. In a 1914 essay, he explained the more far-reaching effects of surnames in terms that reflect core values of Thai culture and Thai nationalism, as he defined them:

> The cohesion of the family, the growth of love and respect along family lines, the proper governance of a family—all of which, [the king] said, would be promoted by the use of surnames—would be means for instilling respect for government. A family, the king stated, is bound together by love. Younger members of the family respect their elders because they know that their elders act only for the benefit of the family as a whole. The strengthening of such attitudes on the family level could not help but find expression in attitudes toward government. Inculcation of love in the family would inevitably promote inculcation of love toward the head of the government of the nation.[40]

One example of the king's personal involvement in the surname project is the Viravaidya family, prominent for over a century in medicine and in the development of social welfare programs throughout Thailand. A member of this family, the son of a Chinese immigrant father and a Thai mother, was a physician who treated Queen Saowapha, the king's mother. In 1926, the king presented the family with the surname Viravaidya, comprised of "vira," a Sanskrit term meaning "hero/heroic," and "vaidya," a term meaning "one who knows" and used in present-day India to refer to Ayurvedic physicians, as opposed to those trained in Western medicine.

A miniature town called Dusit Thani, which the king designed and had built in 1918, was aptly described by historian Walter Vella as "one of the world's most unusual expressions of political thought."[41] The king was chief planner and chief architect of this small town, a creative masterpiece built on a scale of 1:20 that had everything an ordinary (albeit extraordinary) town would have: houses, palaces, temples, roads, rivers and canals, trees and parks, fountains, waterfalls, and electric lights. It had not one but two newspapers, and it had fire, electricity, sewage, and health departments. Grand parties were held, and there were nightly boat races with miniature boats competing on a miniature river.

> The preamble to [the] constitution [of Dusit Thani] stated that Vajiravudh's purpose was to offer "residents" of Dusit Thani, i.e., his courtiers, the opportunity to study self-government. . . . Ultimate power was retained by the king, who might at any time revoke any action at Dusit Thani that he disapproved of.[42]

Dusit Thani was fantastic in every sense of the word and fantastically expensive. But it was dear to the king's heart, for this was a completely manageable realm within which he was unquestionably obeyed and appreciated by all subjects.

Vajiravudh's most problematical, unpopular, and ultimately self-defeating enterprise was a private militia called the "Wild Tiger Corps," ostensibly modeled on men who had, centuries earlier, kept watch on the frontiers of Siam. The purpose of the contemporary Wild Tigers was to "[create] among the Thai people a new national spirit, the spirit of the Wild Tigers."[43]

> The very structure of the Wild Tigers was designed to shake up the loyalties and ranks of the civil bureaucracy, for Wild Tiger positions did not correspond to regular department positions. A person high in a ministry might well be a common soldier in the Wild Tigers—a revolutionary approach to station in Siam, where customarily a person's rank in the bureaucracy determined . . . virtually every . . . aspect of his social status."[44]

At first, regular military officers were shut out completely, and when they were at last invited to join, a graying colonel might well find himself taking orders from one of the king's young companions, and with what results in terms of military morale may be easily imagined.

Decades after his death, Boonlua could become quite querulous on the subject of King Vajiravudh. She seemed to expect criticism of him and she was well prepared for it. She could not be led into agreeing that his policies were often questionable and sometimes disastrous. She defended even the Wild Tiger Corps, insisting that "people didn't really understand what Rama VI was trying to do with the Wild Tiger Corps. He was trying to teach people about discipline . . ."[45]

Could she have been so naive as to believe that the detestation in which the regular military and many other Thais held this private militia of the king was due to their "misunderstanding" of his objectives? On the contrary, she was defending her king and being loyal—whatever her private thoughts may have been. A Thai man who knew Boonlua for many years made these remarks on her unconditional support for King Vajiravudh:

> Of course, of course—Boonlua knew all about the king and that he wasn't a very good king. But if you said that her statements about him were "lies," or "naive," you would be taking a culturally blind stance. The rule in Thai society is this: you tell everything you think or know to the appropriate people, you say nothing to the inappropriate people, and finally, you never write anything down if it is negative or could be construed as negative. When you remain silent or describe someone in a "good light," you are being *loyal*—not a *liar*. There is an absolute difference.[46]

The first attempted coup d'état of the twentieth century took place in 1912 and was led by a group of young regular military officers. Because one member of the group reported the plot in advance, all were arrested before they could take action.[47] Although the king could justifiably have had all the individuals involved put to death at once, no one was executed. Three of the men received sentences of life imprisonment, twenty were sentenced to twenty years, and the rest received suspended sentences. The major causes behind the coup attempt were disapproval of the king's lifestyle and the military's feelings of marginalization, disrespect, and shabby treatment by their king—beginning with that never-to-be-forgotten incident years before when loyal regular soldiers were cruelly punished after a run-in with some of the then crown prince's pages.

From the early 1920s on, state finances were in a very bad state. Budget deficits were growing at an alarming rate, and in 1924 a commission of three princes was appointed, at the strong urging of British advisors, to study and consider appropriate corrective measures. One great area of concern was the matter of royal expenditures. Among other voices calling for financial prudence was that of the king's younger brother, Prince Prajadhipok. In a May 1925 cabinet meeting on finances, only one prince dissented from an otherwise unanimous challenge to the king.[48]

Even as staunch a champion of King Vajiravudh and his intentions for his nation as Walter Vella gave this appraisal of the king's tolerance for criticism: "Although he claimed that 'I do not and cannot possibly object to . . . fair comment or criticism,' in fact he objected to all criticism."[49] Criticism of his financial policies was certainly no exception. He considered Sir Edward Cook, the new financial advisor and one of many British and European advisors who were employed at the time, to be his particular enemy. After a thorough study of the situation, Sir Edward reported that "Siam is living beyond her means." Expenditures had risen dramatically throughout the reign, largely because of the king's lavish spending habits, including the giving of enormously expensive presents to his favorites, and if nothing were done, Sir Edward insisted, Siam would soon face the odious necessity of raiding currency reserves, "the last refuge of bankrupt governments" which "would reduce Siam in prestige and credit to the level of China."[50]

The king reacted angrily to this report, stating that he would continue to act as his own prime minister, that the budget commission was nothing but an advisory body with no authority, and that he would under no circumstances allow himself to be removed, "like the Mikado in Japan."[51]

The British, by far the most important foreigner advisors then working with the Siamese government, appraised King Vajiravudh entirely in terms of his administrative ability. They had little if any interest in his contributions to the arts and education, and no interest whatsoever in his attempts to create and shape a nationalist ethic. But the tenets of this king's nationalist ethic would be re-created and re-shaped throughout the twentieth century and beyond.

In November 1920, when he was nearly forty years old, the king announced his betrothal to Princess Vallabha Devi, publically declaring his support of monogamy. He and his bride, who wore a Western-style white gown, walked arm-in-arm under crossed swords as a band played Wagner's Wedding March from *Lohengrin*.[52] Four months later the betrothal was annulled owing to "incompatibility of temperament."

Four women succeeded Princess Vallabha Devi as royal consort. In September 1921 the king was betrothed to Princess Lakshami Lavan, and she became consort in August 1922.[53] Two sisters became concubines in 1921 and 1922, despite the earlier pronouncements regarding monogamy; one of them reportedly had several miscarriages and was elevated to queen late in 1922, but was demoted in September 1925. His last wife, Suvadhana, was named consort and, in the eighth month of her pregnancy, she was elevated to the status of queen.

From 1918 on, King Vajiravudh had frequently been ill with kidney disease and a number of other ailments. On November 26, 1925, at the age of forty-four, he died of peritonitis. Only thirty-six hours before the king's death, Queen Suvadhana gave birth. The baby was brought to the king's bedside, and the king motioned to have the infant laid beside him. He asked, "Is it a boy or a girl?" and when told that the child was a girl, he replied, "It is just as well" (*di mueankan*).[54] This child, who was named Bejaratana, survived but never married and did not produce a son who might inherit the throne. She died in 2011 at the age of eighty-five.

During the last six years of Vajiravudh's reign, the royal family and the king reeled from one unexpected death to the next. Six of his half-brothers, three full brothers, the queen mother, and the Supreme Patriarch Prince Vachirayana all died within those six years. Vajiravudh had declared when he ascended the throne in 1910 that succession henceforth should pass through the line of his own mother, Queen Saowapha, never dreaming that he would see all but one of his full brothers die young: Prince Chakrabongse died in 1920 at the age of thirty-seven (and, in any case, had married a Russian woman so his children were ineligible.) Prince Chudadjuj died in 1923 at the age of thirty-one; and Prince Asadang was thirty-three when he died in 1925. By the time Vajiravudh himself died, a circumstance had come to pass that no one would have believed possible when King Chulalongkorn died in 1910: of the numerous sons of the major queens, only one, Vajiravudh's younger, full brother Prajadhipok, was alive to assume the throne.

In 1910, when Vajiravudh succeeded his father, the Chakri dynasty was at the height of its power and prestige, both within the nation and abroad. During the fifteen years that followed, that power and prestige of the monarchy suffered a drastic decline. Vajiravudh's brother Prajadhipok, the most reluctant king of the dynasty, would face overwhelming odds in trying to right the ship of state, and he would not succeed.

PRAJADHIPOK, THE MAN WHO WOULD NOT BE KING

Prince Prajadhipok was a mild-mannered, intelligent, rather frail man who had grown up comforted by the knowledge that there were many brothers between himself and the throne. He had never wanted to be king, but he accepted his fate with resignation and a strong sense of duty.[55]

The prince was educated at Eton and Woolwich Military Academy in England, then at the École Supérieure de Guerre in France. David Wyatt described Prajadhipok's probable expectations on the eve of his return to Siam from England in 1917:

[He was] probably . . . expecting a staff career in the army, certainly not [expecting to become] king; but within months he was rising rapidly up the ladder of succession to the throne. . . . All he had in his favor was a lively intelligence, a certain diplomacy in his dealings with others, a modesty and industrious willingness to learn, and the somewhat tarnished but still potent magic of the crown.[56]

Shortly after returning home, Prajadhipok became a monk for three months under the tutelage of the Prince Patriarch Vachirayana, who also was his uncle, a son of King Mongkut. At the end of his monkhood, the prince patriarch, greatly impressed with the young prince, urged Prajadhipok to consider remaining in the priesthood permanently and eventually becoming prince patriarch himself. According to Prince Chula Chakrabongse, "[t]he young Prince-Priest was the *fourth* full-brother of the monarch, thus he was not likely to attain a high position in the Army or Civil Service, for good positions would be taken by his elder brothers and half-brothers."[57] Much less could he expect to be king. Still, the prince patriarch could have made this suggestion to a number of young princes, and the fact that he chose to approach Prajadhipok and urge him to consider a permanent future in the monkhood, culminating in becoming the prince patriarch, speaks to the matter of the prince's character. Unfortunately, the time he spent in the monkhood had permanent negative effects on his chronic ill health.[58]

Prajadhipok declined the prince patriarch's request respectfully, confessing that he had long been in love with his cousin, Princess Rambhai Barni, and wished to marry her. In 1918, when Prince Prajadhipok and the princess were married, his mother, Queen Saowapha, presented all the female guests at the wedding with diamond rings. The marriage would be a happy one, but the grandsons for whom Queen Saowapha longed never came.

As king, Prajadhipok summed up the first year of his reign in his inimitably droll manner:

> People seem to have the idea that [I am] a sort [of] nonentity who is easily influenced by anybody and that he has no opinions of his own whatever. This statement may sound exaggerated, but it is really very near to the truth.[59]

It is difficult to imagine a more accurate summing up of the situation Prajadhipok faced when he ascended the throne than these words of his uncle, Prince Damrong, in 1926:

> [His Majesty received a] deplorable inheritance when he ascended the Throne, because the authority of the sovereign had fallen much in

respect and confidence, the treasury was on the verge of bankruptcy, and the government was corrupted and the services more or less in confusion.[60]

While King Prajadhipok has been charged with an excessive dependence on his royal relatives and advisors, indecisiveness, timidity, and a host of other failings and incompetencies, it is not at all clear what blend of intellectual qualities, personal abilities, and clever decisions might have enabled him to prevail over the economic and political disasters that attended the early years of this reign. Revolution was no longer unthinkable, because revolutions had succeeded in several other countries. Not only could one *think* about such possibilities, but journals and newspapers now proliferated in Bangkok with "criticism of the government increasing and . . . elite opinion . . . being both expressed and shaped in the popular press."[61]

At the outset of his reign, to restore confidence in the monarchy after the excesses of his brother, King Prajadhipok (or his agents) immediately set about dismissing most of the men who had surrounded Vajiravudh. A Supreme Council of State was created, an advisory body consisting of five members of the royal family including the king's conservative uncles Prince Damrong and Prince Boriphat, two of his brothers, and the prince of Chantaburi, all men with long experience in (pre-Vajiravudh) government. Beyond the Supreme Council of State, all senior government positions were filled by titled or at least royally connected individuals who had been waiting impatiently in the wings after having been shut out of government for over a decade. Now they were free to move in any way they deemed suitable—and they moved with a vengeance.

To be sure, there would be no more Wild Tigers, no miniature kingdoms, no lavish expenditures on personal favorites at court. Power was at last returning to those who, in the opinion of these new leaders of the old order, ought to have it. The attitude of the senior princes was sharply reflected in an incident that occurred in May 1925, shortly after King Vajiravudh's death. Prince Boriphat and other members of the cabinet were meeting to discuss possible names for the new reign; the British minister was also present. Prince Boriphat is said to have pointedly remarked, "not Rama anyhow—we have done with Rama's (sic)—It must never happen again."[62] Yet, despite Prince Boriphat's ridicule of "Ramas" and King Prajadhipok's flat refusal to be identified by anyone, ever, as Rama VII, Vajiravudh's innovation proved convenient and was carried forward.

The decision to return the reigns of power to senior princes was just one example of King Prajadhipok's proclivity for making poor decisions grounded in honorable motives. He hoped to regain the confidence of his subjects after the years of wild spending and peculiar events. But nothing seemed to work for this king. All that most people understood was that at least, under the previous reign, there had been a sense of well-being, a feeling that generosity and abundance defined Siam. Now, the populace was expected to live with less, and the gap between the elite and everyone else in the country suddenly became starkly visible.

Yos Santasombat describes the loss of faith in the monarch that was caused by the economic crises of the years just preceding the overthrow of the absolute monarchy.

> The Thai people . . . expected the monarch to solve even the [unsolvable] problems. The worldwide economic recession, however, was beyond the capacity of King Prajadhipok . . . to remedy. In fact, the royal government's handling of these economic problems was most inadequate. . . . In an effort to reduce the national budget deficit . . . many officials, both civilian and military, were dismissed . . . Furthermore, the royal government imposed a new "salary tax" which affected mainly the educated middle-class government officials and employees of Western-style firms. The discontent of the salaried classes, and especially the civil and military officials, clearly [mattered] most in the 1932 coup d'état. . . .[63]

Not only were the Prajadhipok government's financial reforms inadequate to put Siam firmly back on firmer ground, but middle- and lower-class people suffered, while from their perspective the elite seemed completely unaffected. In 1932, an "Announcement of the People's Party," written by Pridi Banomyong, one of the Promoters, would claim:

The king's government hold people as slaves . . . animals, and did [sic] not consider them as human beings. Thus, instead of helping them, it continued to "plant rice on the back of the people.". . . It can be seen [that] taxes extracted from the people were channeled by the millions for the personal use of the king. For the people to earn anything, they had to toil until blood pours [sic] from their eyes.[64]

But it was not "the people," however disgruntled they might be, who were preparing for major changes. Those changes would be planned and implemented by a small group of European-educated, middle-class urban men who meticulously and patiently laid the groundwork for revolution.

OVERNIGHT, A NEW PARADIGM OF POWER

On June 24, 1932, the day of the coup, Boonlua and most of the Kunchon family were living temporarily in Phetchaburi. Very early that day her brother, Colonel Khap Kunchon, then stationed in Bangkok, woke to find that he had been summoned to the Throne Hall by leaders of the coup d'état—the Promoters. Terrified, he struggled to imagine what the future might hold—life or death, compromise or civil war.[65]

The coup promoters may be divided into two factions: a senior faction comprised of older military and civilian officials who were willing to join the venture because they had no faith in the ability of the current regime to deal with the political and economic problems of the time, and a junior faction of more ideologically motivated intellectuals and organizers, both military and civilian, who would soon overtake the senior group in assuming positions of the greatest influence and power in the post-absolute-monarchy era.

From the standpoint of Boonlua's life and work, the most important of the Promoters would prove to be a young army officer of modest background named Plaek Kittisangka. Born in Nonthaburi in 1897, he was educated in the Military Staff Academy and the General Staff Academy in Bangkok, then sent to study military science in France.

When he returned, he became an instructor of military science—and, ironically, equerry to Prince Narit, a position that mirrored one of the duties of the Kunchon family, vis-à-vis the royal family.

An idealistic and ambitious army lieutenant at the time of the coup, Plaek's appointive title was (Lieutenant) Luang Phibun Songkhram.[66] His star would rise steadily during the 1930s until he emerged as Field Marshal Phibun Songkhram, the all-powerful head of the nation during the first two decades of Boonlua's career. Long after the events of 1932, her most popular and most critically acclaimed novel, *Thutiyawiset*, would be suggested by the life of Phibun's wife, Than Phuying La-iat Phibun Songkhram. Aside from its believable and appealing characters, the novel is interesting and important for its examination of political and social power in Thailand and the effects of power on individual lives. Like many other Thai fiction writers, in her novels and short stories Boonlua revealed feelings and opinions that she never fully expressed in essays or other nonfiction writings, much less in public speeches.[67]

Although many of the military members of the coup group were educated in Germany, most of its ideological leaders were trained in France. The undisputed head of the latter group, Pridi Banomyong, was a lawyer who was first trained in Bangkok at the Law School located at the Ministry of Justice, and then in France, where he received a doctor of law degree and an additional degree in economics. An excellent student, he was very popular among his fellow Thai students in Paris. He was elected president of the Thai students' association, a position in which he shared his enthusiasms and his democratic hopes with several young men who would become his colleagues in revolution. Upon his return to Siam, Pridi became an official in the Ministry of Justice and also a law professor at Chulalongkorn University, an ideal position for a man who wanted to influence and educate young Thai intellectuals.

The Siamese absolute monarchy was toppled by 114 men in what may fairly be described as one of the great political bluffs of the twentieth century. They used their understanding of Thai political culture and behavior in preparing and implementing an extremely audacious plan, and they were proven right.

[The] leaders of the 1932 Revolution clearly perceived that Bangkok, as the center of the political, economic, and financial affairs of the country, was the center of real power. They maintained that if they could seize power in Bangkok, the absolute regime would almost certainly collapse.[68]

On the evening of June 23, the home telephone lines of all key government leaders were cut. In the navy, every military unit and battleship in the Bangkok area was given false orders by lower-ranking officers who were members of the coup group. Their superiors, whom the Promoters assumed would be loyal to the Crown, were called away from their posts to investigate a non-existent "Chinese uprising." In their absence, the rebel junior officers were able to quickly mobilize five hundred sailors and take them to the Throne Hall, the agreed-upon meeting place, at 6 a.m. With these unarmed sailors safely corralled, a rebel gunboat moved up the Chao Phraya River to face the residence of Prince Boriphat, minister of the interior, a half-brother of the king, and the most important man in the government. The Promoters particularly detested Prince Boriphat for his well-known arrogance. In return, he despised them as upstarts with ambitions inappropriate to their station.

Prince Boriphat was arrested and taken away—*in his pajamas*, a detail that is rarely left out of the description of events. All leading members of the royal family in Bangkok, including Prince Narit, were taken from their homes and detained as hostages at the Throne Hall. Boonlua's brother, Colonel Khap, reportedly was overcome with despair when he arrived at the Throne Hall and saw Prince Narit, now a captive. Prince Narit—the great man whom he had known and respected all his life, who had built a home at Wang Khlong Toei and lived with Chao Phraya Thewet's family! But when Prince Narit called out to him to come near, Colonel Khap stayed on his knees at a distance, afraid to approach him and ashamed not to.[69] This small incident involving Boonlua's own brother demonstrates several of the coup leaders' astute presumptions about how the Thai elite would react to the coup. Even senior Thai officials were used to following orders and would not immediately resist an authority that called itself legal and that was not visibly opposed

by anyone superior to them. Rather than taking it upon themselves to
defend the absolute monarchy by refusing all of their captors' demands,
regardless of what other individuals who were present might do or
say, they submitted. Even Prince Boriphat affixed his signature to a
public announcement "requesting that all military and civil officials
and employees cooperate in preserving law and order so as to avoid
unnecessary bloodshed."[70]

Pridi Banomyong issued a manifesto to the people at large
denouncing the old regime as exploitative and cruel. It denounced the
king for appointing to high office "close relatives and flatterers, who
had no virtue nor knowledge, to important positions"; and the royal
government for "deceitfully and dishonestly [ruling] the people by saying
that it would promote better living."[71] The aggressive and angry tone
of this communiqué is perhaps most interesting when contrasted with
the far milder messages that would follow, as coup leaders realized the
enormity of what they had done, struggled to assess what they would
in fact be able to achieve in the near future, and worried about how the
international community would respond to their actions—especially
the British. Several months later, when the king criticized the manifesto
as "unkind," Pridi apologized—repeatedly. Nevertheless, the manifesto
provides a stark view of Pridi's (if not all of the Promoters') feelings and
attitudes toward the monarchy on the eve of revolution. It is difficult to
avoid concluding that Pridi and his followers believed that the monarchy
would soon wither away entirely, if only the "Thai people" could be made
to see it as they did—an evil, exploitative institution.

On the afternoon of June 24, an official letter written by Pridi was sent
to King Prajadhipok at his seaside residence in Hua Hin, a residence
ironically named "Klai Kangwon," or, "Far from Care."

> The People's Party, consisting of civil and military officials, have now
> taken over the administration of the country and have taken members
> of the Royal Family, such as [Prince Boriphat] as hostages. If members
> of the People's Party receive any injuries, the Princes held in pawn
> will suffer in consequence. The People's Party have no desire to make
> a seizure of Royal Possessions in any way. Their principal aim is to

have a constitutional monarchy. We therefore enjoin Your Majesty to return to the Capital to reign again as king under the constitutional monarchy as established by the People's Party. If Your Majesty refuses to accept the offer or refrains from replying within one hour after the receipt of this message, the People's Party will proclaim a constitutional monarchical government by appointing another Prince whom they consider to be efficient to act as king.[72]

The king was asked to return to Bangkok on a Coast Guard ship. This he refused, unwilling to appear as a hostage of the party. This is the full text of his reply to their invitation:

I have received the letter in which you invite me to return to Bangkok as a constitutional monarch. For the sake of peace, and in order to save useless bloodshed, to avoid confusion and loss to the country, and more, because I have already considered making this change myself, I am willing to co-operate in the establishment of a constitution under which I am willing to serve.

Furthermore, there is a possibility that, if I decline to continue in my office as king, the foreign powers will not recognize the new government. This might entail considerable difficulty for the government.

Physically I am not strong. I have no children to succeed me. My life expectancy is not long, at least if I continue in this office. I have no desire for position or for personal aggrandizement. My ability to advance the progress of the Thai race alone constrains me.

Accept this sincere expression of my feelings.

Prajadhipok[73]

A special train was sent to bring the king and queen to Bangkok. Many of his generals and relatives pleaded with him to resist, but he would not.[74] Two days later at the Grand Palace, the king received the People's Party representatives with the words, "I rise in honor of the People's Party."[75] The king then signed an edict Pridi had prepared pardoning all of the group's actions. Pridi also presented the king with a Provisional

Constitution providing for limited monarchy—under the temporary
dictatorship of the People's Party.

The overthrow of the absolute monarchy has been described in a
variety of ways. Thawatt Mokarapong believed that it was:

> . . . merely the result of action taken by a group of conspirators
> whose relationship and cohesion were maintained by personal ties
> and friendship among the leaders of the factions—the senior and
> junior factions in the Army, the Navy, and the civilian. . . . [I]n terms
> of organization, the revolutionary party of 1932 must be described
> as a very loose and informal one, ruled by strong personalities with
> suitable personal connections.[76]

According to political scientist Chai-anan Samudavanija:

> The coup d'état of June 1932 replaced rule by the princes with rule
> by generals. Ever since, Thai politics has been characterized by the
> dynamics of military dominance, punctuated by the occasional
> elected legislature in the military-bureaucratic polity, with only a
> short life-span.[77]

No contributions of thought or opinion were solicited from rural
Thais, or from anyone with less than a university education. No attempts
were made to develop popular support for ideological change.

> [There was no attempt] to establish a new belief system, a new
> political culture which could give meaning and significance to the
> newly established parliamentary democracy. Once in power, the coup
> leaders—especially the army leaders—were concerned mainly with
> the problems of maintaining their power and personal interests. Thus
> the system of personal rule—albeit in an altered form—continued.[78]

On the day following the overthrow of the absolute monarchy, the
Bangkok Times summarized the event from a completely different
perspective—as a "demonstration."

There is no evidence that the masses took any part in the recent Demonstration. The discontent of the salaried classes and especially of the officers of the Army and Navy clearly counted for most in the movement. At the same time a contributory cause is to be found in the extension of education in Siam. Since the middle of the nineteenth century, when King Mongkut introduced Western methods and technique, increasing numbers of Siamese students have been trained in Europe. An educated class of officials, administrators, and officers, having once been formed, it was only a question of time and opportunity before they demanded a share in the government of the country.[79]

In 1932, the People's Party stood ready to educate the masses until the time when they might stand ready to govern themselves—but even before the year was out, they had already begun to see that this process might take longer than they had first thought.

In 1933, Pridi announced his economic plan for the nation. It begins:

In seeking a means to promote the welfare of our people, I have taken into consideration not only their present mode of existence, but also those peculiar traits which characterize them as a nation. I have come to the conclusion that, *for the advancement of their well-being,* only one course is feasible; namely, *the government must undertake to administer* a national economic policy by which the economic system will be sub-divided into diversified co-operative associations.[80]

Following the announcement of Pridi's Economic Plan, there was an abortive attempt at restoring the monarchy known as the "[Prince] Boworadet Rebellion." In 1966, Boonlua recalled its effects on her family and friends.

Very few people . . . have been through this stress. In my family, we had a brother-in-law who was in prison a long time because of the Boworadet Rebellion, and it so happens that other friends in Korat— my brother-in-law used to be governor of Korat, not like present day governors, but like a representative of the king over several provinces. He was stationed in Korat, and we knew lots of people there. Well, it so happened that Prince Boworadet took Korat as his headquarters. And then we went to live in Phetchaburi, and it so happened that the Phetchaburi Regiment—a battalion they were, really—they decided to join Boworadet. And so you see it happened that all our friends went to prison—because—well, *they lost*. [Laughter.] But you know, I have tried to follow them, each of them, to learn what happened to them, and very few of them really suffered. The people who went to prison, I suppose *they* suffered. It's not pleasant to be in prison, but their families adjusted to their—well, to what happened to them—so easily, so quickly.[81]

The Boworadet Rebellion greatly advanced Phibun's career, for he played a key role in putting it down and as a result soon emerged as the strongman within the army, eventually rising to field marshal. For all of which no one in the Kunchon family would ever forgive him. The most courageous of those loyal to the king had moved against newly entrenched power, knowingly sacrificing all, knowing that they probably would lose everything, and they had been beaten down by men who could have shown them mercy and lost nothing.

In January 1934, when King Prajadhipok, suffering ill health and nearly blind, left Siam for England, Prince Narit was named as regent. A newspaper report quoted the king's characteristically sardonic comment that he was "quite touched at the spontaneous outburst of goodwill on the part of everyone assembled to see him off, and remarked that Luang Pradit [Pridi Banomyong] was foremost in the crowd and shouted *Chaiyo* ['hurrah'] the loudest of them all."[82]

At first, King Prajadhipok had been willing to hand power over to the coup group, both to save bloodshed and because he saw clearly that constitutional monarchy was inevitable, and that, after all, it had been achieved with mercifully little bloodshed. He had never wanted to be king in the first place, and his experience of the office had certainly proved to be worse than even he had anticipated. After 1932 he stayed in office for three years, in the hope of giving the new government legitimacy and stability. As time went on, however, he became increasingly irritated by the behavior of the People's Party.

In 1935, King Prajadhipok announced from his home in England that he was abdicating the throne, writing, "I am willing to surrender the powers I formerly exercised to the people as a whole, but I am not willing to turn them over to any individual or any group to use in an autocratic manner without heeding the voice of the people."[83] If Siam was to become a constitutional monarchy, very little that he had hoped for—meaningful public participation, transparency in the political process, a respected and robust legislative body—seemed likely to develop anytime soon. Henceforth, he was pleased to be known as the Prince of Sukhothai, which had been his title before he became king. He and his beloved wife adopted a young cousin, Prince Chirasakti, and they lived a quiet life in a country home. Six years later, in May 1941, Prajadhipok died of heart failure, just seven months before Thailand's alliance with Japan and its subsequent declaration of war on Great Britain and the United States. In 1949, his widow took his ashes home to Thailand.

After King Prajadhipok's abdication, the National Assembly invited ten-year-old Prince Ananda Mahidol to ascend the throne. He was the son of Prince Mahidol, who was a son of King Chulalongkorn and Queen Sawang Watthana.[84] Prince Narit was asked to become regent for the young king but declined on the grounds of his age and his earnest desire to continue preserving the theatrical and artistic legacy of an earlier era. When Prince Narit died in 1947, Boonlua told many friends, both Thais and foreigners, that the nation had lost its finest remaining example of Siamese leadership, grace, and character, and that such men would not be seen again. It was her way of saying that in the fifteen years that had passed since the momentous events of 1932, she had seen no evidence to the contrary.

4

THE YEARS OF OPPORTUNITY

PREPARATION FOR A CAREER

Boonlua never credited the 1932 overthrow of the absolute monarchy with the expansion of her own opportunities in the world. To do so might have suggested, however indirectly, approval of the Promoters' actions, and she was careful not to say or write anything that could be interpreted as disloyalty to the royal family, which after all was *her* family. How could people of her class feel a distance between themselves and their nation's leaders, when the palaces were filled with their cousins, aunts, and uncles? Boonlua's sister Chalaem, according to one of the great-nieces, always reminded her younger sisters and nieces to be mindful of their place in society: "When you go out . . . say to yourself, 'This land is *ours*.' Then, you will always feel confident." This point of view would be challenged when the nation came to be ruled by men who were not related to them, not of their lineage and not of their class. Nevertheless, the end of the absolute monarchy and the opening of greater opportunities to the population at large, including women, had a direct and dramatic effect on women like Boonlua (few as they might be), who suddenly became eligible to apply for entrance to Chulalongkorn University. After graduation, Boonlua would be able to pursue a career in government as her male relatives had always done.

Whatever Phraya Thewet's thoughts and feelings may have been, he finally gave his blessing to Boonlua's plan. She would go first to a local college where she could prepare to take the university entrance examination. The only remaining difficulty was the matter of where she would live in Bangkok, with nearly everyone in the family now in Phetchaburi, but this problem was solved when she was invited to stay at Saint Mary's College in Bangkok and teach botany while studying to pass the entrance exam. It was an arrangement that benefited everyone. Boarding with the Sisters was socially acceptable, Boonlua had studied a little botany at Penang, and there was no one else at Saint Mary's capable of teaching the subject at all. Before long, she was also teaching English. From the day she stood before her first class comprised of girls not much younger than herself, her destiny was clear. She loved the students, they loved her, and no one could doubt that she was born to teach.

SAINT MARY'S COLLEGE

It was at Saint Mary's that Boonlua formed the first of many professional friendships with Western colleagues.[1] A French professor, Georges Vian, twitted her for teaching without pay. Famously cranky and witty, he delighted her with his curmudgeonly views, railing against the Christian missionaries and disapproving in general of people trying to convert other people to their own religion. Boonlua jokingly retorted that, on the contrary, the missionaries were most admirable. She admired them for their many sacrifices—and he shouldn't be surprised if she decided one day to become a Catholic nun herself. When she suggested to Professor Vian that he ought to give Buddhism a try, he replied that it was just as bad as any other religion. The monks taught the people to believe in karma and merit—but if they believed or didn't believe, *so what*? The priests in France were no better, he told her, and responsible for all manner of chaos. And the Brahmans in India? Charlatans, the lot of them!

Boonlua adored this kind of banter, reveling in exchanges of smart remarks reflecting a sense of humor with which she was familiar due to her Western education. Vian's slighting remarks about Buddhism might well have offended a Thai who had never been a *nakrian nok*—and some who had.

Many young Thai women had attended Catholic convent schools, but Boonlua's experience was unusual in two respects. First, she had spent all of the years between ages five and seventeen in daily contact and conversation with English- and French-speaking people—and during her entire adolescence she spoke only English with teachers who could not speak Thai. Perhaps most important to her intellectual and emotional development was the fact that she read more widely than most girls, even girls in the convent schools. She was continually asking the nuns for books that had not been assigned, and she devoured them. Her understanding of and attraction to Western (post-Enlightenment) attitudes and ideas was at least partially the result of reading a great many English and French novels, poetry, short stories, essays, and even the formulaic English detective mysteries that she would always love and turn to during her illnesses. As several photographs taken by friends in her middle and later years attest, the recovering Boonlua could invariably be found reclining on a chaise longue in her garden with an Agatha Christie or Dorothy Sayers mystery in hand, and at least one of her devoted dogs curled up on the ground beside her.

Professor Vian and his wife offered to support Boonlua in applying for a scholarship to study in France, but Phraya Thewet's tolerance did not extend that far. He might be willing to change his mind about some things in this new and still quite unfamiliar world but—a young Thai woman in France? His own sister? Never. Issues of propriety aside, Phraya Thewet nurtured an intractable grudge against France, based upon the Franco-Siamese Crisis of 1893. After several years of French demands for territories that had long been held by Siam, but which were now contiguous with the western edge of French Indochina bordering Laos and Cambodia, the French moved a gunboat up the Chao Phraya River to Bangkok and exchanged fire briefly with defense forces at Paknam, at the mouth of the river. This event was traumatic for the Siamese, who had been watching the British and French carve up and appropriate neighboring kingdoms for several decades. According to the terms of the Treaty of October 1893, some territories then under the control of Siam would be ceded to France in return for a guarantee that Siamese sovereignty would be respected thereafter. Immediately following this crisis, King Chulalongkorn had withdrawn from public view for several months in a state of severe depression. Forty years later, in 1933, Phraya Thewet still was unable to speak of France without going into a rage.

The issue of Boonlua pursuing a scholarship to study in France ended when Professor Vian's wife died unexpectedly, and it was not spoken of again. Boonlua was not unhappy at the thought of staying in Siam; on the contrary, she thoroughly enjoyed teaching at Saint Mary's and looked forward to entering the university. One of her favorite Sisters at the convent school back in Penang had made the subject of botany fun for her; now, she would repay the Sister's efforts by making botany fun for the girls at Saint Mary's, who loved their young, enthusiastic teacher.

Boonlua passed the entrance exam, and as she prepared to become a student at Chulalongkorn University in the first class to admit women, she felt that the extraordinary changes in the direction of her life were somehow both amazing—and inevitable.

CHULALONGKORN UNIVERSITY

During her first year, Boonlua's English professor, Arthur Braine Hartnell, took her out of the regular English literature class and paired her with another advanced student. This student was half Thai, half English, and had names in both languages: Tom Johnson and Pathom Chansan.[2] Tom and Boonlua met in Professor Hartnell's office and were assigned readings about which they had to write essays. The readings began with Medieval English literature, and after the two advanced students reached the literature of the eighteenth century and the rise of the novel, they rejoined the regularly scheduled classes. An event which incensed Boonlua, and about which she apparently remained incensed fifty years later when she wrote her memoir, *Successes and Failures*, was a gossip campaign started by a few people in her class on the subject of Tom Johnson. Coming into class one day, Boonlua read the words penciled on a windowsill: "Boonlua Loves Tom."

> I was as amazed as I was angry. The person who wrote those words—
> what benefit did he or she expect to derive from such an act? At the
> time I did not understand that many of the university students still
> had the characteristics of teenagers. They lacked the capacity to think
> as adults. *And they had not received an upbringing that would give
> them higher tastes* than to find pleasure in playing children's [games].[3]

It was a polite but unmistakable clarification of the distance between the origins, ideals, and behavior of her family and theirs. She had explained the rude, mean behavior of some classmates at Convent Light Street in much the same way. Her attitude toward them had become a self-protective strategy: instead of being angry with such people, one should pity them for the inferiority of their upbringing and of their genetic inheritance. This was the way she would henceforth explain and deal with people who did her wrong. One must not blame people for meanness or the inability to comprehend certain things when they were clearly not equipped to do better.

When she entered the university, Boonlua did not immediately pursue the curriculum that would lead to a bachelor's degree, choosing instead to work toward a secondary teacher's certificate, which required only two years in the regular liberal arts program and one year of education courses. Before long, she regretted this decision and transferred to a five-year program that would give her a BA plus her teaching credential. Thereafter, she could look forward to a government teaching position and a modest salary. Curiously, she would always claim that she never had career ambitions during her years at the university (or ever) but was "pushed" by her older sisters. She portrayed herself as "giving in" to their pressure. This attitude had to do with her deep feeling of noblesse oblige. She would imply that, while it might appear to be unseemly for the daughter of a *chao phraya* to be mingling on a daily basis with the hoi polloi, members of her family were ready to do their duty under the new form of government. Boonlua believed that everyone ought to learn appropriate and professional teaching techniques, which she rendered phonetically in Thai (*theknik*); apparently, no Thai word struck her as adequate. This fixation on efficient techniques and proper methods was in no small measure the legacy of the convent schools.

> When one wishes to do a thing, one ought to learn appropriate *theknik*. When I wished to learn typing, I went to the best school at which to learn "touch" typing. . . . I feel great gratitude to my teacher, not only for the *theknik* she taught me but also for her explanation of the rationale for each. Later, I was able to teach my own secretaries properly, for some of the [typing] schools do not teach the things they ought to teach.[4]

Few of the young women with whom she studied at Chulalongkorn University became permanent friends. Just as she would later refrain from joining the "old girls" of St. Joseph Convent in Bangkok or Convent Light Street in Penang for tea, lunch, card games, or travels, Boonlua chose to let slip such ties as she had with her Chulalongkorn classmates. She related to her instructors, not to her classmates.

> I was older than most of . . . my classmates. There were only twelve girls anyway in my class. . . . And then, the university course wasn't much. In my third year I was very pleased to study with Phya Anuman, and I was pleased also to study with Phya Upakit, but all the time I knew that it was no use, that they gave us not actually Sanskrit but the Sanskrit used in Thai [i.e., written using the Thai alphabet], which was quite practical but which I knew I would forget as soon as I left the university. It was sort of too old-fashioned somehow, but I was grateful to [Phya Anuman] for all the trouble he took to make it clear to us.[5] He was a good teacher for the students in those days, but a friend of mine who . . . went to the university after me . . . was disappointed and said there were only two lecturers who gave her something that she expected to get from a university. So I probably was disappointed, yes, but I usually try to adapt myself to things, enjoy things . . . [6]

The following passage from an interview with a former Chulalongkorn classmate illustrates one peer's view of Boonlua in her early twenties.

I didn't like Boonlua and she didn't like me. She was very stuck up. I sent a note to her once, addressed to "Khun Boonlua," and she was furious that I had not written "*Mom Luang* Boonlua" on the envelope, just "*Khun* Boonlua." She went around and told many of the other girls, "It appears that some people like to pull other people down from their proper rank."

Most [other students] thought she was conceited and hard. Many of them respected her for her brains, for being a *nakrian nok*, and for being the daughter of a *chao phraya*, because it was the highest title a person could have [under the former system of absolute monarchy]. By the third year she was a little less stuck up, and she would share a taxi with some of the other girls instead of always coming in a car from Ban Mo "Palace" [Wang Ban Mo]—people used to say *house*, anyway—and I never thought Ban Mo looked like any kind of a "palace." Anyway, Boonlua and her sisters Buppha and Chalaem all slept in an old wooden *house* near the main building.

I remember the mornings when we were going to share a taxi, and I would meet her at her house. She would be sitting out there in the *sala* having her breakfast. A servant brought it on a tray. Boonlua ate breakfast just like a *chao wang* [a lady of the royal palace]. And she never offered me anything to eat—not a bite! She always wore the correct color for the day, just like a *chao wang*, every day[7]—and she wore silk stockings all four years.

I was a better French student than Boonlua, but in the first year her grade was higher and so she ended up winning the Alliance Francaise award and going to the reception. I was so angry—I thought it was very unfair.

I remember Tom Johnson, that *luk khrueng* [Eurasian] she had the special classes with. He wasn't much. He was just very—*ordinary*. Once he went to visit Boonlua at Ban Mo and he didn't even know enough to take his hat off. And Phraya Thewet was there, walking around outside, and Tom Johnson thought Phraya Thewet was the gardener! Hah! Phraya Thewet was furious!

One person who could just go up to Boonlua and talk to her was Mom Luang Chitrasan Chumsai. He could approach her because he was another *mom luang*, the same rank as she was.

The one thing that I will never forget is the awards ceremony when we graduated. The man reading out the names was wrong about her in two ways: when it was time to give her her awards, he called out, "*Nang* Boonlua"! I had to laugh to myself watching her walk up there because I knew she was angry—and there was nothing she could do about it, just walk up there and accept the awards—for *Nang* Boonlua!"[8]

The classmate who made these remarks was a little older than Boonlua and from a middle-class rather than a royally connected family. All her life, the Thais with whom Boonlua would get along best were at least three or four years her junior, which is a considerable age difference in Thailand, where being "elder" (*phi*) or "younger" (*nong*) by so much as a minute has significance: the elder of twins will be *phi* forever, the younger, *nong*.

One woman who later became Boonlua's good friend and confidante was her classmate at Chulalongkorn University for one year. This was Khunying Ambhorn Meesook, born in 1920 into a family at approximately the same social level as the Kunchons.[9] She remembered Boonlua from her own first year at Chulalongkorn University—1938, the year in which Boonlua graduated.

Boonlua and I were fortunate to be there. Parents seldom sent their daughters to university in those years. Most girls only went to convent schools like St. Joseph or St. Francis, or [Convent Light Street at] Penang. Boonlua's family and mine were a little different from most of the others. Chao Phraya Thewet was quite "enlightened," you know, encouraging the children to "talk back," and then her brother Phraya Thewet continued this tradition. Everyone had to eat dinner together, and this was the time for discussion. But talking back went

only so far. In my family, it was the same way. You "talked back"—
but only within well-understood parameters. You had to understand
the rules.[10]

In middle age, Boonlua would turn to this kindly, shrewd, and wise
friend for good advice on some of the momentous decisions of her life,
and she was never disappointed.

If many of her fellow university students found Boonlua to be austere,
self-important, and snobbish, there was one who regarded her with
unalloyed admiration. He was Chom Debyasuvarn, a pre-med student
who attended a debate in which she took part. The topic was, "Is It Better
to Be a Daughter or a Son?" Boonlua's team spoke to the advantages
enjoyed by the daughters and won handily. Chom, the son of a provincial
official, was happy simply to sit and stare, astonished at the way this
young *mom luang* walked and talked and made everyone laugh with her
witty and sometimes stinging remarks. He had never imagined that there
could be a woman like her. She was unaware of his presence, but more
than twenty years later, when she was forty-eight years old, Boonlua
would become very aware of Dr. Chom.

Before Boonlua completed her university education, Phraya Thewet
moved the family back to Bangkok from Phetchaburi. While she prepared
for graduation, weddings were being planned for two sisters and a
niece, and Wang Ban Mo again was filled with activity and youth. Soon,
however, Chalaem, Buppha, and Boonlua would be the only women of
their generation who were still at home with no weddings in sight.

During her last year at the university, Boonlua accepted a part-time
teaching position at Rajini School, a long-established private school
for girls of elite families. It was an ideal place for her and she enjoyed
sharing her modest salary with family members. In a rare reference to
one of her maternal relatives, she used the necessity of helping to support
her maternal grandmother as an exculpatory factor in her decision to
accept salaried employment.

I can't say exactly why I taught. I needed the money for my grandmother. My life is such a complicated thing. I felt that my grandmother

should have been properly taken care of. I didn't like her at all. In character, we didn't sort of—we had no sympathy at all. She used to be wife of a governor, and in the old days she probably could do a lot of things in her own way. She became poor, but she still behaved in a demanding way, as if she was the governor's wife, and I didn't like her at all. But I was very conscientious. I felt that I had to take care of her properly. I had to give her enough money to spend. Other people seemed to think that I was exaggerating goodness, that she really didn't deserve all the attention I gave her. And I have a funny character . . . I'd rather . . . have my way and [let other people] also have their way.[11]

Although Boonlua "didn't like her at all," she shows sympathy, or perhaps empathy, toward this woman whom she describes as difficult to get along with. Of course, the rest of Boonlua's family would have had little interest in this grandmother, who was not a Kunchon at all, simply the mother of Mom Nuan, who had borne Chao Phraya Thewet's last child. There was no real status in being the widow of a provincial governor.

These remarks about her grandmother were made in an interview; she does not appear at all in Boonlua's memoir, in which she states that during this period a good bit of her salary went to nieces and nephews whose many projects were constantly in need of funds. Whether the money went to the grandmother or to the younger relatives, or both, the fact remains that Boonlua was a generous person. Later, when she traveled abroad, she would spend a great deal of time looking for just the right book, jewelry, or special gift to bring relatives and friends as well as servants and their children, and while gift-giving surely is an important aspect of friendship and family life in Thai society, Boonlua took unusual pains. It was while teaching at Rajini School that Boonlua was able to afford, for the first time, the luxury of providing for others—not only money, books, and trinkets, but also opportunities and advice.

BIRTH ORDER, CULTURE, AND CHARACTER

From one Western psychological perspective this thirty-second child in the family exhibited many of the traits often associated with a firstborn child. Frank J. Sulloway, in *Born to Rebel: Birth Order and Revolutionary Personality*, presents a profile of the firstborn that fits Boonlua very well.

> In particularly, eldest children tend to identify more closely with parents and authority. This well-documented tendency is consistent with the general profile of firstborns as ambitious, conscientious, and achievement oriented. Relative to their younger siblings, eldest children are also more conforming, conventional, and defensive—attributes that are all *negative* features of openness to experience.[12]

In Thai society, the roles of elder and younger siblings are generally more formalized than they are in Western societies. Expectations of behavior are well known and children are constantly reminded of them. Every Thai who has a younger sibling is in some sense an additional "parent figure" expected to protect, provide for, and even discipline that sibling, while every child with an older sibling has someone upon whom to rely and obey beyond parents, teachers, and other important adults. Depending upon circumstances, the Thai sibling relationship can be more complex than it is in most Western societies, where the nuclear family is the rule and "siblings compete with one another in an effort to secure physical, emotional, and intellectual resources from parents."[13] To be sure, siblings competed in Chao Phraya Thewet's household, sometimes with a vengeance. But there was an element in the culture of this household that was, from a Western perspective, unique. Few of Chao Phraya Thewet's wives had more than one child. Therefore, nearly every child in the family was simultaneously one of a large family—and also his or her mother's first, and usually her only, child.

Boonlua could not be an only child to her father, but she could be the favorite, by virtue of her intellectual accomplishments, wit, and charm. As for her relationships with siblings, she did not receive (or, did not think she received) the degree of nurturing and comfort that she believed could ideally be provided by *phi* to *nong*. On the other hand, she did not display the kind respect and obedience that they, as *phi*, expected from the youngest of all the *nong* in the family. Phi Buppha, five years older than Boonlua, would gladly have been a guide and mentor to Nong Lua, and apparently she tried to be, but Boonlua resisted. If there was to be any "leading" Boonlua was determined to do it—a desire that was foiled at every turn by the culture of her household and by her entire society: *phi* leads and *nong* follows.

Boonlua continued to protect her niche—the precocious, provocative, and amusing daughter—because it had been so successful when she was a small girl. The strategies she had developed to hold onto this special place in her father's heart—straightforwardness, speaking her mind without considering the result, "performing" to make her talents visible—all amusing and gratifying to the elderly Chao Phraya—became fixed elements of her personality that would not always serve her well.

Sulloway's studies on birth order make almost no mention of cultural differences that might affect sibling and parent-child relationships, and they give scant weight to innate talents or behaviors. The bossy, teacher-ish manner about which Boonlua's friends would (gently) chide her all her life was plainly not, in the beginning, a behavior she selected; it was innate. "She was always like that," her same-age niece Anuwong had said. Sulloway's subjects are shown seeking out "activities that older siblings have not already cultivated." He even suggests that this is "how Voltaire got his start as a poet."

> "I wrote verses from my cradle," [Voltaire] once commented. . . .
> His family used to pit him in verse making against his elder brother
> Armand. Voltaire won easily. . . . The example of Voltaire is instructive
> from another point of view. His whole personality was a mirror image
> of his brother's.[14]

Voltaire's relationship with his brother is not as different from Boonlua's relationships with her siblings, especially the girls, as we might assume. Voltaire's innate genius as a poet is presented by Sulloway as secondary to the selection of an activity in which the brother did not excel, rather than primarily as an expression of Voltaire's own intellectual gifts and predilections. As a child, Boonlua concentrated on literary pursuits in a household dominated by sisters who were beautiful dancing girls. She too loved dancing and singing but knew that she could never compete with them in that arena. As a child and then as an adolescent in the convent schools, Boonlua dreamed of being a novelist when she grew up. That hope was dashed when she returned from Penang and found that her sister Buppha, who once had been the beautifully turned out "palace lady" whom she envied and admired, remained all of that— and was a famous novelist besides. Of course, she could have written her own novels with her own original plots, characters, and narrative. But the thought that she would be compared unfavorably with her sister was unbearable.

"Dancer" and "novelist" were no longer appealing to her, as she could never be "best" at them. Instead, she pursued education as a career, not only because that career was available but also because she knew that she could and would be *outstanding* as a teacher.

There was another extremely important influence on both Boonlua's and Buppha's behavior that I did not fully appreciate until I had been studying the lives of both women for some years. Despite the overwhelming personality and power of their father and his exalted place in their lives, and the dominance of males in their society and era, both women were strongly influenced by mothers whose behavior was distinctly "contrary." It was not their father who was unusual in his society. Indeed, he was the archetype of a Siamese nobleman. It was their mothers who were unusual: gifted, creative, defiant, and courageous. Buppha's mother, Malai, had caused a great scandal by leaving her husband, setting up her own dancing school, supporting herself, and marrying a Western foreigner, actions that should have been unimaginable in 1910 Siam but were not, since Malai had planned and implemented them.

Boonlua's mother, Nuan, did not live beyond the age of twenty-five, and little is known about her. But we do know that she taught her three-year-old daughter to read and was strict with her, at a time when little was expected of small girls of the elite beyond docility and charm. Boonlua recalled that neither docility nor charm was as important to her mother as literacy and self-discipline, and this was quite remarkable. Beyond their unusual mothers, both girls were influenced by other strong women. Buppha was raised by the *chao wang*, the ladies of the inner palace, where she spent several of her early years living with her aunt. These women had high standards and strictly followed countless rules pertaining to appearance and behavior. Both girls were subjected to the high expectations and strict discipline of Catholic nuns in the convent schools. The truth was that their young lives were controlled almost entirely by strong, demanding, opinionated women who expected much of other women and of themselves, and no less of the little girls who were in their charge.

Boonlua and Buppha were to become the most recognized and successful members of the Kunchon family in their generation. Whence the ambition, the drive, the determination, and perfectionism of these two women? They looked to their father and to their eldest brother as examples of character, accomplishment, and leadership. But it was their mothers, the ladies of the palace, and the Catholic nuns at their schools who provided the most influential examples of how a woman might live and ought to live. When I first heard Boonlua say, "I was raised by men, you see…," I took her at her word. But the more I learned, the more I realized that both she and her sister were influenced, and their characters shaped, by a series of extraordinary women.

Buppha and Boonlua created successful careers without ever leaving Wang Ban Mo. While it is true that ladies (and most gentlemen) of their generation lived at home until marriage—or death, if marriage never came to pass—it is equally true that there was no other place Boonlua or Buppha could live where they would be treated with the respect and deference that were important to both of them and to which they were accustomed. "A room of one's own" was something that Buppha and Boonlua both longed for and talked a great deal about but that neither sought until late in life. Wang Ban Mo and all that it stood for was a source of great pride to them both.

When she left Wang Ban Mo to go to work every morning, Boonlua stepped into an entirely different life from that of either Buppha, who wrote by night and slept by day, or Chalaem, who was now running the household, a demanding job. Boonlua wrote:

I am the only woman who came out of our house to get into the world. [My sisters] know only people who belong to the same type of families, who've had almost the same background; they know people who have grown up with them. Or if they know new people, they know them from sort of a—well, not an equal status. . . . But when I go up and I travel all over the country, and I meet a lot of primary school teachers, for example, I know teachers all over the country who are entirely different *from us.* . . .

With regard to life experience, there is very little possibility of exchange of ideas with [my sisters]. I listen to them, and sometimes I put in a few words to say, "Well, it's not exactly like that," or something like that. For example, they are offended by certain manners. And I say, "Well, nowadays about 90 percent of the Thai people do this, and *we* belong to the 10 percent." In fact, we belong to the 1 percent—or even less.[15]

By day, she may have lived in a different world from Buppha and Chalaem, yet when Boonlua spoke of the 10 percent, or the 1 percent of society that comprised the elite, there is no question that she included not only her sheltered sisters but also herself in that small number.

Although she had prepared to be a teacher and made her reputation as an excellent teacher, she insisted all her life that she had never "really" wanted to be one. It was Buppha, she would always say, who had really wanted to be a teacher but was unable to do so.

Call it karma or fate if you will. . . . My older sister, M.L. Buppha, wanted to be a teacher. She thought it was a good and useful career. But I didn't think about becoming *anything,* really. If I were to say what career I really wanted, I would have to say: dance the *lakhon!* *That* was the ambition buried deep in my heart![16]

Could she really have believed this? Many people were startled and amused when she said such things. It was so difficult to imagine the Achan (Professor) Boonlua they knew in her middle age—wool cap pulled down around her ears to keep out treacherous drafts at the onset of the hot season, briefcase in one hand and bulging knitting bag in the other, sensible shoes on her feet, and a worn sweater over her shoulders—impossible to imagine their Achan Boonlua costumed and bejeweled, floating across the stage on quick bare feet, dancing the *lakhon*. But she was not joking at all when she shared this old dream with others. As a girl Boonlua had rejected the dancing sisters whom she felt often rejected her, and she insisted that she preferred to play with the boys in the house. Yet whenever the girls gave her a role in their amateur performances, she responded with intense pleasure and gratitude.

> When I was born my father had given up his [classical dance] troupe and he was in retirement, but my sisters remembered the things they had seen, the songs they had heard. They would sing them together and then they would write plays and make the younger children in the house act them. I would be one of the principal actresses.[17]

Remarks of this kind hardly reflect the childhood environment she described as "roaming with the boys in the family." Her longing to be like her beautiful, graceful, charming sisters was matched only by her determination not to be unfavorably compared with them. If it was true that her real ambition, deep in her heart, was to dance the *lakhon*, she solved the problem with a perfect compromise. As a teacher, she composed and directed dance dramas with her students, and composed original plays for them based on classic models. Later, as a literary critic, she would write essays about classical Thai drama that would earn her the title of "the inventor of Thai literary criticism."

THE MATTER OF MARRIAGE

Boonlua was twenty-seven years old when she graduated from Chulalongkorn University. For young women of the time, the primary age for engagements and marriages was from about seventeen to twenty, with thirty representing the outer edge of marriageability.[18] Engagements and marriages had been the topic *du jour* throughout the three years between Boonlua's return from Penang and her enrollment at the university. Her sisters, cousins, and nieces talked of nothing else: Would this girl or that one marry? And if she did, would she be able to hold up her head in society? Or might she have to swallow her pride and accept a second-rate suitor for fear that no more acceptable one would come along? The romance novels of the time are surprisingly close to the truth, at least in regard to marriages within the aristocracy.

Chao Phraya Thewet's attitude toward marriage was one that even his peers had found bizarre. He frankly announced that he wanted none of his children to marry, whether sons or daughters. There is nothing culturally familiar in this attitude; most Thai men of all social classes have considered involvement in the marriages of their children, if only to the extent of giving final approval to the match, to be an aspect of parenting that was mandatory and also pleasant.

Boonlua, who would always be quick to defend her father's memory when she thought it needed defending, managed to come up with an explanation: he had once agreed, she said, to an engagement between one of his daughters and the son of a colleague. The young man then went abroad to study and returned with a foreign wife on his arm.[19] From that day, Chao Phraya Thewet was unwilling to agree to any engagement for any daughter. Almost all marriages within the upper class were still arranged during and well beyond the 1930s. One loophole did exist: young men he liked often visited him at Wang Ban Mo, and occasionally one of them would fall in love with one of his daughters and they would become engaged. He would then insist that whatever happened after that, no one could blame him for it. The downside of this system, which in fact was no system at all, was that his daughters had no organized help in making good matches. The fortunate (or beautiful and/or bold) found husbands on their own and enlisted sisters and stepmothers in planning weddings.

By the time Boonlua was in her late twenties, Chao Phraya Thewet was gone, and his son Phraya Thewet (Mom Luang Wara Kunchon) was in the position of approving or disapproving suitors for his younger sisters and his own children. He and his wife arranged a brilliant marriage for their daughter Mom Anuwong, and other girls in the family also married well. But marriage possibilities in the case of Boonlua were not spoken of. She openly blamed her plain looks for her lack of suitors. But it was not that simple.

> I had been hearing for so long that I was not pretty that I had become quite used to it. I didn't much care about getting married anyway. But I was very annoyed when some of the women who came calling insisted on bringing it up. Some had good intentions, but some were rather sneering, and to this day I don't know why. If I had to guess, I'd say it was because I did things that irked them. . . .
>
> At social gatherings, instead of staying with the other women I entered into the conversations of men—men who were the ages of my older brothers—which in my case meant that they were often as old as my friends' fathers. . . . Women didn't do that, didn't talk about affairs of government, or the history of one official or another—who was up, who was down, that sort of thing.
>
> And also, I was so—direct. What I liked best of all was to talk with my nephews. You see, they were older than me—but because I was their aunt, they would talk to me about anything, and I do mean anything.[20]

Plain or not, unfeminine in her behavior or not, the fact is that there were suitors for her hand. She later learned that Phraya Thewet had turned them all down without ever consulting her. It seems unlikely that he simply wanted to control his sister's life to the extent that anyone could, but thus far he had let her choose her own path. At first he had opposed her plan to enter the university, but in the end he had relented and after that was quite supportive. After she graduated he often confided in her, valued her opinions, and trusted her. Why would he have wanted to deprive her of a home and family if that was what she wanted? True, she kept saying that she didn't care if she married or not, but that did not mean much. She was a proud woman. Why didn't he ask her opinion on the subject of her own marriage prospects?

A man who worked for Boonlua when she was in her sixties, the dean of the Faculty of Arts of Silpakorn University at Nakhon Pathom, offered this speculation:

I think that Phraya Thewet thought she would be unhappy in marriage, and that she would make whoever married her unhappy as well. She had never been trained to run a household—she had been going to school all her life. She didn't know how to do anything in the house. She was always reading and telling everyone her opinions about politics and everything else. If she didn't agree with her husband, wouldn't she behave in the same way? Who would want a wife like that? I think that Phraya Thewet believed he was doing the right thing. He was not just trying to thwart her or keep her under his control. Maybe he thought that she would be better off teaching and living at home. And maybe [laughter] he was afraid that if he did arrange a marriage, the man would never forgive him![21]

There was no opprobrium attached to spinsterhood in Thai culture, especially for women of Boonlua's class who could depend upon their extended family indefinitely. It was never assumed that all the women in a large family would marry, and these spinsters always became involved, emotionally and financially, in the lives of nieces and nephews. In fact, they often ended up doing more "mothering" than the mothers themselves, who were all too glad to have a sister willing to share the tasks of bringing them up.

One bright spot in Boonlua's personal life during her twenties was the warm and open nature of her relationships with the numerous nephews, who were a most entertaining and satisfying source of information about the supposedly "good matches" some of her sisters and cousins had made. "Many of the husbands who were thought to be quite marvelous soon became naughty—some within only two years of the wedding," she wrote gleefully in her memoir.[22]

I suspect that the most significant reason why neither Buppha nor Boonlua were married when they were young was that they did not want to be married. They had grown up in a polygamous household rife with enmity and hostile factions that bridged generations. Their observations of the relations between men and women in their family, as well as in the families of their friends, may not have made them eager for matrimony.

Finally, both women were recognized for their own accomplishments and were very busy on a schedule of their own devising.

In the convent schools, Boonlua and Buppha had absorbed ideas about marriage not only from the nuns, but also from Western romantic fiction. This is reflected in the plots and points of view expressed in their own novels. They equated true love with monogamy, although a few of their female characters were presented as contentedly married to men who had minor wives. The leading female characters in Boonlua's novels would often mirror her own life—single working women who held their family together with pluck, common sense, and wise advice.

Something that may not occur to the modern reader is that marriage was dangerous. As girls, Buppha and Boonlua had seen many women in the household die young of childbirth or its effects, or of tuberculosis, which was rampant where many women lived in close quarters, and was essentially incurable. In their fiction, we see how terrible and traumatic these experiences were, not only for the women who suffered but also for the women—daughters and nieces—who were at hand to witness the suffering and death of women.[23]

Altogether, marriage was undeniably a risky proposition, though their sisters and nieces seemed to regard it as the most desirable life for a woman. Buppha and Boonlua could relate quite well to Jane Austen's Emma. Failing the appearance of a Thai version of Mr. Darcy, useful and comfortable spinsterhood seemed far from the worst way they could spend their lives.

BECOMING A TEACHER

Upon her graduation from Chulalongkorn University, on April 1, 1938, Boonlua and every other graduate in education automatically became a *kha ratchakan, chan song*—a (royal) civil servant, second grade. Not only people working in the Ministry of Education but all doctors, lawyers, teachers, professors, and other professional people also became civil servants upon graduation from university. The handsome government uniforms, which might only be worn on official occasions, depending upon one's occupation, were a source of great pride. The new government had skillfully managed a confluence of the old, prestige-laden royal government service and the newly conceived civil service.[24] It was not until the 1970s that ambitious university graduates seriously considered other careers—in commerce, advertising, and other fields entirely disconnected from the royal civil service and military network. Careers in the commercial sector might provide a good deal more money, but they lacked the prestige that continued to go along with being a *kha ratchakan*, "servant of the *royal* government."

At the time Boonlua attended Chulalongkorn University, the head of the Secondary Teacher Training Department there was Mom Luang Pin Malakul, who was a few years older than she, and whom she had known all her life. Their relationship, begun simply enough in childhood, would become difficult. Many people thought that they would make a perfect couple and expected more than a professional relationship to develop. But M.L. Pin married someone else, and his "cousin-like" relationship with Boonlua began to deteriorate when they worked together as civil servants. Boonlua never could understand that their relative positions required a difference in how they would or could relate to each other. Later, when M.L. Pin became minister of education, she was unable to show the deference toward him that his position required. "Phi Pin's" family and hers were on the same social level and she had known him all her life; why on earth should she suddenly defer to him and start calling him by his title just because he had been appointed minister of education? After all, he was still Phi Pin!

When it came time for the senior teaching students to be evaluated, M.L. Pin told his staff that they should see to the other students; he would evaluate M.L. Boonlua himself. To her surprise and annoyance, his evaluation was critical and, in her opinion, petty: one suggestion was that she really ought to use colored chalk to write on the blackboard. He finished his evaluation with the remark that he trusted her to make the necessary improvements in her teaching manner since he had no time to follow up.

Why did she need advice from Pin about the best ways to tend her flock at Rajini School? Boonlua made whatever improvements she deemed suitable and continued to teach her class of some twenty-five girls as she pleased.

At last, she felt herself to be fully an adult. The fact that she had to share her living quarters with her older sisters just as she had during her childhood was a common enough situation, one without remedy, and she accepted it. She was happier at home than she had been for some time and, for the most part, happy at work too.

Boonlua was impressed with the methods she saw in use at Rajini School, and especially with the headmistress, Princess Pichit-jirapa Thewakul, a woman who could instantly silence loud, unseemly, or sarcastic talk between girls by giving the gentlest of corrections in the kindest of voices. In response, the nicely raised girls would giggle a little and desist.

It is interesting that although Princess Pichit-jirapa's behavior modification methods took place in a school, Boonlua described them as examples of *oprom*, or "upbringing," the term she had used to describe her father's child-raising practices. The princess's moral guidance, which Boonlua considered to be a vital part of education, was orally conveyed and not learned from books.[25]

Boonlua was highly gratified and flattered by the praise she received from the princess, a woman who was in every way her ideal: intelligent, kindly, exquisitely well-mannered—and very well-born. Her relationship with this lady stands in great contrast to several later relationships with superiors who would fail, in numerous ways, to meet her standards. Princess Pichit-jirapa was that rare and difficult-to-define human being, the true *phu di*—one of the "good people" who was truly good in every way, whom Boonlua could respect with all her heart.

She was invited to stay on at Rajini after her graduation from Chulalongkorn University, but by then she was not sure that she wanted to stay. Princess Pichit-jirapa was wonderful, the teachers did not gossip (one of Boonlua's principal conditions for a place in which she would want to work), and everyone treated her well. Still, it was not a perfect situation. The problem, as Boonlua identified it, was that the teachers firmly believed Rajini School to be the best school in Thailand, and thus they saw no need to change or improve anything.

Just as she had become disappointed in the curriculum at Chulalongkorn University when she was a student there, she now began to find fault with the policies and objectives of Rajini School. She would go on to find fault with the administration at her next school, and the next. In every case, she was positive that she knew how to remedy the situation, if only her superiors would recognize that obvious fact and allow her to lead the effort to make the changes that anyone should be able to see were necessary.

As much as she admired the headmistress, it became impossible not to see that, after all, the princess had her faults. She was more of a scholar than an administrator and particularly unsuited to meet the demands of the swiftly changing times. "I knew that Thai society had many obstacles to overcome. And this could not be done through the kind of sheer 'goodness' the headmistress exuded."[26] The focus remained on the teaching of nice girls from good families. Although Thai society had changed drastically since the overthrow of the absolute monarchy and the diminution of royal influence—and, by association, the diminution of the fortunes of many of the royally connected families whose daughters attended Rajini—Boonlua felt that the administration of the school seemed all but unaware of the changes.

In the end, the decision of whether to stay on or to move on was not Boonlua's to make. Within the year, the Ministry of Education made sweeping changes in its national plan. No longer would Mathayom 7 and 8, the level at which she was then teaching, be taught as the last two years of the Thai equivalent of high school. Instead, the universities were to design special schools for university-bound adolescents which would be called "Triam Udom" ("preparatory schools"). The director of the Mathayom level Teacher Training Department at Chulalongkorn University, Boonlua's old friend and sometime nemesis M.L. Pin Malakul, was given the task of creating a Triam Udom there and he would administer it once it was in place. When all was ready, he wanted Boonlua to join his staff.

Boonlua was amazed to find that when she began to teach at Triam Udom, female relatives and family friends immediately lost interest in the matter of whether she would marry or not. They saw her in a different way. She was now twenty-seven, and most of her former classmates from the university were already married. Their mothers, who previously had had to assess the slight if not quite negligible threat Boonlua posed to their daughters' marital prospects (after all, she was titled), could now relax. Here, she records "for the sake of social history," as she put it, the sort of comments those mothers gradually ceased to make:

> Khun Boonlua is not at all as pretty as Khun (___). She simply can't compare. Probably because she studied too much.[27]
>
> Why *does* Khun Boonlua wear such a color! It doesn't go at all with her complexion and makes her look quite *pale* and *drawn*—not at all like Khun (___). Now, *that* girl looks fresh and lovely whenever you see her.

And, last but not least:

> Khun Boonlua, do you think that you will live with your brother for the rest of your life?[28]

Boonlua chose to reply to such remarks by smiling politely and murmuring vague comments that further irritated her tormentors. The Thai tendency to make direct personal comments on other people's appearance, activities, and more personal matters often comes as a surprise to Western foreigners who harbor the idea that Thais (and Asians in general) behave in a more reserved and subtle manner than they do themselves. In fact, personal remarks comprise a fairly large part of Thai small talk, although the "rules" for appropriate personal remarks must be understood. Comments and questions concerning another's appearance, spending habits, health, or marital status are often meant to show kindly interest—but, not always. Boonlua understood the rules perfectly, including the rules for responding.

When she had been teaching for about a year, Phraya Thewet began to talk with his sister more and relate to her as an adult, and in some ways, a peer. He offered advice and shared his thoughts about government service, even though he had served during the reign of

King Prajadhipok before the overthrow of the absolute monarchy, when conditions had been quite different. He confided that he would always feel bad about leaving the service of his king. He had resigned over matters of policy about which he had very strong feelings indeed— although he had never shared them with His Majesty, giving his own increasing deafness as his official reason for retiring early. He also confided a curious bit of information: ever since the ceremony in which, as a young page, he had drunk the Water of Allegiance, he had felt— and would feel all his life—that service to his king was his ultimate purpose in this life. But one aspect of the ceremony had made him uncomfortable. If the king were to order him to kill someone, unlikely as such an event seemed, it would require him to disobey the first of the five Buddhist precepts against the taking of life and he would have to comply.[29]

When Phraya Thewet's own son returned from his study in the United States (before the overthrow), he urged him not to become a civil servant for this reason. It is an interesting cultural contradiction: Buddhism forbids taking life, but loyalty to the king may require that one do so. Phraya Thewet, by any reckoning a "royalist," withdrew from the system partially for reasons of conscience. In this, he demonstrated the independence—and eccentricity—for which the family was known. In any event, by the time Boonlua joined the royal civil service, the ceremony of drinking the Water of Allegiance had been discontinued on the grounds that it was incongruent with democracy (and because it was so closely identified with the absolute monarchy and so blatantly "pre-modern").

After the royalist countercoup called the Boworadet Rebellion had been crushed in 1933, the political fortunes of Field Marshal Plaek Phibun Songkhram, the officer most responsible for defeating it, rose swiftly. By the time Boonlua graduated from the university, Phibun was prime minister. He and his closest advisors were wary of the old elite, in general; in turn, many Thais of the elite class saw Phibun as a mountebank and a demagogue, although they would never say so in public. The punishment for speaking against the nation's leaders had become more draconian than it had been before the absolute monarchy was overthrown.

The political situation in Siam was very complex during the 1930s, not simply a matter of who was "royalist" and who "anti-royalist." The "flexibility" that is famously attached to Thai political and social culture was very much in evidence during this difficult period of transition. One did not publically denounce anyone in a position of power, or any policy suggested or implemented by that person. This had always been the case, and so it remained under constitutional monarchy.

The Kunchon family reacted to the political realities of the late 1930s in various ways. As a teacher and civil servant, Boonlua was responsible to the government, to the dismay of her sister Buppha, who bitterly criticized Field Marshal Phibun Songkram, his advisors and followers, and all their works. Boonlua was pragmatic and more realistic about what the prime minister could or could not do, as head of the government of Siam. Moreover, she was frankly enthusiastic about at least some of the new administration's social and educational ambitions. Her brother, Colonel Khap, now also serving in the Phibun government, got along well with the prime minister himself and soon would be assigned to Washington, DC as a military attaché.

Buppha kept to her novels, was unrelenting in her disapproval of the New Siam, and began filling notebooks with angry patches of narrative and dialogue that she planned to use later in a novel that would reveal the upstarts, showing them for what they were.

POLITICS AND EDUCATION

Boonlua embarked upon her teaching career in the belief that it would take most of the Thai people a long time to fully participate in democracy, and in the further belief that it would be the teachers of the nation who would prepare them to do so. She believed that personal behavior and national objectives ought to be congruent, and in this she was very much in line with the basic philosophy of the Phibun administration—a philosophy that was not at all new as regards the relationship of nationalism to education in Siam.

Thai historian Nidhi Aeusrivongse, in an essay (in Thai) on the role of primary education in the development of Thai nationalism, traces its development from the reign of King Chulalongkorn (1868–1910) to the present day.

In the year 1906, Prince Damrong[30] . . . wrote that the chief objectives of education were to develop the character (*uphanisai*) of students in two respects. Students should learn to . . .

1) Love and cherish national sovereignty and exhibit honorable behavior (*praphruet ton yu nai sucharittham*);

2) Acquire academic knowledge.

The most efficient and economical means to these ends, by far, was the writing of school textbooks.[31]

The conviction that building and defending the nation must be paramount, with the acquisition of academic knowledge relegated to a not unimportant but necessarily secondary status, has not changed from 1906 to the present day. Making reference to eminent political scientist Benedict Anderson's seminal work, *Imagined Communities: Reflections on the Origin and Spread of Nationalism*, Nidhi goes on to say that if Thailand has constructed itself as an "imagined community" over the past century, it is Thai leaders (and their close aides)—from King Chulalongkorn to King Vajiravudh to Field Marshal Phibun Songkhram—who have done the "imagining," introducing their vision to citizens at their most impressionable age: from six to fourteen. Nidhi quotes passages from primary school textbooks from which students learn that Thailand is a larger extension (or, version) of the student's own family. There is, regardless of any specific era, a father / leader who is to be obeyed for the good of all, while everyone else in the family / kingdom is to work together—each according to his station. Teacher and policeman, farmer and bus driver, represent a community within which one heart beats.

The "nation" (*chat*) in the school textbooks . . . consists of a group of people among whom there are no problems. There may be diversity (*khwam taek lai*), but it is always "harmonious" (*klomkluen*) diversity.

There is peace under the rule of efficient leaders. And this image
prevails through sixth grade.[32]

Boonlua was a child during the sixth reign (Vajiravudh) when
Prince Damrong's view of the purposes of education was already well
entrenched. Even in the missionary schools these ideas were never
challenged. When she became a teacher herself, and Field Marshal
Phibun Songkhram was prime minister, education as an element of
nation-building was at least as important. Now, instead of learning from
textbooks, Boonlua was writing them, and although the leaders of the
nation might be very different from the leadership of her childhood,
the messages were almost identical.

Nidhi demonstrates the fact that in textbooks throughout the modern
era great stress has been laid on "we [Thai]" (*phuak rao*), our nation/
family, as opposed to "they" (*phuak khao),* the enemy who would harm
us, if it could. To this day, fourth graders learn these words penned by
King Vajiravudh: "If it is my nation's secret, though I should be beheaded,
I would not tell."[33] Nidhi wryly adds that although ten-year-olds are not
entrusted with many state secrets, they do not fail to get the point.

The cultural paraphernalia of nationalism is also strongly emphasized
in textbooks, and in this realm also Boonlua would have influence. This
statement appears in a fourth-grade reader of the 1930s:

> Each part of the (Thai) nation has its own geography, its culture, its
> customs and its languages. But we are all Thai. Every one of us lives
> upon the same (Thai) soil, as one nation. Every one of us has the same
> king. And Thais, no matter what region they live in, have an important
> part in making our nation productive and stable . . .[34]

Boonlua accepted as natural and beneficial the idea of education as a
medium of teaching monolithic Thai culture and engendering feelings
of patriotism. Although Thailand has always been a multicultural,
multiethnic society, in the last century the official attitude has been that
the more quickly and thoroughly people of other ethnicities could be
assimilated, speak Thai, and come to see that "we are all Thai," the better.

This policy was meant to include upland peoples such as the Hmong and Akha, as well as ethnic Chinese, Burmese, Cambodians, and Malays living on Siamese territory, and the single largest ethnic group residing in Thailand—the Lao, mainly in the Northeast on the Lao border. Siam had to be a successful "melting pot" if it was to survive.

The nationalist ethic that Phibun and his chief advisor, Luang Wichit Wathakan, painstakingly developed during the latter half of the 1930s was a strange blend of traditional and contemporary Thai, Western, and Japanese ideas. It was a grand attempt to define and refine the entire understanding of what it meant to be Thai. A good many strange bedfellows were involved in the creation of national policies and their implementation. The creators of these policies and those who implemented them included the self-made sons of provincial farmers and businessmen like Phibun and Luang Wichit, and the descendants of kings like M.L. Boonlua Kunchon, her brother M.L. Colonel Khap, and M.L. Pin Malakul.

By 1939, Boonlua felt that she wanted to teach Thai language, literature, and culture instead of being restricted to the teaching of English language and literature. It was the teachers of the Thai subjects, she now saw, who had the greatest opportunity to help the students understand their own culture (*watthanatham*). She also believed that those who were now teaching Thai language, literature, and culture lacked attitudes and methods that were sufficiently up to date. Although she tried very hard, she was unable to convince her superiors that they should allow her to change her teaching focus, not because she was unqualified but because her fluent English and adequate French made her too valuable a resource to "waste" on Thai. Nevertheless, she counted this as the "first failure of my life as a teacher."[35] Apparently it did not occur to her that the current administration might have misgivings about how a descendant of the Chakri kings might introduce the children to "Thai culture."

In addition to her teaching duties, she was made a liaison person between Triam Udom and the university, and in the following year she was made director of the English Department. Boonlua's years at Triam Udom were successful in many ways. She got on fairly well with most of her colleagues and, as always, she was loved by her students, who were enthusiastic and grateful. But one event that occurred during her first year at Triam Udom foreshadowed the kinds of problems she would encounter throughout her career. It also suggested the kinds of misgivings on the part of her superiors that may have led them to reject her request to teach Thai subjects.

It was the custom for students to recite a long Buddhist prayer once a week in homeroom. In a teachers' meeting an argument arose over whether the homeroom teacher should remain in the classroom and recite the prayer with the students. The final decision was that the teacher should not remain in the classroom, because if the teacher faced the class while praying, placing her palms together before her face in a *wai* to honor the Buddha, it would appear as though she were in fact *wai*-ing the students, which would be most inappropriate. (A teacher or other elder would never initiate a *wai* toward a student.) On the other hand, if the teacher turned around and *wai*-ed the blackboard, that would look equally ridiculous. Boonlua thought that this discussion was very silly and she said so. She explained to the other teachers that when the whole class offered praise to the Triple Gem (Buddha, Dharma, and Sangha), it made no difference which direction anyone faced, since these were *concepts*, and thus could have no *location*. Her argument was ignored, and the group decided that it was better for the teacher to remain outside the classroom until the prayer was finished.

> This kind of issue was of little importance to most of them, but I felt that when the teacher did not join the students in the prayer, it made the students understand that prayer was for children, and that when they grew up they wouldn't have to pray anymore. Besides that, some teachers worried that the children wouldn't pray properly and would pop in to be sure that they were behaving, also an inappropriate thing to do, not understanding that when one hears the words of respect for the Triple Gem, one is supposed to join in and show one's own respect. For that reason, unlike the other teachers I stayed completely away from my classroom while the students were praying [so as not to have to show disrespect for the Triple Gem by not participating]. If

you want young people to respect something, you must show respect for it yourself.[36]

THE "SOCIALIZATION" OF THE *PHRAI*

Even though she was a new teacher, Boonlua was concerned about many aspects of the school's mission. The students were all teenagers, and she felt that a main teaching objective ought to be "socialization"—especially for the students from upcountry. Some people, she pointed out, had gone through the entire Thai education system and were now teachers and still did not know how to properly perform the various prostrations to a Buddha image, to an elder, to a monk, or to a corpse at a cremation ceremony, for example. In a society that claimed to value and respect tradition and the proper observance of customs, students should be protected from future discrimination based on not knowing how to conduct themselves.

In this world, she patiently pointed out to her colleagues, there are *phu di* (those who know how to behave properly and do so), and there are *phrai* (commoners, who may not).[37]

> *Phu di* know how to perform myriad forms of the *wai*; *phrai* do not—but, they can learn. Of course, in some ways, *phrai* may be said to have an easier life—in a sense they are more "free"—and therefore it is understandable if some people might wish to follow the *phrai* way of life, but it was doing the students real harm to encourage such thoughts. They ought to learn such things as the different forms of a *wai* and why one does certain things, such as *wai* one's teacher at the beginning and the end of every school day.[38]

This is one of the more stunning examples of Boonlua's lack of sensitivity in working with others. It seems unlikely that she pondered whether her colleagues might feel insulted by these remarks. While the *phu di/phrai* incident was not quite typical of her behavior with her colleagues, such incidents did occur from time to time, and when they did, they were never forgotten. She judged her inability to convince people of the rightness of her beliefs in such situations as "failures" in her life. Had she presented a better argument, she reasoned, they would have been convinced of the rightness of her position.

What really was the issue at stake in the *phu di/phrai* incident? For Boonlua, it was a matter of *oprom*, proper upbringing, versus *sueksa*, book learning alone. This issue went to the very heart of preserving the sacred traditions that permeated Chao Phraya Thewet's household and that she felt were, and should remain, above and beyond changing curricula, or even evolving social and political systems. Another way of understanding the incident is that to Boonlua, the swiftest path toward "equality" and "democracy" was simply to pull everyone up to the highest level and make everyone into a reasonable version of a *phu di* by way of the national education system, a tide that would lift all boats.

At the outset of her career, Boonlua had two important goals: first, to help Thai youth live in the modern world under an ostensibly democratic government, and second, to impress upon Thai youth the beauty and importance of Thai traditions—as they had been imparted to her by her elders.

The new leaders of Siam, however, were no great admirers of Boonlua's heroes, men like Chao Phraya Thewet, or even Prince Narit, who was still alive and being treated with a reasonable degree of respect. They were working diligently to alter the old paradigm of "nation, religion, king," refashioning the basic idea to better reflect their modern objectives.

In 1941, the year Boonlua was appointed head of Foreign Languages at the Triam Udom school of Chulalongkorn University, she and the entire nation were stunned by an unexpected, unimaginable, and terrifying event: the Japanese invaded and occupied Thailand, putting the nation quite literally at the crossroads of war.

5

CULTURE WARS

The years between the late 1930s and the end of World War II were dangerous and difficult years for Thailand. No one imagined that the nation's growing and comfortable relationship with Japan would culminate in the invasion of December 1941. Thai leaders had been convinced that the Japanese saw them as their equals and saw the Thai nation as the emerging natural leader of Southeast Asia, just as the Japanese had emerged as the natural leaders of East Asia. Now, it seemed clear that all along, the Japanese had planned to use Thailand as their base of operations when they were ready to attack and occupy Southeast Asia. For the next four years, air strikes by the British, French, and Americans caused terror and destruction, exacerbated by unprecedented floods in 1942 that crippled communications, spread disease, and transformed Bangkok into a vast riparian village. It was a miserable period in modern Thai history, followed by a frightening postwar period in which Thailand struggled to repair badly damaged relations with the Western powers.

These years were unforgettable for another quite different reason. A new nationalism had taken shape during the years of Japanese courtship. Field Marshal Phibun and Wichit Wathakan, his closest associate, changed the name of the country from Siam to Thailand, "the land of the Thai," in 1939. By 1942, a National Institute of Culture had been established, and many policies and laws were enacted that affected virtually all aspects of Thai life. Boonlua became officially involved in this effort in 1943, when she was appointed to the Committee on Women's Dress under the aegis of the Bureau of Customs and Women's Culture. This bureau particularly reflected and expressed Phibun's great concern with *appearance*, with suitable attire for all occasions, including hats, gloves, socks—all the sartorial paraphernalia of the West—and also with etiquette. To Phibun, these were hallmarks of a modern, progressive nation and they were every bit as important in building the image of the Thai nation as were the economic or agricultural aspects of his national program. Eventually, Boonlua would explore her feelings and opinions about this era through the medium of fiction, producing two fine novels that are also valuable contributions to the social history of the period.

LIFE ON THE EVE OF WAR

In Thailand, the most noticeable effect of the outbreak of war in Europe was a rise in the prices of consumer goods. If the war was a nuisance, it was far away. Thailand had long enjoyed a close, if cautious, connection with Great Britain, and more Thais had been educated there than in any other country. Yet, many urban, educated Thais admired Germany and felt certain that Germany would be victorious.[1] In any event, Thais who thought about the war at all felt that it was up to the British and the nations of Europe to solve their own problems and end the hostilities.

Before the war, few Thais saw their leaders' fascination with Japan as ominous. On the contrary, Thais like other Asians were thrilled by the example of Japan's demonstrated ability to beat the colonial powers at their own economic and military games, beginning with their triumphant performance in the Russo-Japanese War of 1904–5. Perhaps, in these times, Japan might well be the nation to emulate, and the Thai government was certainly doing its best. Frankly imitative social programs were conceived to encourage or even order Thai citizens to be more organized, productive, tidy, thrifty, and brave—in short, to be as much like the Japanese as possible, but in a distinctly Thai way.

Boonlua's life was focused on family life at Wang Ban Mo and on her busy teaching schedule at Triam Udom. Prince Subhadradis Diskul remembers Boonlua in 1938, the first year in which he was a student there, and she a teacher.

> I was in the first class of the high school level at Triam Udom, and it was the first co-ed class in Thailand. I don't know why, but we believed that Achan Boonlua established all the school regulations for the girls. For example, if a boy was talking to a girl, they had to be located where the wind could blow from eight directions! I still remember how she was not very healthy, and sometimes had to lie down on the beach chair at the back of her office. She was so interesting. She was the kind of person who could make even a pot of *nam phrik* seem interesting.[2]

The first class of Triam Udom graduates was about to be sent up to Chulalongkorn University at the end of 1939, and to celebrate this event it was decided that the graduates would stage a *lakhon*, a theatrical production including both Thai and Western elements. Boonlua was asked to create and direct, a responsibility that she accepted with a sense of duty and high purpose. She assumed that she would receive all necessary help from colleagues in matters of costuming, scenery, prop management, and even curtain-pulling procedures. In the end, the *lakhon* that Boonlua produced in 1939 at Triam Udom was "an event in which I simultaneously achieved success and failure."[3]

During her childhood she had to struggle for autonomy against the constraints of the elder-younger sibling relationship. Now it was she who was completely in charge, casting colleagues as assistants and students as disciples. The ideal she taught was "one for all, all for one," but the production was rigidly hierarchical. She continually reminded the students of the ethic of the troupe: no one was more important than anyone else, whether it be leading lady or curtain-puller. Yet, it soon became clear that fits of temper and sulks would be tolerated in the case of leading ladies, while curtain-pullers were expected to carry out their tasks promptly, skillfully, and silently.

Boonlua never mentioned, in her writings, the traditionally severe discipline meted out by teachers and directors of *lakhon*. But her distant relative and contemporary, M.R. Kukrit Pramoj, an expert on and performer of *lakhon*, recalled the kind of training he both observed and endured during his own childhood: "The masters beat the children to bits. It was terrible. It should *never* have been allowed, but that is how it was in those days."[4] Whether or not such behavior was *de rigeur* in Chao Phraya Thewet's *lakhon* troupe, Boonlua herself was never mean or even unkind to performers, but she was unapologetically demanding. To their astonishment and dismay, prop masters and curtain-pullers learned that they were expected to attend every rehearsal, on the grounds that less than perfect timing could change a fine performance into a ridiculous one, and ridicule was to be avoided above all.

A few of her colleagues were genuinely supportive, devoting their spare time to the preparations, and the school director contributed a gratifying amount of money. She was thrilled when a fellow teacher was able to borrow a car and even find precious gasoline so that they could go on shopping expeditions to buy fabric for costumes. Other teachers sewed the costumes and one wrote original lyrics for folk songs. Some of the teachers, however, were shocked at Boonlua's insistence that country music be included. They asserted that such singing was coarse, an opinion she dismissed scathingly as nonsense, the result of a lack of understanding of the very elements of Thai theater. Despite the generous help she received, she later wrote, "Instead of being delighted with my triumph, I was sad, disappointed with the lack of knowledge of things Thai on the part of some people of my own generation."[5]

Even a document as self-justifying as her memoir *Successes and Failures* vividly demonstrates how rigid and condescending she must have appeared to colleagues she found disappointing, incompetent, or simply ignorant.

People who knew her during her Triam Udom days, and who would be her great admirers and friends decades later, were not her former colleagues but her former students. Although she had warned them at the outset of rehearsals about the legendary fierceness of *lakhon* directors, the student performers were inspired by this woman who seemed to understand them and who displayed a firm but caring attitude throughout rehearsals and performances. Some were taken aback, at first, to learn that Achan Boonlua had been selected as the director, including Prince Subhadradis:

> I was surprised to find that Achan Boonlua was going to be the director of the *lakhon*. I had thought that all she knew was English, like a *farang* woman. Some of my older sisters didn't really like her; they called her "Miss University." But she always showed compassion for me.[6]

Boonlua introduced the teenaged cast to a world they had scarcely known existed and convinced them that they were capable, and could be successful, both as individuals and as members of a team. She poured nearly all of her energy and her salary into the production, and when it was over she was exhausted. She blamed symptoms of weakness, malaise, and nervousness on "lack of knowledge of the world. I had thought that my colleagues would understand the young people [in the *lakhon*] as well as I did. . . . I allowed these matters to gnaw away at me needlessly, until finally I became quite ill."[7]

Throughout 1939 and 1940, Boonlua consulted various specialists about her debilitating physical ailments. In a phrase that is almost identical in Thai and in English, one physician told her to "wise up" about her own personality and the environment in which she had chosen to spend most of her hours, advice that she claimed she accepted—whether or not she then followed it or fully understood what the doctor meant. She was offended by advice she received from well-meaning friends and coworkers. Some assured her that she would get well if only she would get more exercise. Achan Boonlua should take her mind off her symptoms by working in the garden, learning to cook, or—the advice she found most absurd—taking up running! Most irritating of all was the remark, "I never get sick because I'm a *phrai* (commoner), not a *phu di* (person of the elite) like you. She even went to occult healers, one of whom told her that the dark arts were unsuitable for the daughter of a *chao phraya*. She should stay away from charms and spirits and the people associated with such things and confine herself to the company of intellectuals (*banyachon*).

She was only twenty-eight years old, but in some ways, people said, she already seemed to be slipping into old-maid behavior. For that matter, so was her thirty-four-year-old sister Buppha, despite her enviable fame as a novelist. What was wrong with these titled, accomplished women who appeared to have everything? Buppha also suffered from spells of generalized weakness, headaches, muscle aches, dizziness, nervousness, feelings of despair, and a host of other vague symptoms that had been diagnosed, since the Victorian era, as "neurasthenia"—at least by doctors trained in Western medicine and familiar with maladies common to ladies.[8]

Neurasthenia, understood to be an ailment that one could develop, endure, and finally surmount, did not carry the stigma of mental illness, which was generally understood in Thai and other Asian cultures as the result of a bad genetic inheritance, or moral weakness, or a lack of mental and/or emotional competence. There also is a "princess and the pea" aspect to the matter, reflected in Boonlua's friend's comment that she was glad to have been born "a *phrai*, not a *phu di* like you," and therefore less prone to such ailments. Women of the lower classes were bound to be sturdier and less sensitive than women of Boonlua's class, who might well be more delicate physically. On the other hand, elite women were more likely to be intelligent, artistic, graceful, and courageous. Courage was a highly valued quality in the Kunchon family, and not only for men.

Medicines and tonics began to play a bigger role in Boonlua's and Buppha's life at this time, notwithstanding the scarcity of such things during the war that was about to descend upon them. For the rest of their lives, the sisters would suffer from many physical ailments and from depression, compounded by the effects of the many medicines and tonics they consumed to relieve an ever increasing number of mysterious symptoms.

During the next year Boonlua's health improved somewhat. She even dared to take up bicycling during a holiday at the seashore, but soon regretted this bit of adventurousness when she developed areas of mysterious numbness in various parts of her body. Neither entirely well nor seriously ill, by late 1941 Boonlua looked forward to the coming semester with cautious optimism—until December and what Boonlua would always call "the biggest event in the history of Thailand." It may seem perplexing, after the events of the preceding three or four years, that Thais could have been dumbfounded by the invasion of the Japanese. Nevertheless, they were.

"THE BIGGEST EVENT IN THAI HISTORY"

On December 9, 1941, Field Marshal and Prime Minister Phibun Songkhram addressed the citizenry in a radio broadcast that left the entire Thai nation reeling.

> On December 8, 1941, since about 2 o'clock a.m., Japanese forces entered Thailand by sea in the [southern provinces]. . . . Almost everywhere the Thai military and police forces put up a sturdy struggle . . .
>
> [T]he Japanese Ambassador [had come] to the Official Residence of [the] Prime Minister on December 7, 1941, at 10:30 o'clock p.m. and explained to the Minister of Foreign Affairs that war had been declared on Great Britain and the United States but that Japan did not consider Thailand as an enemy but she was obliged by necessity to ask for passage through Thai territory.
>
> Having thoroughly examined the matter, His Majesty's Government consider that the events which [have] thus occurred could not be averted. Although Thailand had tried all she could, she could not get clear of them, and from the nature of the events which had occurred, further struggle would entail the loss of Thai blood without achieving its purpose. It has therefore been necessary to . . . concede passage to the Japanese armed forces.[9]

Within one week the Thai government would further agree to fight alongside the Japanese in Burma, and both governments agreed to mutually support each other in the event that either was engaged in an armed conflict with another country. The final Treaty of Alliance begins:

> The Royal Government of Thailand and the Imperial Government of Japan, firmly convinced that the establishment of a new order in East Asia is the only way of realizing prosperity of that region and the indispensable condition for the restoration and promotion of world peace, [are] animated by a firm and inflexible determination to eliminate all baneful influences which are obstacles to such purpose . . .[10]

The treaty was signed in the Temple of the Emerald Buddha adjacent to the Grand Palace, a decision that was shocking to many Thais because the temple is one of the holiest sites in the kingdom and a great source of national pride. A year after the signing, Wichit Wathakan, then foreign minister (among his many other titles and posts) and most enthusiastic about the alliance, would justify this location in a statement that suggests a perceived need for some justification.

> . . . We believe in the truth of the Lord Buddha, therefore, any act performed before him must be considered that we will always abide by the truth and nothing but the truth. We shall honour our words and respect the pact literally, spiritually and honestly.[11]

On January 25, 1942, Thailand declared war on the Allies, giving its reasons in a widely published government communiqué:

> . . . In the past Thailand has been oppressed in many ways by England. The British did everything to prevent the development of the country, especially in the industrial field. . . . As far as the United States is concerned, all Thais should remember that during the Indochina War, the American Government refused to sanction the delivery of a shipment of airplanes, previously paid for by Thailand. History also reveals that the United States failed to mediate or to assist our country when we were at loggerheads with France in 1893 . . .[12]

Sir Josiah Crosby, the British Ambassador to Thailand, would later describe this document as "a record of childish insincerity which must be well nigh unique in the history of international relationships, and future generations of Siamese will assuredly blush to recall it."[13]

Phibun and his top aides, especially Wichit Wathakan, were ambivalent about the relationship with Japan, before and after the invasion. Admiration for Japan remained throughout the war. Even in the early days of the occupation, Wichit Wathakan defended the alliance and bitterly castigated the British and the Americans for past wrongs. Many of the social programs that he would continue to develop and refine throughout the war years reflected Japanese ideas about the relationship of the individual to the state and about the proper conduct of the self. However, this admiration and emulation was combined with a fierce determination to cling to the trappings of independence, and to identify and interpret a native Thai culture.

One aspect of the alliance with Japan that strongly appealed to Thai leadership and also to the population at large was the prospect of a solution to the problem of the "lost territories": areas of Malaya, Burma, Laos, and Cambodia that Thailand had occupied and ruled for considerable periods of time in the past, but had been forced to cede to France or England in the late nineteenth century in return for guarantees of continued Thai independence.

After the invasion and occupation of Thailand and the subsequent invasion of French Indochina, British Burma, and Malaya, Japan was in a position to demand the return of the "lost territories" to Thailand. It is difficult to imagine what other scenario, besides the Japanese invasion of Thailand, Wichit Wathakan could have envisioned to realize his irredentist dreams. Prior to the invasion, Wichit had meticulously mapped out and justified Thailand's claims to these territories. Days after the invasion, immediately following the Declaration of War on the Allies in Bangkok, an English version of his book, *Thailand's Case* [for the return of the lost territories] was published so that the Western powers would know what to expect.[14]

If this seems cynical, there is at least one other way to view the statements and actions of Phibun and Wichit Wathakan during the late 1930s. Perhaps they thought that they could follow, update, and even improve upon earlier models of Thai diplomacy in these difficult times. King Mongkut had compared dealing with the English and the French as standing between the crocodile and the tiger. Yet, he had succeeded in leaving a sovereign kingdom to his son Chulalongkorn, who in turn left a sovereign kingdom to his sons, minus the lost territories. Perhaps now, eighty years later, they could do better, standing beside Japan and yet apart from it, figuring their odds, and playing all sides against the center. However, the crocodile and the tiger had been one thing; the Rising Sun was quite another.

THE WAR IN BOONLUA'S FICTION

Boonlua's 1962 novel, *Western Daughter-in-Law* (*Saphai maem*), is set before and during World War II.[15] Through the relatively safe medium of fiction, and with the perspective she had developed over the intervening years, Boonlua was able to explore and share her own feelings about the Thai government, the Japanese, the war, and the life of her nation during the 1930s and 1940s. The fears, beliefs, and prejudices of the characters in *Western Daughter-in-Law* mirror those of Kunchon family members and friends. Boonlua's own attitudes are clearly expressed through the leading female character, Kanika—an unmarried teacher whose family members rely upon her wisdom and common sense—and even more forcefully in the attitudes of older men in Kanika's extended family. Although Boonlua may not have thought of it in quite this way, because they are male and middle-aged or elderly these characters have the "right" to make highly critical and angry statements about the government, the war, and the state of the nation in general. Other women in the novel besides the independent-minded Kanika all have a son, brother, or fiancé who is studying in either England or in Germany, and their views appear to be entirely formed by the men whose letters they avidly read.

Sirima's older brother in Germany assured her in his letters that the Germans would be the victors, certainly and soon. . . . When Sirima cheerfully shared this news, Suthira said . . . "I wonder . . . if the Germans are victorious, what will become of us."[16]

Kanika is not worried about a fiancé in Europe, but about the fortunes of her nation, and often ponders the path that has led to the terrible situation that she, her family, and her countrymen and women now face. "Victory" and "defeat" have become words that no one can define with certainty, and about which everyone argues.

[Kanika thought] that Thailand itself was adrift between the politics of the great nations. . . . Thais must live in fear of both outcomes: Should its own allies, the Axis powers, win, democracy would disappear altogether in Thailand. But should the Allies win, the nations in which democracy thrived, Thailand would be thrown into a terrible position. Surely, the French would exact their revenge . . .[17]

There is little doubt where Kanika's, or Boonlua's, sympathies lie, as in this scene, where she divides what is obviously her own opinion between Kanika and her uncle.

Kanika and her uncle whispered together on the veranda, far from the other relatives.

"Uncle, what do you think will happen?"

"Catastrophe, I say. The damned Japanese—who can trust them? If they win, we'll be their slaves, and no mistake about it. And our leader with them, the instigators and power lovers, men who cannot talk like men but speak with knives."

Kanika asked, "Is there hope that the British will win, do you think?"

"The damned Germans have poked a wasp's nest. Child, do you think the Americans will be defeated? With the Americans supporting the British, the British must win eventually. And Russia? The Germans can never defeat Russia. . . . And as for us, we will be dragged down into the catastrophe of Japan's defeat."[18]

Boonlua was able to castigate the Thais for their gullibility about the Japanese through Uncle's angry statements.

Most Thais privately believed, or hoped, that if worst came to worst the Americans would forgive all, and the British would follow their example. But Kanika's uncle was infuriated by this idea.

> "The Thai think like thirteen-year-old children!" Uncle announced. "Do they believe that the Japanese will die alone before they destroy everything and everyone they can reach? How could the Thais have imagined that they could declare war with the Japanese and then be allowed to skip away, singing their crazy songs?"[19]

There was a pronounced "ethnic" aspect to the new version of nationalism. The Chinese were vilified in a campaign that echoed the kind of nationalistic rhetoric espoused by King Vajiravudh in his 1914 tract, "The Jews of Asia." Certain occupations were reserved: for example, only "Thai" were allowed by law to make or sell Buddha images; sell bricks, firewood, charcoal, or torches; make women's hats or dresses; weave wicker items or furniture; cut hair, make toys or dolls; or be a lawyer.[20]

Who were the "Thai?" Siam always had been what is now termed a multicultural state. The single largest ethnic group in the nation consists of Lao people in the Northeast. In the South, many Thai citizens are of Malay descent, while on the eastern border, in Surin province for example, Thai citizens speak both Thai and the Khmer (Cambodian) of their ancestors. Ironically, both Phibun and Wichit Wathakan were of Chinese descent, but they were born in Thailand and considered themselves to be fully Thai. As before in modern Thai history, it was "new Chinese," people who sent money to their homeland, who were mistrusted, not people of Chinese descent who were born in Thailand and had grown up studying in Thai schools and speaking Thai. In any event, Thai leaders, of whatever descent, would decide who was and who was not a real Thai.[21]

There is no question that Phibun and Wichit admired fascism—but does their admiration mean that they were fascists? Is it reasonable to call this a "fascist era" in modern Thai history? There is disagreement on the subject, with reasonable opinions on both sides. People who study Thai leadership during this era tend to answer either, "Of course they *were!*" or "Of course they were *not!*" Thamsook Numnonda contends that rather than identifying Thai wartime policies as first "pro-Japanese" and then, near the end of the war, "pro-Allies," they should be identified as "pro-Thai" from first to last. After the war, Phibun, who had been so pro-Japanese, would return to power in 1947. His administration would enjoy greater support from the Western powers than ever before, especially from the United States. Thailand, in the Cold War environment, would be positioned as the frontier of the Free World in Southeast Asia, resisting and repelling grow communist insurgencies on its borders—as anti-communist a stance as it was pro-Thai.

During the war, Thailand was the only country in Southeast Asia that maintained its sovereignty and the management of its own affairs even under the occupation of the Japanese, in that the administration of the country continued to be vested in Thai authorities, especially in the person of the prime minister. Moreover, Thailand was the only Southeast Asian country with an indigenous army operating independently of the Japanese army. "Hence, in [the] Thai view, the Japanese army was not an army of occupation but rather, a 'guest' army. . . . Pro-Axis throughout the greater part of the war, the Thai Government was nevertheless seen by the Allies to be pro-Allies towards the end of the war."[22]

A literary example of how the Japanese saw Southeast Asians is found in Hayashi Fumiko's 1941 novel *Floating Cloud (Ukigumo)*, the first part of which is set in Vietnam, where Hayashi spent some time as a correspondent. Her cast of characters is divided into three distinct groups: the Japanese (new masters), the French (old masters, sometimes friendly with the new masters), and the natives, who serve drinks during conversations between old and new masters and knock politely on hotel-room doors to warn occupants before coming in to collect laundry.[23]

Thai attitudes toward the Japanese were diverse. Within a few months of the invasion in 1941, fear about personal safety at the hands of the invaders was much diminished. The complexity of people's feelings is illustrated in this passage from M.R. Kukrit's *Four Reigns* (*Si phaendin*), which is both descriptive and ironic.

> Phloi recalled that after the Japanese invaded Thailand, it was strange. At first, no one felt anything but grief, and everyone agreed that the Japanese were monsters. Then, many Japanese people, soldiers and civilians, came to Thailand, and began to work closely with Thai people, and Japanese soldiers walked about everywhere, without incident. And at last, life became ordinary again. The *farang* decreased in importance, as [her son-in-law] Khun Sewi had said they would, and had become the enemy, or had become people one could speak of without respect, or fear. As for the Japanese, they became the important ones, the great friends. They had important work. Soldier and civilian alike, the Japanese had assumed the status of honored guests.[24]

The Thais were not treated with the level of brutality that occurred, for example, in the Philippines. I do not mean to minimize the experience of Thais during the Japanese occupation, much less to excuse the appalling treatment of British, American, and other people in Japanese internment camps in Thailand, Burma, and elsewhere. However, it is a fact that most Thais, by comparison with other Southeast Asians, did not suffer directly and greatly from the Japanese occupation. I have spoken with Thais who were children during the war, and who have neutral or positive memories of the Japanese, especially the educated officers. One Thai woman recalled the ordinary and frequent visits of "a Japanese officer who would come to play chess with my father. He had heard that my father liked to play chess, and he came to our house, and he spoke to my father in English. They would play chess, and sometimes he would swim in our pond. I was a little girl, and I didn't think anything much about him. He was very polite."[25]

One of the most beloved novels of the twentieth century, *Khu Kam* by Tomayanti, is a sentimental tale about the tragic wartime marriage between a Thai woman and a Japanese officer.[26] It is the only novel I know of in which the hero is a member of an invading army. The message of the novel is very "Buddhist": all human beings are at the mercy of *kilesa* (in Thai, *kilet*), attachments and desires; nations and their leaders are likewise subject to attachments and desires—for power, for glory, for territory; and thus all wars are the result of *kilesa*. Kobori, the Japanese officer, and Angsumalin, the daughter of a Thai official who has arranged the marriage against her will, are both victims in this tragic tale, and both are trying to do their duty under terrible circumstances. The Japanese may be the enemy, but the real and permanent enemy is human nature.

At war's end, it would appear painfully obvious that not only had the Thai government been blinded by opportunity during Japan's beguiling courtship during the late 1930s, but also that Japanese dreams of empire were too vast to succeed. But in 1941, when Japan was successfully attacking Hawaii, the Philippines, Malaya, and Singapore, when empires that had seemed eternal appeared to be crumbling under the weight of Japanese military might and scrupulous organization, from the vantage point of Southeast Asia there was nothing at all obvious about Japan's eventual defeat. Moreover, there was so much to gain if Japan won—or so it seemed in 1941.

BOONLUA'S WAR

The very first government building to be seized by the Japanese after the invasion was the Triam Udom school. Chulalongkorn University had to disassemble the school, locating departments wherever it could. Both the Accounting Department and the Liberal Arts Department, where Boonlua taught, were temporarily relocated in Chumphon Palace, but soon the students had to be sent home because of the widening scope of air raids. Everyone who had been absent less than 20 percent of the time was automatically passed on to the next level.[27]

In addition to the English courses she taught at Triam Udom, Boonlua was involved in teacher training at Chulalongkorn University and also had been given the task of developing materials for the teaching of Thai language.[29] Although she had resisted the job of developing Thai language teaching materials in the past stating truthfully that she was competent to teach Thai literature but was not a linguist, once she had taken on the task she did her best, calling upon everyone she knew who was reputed to teach Thai successfully, and reviewing the few materials that were already in use. Gradually, she and her friends developed a new Thai language curriculum that would remain the standard for many years.

The war and the catastrophic floods of 1942 would always be inextricably linked in the minds of those who lived through the war years, as illustrated in this passage from *Western Daughter-in-Law*:

> All her life, Kanika would remember October of the year 2485 B.E. [1942 C.E.], when the great flood came to Thailand. Fighting between the Germans and the Russians was then fierce, and the hope of the Germans for an easy victory was forgotten. The further the German forces moved on Russian soil, the more wretched their condition. . . . As for the Japanese, they were stopped at the Burma-India border . . . unable to advance upon India, or toward Australia.
>
> But here at home, they were surrounded by water, the garden had become a lake, and earthworms escaping the flood slithered up the stairs, covering them with their long white bodies. On the night of October 22, 1942, Kanika and her mother lay in the bedroom listening to the BBC on the radio. Her father did not like it because it was forbidden by the government. But in his household there was only one "good citizen": himself. Everyone else listened avidly. On that night, Kanika tuned in to the BBC, put her head close to the radio, and heard something that she had not heard before: a new clarity and resonance in the tone of the announcer's voice as he said, "The British Eighth Army has carried out a successful attack [on the Germans] at El Alamein."

"Oh!" Kanika cried out.

"What is it?' her mother whispered, alarmed.

Kanika turned to her mother, her eyes shining. She smiled as she whispered, . . . "The British Eighth Army has won a victory over the Germans." She continued listening for awhile, turned back to her mother and said, "They say that it was a great victory. Now, there may be reason to hope."

From that day on, the fortunes of democracy began to change. . . .[29]

Although there is never any question of where Kanika's loyalties lie, her hopes for the future are always expressed vaguely in terms of "democracy." Great Britain, France, and the United States are mentioned only in specific examples, as in this passage about the Battle of El Alamein.

On the last day of the 1942 school term, Boonlua and her fellow teachers climbed into a boat and paddled their way to the home of the Triam Udom president to work together on the tasks of grading and student evaluations. Although she was too physically weak to do her share of the paddling she worked as diligently as the rest of them, grading exams and writing evaluations until two o'clock in the morning. The next day, after the principal had studied the grade list, he instructed the teachers to add 10 percent to each student's grade. Because everyone passed that year, unofficially it would always be known as the "Tojo Class."[30]

WATTHANATHAM THAI: THE NATIONAL INSTITUTE OF CULTURE

Few Thais today realize that the familiar word watthanatham, meaning "culture" as used by Western anthropologists, was fashioned from Pali-Sanskrit roots during the 1930s. Before and during the war, the Phibun administration was deeply involved in an immense task: the definition of Thai culture and the construction of a National Institute of Culture to explain and implement new policies. Most aspects of this effort reflected Phibun's dreams for the nation and his deeply felt beliefs about governance and civilization, but the architect of the great nationalist project of the era was the second most important person in the government, Wichit Wathakan.

In 1943, Boonlua and her colleagues on the National Committee for Women's Dress were given the mission of deciding upon and writing guidelines concerning which articles of Western or Thai clothing a woman should wear for various social occasions. (Japanese clothing was never worn.) How should one assemble an outfit for a social occasion, when one's husband would be wearing Western attire? If Boonlua thought that her appointment to this committee was perplexing, her sisters Buppha and Chalaem thought it was hilarious, because she had never cared for clothes and her efforts to dress up, on the rare occasions when she did try, were notorious. She spent practically nothing on herself because she gave most of her salary away to her young relatives, indulging herself only in the acquisition of books, her lifelong passion. Given these circumstances, Boonlua turned gratefully to her sisters for advice. Those who had married high-ranking officials often attended state functions. Moreover, her brother Phraya Thewet, before his retirement, had occupied a position similar to "chief of protocol" and had often received foreign visitors at Wang Ban Mo on behalf of the government, so he too was a source of useful information. Nearly all of the Kunchon family, with the exception of Boonlua, were not only interested in such things but were *au courant* on the innumerable details of correct dress, jewelry, and footwear, both Western and Thai, for formal and informal occasions.

Boonlua and her colleagues wore a civilian uniform to work, which was of Western design, and the rest of the time they wore a combination of Thai and Western clothes. Ever since the 1870s—at least, for those middle- and upper-class urban women with a "social life"—it had been the fashion to dress in modified Western style from the waist up, and in Thai style from the waist down, and this fashion had been updated. During the Phibun era, one could wear an entirely Western outfit, or Western upper garments above a Thai skirt—but only a Thai skirt *with side seams*, never the traditional Thai wrap-around style, because Phibun had declared that it looked "primitive."

At first, Phibun's great concern with appearance did not seem strange to Thais. Looking as good as one could was seen by most people as laudable, an old-fashioned attitude of respect for oneself and for others. Coming into another's presence looking unkempt and disheveled was disrespectful. "The Leader" (*phu nam*), as Phibun preferred to be called, expected all Thai citizens to practice neatness, cleanliness, and meticulous personal habits, as reflected in this passage from the National Cultural Maintenance Act of 1940:

> Whereas it is expedient to prescribe customs and traditions for the Thai people for orderliness in dress, behavior and etiquette when appearing in public places . . . the National Cultural Maintenance Act B.E. [Buddhist Era] 2483 [1940 C.E.] issues the following Royal Decree: . . . In public places or areas within the municipality people must not dress in improper manners which will damage the prestige of the country, e.g. wearing loose-ended sarong, wearing only underpants, wearing sleeping garments, wearing loincloth, wearing no blouse or shirt, women wearing only undershirt or wrap-around. . . . The Prime Minister shall have charge and control of the execution of this Royal Decree. (Countersigned by) Phibunsongkhram, Prime Minister.[31]

This pronouncement is strongly reminiscent of this proclamation from King Mongkut, nearly a century earlier:

> People who wear no upper garments seem naked; the upper torso looks unclean, especially if the person . . . is sweating. Other peoples of *civilized* countries wear upper garments with the exception of the *lawaa* and the Laos people who are forest dwellers and *uncivilized* and do not use clothing. . . . Let everyone, therefore, wear upper garments when coming to royal audience.[32]

A properly dressed man in one widely distributed government poster during the war is shown wearing walking shorts, shirt, socks, shoes, a pith helmet, and carrying an attaché case, looking for all the world like a colonial functionary on his way to inspect the natives. The results of improper dress and unclean habits were described as nothing short of catastrophic to national interests in one of hundreds of Wichit Wathakan's radio plays starring two Thai citizens named Man and Khong who discuss issues of the day and how Thais may advance their nation through proper behavior.[33]

KHONG: To wear proper dress would show that we do not have barbaric minds as those wild people of Central Africa.

MAN: That is right. If we go to Central Africa, we will see that those barbarians do not dress themselves orderly and beautifully. Their barbaric minds are indicated by their [dress]. On the contrary if we go to London, we will see beautiful people wearing beautiful and orderly dresses. And we will see that the British are a people who are cultured and are good in every aspect. Whether the mind is civilized or not is expressed through [dress]. Very few of those who are badly dressed are civilized. . . . You must understand that to safeguard our country's independence, we cannot only rely on a strong military or the ability to fight. . . .

KHONG: And the fact that we do not have good culture would serve as an excuse for them to introduce [their ideas of] culture to us. . . .

MAN: Our country must not be filthy either. . . . We live in the community of nations. If we frequently have epidemics, they would take it as an unfavorable aspect and would try to destroy the source of diseases in our country for the happiness of other nations. *This is . . . [a] raison d'être for colonization.*[34]

The views expressed in this bizarre and unapologetically racist radio play appear all the stranger in light of the fact that Thailand had declared war upon the British and was currently being bombed by "the British . . . who are cultured and are good in every aspect." Never is there a reference to the cultural or behavioral excellence of the Japanese, who perhaps are no longer to be seen as "good in every aspect." Or do these strange radio plays reflect, more than anything else, a fierce determination to preserve at least the appearance of autonomy despite the betrayal and humiliation of the Japanese occupation?

At last, the obsessions with ideal appearance and behavior came to seem excessive, and in some regards even silly. Citizens began defacing the posters showing ideally dressed Thais, in creative and sometimes crude ways. They made fun of the perplexing regulations about hats and gloves, the fines for being caught downtown in one's sarong, and the consequences of daring to chew betel nut, which Phibun hated and banned.

It was during the bombing of Bangkok that Boonlua was visited by a "serious suitor"—meaning that negotiations were underway between the families—but she decided against him.

> The family was sort of negotiating. He was a social equal, the son of a *chao phraya*. But whenever the air raid siren sounded, he was the first one into the air raid shelter. I said to my sisters, "I don't want to marry a man who is first into the air raid shelter! I would prefer a man who would be the last." Anyway, I didn't feel . . . well, in Thai we would say that you feel a person is just "not *nuea khu*"—you know, it means not your mate from your last existence.[35]

The Siam Society, a prominent and prestigious organization of Thai and Western scholars founded in 1904 continued on during the war. However, in December 1939, following the country's name change from Siam to Thailand, it had changed its own name to the "Thailand Research Society."[36] Until the end of the war, the organization's publication would be called the *Journal of the Thailand Research Society*. Immediately following the war, both the organization and its publication would quietly return to their original names, the latter being known from that day to this as the *Journal of the Siam Society*.[37]

It was not difficult for upper-class Thais such as Boonlua, her brother M.L. (Colonel) Kap Kunchon, Prince Dhani Niwat, and Prince Wan Waithayakon (both sons of King Chulalongkorn) to play active roles either within the wartime government or within such organizations as the recently renamed "Siam Society," because they did not have to do or say anything that flatly contradicted their own deepest beliefs. After all, the king remained upon the throne (even if he was a boy and lived in Switzerland), the present government continued to strongly support Buddhism, and most Thais related to each other much as they ever had. The common people continued to show respect for their betters, be they members of the royal family or top officials in the current government.

In 1944, Prince Wan was elected president of the Thailand Research Society. He celebrated the event in the September 1944 issue with an article entitled "Thai Culture" (in English), which comprises a valuable text on the evolution of Thai thinking about "Thai values" during the war years.

> Culture [*watthanatham*] is a word which is very much in vogue nowadays. . . . [T]he third principle in the Joint Declaration of the Assembly of Greater East-Asiatic Nations reads as follows: "3. The countries of Greater East Asia by respecting one another's traditions and developing the creative faculties of each race, will embrace the culture and civilization of Greater East Asia."[38]

The remainder of this essay may be most significant for what is left out, for example, any mention of the present king, Ananda Mahidol, or of the sacred symbols of nationalism that had been paramount during preceding decades—particularly, King Vajiravudh's constant refrain of "nation, religion, king." "Nation" is very much in evidence in Prince Wan's essay, and "religion" is treated with respect, but all mention of "king" is limited to those long dead. King Mongkut (1851–68) and, even more prominently, King Ramkhamhaeng (?1279–98) are mentioned in the course of this article by way of suggesting a smooth continuum of "Thai culture" over the centuries, culminating in the current policies and philosophies of Field Marshal Phibun Songkhram. Prince Wan states that in addition to "the Pact of Alliance covering political, military, and economic fields of collaboration between Thailand and Japan, a Cultural Agreement between the two countries was concluded on October 28, 1942." He goes on to say that no definition of "culture" accompanied this agreement, but that fortunately this matter has been thoroughly considered by Thai leaders:

> Ever since his assumption of office as Premier, Field-Marshal P. Phibun-Songkram has attached the greatest importance to the development of culture among the Thai people. . . . His desire is to inspire and instill into the people the spirit of . . . united patriotic action looking to the greatness and prosperity of Thailand. . . . [He] said that education and patriotism alone were not complete qualities in themselves: they had to be complemented by national traditions, which the Government would notify to the public from time to time, under the name of *Rathaniyom* for their own observance as well as for the observance of generations to come. . . . His Excellency went on to explain that State custom and convention is similar to the moral code of etiquette of civilised people . . .[39]

TWELVE *RATHANIYOM*, FOURTEEN *WIRATHAM*

The *rathaniyom* mentioned by Prince Wan were developed by Wichit Wathakan. They have been translated into English using various terms, including "national traditions," "notifications," and Wichit Wathakan's own favorite, "state conventions."[40] The first *rathaniyom* is comprised of a pronouncement and a definition: The nation shall be known as Thailand. Other *rathaniyom* concern the definition of patriotism, the desirability of buying goods produced in Thailand, and, last but not least, the need for proper dress and etiquette.

Prince Wan explains the difference between royal pronouncements of "former times" and the *rathaniyom* of the present day:

> *Rathaniyom* has similar characteristics to those of *Phrarachaniyom* (Royal custom and convention) in former times; the only difference is that *Phrarachaniyom* constituted the opinion of the king alone, while *Rathaniyom* constitutes the opinion of the State formed in conformity with public opinion as a national tradition.[41]

This is a curious statement in that the *rathaniyom* supposedly "formed in conformity with public opinion" had to be explained to the public so that public opinion could conform itself to the newly announced national "tradition." If, among the twelve *rathaniyom*, there was not a single mention of the monarchy, neither was there any suggestion that the monarchy was unnecessary or even absent. The coup group had learned during the 1930s that the Thai populace at large was very unlikely to rise up to destroy the monarchy (or sanction such actions), even after they had been told repeatedly that the Chakri dynasty and the aristocracy in general had been exploiting ordinary Thais for centuries.

Prince Wan had little difficulty in conforming himself to the new realities of life or in assuming the high position in the National Institute of Culture to which Field Marshal Phibun Songkhram and Luang Wichit Wathakan had assigned him. Nor did Boonlua find her own role on a committee of that institute to be onerous, much less impossible. Why were these people so willing to compromise with a regime that they criticized privately while it held power, and then publicly when it no longer did? They could have simply refused the positions that were offered to them, gone home, and lived approximately as they always had in a microcosm of the Siam of olden times.

As a child, Boonlua had absorbed the monarchy-centered patriotic values of the Thai ruling class in her father's home, and then the early-twentieth-century nationalist rhetoric—also monarchy-centered—so rigorously developed by King Vajiravudh. A good part of the reason that Boonlua and other Thais of the old elite were able to adapt to the Phibun Songkhram regime's vision of a nationalist ethic, and of the duties of leaders and citizens in Thai society, was that this program was in its way quite flexible—and also far more "traditional" than one might assume.

For the majority of Thais, the nationalist rhetoric of this administration was perceived as not only acceptable but actually stirring. All of the new attention to "the Thai race" had its gratifyingly inclusive aspects. Certainly, no one rose up with so much as a murmur of disagreement after the 1944 promulgation of the "Fourteen *Wiratham*," or the Thai Code of Bravery[42] (or "of Valor," depending upon the translator), one

of the most important of the many pronouncements on Thai culture
that were produced during the Phibun years. It is important less for
its obvious debt to the Japanese code of bushido than for what it
demonstrates about the durability of Thai values over time and through
periods of great change and peril. Following is Prince Wan's translation:

The Fourteen *Wiratham*

Valour of the warrior

The Thai love nation above life.
The Thai are eminent warriors.
The Thai, as a nation, are good to friends
and most terrible to enemies.

Valour of religion

The Thai, as a nation,
worship Buddhism above life.
The Thai, as a nation,
are people whose word and thought correspond.
The Thai, as a nation, love peace.
The Thai, as a nation, are loyal and grateful.

Valour in economic activities

The Thai, as a nation, are diligent
in agriculture, industry and commerce.
The Thai, as a nation,
cultivate foodstuffs for their own consumption.
The Thai, as a nation,
accumulate heritage for their descendants.

Valour in culture

The Thai, as a nation,
like to live well.
The Thai, as a nation,
like to dress well.

The Thai, as a nation,
honour children, women and the aged.
The Thai, as a nation,
follow each other in what they say
and follow the leader.[43]

This document was entirely new, yet completely familiar to Thais. It reflected an overall orientation to life that may appear to be contradictory in some particulars (terrible to one's enemies while loving Buddhism more than life), but it seemed perfectly reasonable to the audience for which it was intended, in terms of both fundamental values and suggested behaviors. If we imagine the Fourteen *Wiratham* appearing either fifty or one hundred years earlier—or during the first decade of the twenty-first century—they would reflect the primary values of most Thais and assimilated members of other ethnic groups, regardless of the details of the nation's leadership from one era to the next.

In support of Phibun's postwar insistence that such proclamations as the Twelve *Rathaniyom* and the Fourteen *Wiratham* were in fact directed against the overwhelming impact of Japanese occupation, Thamsook Numnonda writes:

Spurred by his ardent nationalism to build a new Thailand, Pibul was determined that Thais should be masters in their own house. The Rattha Niyom were also aimed at inculcating a greater sense of economic self-help among the Thais. They were advised to choose an occupation and "work at work" rather than "play at work and work at play". Most of the rules and regulations were geared to ensuring a better life for the Thais. . . . [They] were encouraged to earn money in their free time by tending vegetable gardens and raising domesticated animals like pigs, poultry or oxen, washing clothes and selling noodles.[44]

There was little in the documents, speeches, radio plays, and other mass media products to which Thai leaders were so attached—with the possible exception of the marginalization of the role of the monarchy—that was in conflict with the essential view of life most Thais considered reasonable and desirable.

There is little question that Phibun relished the role of The Leader, the *phu nam*. Citizens were to look to their *phu nam* as their pilot and guide. Before the abdication of King Prajadhipok and after the rise of Phibun, people were forbidden to hang pictures of the king in public places or in their homes. After the abdication, they were advised to hang pictures of Phibun rather than pictures of the young King Ananda. A photograph of the *phu nam*, not the king, was flashed onto the screen at movie theaters before film showings, and theatergoers stood and bowed. The tacit message was that the boy king was of little use to the Thai people, whereas the *phu nam* had the strength and wisdom to lead the Thai nation through the perils of the time—perils that were all too evident to Bangkokians, who had never expected to find themselves building bomb shelters.

Even after the disasters at war's end, Phibun would recover his power within two years, coming to power again in 1947 and remaining prime minister until he was finally overthrown by Field Marshal Sarit Thanarat in 1957. Kobkua Suwannathat-Pian chose an apt title for her 1995 biography of Phibun: *The Durable Premier*. Whatever else Phibun may have lacked, he was a durable leader and seemed to have formidable reserves of *bun* (merit).

The Phibun administration wanted to "restore Thai-ness," after decades of rule by the "European" kings Vajiravudh and Prajadhipok, both educated in England. Great efforts were made to support rural customs, regional dancing and music, and traditional costumes. Yet, the consonant goal of homogenizing Thai culture and setting boundaries between what was Thai and what was not had some curious results. There are questions as to the legitimacy of the *ramwong* as the Thai national dance, since folk dances were, by definition, regional. Many of the popular *ramwong* songs were written by Than Phuying La-iat Phibun Songkhram, the prime minister's graceful and popular wife. Complicating the "Thai-ness" issue was the constant pressure to adopt selected Western customs and habits.

In retrospect, Boonlua would see the efforts of the National Institute of Culture as laudable, well intentioned, frequently misguided, and ultimately unsuccessful. Still, she remained proud of the role she had played, expressed disappointment that the Phibun government had not come up with better objectives that might have led to better results, and recalled the era as a would-be Camelot defeated by the vulgar excesses of human nature.

> Those who are of an age will remember that during the great war in Asia, while the world burned and destroyed itself with horrific weapons and bitter animosities, Thailand had an opportunity to *prap-prung* [refine, improve, rectify, reorganize] its own Thai culture through the government's establishment of the National Institute of Culture. The task of this institute was a vast effort which might now be called "adult education."[45]

The mission was misguided, in her opinion, in its demands that people give up some of their most cherished and harmless habits. Gradually, the campaign to define, interpret, and regulate "Thai-ness" turned upon itself and was consumed by its own inane details.

> Some people insisted that you could not even enter a hospital as a patient without your hat since a hospital was a public building and one must always wear a hat in a public building. This may have been an exaggeration, but it was certainly true that you dare not go hatless as a *visitor* to anyone at a hospital, for the guard was under orders to turn you away, and he would.[46]
>   . . . Stopping the chewing of betel was reasonable enough, for spitting betel juice makes public places filthy, and what is more the doctors tell us that it causes cancer of the mouth. Wearing shoes is also a healthy thing to do. Dressing like a *farang* was suggested to show the Japanese that the Thai people are free [of Japanese influence, choosing Western dress over Japanese], that we could follow the *farang* in some ways [rather than the Japanese] if we wished to do so. But what was the reasoning behind the requirement to wear *farang*-style

hats, in a country with a hot climate? It wasn't done to protect one's head from the sun. Hats were worn socially, to emulate *farang* notions of beauty—even at funerals![47]

Boonlua vividly recalled one of the strangest products of the national cultural program, the modern mass weddings. Several dozen couples would be transported from rural areas to Bangkok to be married in one large Western-style ceremony.[48] The brides wore white wedding dresses, white veils to the waist, and white shoes. Since most of the village brides had never before worn shoes or underwear, much less Western-style formal wear, the Women's Bureau ladies who were in charge had to take the brides in hand and "polish" them for the occasion; Boonlua used the term *khat si chawi wan*—literally, "to rub with a wet towel."[49]

When they had been adequately polished and suitably attired, the brides were led out of their dressing room by a *thao kae*—presumably, "an elder," but in fact a female civil servant. One of my friends who acted as a *thao kae* said that by the time a bride was ready to march to her wedding, dressed and powdered and white from top to bottom, she looked "just like a Vietnamese girl going to her first communion."[50]

Boonlua was personally affected by regulations concerning the appearance and deportment of civil servants. They now wore Western-style uniforms, and of course hats, but they were strictly forbidden to carry umbrellas against the sun, which was derided as a practice of uncivilized people in tropical climes. Umbrellas were to be used only on rainy days, as people did in England, and so Boonlua had to walk great distances on campus each day wearing only her uniform hat, which was not adequate to protect her from the fierce mid-day sun. The dwindling supply of her usual medicines and vitamins, combined with forced marches across campus in the heat of the day, caused her real suffering.

When the bombing increased to a level that seriously threatened their safety, Boonlua and her fellow English teachers turned to writing an English textbook that would be used for many years thereafter. This effort was a rewarding one, not only because it was one of the "successes" that she kept track of so carefully throughout her life, but also because it gave "proof that Thai people could work together toward a common goal."[51] It is an interesting comment, in light of the fact that Phibun constantly emphasized teamwork as a fine and "civilized" thing. At least, the textbook-writing project assured Boonlua that she could work in collaboration with others toward a common goal, whatever some of her coworkers might have said, or intimated, in the past.

In 1943, Triam Udom was separated into several campuses outside of Bangkok and far from the allied bombing. Boonlua was by now quite weak and very aware of the fact that sickly civil servants were frowned upon as a bad example to the populace. Not only was she ill, but she was also increasingly depressed over the state and the probable fate of her nation. The following passage from her memoir echoes a passage from the novel *Western Daughter-in-Law*, quoted earlier in this chapter:

> Listening to the BBC, I heard of the British victory at El Alamein and the retreat of the Germans. It was becoming clearer every day that the tide was turning, and that Thailand was going to meet an evil fate, but the group in power never changed its policies. And no civil servant would dare to say anything contradicting the leaders. I wondered, *how were we ever to progress under such leadership?*[52]

In the novel, she had shown how Thais at the end of the war began to fear the worst and hope for the best. The novel also calls into question the positive remarks she made in public about the good intentions of the wartime government.

> "The *farang* will invade through Burma," Jit said dispiritedly, "you may be sure of that. But there are so many places along the border where it could be done—it is impossible to guess. But the idea that we all will be their slaves—no, we need no longer fear it. The era of colonialism is gone. But as for killing and death? The others have suffered it, and now it is our turn. What will happen depends entirely upon whatever merit we now possess [Thai: *ton ni man laeo tae bun laeo tae kam*]."[53]

Giving the excuse that her health was very bad, which was well known, Boonlua asked to resign her government position. Her request was officially denied and she began to work part-time, but when allied bombing again increased in early 1944, like many Bangkokians who were able to do so the Kunchon family decided to leave Bangkok, relocating their household thirty miles upriver in Ban Phaeng, a village not far from the ancient capital of Ayutthaya and very near Bang Pa-in, the site of King Chulalongkorn's famed summer palace.

Boonlua's niece Rukchira, who was fourteen at the time, remembered the inauspicious beginning of the great journey. Her beloved aunt, now thirty-three years old, was the organizer of this family event.

> Auntie Boonlua was in charge of getting us all into the boats and packing everything, but she didn't have a very good idea of how to pack boats and one of them sank as soon as it left the dock. Dried fish were floating around everywhere and quite a lot of our silk clothing was ruined.[54]

Boonlua decided to stay with her family at Ban Phaeng until the end of the war. Determined to rebuild her health, she swam in the river for twenty minutes every day. It was a healthy interlude in her life. The village itself was almost unchanged by the war, except for the scarcity of medicine and the difficulty of travel. But rice was planted and harvested, and there was a constant supply of fresh vegetables and fish. Boonlua and her sisters and nieces bought handwoven material from local women and passed the time cutting, sewing, and embroidering blouses, and they experimented with making condensed milk and butter from water buffalo milk, and bread from rice flour. A new cottage industry sprang up in the village as local women learned to style the hair of the Bangkok refugees and made house calls by boat, carrying curling irons that they heated over charcoal fires.

If Boonlua was tired and ill before the journey to Ban Phaeng, Buppha was all of that and dangerously depressed as well. The shortage of medicines during the war had led to the deaths of several of Boonlua's relatives and close friends. Before the exile to Ban Phaeng, an elder sister, M.L. Apha Aphaiwong, died in Buppha's arms of tuberculosis, as had her friend M.L. Chup Chantharaprapha. Buppha also kept a vigil at the side of Khunying Prik Warunrit, whom she greatly admired, until her death from cancer, which occurred while they were in the village.[56] Like Boonlua, Buppha found life in the village soothing and restorative, and despite all, it was there that she wrote the most famous of her short stories, "The Good Citizen" (*Phonlamueang di),* which has been translated into English and several other languages.

Many years after the war, in an interview conducted to honor her seventieth birthday, Boonlua made some interesting remarks about the funeral rites for one of her sisters, Khunying Prik, who died at Ban Phaeng. Her remarks also display the quirky sense of humor and droll remarks for which, by the age of seventy, she had become famous. The interviewer had just asked her what she thought about the direction of *watthanatham khong khon thai rao,* our Thai culture.

> BOONLUA: You are thinking in the *farang* way. You mean "*cultural life,*" right? [Boonlua uses the English words "cultural life" in her otherwise Thai sentence: "*Mai khwam wa cultural life, chai mai?*"]

> INTERVIEWER: Well, for example, let us talk about the custom of wearing black at funerals. What do you think of it?

> BOONLUA: I absolutely hate seeing people wear black at funerals. It's not at all a Thai custom. Before, no one wore black. If one owned white clothes, and the king died, one shaved one's head and wore the white clothes for two or three days. . . . But, in fact, wearing white for mourning is a Chinese custom, not Thai. Before they started wearing white—well, whatever clothes you owned—that's what you put on and wore to the funeral! [Audience laughter] And it was not a sad affair, either. . . . The most jolly occasion one could imagine was a royal cremation, with puppet shows and masked plays and all sorts of amusements. But in the Fifth Reign, it was decided to change all that and do funerals in the *farang* style. But, you see, they couldn't *really* do it in the *farang* style because Thais are simply—simply *not farang.* [More laughter]

INTERVIEWER: You mentioned the fun of Thai funerals. What is it in our philosophy that causes such behavior?

BOONLUA: The fun aspect of funerals? Well, all our lives we have heard [the essential facts of life]: be born, grow old, suffer, die [*koet kae chep tai*]. When someone dies, people come to be with the mourners and alleviate their loneliness. My family moved to the countryside in Ayutthaya [in fact, the nearby village of Ban Phaeng] during the war, and one of my sisters died there. At dusk, we put her body into the coffin. The neighbors came bearing lanterns and put them into the ground with stakes. All we had during the war was coconut oil lanterns. Gradually, the place was filled with neighbors. And then they all began to dance, everyone danced the *ramwong*—except for one of my sisters, who stayed in the house, crying. But that's what people did then—neighbors would come when someone died, and light the lanterns, and dance—quite cheerfully. And I said to myself, "How nice. My sister has gone to the trouble to die and given us all the opportunity to dance." [Laughter][56]

One curious aspect of village life was the presence of some Thai men who would appear one day and disappear the next. Everyone knew that they were involved in some mysterious business, but it was never discussed. In fact, they were members of the wartime resistance. Boonlua's family was deeply involved in this effort by way of her brother Kap Kunchon, who was active in the Free Thai Movement (*Seri Thai*), first in the United States and then in China. He had been appointed Phibun's military attaché to Washington in 1941. When Phibun sent the declaration of war to M.R. Seni Pramoj, the ambassador to Washington, neither Kap nor Seni was willing to recognize it, and both later became prominent leaders in the resistance.[57] Seni remained in Washington, but Kap did most of his work from China.[58] Although Seni at first vouched for Kap to the Americans, who were suspicious of his connections to Phibun (one of Kap's direct responsibilities was looking after Phibun's children, who were studying in the United States), Seni gradually came to consider Kap a potential rival and sought to minimize his influence and his image in the eyes of the Americans and the British.[59] Colonel

Kap would again become a personal advisor to Phibun when he returned
to power in 1947.

In 1945 the bombings continued, and train trips to Bangkok from
Bang Pa-in took at least nine hours because train lines were prime
targets. Allied planes began to fly over the countryside, dropping not
bombs but the leaflets known as "cloud ambassadors" (*mek thut*).
These brought great joy and relief to the frightened Thais, for the
"ambassadors" proclaimed that when the allies won, Thailand would
not lose its freedom.

In her novel *Western Daughter-in-Law*, Boonlua gives the last word
on Thailand's narrow escape from catastrophe to a very old man who
so far had offered no opinions about the war or the state of the nation
over the past decade, preferring to study the Dharma in silence.

> "Listen to me," he said, putting down the book of [Buddhist] scriptures
> he had been studying. "I am old. When they changed the government
> [in 1932] I said nothing. I knew that I was out of date, an old-fashioned
> man. But what has happened now? Remember this . . . long ago we
> shed our blood fighting the Burmese, but in time we recovered all
> that we had lost. But when a man sheds his honor, it is very difficult
> to recover it. And I fear that [in this war], we lost more than blood,
> more even than our independence. We sold our souls."[60]

When the war was over, many people feared that the legendary skills
of Thai diplomacy might fail at last. M.R. Seni Pramoj became the Allies'
choice for the position of prime minister, but he had almost no political
experience and the postwar diplomatic situation was a shambles.[61] How
could Thailand's formerly close relations with the Allies ever be mended?
The British, in particular, angrily demanded that Thailand pay a heavy
price for its collaboration with the Japanese.

> [T]he British pressed Thailand to comply with a series of punitive
> demands, presented ostensibly as reparations but resembling
> more a blueprint for British colonization. . . . Lord Mountbatten

... informed [the Thais] that, in addition to the military agreement, there was "a little paper" he would like them to sign, after which Britain and Thailand would once again be at peace. To the delegates' shock and dismay, the "little paper" Mountbatten spoke of was a list of 21 demands which would impose British control over Thailand's economic, political and military affairs for an unspecified length of time. . . . Britain was trying to hold Thailand accountable for helping Japan to invade Malaya and Burma, and intended to make Thailand pay dearly for what Britain perceived as a base betrayal of prewar trust and friendly relations.[62]

Boonlua made very few overtly political remarks in her lifetime, choosing to use the safer and more flexible outlet of fiction writing for this purpose. The following opinion about Field Marshal Phibun Songkhram in her memoir is an exception to that rule.

I do not believe that one man in a position of ultimate power could have caused all of the bad things that happened. I say that this was a powerful man who had stupid friends and clever enemies. His stupid friends gave him his head in all things, and the clever enemies were right behind them, encouraging his arrogance, until he appeared to the public to be insane. . . . He needed friends to give him honest advice, but they would have had to do so from the very beginning, for after a man has achieved power, no one will dare to begin to say things that he will not want to hear. . . . My father always told us that it is impossible for an honest man to agree with his superior all of the time. As long as I was working in the National Institute of Culture, I despaired, seeing that the nation was in the hands of a small group of dishonest men—dishonest to their leader, dishonest to their friends.[63]

At the end of the war and not for the first time, Boonlua submitted her resignation to Chulalongkorn University, on the grounds of serious health problems. This time, her request was immediately granted, a response that left her feeling inexplicably peeved.

6

LIFE AT MID-CENTURY

From 1945 to 1960, the Thai nation would reorient itself as a strong partner of the United States on the frontier of the "free world" in mainland Southeast Asia. Boonlua, who had spent at least some of her time during the war years contributing to Phibun and Luang Wichit Wathakan's grand cultural program, would spend a far greater percentage of her time during the following two decades working with American and other foreign advisors toward the goal of "national development." In 1950 she would receive an MA in education from the University of Minnesota, and during the next two decades she would collaborate with Thai and foreign colleagues on projects designed to upgrade and modernize the Thai education system. By 1960, when she was appointed vice rector of a new provincial college, Boonlua would have developed her own, unique view of the processes and fruits of national development and modernization. Her thoughts about these subjects would one day culminate in the strange, futuristic novel *Land of Women (Suratnari)*, published in 1972, about a land in which women rule, the environment is sacred, and human beings frequently pause to discuss the direction of life on earth.[1]

AFTER THE WAR

When Phraya Thewet was sure that Bangkok was safe, he moved the Kunchon family back to Wang Ban Mo.[2] Boonlua and Buppha were still in poor health, as they had been throughout the war, but life was more or less comfortable, and although some might grumble about the inconveniences of the postwar years in Bangkok, the Kunchons did not, for they had become accustomed to life in a village, where electricity and running water did not exist, much less telephones. Allied bombing had nearly severed Bangkok from the rest of the country. Railway bridges south of the capital lay in ruins, as did the single bridge spanning the Chao Phraya River between Bangkok and Thonburi.[3] The supply of electrical power and potable water were unpredictable at best, and the telephone system was a shambles. Prince Prem Purachatra wrote:

> [Bangkok has become] a city of oil lamps, with a population . . . of early sleepers and sturdy walkers . . . [living] a simple, rustic, one might even say mid-nineteenth-century existence, without electric light, without a dependable water-supply, without trams, refrigerators, and the radio. . . . We are back now where our fathers and grandfathers were . . . Such are the wages of war.[4]

Anxious months passed after the fall of Japan, as Thailand struggled to restore its prewar relationships with the Western powers. At the outset of the war, M.R. Seni Pramoj, the Thai ambassador in Washington, had refused to deliver the declaration of war on the United States. Throughout the war, Seni conducted the Free Thai resistance movement from abroad, while Pridi Banomyong organized the movement within Thailand.[5] On August 16, 1945, with the unanimous approval of the National Assembly, Pridi Banomyong issued this proclamation:

> The will of the Thai people does not approve of the declaration of war and of acts adverse to the United Nations (and that of the Regent [Pridi himself], acting for the King) proclaimed on behalf of the Thai

people that the declaration of war on the United States of America and
Great Britain is null and void and not binding on the Thai people . . . [6]

The United States responded four days later with the assurance that
they "regarded Thailand not as an enemy but as a country to be liberated
from the enemy." Nonetheless, Pridi, Seni, and Thawi Bunyaket, who
had been active in the resistance while he was Phibun's minister of
education and also minister attached to the Prime Minister's Office,
continued quite justifiably to fear the British, who were angry and
noticeably unmoved by Thai protestations that they had been forced to
collaborate with the Japanese. The British insisted that there could be
no question that Thailand had made its choices early and had not been
suddenly overtaken and invaded, as its neighboring nations had been.
On the contrary, for at least a decade Thai leaders had enthusiastically
pursued the alliance.

If these facts were unarguable, the United States offered the counter-
argument that British and French former subject populations in Burma,
Malaya, Cambodia, Laos, and Vietnam had no intention of returning
to their prewar subjugation, and that unfortunately the nationalist
movements in those countries were full of communists, whether by
intention or default. Existing governments throughout Southeast Asia—
with the sole exception of Thailand—were in a state of chaos. Before and
after the overthrow of the absolute monarchy, the Thai leadership had
been opposed to communism, notwithstanding a few failed flirtations
with socialist legislation during the early 1930s drafted—his American
supporters were somewhat chagrined to admit—by Pridi, more recently
a hero of the resistance. But, the Americans insisted, he had learned his
lesson, he had always opposed the alliance with the Japanese, and he had
always been a champion of close relations with Great Britain and the
United States. Pridi, they concluded, was regarded by Thai and foreigners
alike as an honorable, idealistic man.[7] American arguments prevailed so
that in a remarkably short period of time Thailand was able to rise like a
phoenix from its darkest hour in 1945, emerging, depending upon one's
point of view, either as a beacon of anti-communism in Southeast Asia
or as an accomplice in the pursuit of US Cold War objectives.[8]

In 1946, Pridi accepted the position of prime minister, announcing that he intended to step down as soon as possible.[9] King Ananda Mahidol, twenty-one years old, presided over a ceremony inaugurating the new constitution, and again the balance of official power shifted. Under the 1932 constitution, legislative office had been open to members of the royal family while bureaucrats and soldiers were excluded. Now, fourteen years later, "princes were in, soldiers were out."[10]

When King Ananda Mahidol returned from Switzerland in 1946, the Thai were weary, frightened, disillusioned, and emotionally vulnerable. People wept at the very sight of the new king. They dared to hope that the glorious past might return with him, making it possible for the kingdom to rebuild its honor and erase the memory of the past decade. In many ways it was a constructed glorious past, particularly focused on the visible successes of King Chulalongkorn's reign, when the king saved the country from British or French colonization, journeyed to European lands and visited with royalty, and sent the young princes abroad to Oxford and Sandhurst, the Sorbonne and St. Petersburg. If this longing for an imperfectly remembered golden era made the people eager to support the anti-communist campaign of the years directly following the war, it must be remembered that when King Vajiravudh was on the throne in 1917 as World War I was coming to a close, he watched the Russian Revolution in horror and made anti-communism an integral part of Thai patriotism. Following World War II, Thai military leaders, eager both for military aid from the West and political support at home, lost no time in reviving and amplifying Vajiravudh's definition of patriotism, using young King Ananda Mahidol as their focus. The following description of reaction to a public appearance by the king appears in Rayne Kruger's book, *The Devil's Discus*.

> [Poor Thai] crouched in the dust for hours to proffer their poor gifts of a bunch of flowers or a trussed chicken. Of the realities of the struggle for power in Bangkok they knew nothing and cared nothing. Here was their young king, compassion manifest in his every shy half-smile . . . enabling them to acquire much merit by their grateful acceptance of this opportunity to show their loyalty.[11]

In M.R. Kukrit Pramoj's 1953 historical novel *Four Reigns*, the heroine, Phloi, stands on Rajadamnoen Avenue (literally, the "path of kings") for hours, holding her parasol and straining for a glimpse of King Ananda's motorcade. The worldview espoused by the fictional character Phloi— the daughter of a wealthy Phraya (one rank lower than Boonlua's father, Chao Phraya Thewet) and married to an even wealthier Phraya—mirrors the worldview of the Kunchon family.

The following passage from *Four Reigns* is included for two reasons: first, to illustrate the majority view of the young king; and second, to show how the very language of Thai fiction reflects profound political and social realities. Phrases that are rendered in *rachasap* (language used when speaking about or to royalty) in the original Thai novel are italicized.

Activity in the crowd intensified, imparting the message that *the royal motorcade* was coming near. Everyone began to walk, or to run, eager to find the place from which they might most closely observe the *glorious sight of their monarch*. By chance, the place where Phloi had chosen to stand was very close, and despite the crowd, she thought that if she craned her head she would be able to see him without having to push forward. All down the avenue, the cheer rang out: "Chai-yo! Chai-yooo!" coming ever closer, the crowd around her growing ever more agitated. Phloi stood up straight, thinking that at the very moment he passed she would stand on her tiptoes. Her eyes were fixed on the place where *he* would first appear. She glanced neither left nor right, unwilling to allow anything to distract her from that vision. The cheers grew louder, a crashing in her ears such as might herald the collapse of the world. The *royal automobile*, the color of ivory, slowly passed before her, the royal flag on its hood fluttering, and at that moment Phloi had to clasp both hands to her breast, to keep her heart from flying away. For she had seen *the king quite clearly, and his younger brother [Bhumibol] sitting beside him, waving their hands and smiling slightly. The king's eyes glowed, a glow of utter kindness and beneficence* that many Thais now living had never before seen. Phloi stood transfixed, tears streaming down her face, suffused with a joy so fulfilling that it embraced her heart, and held it. How quickly her *young king had grown up* [since his previous visit, in 1938]. Since the last time she had seen him, *he had grown so handsome, so graceful, incomparable in every respect and possessing,* Phloi felt, *every quality a monarch should have.*[12]

The very act of reading, hearing, or thinking about the king and all royal persons and concepts via the splendid, mellifluous, archaic medium of *rachasap* is for many Thai experienced as an act of devotion to traditional Thai culture. There is no way to talk, write, or think about a king (or any member of the Thai royal family) that does not emphasize, by nearly every word, the unbridgeable gap between ordinary people and royalty. Although most Thais could read the amount of *rachasap* contained in a novel such as *Four Reigns* because they have learned it in elementary school, as time went on very few would be able to use it to converse with royalty, should that unlikely event occur.

Boonlua, and everyone else in her family, was taught to use *rachasap* with ease and fluency from early childhood. In her autobiography, *Successes and Failures*, when she writes about people who have royal titles, Boonlua automatically replaces common pronouns, verbs, and other parts of speech with *rachasap*; when the discussion returns to non-royal people and their activities, her language reverts to everyday Thai.[13]

If the absolute monarchy ended in 1932, *rachasap* went on unscathed. All news broadcasts on the radio and on television continue to and must use *rachasap* in describing the activities of royal persons. It is significant that even the most radical of the reformers did not seem to take into account the immense power of the (royal) word. Regardless of how they may have felt about royalty in general, or individual members of the royal family, I cannot think of a single example of anyone involved in the overthrow of the absolute monarchy speaking or writing to a king, or about a king, using ordinary Thai speech, a fact that speaks volumes about the extent to which they could conceptualize, given their own upbringing, either a true revolution or even a significant evolution of the Siamese polity.

"THE WORST THING THAT COULD HAPPEN
IN MY LIFETIME HAD HAPPENED"

Pridi Banomyong was about to tender his resignation as prime minister, indicating that he much preferred the position of "elder statesman," when an event occurred that Boonlua often said was "the moment at which I knew that the worst thing that could happen in my lifetime had happened." King Ananda Mahidol died, under what would ever after be referred to as "mysterious circumstances."

The king's death was indeed tragic, not least for the rumors, misrepresentations, and injustices that followed, which can never be repaired. Shortly before they were due to return to Switzerland, King Ananda and his brother, Bhumibol, who were interested in firearms and target shooting, awakened early on the morning of June 9, 1946, and were examining a Colt .45 automatic pistol, "a gift from Alexander MacDonald, a souvenir of the royal excursion to the Sriracha guerrilla camp with Pridi Banomyong."[14] A shot rang out, and moments later a servant ran into the king's mother's bedroom shouting that the king was dead. That afternoon, a public announcement was made that the death was an accident, but the story was soon retracted.[15] What really happened remains a mystery or a secret. No one had a motive to kill King Ananda, everyone surrounding him or with access to him cherished the honor of serving him, and the brothers were famously devoted to each other. If an anti-monarchy assassin had somehow appeared (but was never seen), killed him, and then escaped, the result was not the end of monarchy but the succession of Bhumibol as king on the following day. Two years later, three royal pages that had been nearby at the time of Ananda's death were arrested on charges of having assassinated the king, and after six years in jail, they were executed.[16]

The nation grieved over their scarcely known but beloved boy king. Their enthusiastic allegiance was soon given to the new King Bhumibol, but in the days following King Ananda's death the morale of the Thai people was very low.

THE YEARS BEYOND THE WAR

Within a year, Field Marshal Phibun Songkhram would again occupy a powerful position in the army, and by 1948 he would return to the role of prime minister and remain there until he was overthrown in 1957 by one of his generals, Sarit Thanarat, aided by generals who, in turn, would succeed Sarit in 1963. Against all expectations, Phibun was able to shed the ignominy of wartime collaboration with the Japanese and defeat. He had promised, after the government dropped war crimes charges against him in April 1946, never to return to politics, but a year later he founded a newspaper, *Si Krung*, in which the call was raised for a "savior" who would prevent "impending catastrophe" for the Thai nation.[17] Not long after, his announcement of the formation of a new political party, Thammathipat, caused a sensation both at home and abroad.

Phibun's greatest source of support was, as ever, the military. But in order to return to power it was imperative that he garner support beyond Thailand, particularly in the United States. While the British reacted with outrage to the idea of his return, US diplomats, committed to the containment of world communism, saw real advantages to the kind of strongly anti-communist, authoritarian administration Phibun offered. The "clean" heirs of power following the war—those untainted by collaboration with the Japanese—were proving unequal to the tasks of restoring order, rebuilding the economy, and regaining the confidence of a nation that had experienced defeat, destruction, and the privations of war. Corruption was rampant even among Pridi's supporters, despite his own famously clean image.[18] By mid-1947, Phibun and the military "were no longer willing to stand patiently in the wings watching civilian bunglers bicker and quarrel as Thailand crumbled around them."[19]

In the months following the king's death, rumors spread that Pridi had somehow been involved in it. There was no evidence and no conceivable motive for his involvement, yet, in an environment of generalized dissatisfaction with the state of the nation the rumors continued to gather momentum. Three decades later, Pridi would tell his biographer, "From the day I knew of the death of King Ananda Mahidol until the time I learned of the supreme court's ruling on October 12, 1954 [decreeing the execution of the alleged assassins], I honestly believed that the king had ended his life from an accident committed by himself and there were many reasons for such honest belief."[20]

Pridi was not able to recover his reputation, except among a faithful core of followers who continued to defend his memory. Eventually he was forced into exile in China and later moved to France. In recent years his image has been greatly restored, and he is now regarded as an idealistic and ethical intellectual and teacher who was treated unfairly by his political and social opponents.

THE KUNCHON FAMILY IN THE POSTWAR WORLD

In the year following the war, Boonlua and her family, like the rest of their countrymen, had held fast to the rails as the ship of state moved into unknown waters. She was as shocked and grief-stricken as everyone else when the young king died, but it was becoming clear that she possessed inner resources that would see her through. By the end of 1946, ailing or not, grieving or not, Boonlua was back at work, teaching and writing and becoming more and more important to the future of education in Thailand.

Unlike Boonlua, her sister Buppha seemed to have been vanquished by the stunning series of tragic events through which they had come, and from then on she would seem increasingly like a delicate ghost from a former, better world. Her novels had all been written, and although she planned new projects, none of them came to fruition. Too depressed and ill to resume her writing career, she wrote to her nephew Somphop, with whom she had a lifelong correspondence:

As for joining you in the trip to Songkhla [in southern Thailand], I have a distressing reason for not wanting to go that I am afraid my Somphop will not understand—and if you do understand, I fear that you will be needlessly alarmed for me. In short, the fact is that since the war I have had no new clothes made. Everything I am wearing is quite shabby, and for another thing I feel disinclined to go away from home because I do not have enough money! It is my nature, I simply must have money to spend when I travel—I would rather not leave home under these circumstances because any fun I might have on the trip would be outweighed by not having any money. . . . I dream of writing all the time but am simply too ill to write. I was feeling better when the war ended, but when the king died, all my symptoms returned and were worse than ever. I taught a little French for a while, they offered me 600 baht a month, but it is too exhausting. I do not think that I have ever told you that I went to tea with His Majesty shortly before his death, and I think constantly of how graceful he was, sipping tea. I have been ill ever since his death, so tired and so weak with my old madness, the madness that comes over me because of the dreadful affairs of state . . .[21]

Buppha, tired and ill with her "old madness," would live on for seventeen years with a heart condition exacerbated not only by heavy smoking, but also by a depression that was inextricably linked with her sorrow for a life and a world that would never return. During most of these years she lived with her sisters, but Boonlua would never speak about Buppha in personal terms. In public, she would speak of "my sister the novelist" and occasionally comment on her books, but she did not reveal anything about the fading, sickly gentlewoman with whom she spent so many years of her life.

RETURN TO TEACHING

Although she was pleased when the director of the English department at Chulalongkorn University finally wrote a personal letter asking her to return to teaching, Boonlua's first response was to reply testily that since everyone knew her to be a sickly woman and a bad example of a civil servant, perhaps she was not a good candidate for the position. The director replied that perhaps it was so—yet he would much rather have a part-time Achan Boonlua, sickly but competent, than a full-time, healthier individual who was not her equal. And so she returned to teaching, first at Chulalongkorn University and, soon after, at Mater Dei school. She was particularly pleased to be asked to teach Thai literature and composition at Mater Dei.

It was the first time that I was really *allowed* to teach Thai, in a proper way, particularly literature and composition. At last I had the opportunity to put in practice ideas for teaching these subjects that I had long wanted to try. This was one of my true successes, for the school was most pleased with the results of my efforts, and my students at Mater Dei and I grew very close and have remained close ever since.[22]

A well-run school for elite adolescents, most of them girls, was perhaps the best of all possible worlds for Boonlua. By and large removed from the bureaucracy of the Ministry of Education, where she would later suffer the most painful of what she considered to be her "defeats," at Mater Dei she was surrounded by a staff of educated teachers from good families who respected her on both intellectual and social grounds, and a student body that was receptive to new ideas. One of her students, M.R. Supicha Sonakul, recalled the impact Boonlua had on her.

When she taught *Khun Chang Khun Phaen*, she could chant the *sepha* [musical verse form], which fascinated us.[23] None of the other teachers could do it. She had a very good voice, too. Most of the teachers concentrated on grammatical structures. It was boring. But she taught literature in context. In her family she learned the literary tradition. And she had the talent to appreciate her own background. To make Thai literature more fun, she wrote a historical play for us to perform set in the Ayutthaya period. Sometimes she brought dancers into class, folk acts. We borrowed costumes from Phra Nang Lakshmi.[24] She was one of the "Rama VI ladies"—I assume, one of those who acted in [the king's original] plays.[25] Boonlua was a teacher in spirit. She not only taught us—she taught everyone she met. My uncles and aunts played cards with her. They would say, "Now, Boonlua—don't be a teacher during the card game!"[26]

Once again, Boonlua was given the task of producing a theatrical performance, a *lakhon*, but this event, a benefit on behalf of schools that had sustained bomb damage during the war, would be an unqualified success. She still insisted upon her standards, but she had learned a good deal from her unhappy experience with the *lakhon* production at Triam Udom before the war. She composed an original work entitled *Uphayobai*, a traditional poetic drama set in the Ayutthaya era in which male leaders are greatly assisted (saved, finally) by their intelligent and resourceful female relatives.[27] The theme of men depending upon women for information, creative ideas, and sheer strength would become a familiar element in her later novels and short stories. The students were well aware of the "agenda" behind the story, although Boonlua never spoke of it directly. One student later wrote:

> We could see her views about women in society so clearly, from things like the speech of Princess Dok Kaeo, the wife of the youngest prince, who used a smart trick to save her husband's life and prevent chaos in the country. He had to admit that "even a man who is competent needs to have a wife to warn him about dangerous events that might happen."[28]

The entire structure of *Uphayobai* reflected Boonlua's dislike of the way classical literature was taught in the schools. The students did not, in her opinion, have the least idea of how to recite Thai poetry. They read as they had been taught, monotonously droning on line by line, taking a breath automatically at the end of a line even when doing so confounded the meaning or spoiled the beauty of the poem. The idea of combining lines to express whole thoughts had never been considered—until Boonlua did it.

Uphayobai was composed in traditional poetic form, but she intended it to be performed in a nearly conversational style. This combination of old and new exactly suited her: traditional forms should never be abandoned but might benefit from being modified. This was, she said, a direct result of her relationship with and respect for Prince Narit. She often pointed out that with her father's help Prince Narit had composed the *duekdamban* form of *lakhon* during King Chulalongkorn's reign, a modification of old, slow, lengthy classical dance dramas to make them accessible to foreign visitors—and preserving them also for future Thai audiences that would have less patience than their ancestors for twelve-hour productions.

The fact that all of the tasks in this production were given to students, not to grudging fellow teachers or staff, suggests that Boonlua had learned something from her first such effort at Triam Udom. After the *Uphayobai* performances, many people realized that they had made a great mistake in buying the tickets and then giving them to their children, thinking that a "school" *lakhon* would, by definition, be amateurish and a chore to sit through. Too late, they learned that it had been a "real" *lakhon*, and they were sorry to have missed it.

None of the students who were involved in *Uphayobai* would ever forget it.

Achan tried to teach us about good teamwork, cooperation, and responsibility. She was so strict about everything: our pronunciation, our singing and other routines. Even though it was very hard and tiring for us, we thought it was a lot of fun and each of us felt important to be a part of the show because Achan made everyone take charge equally. If you couldn't sing well, she would make you dance. She borrowed the costumes from a princess and taught us not to be jealous of the main character, who would get to wear the most beautiful costume. She trained us so hard on the emotional scenes that I remember crying a lot . . .[29]

TWO YEARS IN AMERICA

In 1948, when Boonlua was nearly thirty-eight years old, she won a scholarship from the American Association of University Women (AAUW) to study in the United States.[30] At the end of the war, the Ministry of Education had decided that henceforth, only university instructors who had studied abroad (in the West) and earned at least a master's degree would be assigned to teach English to upperclassmen; of these, people who had studied in England were most sought after.[31] This was galling to Boonlua, since many of the people suddenly qualified to teach English were far less capable of teaching either English grammar or literature than she was. She made it plain that while she in no way disdained to teach underclassmen, she resented and disapproved of the growing division between people who had studied abroad and people who had not, and of the "degree disease" that was increasingly afflicting Thai society.[32]

Another reason she wanted to study abroad was that she was suspicious of the answers she received when she questioned colleagues who had studied in the United States. Most of them seemed to think little of the Americans they had met, complaining that all of them were bigoted (in terms of race, culture, and religion) and obsessed with whatever degree of status they felt had been conferred upon them by their *alma mater*. But when Boonlua talked with Americans themselves—and there were more Americans arriving in Thailand by the day given the ever-widening and deepening economic, diplomatic, and military relationship between the United States and Thailand—she was surprised to find that not only were most of them quite agreeable, some of them shared her concerns about the superficial and even counterproductive character of certain "development" efforts. They tended to be outspoken, candid, and amusing—all traits that she admired and also possessed. The more Americans she got to know, the more interested she became in going to their country and seeing for herself what life there was like.

Boonlua applied for the AAUW scholarship with the idea that if she won, she would devote herself to her nation's educational efforts, both despite and because of her growing disenchantment with Thai educational policies. If she lost, she "would take it as a message from the *thewada* (celestial beings) that I ought to look into a different career."[33] She now felt that if she were to continue teaching, she wanted to be in a position that would allow her to influence educational policy, and as the holder of BA and BEd degrees from Chulalongkorn University, she was not in such a position.

Boonlua was unhappy with some of the recent changes in secondary school policy, for example, the separation of secondary students into two classes: those bound for the universities and thus studying in the Triam Udom preparatory schools like the one attached to Chulalongkorn at which she had taught; and the vocational students, who were slated for a lifetime as manual workers or farmers but were given little relevant training. She was not alone in criticizing this policy. Writing about education policies from 1932 through the 1970s, Morell and Chai-anan make the same observations that are implicit, although never clearly stated, in most of Boonlua's increasingly disaffected writings on the subject of education.

> The government's system of formal education contributes directly to the development of desired political attitudes. It can be argued, in fact, that this is the primary purpose of the many rural (four-year) schools. So little is done to make instruction relevant to the lives of rural villagers, or to disseminate reading materials to the villages, that the purported goal of rural literacy seems somewhat insincere. Rural primary schools do best at inculcating concepts of national unity: loyalty to king, country, and bureaucracy, and submission to central authority.
>
> Until 1980, all rural primary schools (*rongrian prachaban*) operated under the jurisdiction of the Ministry of Interior rather than the Ministry of Education, which was unquestionably a political rather than an educational decision. Teachers are employees of the central government. The curriculum is standardized throughout the country—metropolis and village, Northeast and Muslim south. By the time a youth finishes primary school, the values and rules of traditional Thai political culture have been learned by rote.[34]

This was not the way Boonlua believed children ought to be educated. In addition to her primary interest in upgrading and updating the teaching of literature, the development of relevant vocational training would become one of her lifelong campaigns. Unfortunately, this campaign would be only occasionally successful against a conservative and rigid bureaucracy.

As for the university-bound students, Boonlua believed that they should not be removed from schools they had attended for years and in which they were comfortable, before being placed—prematurely, she was sure—into the university environment. At only fourteen or fifteen years of age, they should have been enjoying themselves with their peers and acquiring leadership skills instead of struggling to conform their behavior to that of university-age students. A third issue that concerned her was the increasing importance of competitive examinations for university entrance, which she thought exacerbated the "natural competitiveness of adolescents."

> Where there are winners, the number of losers must be equal, but the students were not encouraged to assess the results of the situation with compassion. Additionally, the ordinary schools were continually losing their best students to the "better" schools. Some years later, when I was working with the Education Inspection Unit, at first the teachers I met would not talk about this problem with me, because they knew that I had been a teacher in one of the Triam Udom schools. But as soon as they discovered that I completely agreed with them, they would open up and give free rein to their feelings. Unfortunately, they were to learn that nothing would ever change, so that they might as well simply make up their minds to become better Buddhists.[35] But before I went abroad, I was full of hope and determined to play a part in the improvement of the education system.[36]

Nearly twenty years had passed since the overthrow of the absolute monarchy, but it was clear that Bangkok remained the center and focus of national life, as Thai capitals had been for centuries. Government officials in Bangkok still tried to avoid being posted to Khon Kaen in the northeast, or Pattani in the south, just as their grandfathers had done a hundred years earlier. If "development" was the mantra of the 1950s, its choicest fruits continued to be enjoyed in the capital city, a fact that Boonlua would learn only too well a decade later, when she was appointed head of a new teacher's college in the provinces.

LIFE IN THE UNITED STATES

While Boonlua studied for an MA in education at the University of Minnesota, her sponsors in the AAUW took advantage of her presence to invite (or send) her on several lecture tours around the country. She thoroughly enjoyed her two years in the United States, and particularly enjoyed these tours and the warm reception she always received. Quite a few Americans understood her to be a "princess," having a vague idea of the significance of the title *mom luang*, and they were thrilled to make the acquaintance of a royal personage who spoke excellent English, was possessed of a sharp wit, and told wonderful stories about her exotic homeland, although she seemed oddly reticent when asked about her mother and father or her brothers and sisters. On a tour of Kansas, Boonlua spoke on nine occasions within one week, and when she returned to Minneapolis her American sponsor "was outraged that a scholarship student should be taken advantage of in this way— although the fact was that I had enjoyed myself quite a lot."[37] She also had the opportunity to visit many American public schools, and she made good use of these visits to note the programs and policies that seemed most effective and most transferrable to the Thai environment. She had come to the United States to learn and to earn a degree that she thought would give her a more respected voice in educational policy-making. It was a goal that would be partially realized.

She was comfortable with the Americans, who found some of the personal characteristics that caused Boonlua difficulties in her own culture to be laudable, and even amusing. No doubt, some of her new friends assumed that they were learning a good bit about "what Thais are like" from their association with her. And she found answers to the questions she had once asked of Thai colleagues who had studied abroad.

I returned to Thailand with answers to the questions I had had about *farang*s. Human beings of every nation, speaking every language, turned out to be very similar. . . . The *farang*s have had more opportunities for scholarship and so they have more scholars. But their philosophy is not impressive: they have spent centuries fighting over religion and misunderstand the problem of "sin." As for the Thai, they have always had religious freedom but are rather behind the *farang* in terms of academic knowledge. One could go on and on in this way; I shall simply say that I learned that the percentage of people with an accurate understanding of life seems to be about the same, from one society to another.[38]

Boonlua was impressed with the people she met through the American Association of University Women. She saw them as unselfish, far-sighted, and generous with their time and intellectual gifts, and she made up her mind that when she returned to Thailand, she would become active in the Thai Association of University Women and encourage other members to follow the example of the American women.

She enjoyed unusual good health during her entire two years in the United States, both at the University of Minnesota and during her many trips. Her faculty advisor at the University of Minnesota, Forrest Moore, told me in 1997 that he did not recall her ever being ill. He was surprised to learn that in Thailand she was known all her life as a sickly woman.

Over the years, she would frequently comment on how well she felt when traveling or living abroad, adding that outside of Thailand she never felt the stress and frustration that eroded her health at home. She was quite aware of the fact that frustration and depression inevitably led her into illness. When she returned to Thailand from the United States in 1950, her health began to deteriorate almost immediately, a circumstance that she blamed on the difficulty of adjusting to the hot, humid Thai climate after two years in Minneapolis.[39]

A CAREER IN EDUCATION

Not long after Boonlua's return from the United States, an unexpected event occurred.

> When I first returned from the States, there was a man, a suitor, someone who came through the family—but he only came to visit

twice. The reason was that he came to our house and I met him—and then, when he came the next time, I didn't even remember him! I greeted him as if he were a stranger, and after about five minutes I realized, "Oh dear, this is the man who came the last time . . ." He never came again. And so I said to myself, "Well, there will be no more of this sort of thing." I was getting old.[40]

Boonlua found life at Wang Ban Mo exactly as it had been before her wonderful two years in Minnesota. Her sister Buppha continued to languish, did not feel well enough to write, and spent most of her time with her older sisters, sisters-in-law, and friends—and most of the friends were relatives by definition, people with titles, and of their class. Chalaem, now in her late forties, ran the household and was gradually taking on the role of family dowager. Phraya Thewet's health seemed less robust than she remembered, but he continued to maintain strict standards in the household. His great-granddaughter recalled:

My grandfather [Phraya Thewet's son-in-law, Mom Anuwong's husband] did not like to go there for dinner because of Phraya Thewet's after-dinner ritual: after dinner, all the serving plates would be passed up to him at the head of the table, and he would scrape all the remaining food into one bowl. Then he would mix all the food together—curries, desserts, everything—and pass that bowl back down the table, and everyone would have to take a spoonful of it, and eat it. That was the way Buddhist monks ate. They weren't supposed to think about the food, whether it was good or bad, or how it tasted. And Phraya Thewet thought that the members of his family should observe that, at least to the extent of one spoonful at every dinner. I don't know whether the custom went back to Chao Phraya Thewet's time or not, but I think that it may have.[41]

In 1954, all of the Kunchon family, and Boonlua in particular, were amazed when Buppha decided to take a trip to San Francisco. But that was nothing compared to what *happened* in San Francisco. She proceeded to marry Dr. Sukij Nimmanhemin, an event that must have required a good deal of planning. But if Boonlua knew about this, she never said so.

Two years later, Phraya Thewet died of heart failure, leaving his entire estate to Chalaem, whom he trusted to make suitable provisions for his numerous siblings, nieces, and nephews. It was shortly after this event that Boonlua accepted an assignment to go to the southern provinces of Trang, Phuket, Krabi, and Phangnga to deliver "hot season lectures" to the teachers while the students were on holiday. Virtually all Thai schools, public or private, are closed during March and April, the hottest months of the year, and therefore, teachers are free to pursue professional development. On the first trip, an incident occurred that Boonlua described as amusing, if insignificant; in fact, it is most revealing of the bureaucratic culture in which she worked. As a result of new government regulations, upon her return from the United States Boonlua had been temporarily "demoted" from the rank of bureaucrat second class, the rank she had before she went abroad, to bureaucrat third class. She recalled that when her colleagues on the trip to the southern provinces learned this fact—at the end of the trip—they obviously felt uncomfortable with her, despite the fact that she was titled, and probably outranked all of them on a strictly social level. Fortunately, soon after their return she was reestablished as a bureaucrat second class—after which she said that everyone immediately felt comfortable with her again. The incident exemplifies the importance of official status in Thai society and demonstrates that how one is seen by others, and treated by them, can be altered swiftly and easily by externally initiated changes.[42] While she deplored this competitive attitude, she too was greatly concerned with matters of rank and status, even if she was *most* concerned about doing her very best in every task she undertook, invariably working beyond expectations. Unlike many of her colleagues, she was sincerely dedicated to the wider objectives of national education; even more unusual for a bureaucrat in the Ministry of Education was her preoccupation with the poor conditions under which people had to work in the provinces, far from the center of power.

When she returned to teaching at Chulalongkorn University, Boonlua was at first pleased to be working with people whom she felt were even more educated than she was, but she soon came to feel that they were, for the most part, a complacent lot. One issue concerning this period that she chose to discuss in her autobiography seems a strangely minor event to immortalize, but it is a psychological red flag, predicting problems she would encounter (or create) throughout her life. Boonlua was shocked to discover that the female students' restrooms were in a deplorable state—wet, dirty, and she had even seen lipstick marks on the walls.

She took the matter of the dirty bathrooms to her superior, who nodded in agreement as to the necessity of teaching the female students the importance of personal hygiene and a clean restroom, and how to keep it that way. Boonlua volunteered to personally oversee the restroom cleaning project. Nothing happened. After three or four months, she again approached her superior on the matter. Again, he nodded in agreement and said that she was quite right to be concerned. Nothing happened. From this, Boonlua learned that "It is best to do what you are told to do, and not look for extra tasks."[43]

One of her friends, Khunying Ambhorn Meesook, commented on an aspect of her personality that was clearly demonstrated in the women's restroom incident at Chulalongkorn:

> For a very intelligent woman, Boonlua had absolutely no idea of priorities. It was all the same to her, whether the problem was dirty bathrooms or poor policy-setting at the Ministry of Education. You could not get her to understand that some things are important and need to be addressed, and others are not. This attitude of hers, that *everything* matters, was not a big problem when she began her career, but later on, it was deadly.[44]

Not long after moving into her new position at Chulalongkorn University, the director of the Triam Udom school asked Boonlua to return there and assume the position of assistant director. It was a tempting offer as it would give her the opportunity to put certain of her pet teaching ideas to work, ideas she had wanted to try even before she went to the United States. It would also mean a promotion in terms of both government rank and salary. After thinking it over for a few months, Boonlua accepted.

During the same period of time, she joined and became active in the Thai Association of University Women as she had promised herself she would do, and before long she was asked to become chairwoman. This, she counted as one of her successes in life, although other demands on her time gradually forced her to cut back her involvement, first to vice chairman, then to chair of the committee that coordinated activities with women's associations in other countries, and finally as a consultant to the association.

A minor failure of this time was an abortive project that she and other members of the association initiated as a public service: evening English classes for a modest fee. At first, she had forty students; after three months, the number had dwindled to ten. But teaching English at night after working all day was not pleasant, and even though Thai colleagues and foreign friends who were native English speakers graciously volunteered their time, before long everyone was forced to admit that the project was not a success. Boonlua recalled the nadir of the whole "English class affair":

> One evening, a man who was one of my remaining students took umbrage at my statement that a *farang* woman may kiss a man as a simple gesture of friendship. I had noticed this even when I was a child, in Penang. The gentleman became incensed at the idea, and never returned to the class. If there are people who think that teaching English to adult Thais would be a good way to make money, well, I suggest that they try it.[45]

BOONLUA THE ELUCIDATOR

In her own estimation, the best career experience of her life began in 1953, when she was appointed director of the Education Inspection Unit, responsible for secondary education throughout the kingdom, a position she held until 1959. Throughout the 1950s, the Ministry of Education received substantial US aid through USOM (United States Operations Mission, also known as USAID, United States Agency for International Development). One project was the improvement of national education through the use of "inspectors," small groups of educators who would travel to schools throughout the country, helping teachers to do a better job of teaching and also listening to their problems.

Although the job description is usually translated as "education inspector/inspection," the Thai term, *sueksa nithet*, does not quite convey that meaning. When in 1956 Boonlua attended a meeting of educators from several countries in Geneva, there were rousing discussions over accurate terms to describe this function, in various languages. For example, the Americans used the term "supervisors," the British called themselves "Her Majesty's Inspectors," and the Germans preferred to call themselves "consultants." When someone asked Boonlua what term was used in Thailand, she told them that the Thai term, "*sueksa nithet*," meant something closer to "elucidator." The conferees at once agreed that the Thais had the best term of all.[46]

The 1956 conference in Geneva was one of the highlights of her years as an inspector. The following year, she would attend another conference in Paris. By this time Boonlua was well known for her quick wit and slightly daring remarks, demonstrated in the following remarks about conferences. During the 1950s, the majority of the conferees were men.

There are benefits to being a female representative at a large conference. When you can see that someone is about to ask you a difficult question, you can simply get up and leave the room. People assume that you need to use the bathroom, so no one says anything, and by the time you get back they're on to something else. It is useful not to be too pretty; if you aren't, the others are far less apt to ply you with questions about your country. On the other hand, being pretty can also be useful, because men don't ask pretty women lots of awkward questions about their career. I was in between—not pretty, but not ugly either. When I spoke with men whose English permitted them to ask me too many questions, I could always resort to the bathroom break strategy; and, no one made a pass at me.[47]

These are very unusual remarks for Thai ladies of her generation—especially when committed to print. That Boonlua thought nothing of doing so was partly a matter of her own sense of herself—anything that she felt was worth saying was probably also worth writing, and sharing, especially if it was amusing. Another reason for her openness was the fact that in 1956 she was already forty-five years old, late middle age in her era and society—an age at which spinsters are in some ways "un-gendered" and can say things that women under thirty could never say.

Although Boonlua made several good friends among the American advisors, she was not impressed with all of the USOM "experts." She once dismissed an advisor as being not only too young for his position and entirely uninformed on the subject of *Thai* secondary education—but less knowledgeable than she was on the subject of *American* education. She resented the fact that USOM advisors controlled the purse strings of the projects (although she knew that this was partly to avoid corruption) and that they made all the major decisions, in concert with top people in the Ministry of Education. Boonlua felt that the decision makers wasted money on the wrong things because they didn't know better, and because they were poor decision makers. A senior USOM official once said to her, "I have heard that you hate the National Education Project. Why?" She replied, "I do not hate the National Education Project. But I do think that the ministry's timing is wrong. They ought to be spending their time on developing good curricula for all the grades, and asking for advice on that project, not immediately moving ahead with vast national plans."[48] Another thing that rankled was the fact that not only American money, but also *Thai* money allocated to these projects, was controlled by the Americans. Boonlua shared these concerns with her coworkers, some of whom urged her to go to the minister of education, M.L. Pin Malakul himself, and speak with him alone. In her position, the friends said, she had every right to do so—and after all, their families had always known each other. They were social equals. Occasionally, she would go to speak with him, apparently unaware that he was beginning to dread her visits.

During the 1950s, Boonlua worked in several positions simultaneously, which was not unusual. She was the director of education inspection for secondary schools, as well as assistant director of Triam Udom. Unfortunately, the director was often abroad, so Boonlua had to serve as acting director. She did not feel that she (or anyone) could do justice to both jobs, and finally decided to devote herself full time to the Education Inspection Unit. A third, also demanding, commitment was her participation in a UNESCO-sponsored program to improve the teaching of English in all of Southeast Asia, an activity that required her to travel periodically to Singapore. She was immensely busy, and traveled frequently within Thailand and abroad. During this unusually busy period, her health was comparatively robust, particularly during her trips abroad.

In many ways, the Education Inspection Unit was perfect for Boonlua, and she knew it. She was in charge of a small group of people, never more than half a dozen, all of whom were younger than she was, impressed by her, and grateful to be working with her. She was at her best in a position of authority, and she was a kindly, generous, sensitive boss. As for the task of the inspection unit, the requirement was to do precisely what Boonlua did best: advise, consult, and "elucidate."

It had been decided when the Education Inspection Unit was formed not to give the inspectors authority to promote and demote anyone so that there would be no possibility of corruption. Boonlua had favored this arrangement, believing (naively, she later said) that a position of authority would have negative effects in the field, with some administrators and teachers wasting their time on efforts to impress the inspectors. It would be easy, she felt, for a teacher to fool someone visiting his or her class for a day or two, convincing the visitor that he or she was both effective and admired (even though other teachers and the students would never be fooled). In Boonlua's opinion, it would be a better use of everyone's time if the inspectors concentrated on convincing the teachers that they had come to help and to listen—*not* to promote them or otherwise affect their career path. What was most important, she believed, was to convince the teachers that no one was beyond the need of advice. Didn't the greatest singers in the world all have voice coaches? And the greatest authors—didn't they have editors whom they often thanked, lavishly and publicly, for helping them achieve their greatest successes? Teaching was the hardest job of all because every student is different, and there are so many, many aspects of the teacher's job that no one human being can master all of them all of the time. Talking in this way, she won the provincial teachers over, seemingly every time, and gained their trust.[49]

Because she herself had been a teacher for years, Boonlua, understood very well how teachers might respond to advice.

> If teachers didn't know something because no one had ever told them, they would complain of having been neglected in the past. If you told them something they felt they already knew, they would complain that people were condescending to them. If you went into too much detail about things, they might grow bored, but if you skipped over things too quickly, they might not understand what you were trying to tell them, and they would be embarrassed to admit it.[50]

Boonlua was a good listener, and she astutely included local headmasters and headmistresses in the task of the unit so that they would never feel that "higher-ups from Bangkok" were coming to scrutinize them or to spy on them and their subordinates. She believed that these individuals felt honored to have been sent an inspector who was a foreign-trained professor and a *phu di*—but who, despite her elite background, never talked down to them.

Boonlua's stories about the adventures of the education inspectors often focused on American advisors traveling with the group. On one rural visit, an American advisor came out of his room at the guesthouse, put his finger to his lips, and silently motioned for Boonlua to come have a look at something in his room. When she stuck her head into the room he pointed to the dressing table, where a large mouse sat admiring himself in the mirror and smoothing his whiskers.

> This American was a sophisticated traveler, a man who was not afraid of a little mouse. He made the error of assuming that my response

would be the same and was quite surprised when I took one look—
and bolted for my own room.

Even when they occasionally stayed in the best hotel in town, the
inspection teams could encounter unexpected problems.

After dark, a radio salesman staying at our hotel started playing Indian
and Chinese stations on all of his radios. He had speakers with him,
and for some reason in the middle of the night he put one of the
speakers directly in front of the American's door. The next morning,
the American could hardly answer any of the questions people asked
him. One of the Thai men was also exhausted from being kept awake
all night by the radios and returned to the hotel to get some rest.
But he got an unexpected bonus, he told us later. Through the door
of his room, he heard two Thai men talking about their romantic
exploits, and he said he learned some words that aren't in any of
the dictionaries. None of the other education inspectors knew them,
either—and *they* were supposed to be the Thai language experts![51]

On yet another trip, the inspectors were invited to stay at the home
of a school headmaster who had done everything possible to make the
team comfortable—including installing a standing, full-length mirror in
one corner of the bedroom in which the visiting ladies were sleeping. The
visitors soon discovered that this mirror gave anyone coming up the stairs
an excellent view of the entire room, including any lady who happened
to be dressing. (In a traditional Thai house, instead of a door, there might
be a standing screen placed about twenty inches inside the doorway to
give privacy, but in this case the mirror defeated its purpose.) After the
problem was discovered, before ascending the staircase the gentlemen
would call out "Coming upstairs! Coming upstairs!" which reminded
Boonlua of an old custom in the Inner Palace. When it was necessary
for a palace page to enter the Inner Court, lady guards would precede
him, shouting, "*Phuchai ma! Phuchai ma!*" (Man coming through! Man
coming through!).

The inspection teams had to travel to remote provinces, but rather than weakening her physically, Boonlua thrived. "For the first time in my life," she told her sisters, "I know what it feels like to be a healthy person."[52] It was in the field that the inspectors were happiest, for their good reputation quickly spread, and the rural and small-town teachers felt that at last the government was responding to them, and they reciprocated by showering the visitors with hospitality and gratitude. By contrast, the inspectors received little respect in Bangkok. The budget never allowed the hiring of an adequate number of inspectors or anything near it. They could not set a regular schedule to visit the schools because there were so few of them, and they had no budget authority. "We were like preaching monks," she recalled, "going where and when we were invited." The *per diem* set for upcountry travel was absurdly low, and even then they had to struggle to receive these funds in advance. Too often they had to wait for weeks after a trip before being reimbursed.

Boonlua later greatly regretted having agreed to define the inspectors as a "unit," or *nuai*, because this designation lacked prestige. Typically, she had thought that the importance of the task would earn respect, and when that did not happen, she was frustrated.

She always defended her readiness to speak her mind and stand up for what was right—even if it meant disagreeing with the minister—as the result of "the way I was raised." Her father, she insisted, had taught his children to speak, as it were, "truth to power." He himself had sometimes felt compelled to disagree with King Chulalongkorn, he told her, because a good servant must be truthful, even when the truth might not be well received.

Perhaps the most important consideration in interpersonal relations, at all levels of Thai society, is the necessity to save "face"—another person's as well as one's own. Suntaree Komin's study of Thai personality identifies "ego" as the single greatest determinant of Thai behavior, but "face saving" would seem to be a better translation for the concept that Suntaree and her research group were describing.

Since the Thai give tremendous emphasis [to] "face" and "ego,"
preserving one another's "ego" is the basic rule of all Thai interactions....
*Most important is to avoid public confrontation, regardless of whether
it involves an inferior, an equal, [or worse] still, a superior.* To make
a person lose "face," regardless of rank, is to be avoided at all cost.[53]

DEFINING "THAI" BEHAVIOR

Ironically, although Boonlua was considered by both her countrymen
and foreigners to be an expert on Thai culture and behavior, she often
seemed oblivious to behavior that Suntaree's study deemed "the basic
rule of all Thai interactions." True, she often spoke and wrote about the
importance of politeness in Thai society, once mildly rebuked a Western
colleague for "causing ruffled feelings among . . . Thai colleagues," and
on another occasion told a young Englishwoman that "she had to
remember that we Thais were not at that stage of development where
efficiency matters more than politeness."[54] But for herself, Boonlua was
able to create a quite personal version of "Thai-ness" that was ostensibly
grounded in the teachings of Buddhism, the values cherished by her
family, and the larger value structure of the Thai elite—yet, she often
used her elite status as a trump card, and if she did not respect a person's
intelligence she could be caustic, and she never apologized.

She also displayed the manners and behaviors to which she had been
exposed every day of her life, from the age of four to the age of seventeen,
in the Catholic convent schools. To be sure, obedience and piety were
valued there, just as they were in traditional Thai society, yet the convent
schools also inculcated their students with certain Western values that
shaped their view of the grand purposes of life. The English and French
novels the students read in their leisure time extolled individuals who
were courageous, honorable, independent in both word and deed—and
who were rewarded, at the novel's end, for such behavior.

Compare Boonlua's vision of the ideal bureaucracy, in which patriots
speak truth to power, with Morell and Chai-anan's view of the Thai
bureaucracy:

Thailand is basically a bureaucratic society. Each . . . [Thai] has his place, of which he is cognizant. . . . A child's contact with the polity occurs very early in his life, whether he is an urban resident or a villager. In a sense the polity *is* the executive branch of government, represented by a school teacher, a policeman, a district officer, or a community development worker, all of whom are employees of the national bureaucracy. . . . Through this process, all but a very few Thais have become properly socialized members of a bureaucratic society.[55]

Although I am not suggesting that Boonlua consciously modeled her notions of "Thai-ness" on Western ideas about the self and one's responsibilities toward society, her words and actions suggest that, subconsciously, this was at least partially the case. She saw nothing unacceptable about the idea of speaking up in a committee meeting at the Ministry of Education to state politely but firmly that *the minister himself* did not know enough about the plight of the Education Inspection Unit to make, much less implement, fair and far-sighted policies that would benefit the nation. Her friends were often appalled and bewildered by such behavior. Her best and most admiring friends, including Khunying Ambhorn Meesook, sometimes despaired of Boonlua on such occasions.

She would say anything if she thought that it was important and that she was right; and there was no point in trying to talk to her about compromise. She held few people in awe, you see—even Mom Luang Pin, when he was minister of education. He was of her own social class, minister or not, and she could remember him from their childhood, so she would simply talk to him as to an equal— because he *was* her equal. People who were her peers, in terms of their position in the ministry, and whom she did not respect because she thought they were incompetent—well, it was quite obvious what she thought about them. I said to her, "If you are going to work in a bureaucracy, then you must learn to suffer fools." But she wouldn't. She wouldn't suffer them at all.[56]

Boonlua proudly confessed her differences from other civil servants:

I wasn't like most of the other civil servants. Most of them were fearful whenever they were working with their supervisors. They would never express an opinion until they had been urged repeatedly. With my upbringing, it's the opposite way; if you don't tell the truth, you are a crooked counselor. In meetings, I always gave honest views whether they were likely to go against or along with anyone else's views. In my home, I always heard, "We cannot *not* tell the king."[57]

Boonlua would be admired, loved, and fondly remembered by both Thai and Western friends for the very qualities that led her into some of the most unhappy periods of her life. "Her tongue could be sharp," her friend Doris Gold Wibunsin wrote, "her wit biting, her criticisms devastating, yet her intent was always to enlighten and improve, never destroy."[58]

THE RISE OF FIELD MARSHAL SARIT THANARAT: "SUCH MEN ARE NECESSARY"

One important fact about Field Marshal Sarit Thanarat, who came to power in 1957, and whom Boonlua admired, was that Sarit was raised and educated entirely in Thailand.[59] Every other national leader who had come to power since 1932, whether prince or commoner, had been educated in Europe. As a child, Sarit lived in a village accessible only by boat in the poor northeastern corner of Thailand directly across the Mekong River from Laos. When he was eleven, his father took him to a temple school in Bangkok, and after that his education was purely military, beginning with the preparatory school attached to the Army Officers School. For these reasons, his worldview was uncontaminated by the political and philosophical ideals to which the Promoters had been exposed in London or Paris. He fought on the Burma border during World War II, was given command of the First Army Regiment at Bangkok thereafter, and steadily gained influence.

Sarit's patriotism was focused on the monarchy. He gained the tacit support of King Bhumibol before his coup d'état by promising to restore the royal family to its rightful role and privileges, which had been severely curtailed under the various administrations of Field Marshal Phibun Songkhram. It is unlikely that the corruption that marked Sarit's regime ever occurred to him as immoral. He showed ultimate respect for and devotion to King Bhumibol and he observed the traditional practice of *kin mueang* (literally, "eating the land"), by which governors and other government officials had been expected, time out of mind, to enrich themselves from the place in which they were posted as one of the perquisites of office.

Within a year of the 1957 coup d'état, Sarit dissolved the parliament, declaring that "Thai-style democracy" did not require elections.[60]

Be that as it may, Sarit's persona—the slightly crude but essentially well-meaning and patriotic man of action—was very appealing to Thais at all social levels. Military, bureaucratic, and business leaders and their wives who financially supported royally sponsored charities were presented with awards, decorations, and titles. Thais and their foreign admirers were able to think of Thailand as a real kingdom once again, and it was entirely possible to think of Sarit's excesses (financial, political, and moral) as a reasonable price, after all, for the good things that he had either caused or allowed to occur.

Boonlua supported Sarit, in part because he had greatly enhanced the position and the visibility of the king and royal family—even if that meant "using the monarchy to legitimize his rule," in the eyes of many Thai intellectuals. Morell and Chai-anan describe the relationship between Sarit and the king:

> The king and Sarit, surprisingly, hit it off quite well. . . . Sarit seemed to have decided that a popular, indeed even a powerful king might be advantageous to the nation and to himself. He removed many of the remaining obstructions . . . to the king's freedom of movement. . . . Sarit . . . almost [seemed to be] grooming the young king . . . not just to reign but to rule.[61]

He was good for the monarchy, the king seemed to like him well enough, the country was doing well, and, whatever his failings, Sarit met Boonlua's criteria for "leadership." Professor Nitaya Masavisut, a literary scholar and longtime friend of Boonlua explained her regard for Sarit:

> Sarit was a villain—but you see, Boonlua always *liked* the villain, whether in literature or in life. Villains were interesting. She thought that that was what the country needed, someone like Sarit: a villain, yes, but one who loved the king, and who was strong—Boonlua admired *strength* very much—and who could make the government work. Unlike some of our other leaders, Sarit was very good at getting people to do things.[62]

If Boonlua "always liked the villain," how did she reconcile that attitude with her strict moral code and her reverence for the royal leaders of the past century, whose virtue she so often extolled? In fact, she saw no contradiction, for while a villain such as Sarit might hold the position of prime minister, he was, in the end, merely a functionary. She admired him, but it was a frankly condescending admiration. It was his task to keep the ship of state afloat so that the treasures of Thai culture might be preserved and the monarchy protected. Such men were useful, and necessary.

The year 1959 would be a momentous one for Boonlua, in two respects. First, M.L. Pin would ask her to leave the Education Inspection Unit and take the position of vice rector of the new Bang Saen Teachers College some thirty miles south of Bangkok, on the Gulf of Siam. She would be crushed by this decision, for she had been truly happy with the inspectors.

The crisis began with her request for yet another private interview with M.L. Pin to explain her general concerns about the National Education Program and her specific concerns about the funding and operation of the Education Inspection Unit. M.L. Pin listened patiently and said that he would think about everything she had said and get back to her soon. Not long after this meeting, he informed her that in his opinion it would be best for everyone, including her, if she accepted the position in Bang Saen. The move would involve a promotion for her, and he knew that she would do an excellent job. The position of vice rector was in fact the top position at the college, for in the Thai system the rector of all provincial colleges resided in Bangkok.

However M.L. Pin described the move, Boonlua knew that she was, in effect, being fired. And she knew why, although she could never quite bring herself to admit it: M.L. Pin was no longer willing to put up with her. In view of their often difficult relationship, of all that they had in common and all that they did not, M.L. Pin's contribution to Boonlua's cremation volume is significant, as much for its cool tone and faint praise as for its particulars:

> M.L. Boonlua was a *mom luang* from the second reign, like myself. Therefore, we were related, and at one time long ago she did call me "elder brother," although she later came to address me as "professor" . . .
>
> M.L. Boonlua was a teacher whom everyone respected . . . because of her essential goodness and also her knowledge. Her contributions to her school were always wholehearted. I can recall that after everyone else had retired, in the evening I could always send someone to call her, and she would come at once to take care of whatever needed to be done.
>
> It is my feeling that *it was because she was so highly civilized* that she could barely tolerate ordinary life, and that is why she changed positions so often and finally had to resign from government. . . .
>
> In meetings, her contributions were profound, and when she [was sent to attend] meetings abroad, one could trust her to make significant contributions, in terms both of content and [her use of] language. . . .
>
> There is no one like M.L. Boonlua. What a shame.[63]

What was M.L. Pin suggesting in the statement that Boonlua was so *civilized* that she could not tolerate ordinary life? He emphasized the fact that "in meetings, her contributions were profound"—and, he might think but was far too polite ever to say—profoundly irritating. She was at her best when she was sent to attend "meetings abroad" (i.e., in the West). There, she could be counted upon to "make significant contributions"—contributions that would reflect well upon Thailand as a civilized nation. She had no difficulty dealing with Westerners; where she had difficulty was in dealing with ordinary Thai life, with saving her colleague or superior's face even when she thought that other, more important issues should take precedence. Or agreeing with something that she didn't think was right in order to avoid conflict. Those things, the very stuff of ordinary Thai life, she never believed applied to her.

There was another, very important reason why she was devastated by M.L. Pin's decision to send her to Bang Saen. At the age of forty-eight, she had decided to accept a proposal of marriage from Dr. Chom Debyasuvarn, an epidemiologist in the Ministry of Public Health.

M.L. Boonlua had fallen in love.

7

AN INDEPENDENT WOMAN

During the 1960s, the personal aspects of Boonlua's life changed enormously. The woman whom everyone had expected to end her life as an old maid at Wang Ban Mo did, after all, find her *nuea khu*—the "partner from past lives," her true love. In 1959 she married Dr. Chom Debyasuvarn, and the marriage was a success. By 1970, slightly before the mandatory retirement age of sixty, she would be ready to retire gracefully to a life of writing fiction, serving on committees, appearing on panels to discuss the development of modern Thai life and literature, and enjoying her growing reputation as an iconic figure in Thai society.

THE COURTSHIP OF DR. CHOM

Dr. Chom Debyasuvarn had admired Boonlua since his student days at Chulalongkorn University, but they did not meet during those years, nor did they meet at the University of Minnesota, where he earned an MA in public health two years after she earned her MA in education. A charming man with a droll sense of humor, Dr. Chom entitled the essay he wrote for Boonlua's cremation volume, "Success and Failures in the Married Life of Mom Luang Boonlua Debyasuvarn," paraphrasing the title she had chosen for her autobiography in 1974.[1] The first words in his essay are, "I have often marveled, wondering how Khun Boonlua and I ever came to live as man and wife." He perfectly remembered his first sight of her at the long-ago debate at Chulalongkorn University on the topic of whether sons or daughters were more desired or more valued in Thai families.

> Khun Boonlua, defending the daughters, was victorious. . . . I remember that she was so articulate, and her speech so very witty. After that, I did not see her again until one day during the war. The memory of that day is vivid even now. I saw her on the Hua Lamphong–Banglamphu tram line. She was sitting in first class, and I was in the second class section. She wore a plain white blouse and a dark blue skirt, and her gestures—walking, sitting, getting off the tram—and also her lovely complexion caught my eyes and my heart. However, at that time I did not look at her as a young man looking at a young woman. I looked up to her as a competent person and never imagined we would know each other personally. I went to several panel discussions in which she participated. She was a well-known and honored lady.

Dr. Chom's family was originally from Chiang Rai province in North Thailand. His father was a *nai amphoe*, or district officer, an administrative position that required frequent moves from one part of the country to another. There are several *amphoe,* or districts, within each of the seventy-seven provinces of Thailand. Each district office is responsible for maintaining the civil register of births, deaths, marriages, and individuals residing in each household, and thus, for many Thais, it is the most familiar point of contact with the government. A *nai amphoe* is the head of a district office. While this is an important and respected position at the local level, from the perspective of Bangkok, a *nai amphoe* is a mid-level bureaucrat who spends his career far from the seat of real power in the country.

At one point during Chom's childhood, the Debyasuvarn family was living fifty miles southwest of Bangkok in Phetchaburi, and when his father received his next assignment it was decided that young Chom and his northern-born grandmother should stay in Phetchaburi so that he could finish school there. With her, he continued to speak the substantially different northern dialect, although he was educated in central Thai as all Thais are. Dr. Chom once amazed Boonlua's friends when he accompanied her on a trip to the north and began speaking the northern dialect on the second day of the trip. They agreed that "Dr. Chom is really a genius!" and he and Boonlua decided to keep the details of his linguistic genius to themselves.[2]

Dr. Chom studied at Chulalongkorn University through medical school, then went into the air force, where he remained until after World War II, when he resigned and went to work in the Ministry of Public Health. In 1952, he prepared to go to Tulane University in New Orleans for a master's degree in public health. He was pleased to be going to Tulane, because everyone told him that in the summer, at least, the climate would be similar to that of Thailand. But plans were changed at the last moment, and Dr. Chom found himself on his way to the University of Minnesota, "where the first thing I bought was a Korean War surplus overcoat, which I wore the whole time."

When Boonlua met Dr. Chom at a meeting of the Minnesota Alumni Association, she was impressed. If he was not a person of her own social class, his social *skills* were superb, and this was a quality she admired. The doctor seemed to become everyone's friend upon a first introduction, and his conversation was most amusing. She learned that he had been married but was now divorced, with one grown daughter.[3] As Boonlua and Chom came to know one another through the meetings of the alumni club, she began to think that he was "*mai muean khrai*, "unlike anyone else," and told him so, which delighted him.

[Khun Boonlua and I] met at the alumni meetings, and then we began to meet to have long conversations, and gradually we began to know that we felt comfortable in each other's company.[4] In 1957, we parted for a while because I was sent to England and she went to New Zealand on an education inspectors' tour. When we returned, we decided to marry, and we were married on May 1, 1959, seven years after the first time we met at the Alumni Club.

Although this was not Boonlua's first proposal, it was the first and only romantic relationship of her life. When a suitor had called upon her brother Phraya Thewet during the war for permission to court her, at thirty she already was considered a bit old to become a bride. Yet, there had been another serious suitor a decade later, a man about whom she rarely spoke, for good reason. Dr. Sukij Nimmanhemin, a professor and senior bureaucrat of good family, proposed to Boonlua in 1952, when she was forty-one years old. He was divorced, amicably it seemed, from the well-known owner and head of a prestigious girls' school. He continued to live on the grounds of the school in a house of his own. Boonlua turned him down, saying that she was too old to get married. Two years later, Dr. Sukij proposed to Boonlua's older sister Buppha, who was then forty-nine. He invited her to meet him in San Francisco, where they were married before returning to Thailand. According to friends, Buppha was unwilling to have the wedding in Bangkok, preferring to present her marriage as a *fait accompli* to her family, who were completely unprepared.

Both Boonlua's and Buppha's marriages were viewed as embarrassing by their relatives. When a young lady of an appropriate age accepted a proposal of marriage, she was "establishing a home," and the expectation was that she would become not only a wife but also a mother. The sexual aspect of marriage was the necessary byproduct of nobler objectives. But a middle-aged, post-menopausal woman—an old maid, a "*sao kae*"— would never be a mother, and therefore had no respectable reason for marrying. Such women were expected to become doting aunties. Indeed, unmarried aunties always have played a useful and valued role in Thai families. There was no shame attached to this role, certainly by comparison with what Buppha and Boonlua chose to do instead, at an age when their sisters were busy with grandchildren, nieces, and nephews.

When Phraya Thewet was brought the news of his sister Buppha's marriage to Dr. Sukij in San Francisco, he reportedly laughed and said, "So—the *sao kae* (spinster) has decided that she wants to be a *chao sao* (bride)."[5] And one of his friends remarked that she had been wise to wait so long—she wouldn't have to worry about having her period on her wedding night.[6]

When Boonlua learned that Buppha had met Dr. Sukij in San Francisco—and *married* him—she was astonished and upset. She had told no one except a close friend about his proposal to her two years previously when she was forty-one. She had protected not only her own name but that of the Kunchon family against the scornful laughter of society by turning him down. And now, her sister—*forty-nine years old*—had had the gall to marry this man! A friend described Boonlua's response to Buppha's "betrayal":

> She came to me in tears. She kept repeating, "How could she do it? How could she marry him?" as if it were just an unbelievable thing. I said, "Well, Phi Lua, you turned him *down*—and therefore she has every right to accept him. This is your own fault—if you wanted to marry him, you should have done it." In fact, she did not want to marry Dr. Sukij at all. She wasn't in love with him. She just didn't want one of her own sisters to marry him—and she certainly didn't want *Buppha* to marry him![7]

Years later, Boonlua would go to the same friend to discuss the proposal of Dr. Chom, about whom her feelings were very different. In her friend's words:

> I said to her, "You already know that your family won't approve of anyone." That was the thing holding her back, of course. No doubt at all—her relatives and most of the people who knew her would gossip about her marrying someone of such a low social class, compared with a *mom luang* and the daughter of a *chao phraya* and so on. I said, "You have always been a person who said that you did not care what other people think, as long as you knew that you were doing the right thing. Well then, be true to yourself. If you want to marry Dr. Chom and you think it is the right thing, then do it—for *yourself*. Phi Lua, if you give him up—what will you be giving him up *for*?"

To be sure, everyone would gossip about the marriage. Yet, Thai society always has been characterized by social mobility and flexibility, and a family's fortunes and social status could change vastly within one generation. A general in the army of Ayutthaya could found the Chakri dynasty and become King Phra Phutthayotfa, Rama I. In the modern era, a village boy like Sarit Thanarat could become field marshal and prime minister. A classical dancer from a modest background could bear a child by Chao Phraya Thewet, a descendant of royalty bearing the title *mom rachawong,* and their child, Boonlua herself, would thus bear the royal title of *mom luang.* That was how Thai society worked. Buppha's and Boonlua's marriages, however unusual, were by no means socially catastrophic for their family or for their own reputations. Moreover, their family could not forbid them, which they could have done thirty years earlier. Anyway, when all was said and done, both sisters would be called *mom luang* for the rest of their lives, no matter whom they married.

Dr. Sukij Nimmanhemin was a somewhat more acceptable husband for a Kunchon daughter than was Dr. Chom Debyasuvarn. Although he did not have a royal title, Dr. Sukij's family was distinguished and highly respected, and he was a senior civil servant. A few years after his marriage to Buppha, he would be named ambassador to India, further elevating his social status. Dr. Chom's relatively humble birth was offset in part by his being a physician who had been a *nakrian nok* (Western-educated) and by his holding a reasonably prestigious position in the Thai bureaucracy. Even back in Chao Phraya Thewet's generation, such self-made men had not been unknown.

On the morning of their quiet wedding, Boonlua and Dr. Chom offered food to monks in front of Wang Ban Mo, the bride's home, the customary first act on a Thai wedding day. Boonlua then went to work for a few hours. In the afternoon, they registered their marriage at the local district office witnessed by two close friends, Khunying Ambhorn Meesook and M.R. Sermsri Kasemsri. They then drove to Chao Samran Beach in Phetchaburi, stopping at Dr. Chom's father's home to be blessed in a small religious ceremony.

Dr. Chom wrote:

> We were very happy together at Chao Samran Beach, but there were things that made her feel very distressed during that time: her disappointment in people she respected at the ministry who were taking her away from the Education Inspection Unit and assigning

her to be vice rector of Bang Saen Teachers College [a reference to M.L. Pin Malakul] without thinking at all about the importance of the education inspectors and all the time and toil she had poured into that job. No, the decision was made only on the basis that it would put an end to the enmity that existed between [Boonlua] and certain people while giving her a promotion. Whenever she thought about this, she would begin to weep, and to this very day when I think of her weeping there during the honeymoon at Chao Samran Beach, I am moved still. All we could do was to comfort each other with the idea that if the job at Bang Saen did not work out, she could retire and come home.

From the very first days of their marriage, Dr. Chom worried about Boonlua, comforting and supporting her unconditionally, and this would never change. For her part, she praised her new husband to everyone.

Khun Boonlua was always saying nice things about me, and it made me feel proud, although sometimes I felt I didn't deserve it. But she would just laugh and say, "A good wife ought to praise her husband in all times and places!"

Whereas most people felt that Boonlua spoke too freely, certainly by Thai standards, Dr. Chom always believed that she suffered as the result of not speaking out enough. One wonders whether he had ever attended a meeting where she was present before he wrote, "She hated liars more than anything and she herself would never tell a lie. If there was anything that she felt would be harmful to say, *she would simply be quiet.*"

Some people could not imagine Dr. Chom having any desire to marry Boonlua beyond the desire to effect a connection with the Kunchon family and/or with their supposed wealth, although the family was not wealthy in terms of money or land, and Boonlua had only a modest government salary and looked forward to a modest pension. He could hardly fail to be aware of her family's status, but by all accounts of those who knew them as a couple Dr. Chom was devoted to Boonlua, and she to him. There also were critics who joked that a woman who was forever in frail health and a man who was a doctor were indeed *"nuea khu"*— soul mates—and those who said that Boonlua had married Chom only to avoid ending her life as an old maid at Ban Mo. But their friends, including literature professor Nitaya Masavisut, knew better.

> Several of us had gone to Kanchanaburi for a conference. Achan [Professor] Boonlua was there, and Dr. Chom had come with her. Late on the evening of the first night of the conference, some of us heard the sounds of a ukulele in the distance, and we went out to investigate, and there they were, out on the river in a little boat, and Dr. Chom was playing his ukulele and singing love songs to Achan Boonlua! We were shocked—and so happy for them. They were so cute![8]

In a photograph of Boonlua and Chom taken soon after their marriage, they are sitting close together in the garden of their first home, a house they rented in Thonburi across the Chao Phraya River from Bangkok, and they are beaming. Usually, she looked pensive in photographs, but in this photograph, leaning comfortably against the husband she loved in the garden of the first home she had ever known that she could call her own, Boonlua is beaming with happiness, and so is her husband. After a lifetime of living alone, albeit in the teeming environment of Wang Ban Mo, Boonlua enjoyed learning to live as a couple with Dr. Chom and learning to depend upon him. Fortunately, he was eager to be depended upon. She told everyone that no one had ever understood her so well as "Khun Mo" ("the doctor"), as she always referred to him.

Some of Boonlua's friends recalled a remark of hers that shed light on an aspect of her marriage about which they were all curious.

> We were at my house, talking about a novel that had just come out. It was controversial because there was a scene in which the woman has sex for the first time. All of us had been married for twenty or thirty years, which made it all the more hilarious when Achan Boonlua suddenly announced, "It's completely unconvincing. The author makes it quite romantic. Actually, the first is not romantic at all—it is quite

painful!" And we all sat there trying to avoid looking at each other for fear of bursting into laughter.[9]

SEPARATION: ECHOES FROM CHILDHOOD

With a heavy heart, Boonlua packed her clothes and a few of her favorite books and prepared to leave Dr. Chom and their new home to take her position as vice rector of the new Bang Saen Teachers College. Their fears about her new job were well founded. Chom had no choice but to go on working in Bangkok. During the week he lived alone in the Thonburi house, and every Friday evening he would drive to Bang Saen, leaving at about eight o'clock and arriving at ten or eleven, depending upon the demands of his job and the traffic. Boonlua always tried to wait up for him but invariably he would find her asleep, exhausted from the week's crises.

Ironically, while Boonlua's career was in decline despite her official promotion, the marriage had an immediate and positive effect on Dr. Chom's career. He later wrote, "I suppose that the senior officials in the ministry [of public health] thought, 'Well, there must be something to this fellow if Mom Luang Boonlua would marry him!'" Whether there was anything to his speculation or not, soon after the marriage he was promoted to the position of director of the Department of Epidemic Control.

He felt that his wife was being outrageously mistreated at the education ministry, and she had to restrain him from going to M.L. Pin himself and speaking on her behalf, for this she would never allow. M.L. Pin's motives were fair, she said, and probably even in her best interests, and it was not his fault that she felt as she did.

She struggled to face her circumstances rationally, but she was unable to see what had happened as anything but another exile. She could not help but compare the present events with all that had happened when she was eleven: her father died, and her elder brother and his wife sent her away. Instead of simply moving her from the Khlong Toei residence to the main family residence at Wang Ban Mo, she had been sent to Penang, a foreign country, for six years.

Now, decades later, she was being removed from the work family she loved, the Education Inspection Unit. She was being taken away from Chom and their precious home and sent to Bang Saen, which was on the seashore, as the convent at Penang had been, and she felt abandoned and rejected. She was certain that M.L. Pin "couldn't stand her" for some of the same reasons her elder siblings couldn't stand her when she was a girl: her willfulness, her penchant for speaking her mind, her unwillingness to disguise her feelings to avoid conflict. In retrospect, it was clear that she was primed for an emotional collapse if things did not go well at Bang Saen—and they did not go well at all.

THE YEAR OF LIVING MISERABLY

The moment she arrived in Bang Saen Boonlua was faced with her first problem, and it was a serious one: the college might be located on the seashore, but there was no water—at least, none that they could use. Well-drilling had proved disastrous in the sandy soil, and very expensive, and therefore all water for cooking, cleaning, drinking, and bathing had to be brought in by truck from Bang Phra, twelve kilometers away, because a fresh water pipeline would not be completed until several years later. It is hard to overestimate the effects of this problem on everyone's morale, given the hot climate and the Thai preference for bathing at least twice a day

Another significant problem concerned relations with local villagers. Some of them had been accustomed to letting their livestock roam on what was now the Teachers College campus. Why must their animals now be banished? Others wanted to rent land for rice farming or harvest coconuts from which to make sugar. Still others came to ask if they could set up food stands on campus, understandably interested in this potentially lucrative new source of income. Boonlua did her best to establish good relations with these people, and she was kind and fair in her dealings with them. Her reward was a campaign of rumors started by anonymous individuals in the Ministry of Education to the effect that "some people" at the new Bang Saen Teachers College were taking kickbacks from locals in return for concessions on government property.

Boonlua was beside herself when she learned of these rumors. "Civil servants are the last people," she wrote, "who should have 'light ears' (listen to rumors), or so I was taught from my childhood." She was ashamed that she was unable to control her rage over these rumors and felt that her Buddhist training was being overwhelmed. She was losing whatever *upekkha* she had developed: the important ability to view all events with equanimity. Good Buddhists follow the Middle Path and learn to resist being either overwhelmed by anger or overtaken by unseemly enthusiasm.

Whatever problems she might have to face and try to solve, she found the Bang Saen students to be bright, reasonable, and charming. Days after her arrival, she found a student delegation clustered outside her office asking to negotiate "the food problem." They felt that they had been charged too high a price for the cafeteria food. Boonlua listened patiently, knowing that there was no way she could ever get the government to accede to their major demand: a partial refund of money they had already paid. She explained this to them frankly, then called in the staff in charge of the cafeteria and worked out a compromise. There could be no refunds—she did not have the authority to make that happen—but she did have the authority to assure them that food and service would improve, and they did.

During one trip to the ministry in Bangkok, a senior official teased her by asking, "Is it true that the students at Bang Saen sit under the coconut palms in pairs?" She replied testily, "Since there are no other trees at Bang Saen but coconut palms, they have little choice. The only way Bang Saen differs from Bangkok in regard to romance between the students is that in Bang Saen there is nowhere to hide it."[10]

Aside from the daily difficulties of life at Bang Saen, Boonlua continued to brood about the problems of Thai education in general. She was opposed to the government's four-year teacher training program, which she considered inadequate. She had always supported a five-year, two-degree program that would award both a BA and a BEd. For a while this was done, and she thought that it produced the best teachers ever trained in Thailand. But that effort proved short-lived; the four-year program had become the norm and would remain so.

She also was concerned about a situation beyond the ministry's reach: the effects of industrialization on the teaching profession. "In an industrialized society, there are fewer [of the most] intelligent people working in education because industry takes the best." A related problem she saw was that "In a poor country . . . people who are not quite 'the best' have few opportunities. The super-intelligent people will always [rise to the top]; and if they are in a country where bandits are promoted, they will become the super-bandits."[11]

Perhaps more than anything, she grieved over the loss of her beloved job with the education inspectors. If "the nation"—as she would always say, never "the minister"—had wanted to make the best use of her skills, then she should have been kept in her old position instead of being sent to Bang Saen to do a job that any number of people might have done. If "the nation" had decided that she was not suitable for the education inspector's job (despite the fact that she had been continually and lavishly praised for her work there), then "they" ought to at least take the trouble to explain to her *why* and *how* that judgment had come about.

One problem of life at Bang Saen that could never be resolved was that Bangkok was the center of the Thai universe, as the Thai capital had ever been, and everything beyond it paled in importance according to its distance from the center of power. This was true in all of Southeast Asia, not only Thailand. Whatever "clout" Boonlua may have had in Bangkok, it had melted with each mile she traveled on the road to Bang Saen. If she had been able to make little headway in tackling the problems of Thai education while she was based in Bangkok, in Bang Saen she had no influence at all.

After one year, Boonlua resigned as vice rector. In the end, the whole painful experience was reduced to issues of self-respect, respect from others, and her notions of what was due her.

I do not need to work in a place where I cannot do any good. The way they taught me in my family is a great influence in my thinking about this. The daughter of a government official was considered to have the same privileges and status as her father. As for the son, he had to start working to get his own rank and privileges. But *as the daughter of a chao phraya, I had lowered my rank to work as a teacher*. If I had simply stayed at home, I would have kept the high rank that was mine by birth. If I had not thought that as a government official I could make a difference, I would have stayed at home. What I want to show younger people from all of this is how important it is to prioritize your feelings, and not to confuse yourself and make big mistakes in your life.[12]

A colleague of Boonlua who asked to remain anonymous commented on this statement.

Most women of our generation [and class] were not expected to work, although of course Boonlua and I did. And this was a large part of her problem, working with people in government. After all, she was a *phu di*, and she didn't have to do this sort of thing, and she couldn't quite get beyond resenting the fact that these bureaucrats were incapable of appreciating or even understanding that fact.

On top of all else, while Boonlua was working at Bang Saen there were Kunchon family problems that she had to deal with. After her brother Phraya Thewet died in 1956, Boonlua's sisters had asked her to oversee the task of parceling out some of the family's real estate holdings among themselves and their various nieces, nephews, and stepmothers. None of them had any understanding of the law, and dealing with these matters was a vexing, thankless task. Boonlua begged them to find someone else to take charge, but they tearfully insisted that no one else could do the job as well. This was a typical attitude: involving outsiders in family matters was to be avoided if at all possible.

Near the end of the year in Bang Saen, her health was in a very bad state. Her current doctor told her that she would always respond to stress with a variety of "nervous symptoms"—her problems were essentially "genetic." Boonlua believed that some of her symptoms were caused by factors that young modern doctors simply did not understand. While she respected modern medicine and eagerly accepted all the pills and treatments her doctors suggested, she also believed in the effects of such things as *lom phit* and *lom phi lom phat,* which may be translated as malevolent breezes (or "toxic air"), and various negative forces in the atmosphere that were carried to one by those breezes. The symptoms that she was sure could be attributed to *lom phit* included "red stripes on the skin, as if I had been beaten with a switch, and these red lines could run along the veins very fast. This could happen at any time. If the doctor gave me an injection for relief of allergies, other symptoms might well arise, such as breakage of the small veins in the arms, causing bruises."[13]

It is possible, according to physicians I consulted, that Boonlua suffered from shingles. Certainly, stress could cause the symptoms to keep reappearing. One doctor she saw, who had been her student years before at Triam Udom, insisted that her health would never improve until she left the job, and so at last Boonlua could see no option but to resign her post and return home.

One evening, some months after her return, she was sitting in a movie theater with friends when she suffered a panic attic. She felt unable to breathe and had to excuse herself to go outside and walk around until the frightening symptoms subsided. Some days later she thought about the fact that this movie had been set at the seaside, in a place that looked very like Bang Saen, with sandy beaches and palm trees, and she decided that this had caused her frightening feelings. But if the "beach movie" looked like Bang Saen, it must also have looked like Penang, where as a lonely teenage girl she had sat on her bed in the infirmary listening hour after hour to the sound of the sea and the clacking of palm fronds in the wind. During the Bang Saen exile, it was Khun Mo whom she missed, her dear husband Chom, who—like her father—understood, loved, and admired her exactly as she was.

The great difference between the two periods she interpreted as exile was that after the years in Penang she had been able to return to her home, but she could never return to her father. After the unhappy year in Bang Saen, Khun Mo came to fetch her, joyously carrying her home, and they were seldom apart again.

A FREELANCE CIVIL SERVANT

After her resignation from the position of vice rector at Bang Saen Teachers College, for the first time in the course of her career Boonlua had nothing to do, and not even an office. Once again her old friend, Khunying Ambhorn Meesook, who was now director of educational promotion within the ministry, provided both good advice and practical assistance. She suggested to senior people at the Ministry of Education that Boonlua could be temporarily located in the newly completed Educational Radio Building. Several officials in the new facility happened to be studying abroad for a year, leaving their offices conveniently vacant. It was a perfect solution. Boonlua moved into a new, quiet, comfortable office. She arranged her favorite books on the shelves and unfolded the well-known reclining plastic lawn chair in which she always took her after-lunch nap. Soon, she was receiving phone calls and visits from old colleagues, and within a few months she had agreed to contribute to a number of overlapping part-time education projects. Only a few months before, she had been despondent, but life was now quite satisfactory. She could teach under contract when and as she liked, begin to write a bit of fiction, and involve herself in educational activities that interested her, working with people she respected. Despite all, she still brooded about her career in government. In the following extract from the 1966 interviews conducted by anthropologist Herbert Phillips, Boonlua is candid about feelings and attitudes that she knows are not considered becoming, either in the West or in her own society.

I understand Prince Narit so much better now than when I was younger, and I remember all kinds of things he did that surprised me. The things he allowed a child to do in those days! Especially now when I meet people in government circles. The fear they have of authority— of everything that's come down from above. . . . Without his influence maybe I would have been a successful government official instead of the failure that I am now. But of course my father, too, and my brother too. None of those people could have lasted as government officials in these times. My brother [Phraya Thewet] resigned under King

Prajadhipok. You see, even King Prajadhipok's methods he wouldn't put up with! If I had been a man, I would probably have gone to jail. . . . I probably wouldn't have lasted as long. . . .

Why? You haven't been that critical publicly, have you?

Well, that's because I'm a woman. When you're a woman you just can't do things—you know, it's sort of—you've been, your emotional makeup and so on doesn't permit you.

But weren't you a phu di?

Oh, yes. I think I'm more a *phu di* than lots of people. [She knows that he means *phu di* in the sense of "aristocrat" but she chooses to reply using the term in the literal sense of a "good person."] I really feel emotionally satisfied when I meet a village headman who does his duty very well, or a village schoolmaster and I [compliment] him very willingly and happily. But I feel very unhappy when I meet an upper government official whom inside of me I don't respect, but I have to be polite with. I feel very unhappy.

What's the basis of the unhappiness?

Well, this is a very good question that I wouldn't have been able to answer if I hadn't been ill for many months and been staying home. I think one of the causes of unhappiness is jealousy. Another cause is regret—that this sort of person should have had the luck to be in a position that could have done so much for the country but has done so little. And then the third is, sort of, what Buddhists call *moha*, ignorance at a high level, *illusion*. You still think of "you" as somebody, as *mom luang*, as somebody with such an education, such a background, and so on. If you can manage to think of [any] man objectively, as simply a phenomenon, a symptom of a phase that your country is going through, if you really can do that, then you won't be unhappy. *Moha* is the incapacity to understand [reality], to see things objectively. I try to view things as objectively as possible but I don't succeed all the time. I succeed sometimes. I don't criticize "publicly," you said. Not in public speeches and in writing, no, but at meetings, where I'm put on a committee. I don't know, it's probably my father's upbringing, or I don't know what it is, but I just can't help myself saying the things that are considered very critical. I will just say the things that I think annoy authority. Well, you know very few people like the truth. They think you are being . . . I don't know . . .

Ornery?

Yes—ornery. [Laughter] We have been doing such a lot of wasteful activities, wasting American money, and British money, and UNESCO money, and Thai money, and Thai mentality, and we've been spoiling the American experts who come to help us. Some of them go back and I'm wondering how they find life in the States when they go back. Very difficult to readjust to *what they really are*, in the States. We have done that to them, spoiled them, made them think themselves more important than they as individuals are. *They are ordinary.* A friend of mine said, "Of course, all doctors of education are idiots." I said, "You can't say that!" And he said, "Will you name *one* for me that is not an idiot?" [Laughter] And he named a certain man and then he said, "Do you think he would get any other doctor's degree but education?" I was very annoyed. But at the same time, you know—yes, I was amused.[14]

During the same interview, Boonlua spoke about the influence of theater, and of gender, on the course of her career.

I think with this theater upbringing [i.e., with Chao Phraya Thewet's classical dance troupe residing in his home], you . . . dramatize your own personality somehow. It's been very bad for me in my government career, because when I am speaking, I forget myself, I think of the audience. When I'm asked to take part in a panel discussion . . . I say things that I think would be useful to my audience, and I . . . forget myself as a government official, which is the training you get to be able to be an actor—you lose yourself in the part you play. It's been very dangerous for me. But Thai people, they don't pay too much attention to a woman. If a woman is critical, they take it as a woman's criticism, rather than a professional criticism, and that's why women are much more outspoken than men. . . . But now even the women have learned their lesson. They're sort of fatigued.[15]

Boonlua is criticizing both her own admittedly "theatrical performance" in the bureaucracy, and the bureaucracy itself, which had left the outspoken women "fatigued." Women were not silenced, but their contributions were taken as "woman's criticism" rather than "professional criticism." This, Boonlua contended, gave them more freedom than men—but less power. The facts of Boonlua's career support this perception; she was seldom silent, but she seldom won her battles.

Thais and foreign friends were beginning to trade stories of Boonlua's eccentricities: the time she gave an interview in her garden wearing earmuffs (to protect against unexpected drafts, the dread *lom phit*); her daily after-lunch nap in the lawn chair in her office; the knitting bag that disassembled itself around her feet during meetings; the beloved baggy wool cardigans she bought on her travels abroad. Once in Hong Kong attending a conference, she went on a shopping expedition with a British colleague.

In the department store, dressed casually and topped by her floppy wool "beggar's hat," Boonlua searched carefully through a display of sweaters while [British colleague] John Palmer waited politely nearby—both of them under the increasingly watchful eye of a clerk. Finally the clerk approached John Palmer and asked, "Would you like to buy a sweater for your servant?" "No, no!" the horrified Palmer stammered. "This lady is a princess—I am *her* servant!"[16]

If she was usually less than stylishly turned out, on occasion Boonlua could look smart when she thought it was appropriate. When she attended social or official functions at Bangkok hotels, she would dress in an attractive, traditional Thai silk costume. Almost always, Dr. Chom would pick her up afterwards, and if the affair ended in the early evening, he would come directly from his tennis club.

Khun Mo would come to call for her and off they would go, chattering away, her hand on his arm: Achan Boonlua dressed in her fine silk Thai costume—and Khun Mo in his tennis whites, bare-legged and with a towel slung around his shoulders.[17]

Boonlua continued to spend a great deal of time thinking about and treating her various ailments and syndromes. Her friend Michael Smithies, a Southeast Asia historian, made an astute observation concerning her health problems.

She positively thrived on ill-health, taking baskets of medicines and panaceas wherever she went. She did not allow her ever-precarious physical state to interfere with her appreciation of good food or her desire to smoke; and there would always be a pile of butts in the ashtray in front of her, though in fact she rarely took more than a couple of puffs at any cigarette.[18]

Her first students, many of whom now occupied positions in government and education, would always be grateful for the influence of her teaching on their lives and were flattered by her continuing interest in their progress. She kept track of the ones who had made an impression on her and frequently they came seeking her advice about their professional and personal lives. One of her rules was that she never attended weddings, but she made an exception in the case of one former student.

Achan *never* went to weddings. It was one of her rules, you see. So, I couldn't believe it—I was thrilled when she came to mine. As it happened, I woke up late that morning, and overslept for my own wedding! When I rushed into the hall, I saw that my own mother and sisters were sitting aside, letting Achan manage everything. They didn't mind; on the contrary, they were very pleased. When I went into the ladies' room to freshen up, Achan followed me, and while I sat there before the mirror, with no one else in the room, she began to tell me a long story about one of her nieces. I was shocked. She said, "Her husband has another lady, and she has come crying to me. I told her, 'Don't be a fool. Whatever you do, keep a cool heart (*chai yen*, perhaps the single most important quality one should develop)— and most important, *never leave the house*.'" She paused, then went on telling me about this niece, and I thought, "Why is Achan telling me this dreadful story about her niece on my wedding day?" Many years later, I saw a woman flirting with my husband, and suddenly I remembered Achan sitting beside me in the ladies' room on my wedding day, and I realized that she had been telling me something that I might one day find useful in my own life.[19]

Whether or not Boonlua made an exception to her usual rule and attended this wedding because she knew something about the bridegroom and made up her mind to give the bride some good and necessary advice, there is little question that the "dreadful story" was told to a purpose. Boonlua had unparalleled opportunities, in nearly fifty years of life in the huge family at Wang Ban Mo, to observe the behavior of married men and the disappointments of married life, and she planted a thought in her young friend's mind that might serve her well years after her wedding day: *never leave the house*. Whether or not possession is nine points of the Thai law, an unhappy Thai wife who leaves her home after discovering her husband's infidelity is likely to regret her impetuous decision.

Another way Boonlua often gave advice was to go to the person about whom she was concerned and begin her remarks with the words, "I'm sure that I'm just an old woman in a tumult and there is nothing to be worried about, but . . ." A woman who considered Boonlua her mentor and also a good friend described the following visit, which occurred while she was considering whether to accept an offer to work for a man she had long admired.

I was surprised to see Achan at my door. She said that she had an errand in the neighborhood and thought she would take a chance on my being home—which I thought was rather odd. After we had chatted for a while, she startled me by saying that she had heard about my job offer. She never said who had told her. When she began saying, "I'm sure I'm just an old woman in a tumult, but—," I thought, "Oh, dear! Something is coming!" And then she talked about how unfortunate it is that a woman has to be awfully careful going to work for a man she admires. People loved to gossip and could be quite cruel. She said, "Of course, the only thing that really matters is, is your husband a man who refuses to listen to gossip? Because if he doesn't *listen*, then gossip doesn't *matter* . . ." She never said, "I don't think you should take this job." She was letting me know that I must think hard about the *consequences* of taking the job.[20]

"YOU MUST MEET MOM LUANG BOONLUA"

During the 1960s Boonlua became one of the dozen or so Thais to whom visiting Western scholars were invariably sent when they had questions about Thai society and culture. Her English was excellent, a not inconsiderable circumstance, because Thais who had not been educated in the West and who could not speak English excellently and colloquially were not as impressive to foreigners as those who could converse easily with them and who seemed to share a common sensibility. This was precisely the limitation that Boonlua's father had felt so long ago—the inability to communicate with the Westerners who had become so important to his government and his nation. As a consequence, he had provided at least a basic Western education for all of his children, even his daughters, certain that the ability to speak English (especially) or French (impressive but less useful) would not only benefit them personally but would also allow them to make real contributions to the kingdom, so that its honor and continuing independence would be assured.

By the middle of the twentieth century, education in the West had become mandatory for an ambitious Thai. It was not that there were no fine scholars among those who had completed their studies at home. Indeed quite a few scholars, writers, and painters had been educated in Thailand and had never mastered another language. Perhaps the best known of these was Phya Anuman Rajadhon, often called a "Thai Renaissance man," a friend of Prince Narit's whom Boonlua admired. He was greatly respected for his research and writing on Thai culture and customs. But the contributions of these scholars and writers was scarcely known abroad because few foreign scholars knew Thai well enough to read, translate, or promote their work. As for modern Thai literature, it was almost entirely inaccessible to the West, for most of the Western scholars who could read Thai were historians, anthropologists, or scholars of classical literature, and they were rarely interested in modern Thai fiction and poetry.

Boonlua's particular expertise was in literature, both classical and modern, although she wrote little in English about the subject. Had she been asked to do so, she would doubtless have complied, but it is only at the turn of the twenty-first century that interest in Thai literature beyond the borders of Thailand has become great enough to stimulate the publication of translated fiction and poetry, and virtually all works of literary history and criticism, including Boonlua's, remain untranslated.

Another Thai who was often interviewed and quoted during the 1960s was Boonlua's distant relative M.R. Kukrit Pramoj, the witty Oxford graduate who became a banker, newspaper publisher, fiction writer, and probably the most popular source of information about Thai culture and social history among foreigners. Thais like Boonlua and Kukrit were pleased to reveal their society and culture to outsiders—in large measure, a result of their having been educated in the West, where curiosity about people from other cultures was encouraged—but they were careful about what they revealed and what they kept to themselves. It may not have occurred to most of the foreigners who spoke with them that the opinions expressed by these elite Thais in a strictly Thai setting, with no foreigners looking on, might provide some surprises. For example, Boonlua revealed to her foreign friends almost nothing of the conduct of life at Wang Ban Mo before her marriage, knowing that few Westerners would understand the conjugal arrangements in the family, or the contradiction (in their eyes) between the rigid hierarchy of the household and the casual intimacy of living arrangements. She made some attempt to address cross-cultural misperceptions in the novel

Western Daughter-in-Law (*Saphai maem*), but it was written in Thai for a Thai audience.

Foreign-educated Thais such as Boonlua and Kukrit were carefully taught about their culture and religion by parents who knew that they would be spending many years far from home. They wanted their children to be educated abroad, but not to become Westerners—or to marry them—as reflected in Boonlua's *Western Daughter-in-Law*, Kukrit's *Four Reigns*, and several other novels in which Thai men marry foreign women while studying abroad and bring them home, with dire results for all concerned.

Ever since Thais began studying abroad, they have had to struggle to assert their "Thai-ness" before two audiences: their countrymen and foreign interrogators. They have had to learn to adjust to life in the West and then to readjust to life in Thailand and to (re)define themselves as Thai. In the mid-twentieth century, foreign-educated Thais created a Thai worldview that was in fact an amalgam of all that they had learned to value at home and abroad. And this was nothing new. The process of creating Thai identity went on as it had over the past eight centuries, a process of accumulating and adapting, consuming and assimilating. When Thais of the 1960s looked at photographs from the 1860s, they saw "old Thailand" (the kingdom of Siam) reflected in the images of Thai kings in Western military uniforms and Thai queens in elegant adaptations of Paris and London fashions. But had these kings and queens worn "real" Thai clothing, that is, pre-nineteenth-century garments, they still would have reflected countless influences from the Khmer, the Mon, the Malay, the Burmese, the Chinese, and many other peoples. A rigorous search for an essential culture, in Thailand as in any other society, can only amount to the careful peeling of a cultural onion, one layer at a time, arranging the peels into careful categories. If one persevered to separate the last bits, perhaps one would be left holding nothing. But that is not an idea that appeals to conservative patriots, who prefer their onions whole. For them, there is an essential Thai culture and even a "Thai race." For all her reverence for her family lineage, for the Chakri dynasty, and for the cultural legacy of Siam, Boonlua understood very well that her society was a cultural "onion."

Ted Plaister, her friend of many years and a professor of linguistics at the University of Hawaii, wrote:

> Perhaps the richest memory that I have of Phi Lua (I felt that I had been fully accepted by Boonlua when she told me that it would be appropriate for me to call her Phi Lua . . .) was her ability to stand back from her own culture and mine as well, and be able to laugh at, admire, or scold—whichever was appropriate at the time. She had the remarkable ability to see what was good and useful in all cultures, to see what was frivolous but harmless, and what was undesirable. I always felt that she had respect for all cultures, equal respect, and did not put her own above others. In a sense, I am saying that she was not ethnocentric in any overt sense. Perhaps she was and was just extremely clever at hiding it, but I think not.[21]

THE FACULTY OF ARTS, THAMMASAT UNIVERSITY

During her period of freelancing in the bureaucracy, Boonlua was asked to contribute to the development of the new Faculty of Arts at Thammasat University and to do some teaching as well. At first she protested that she would only develop materials but not teach. Finally, she gave in, developing and also teaching a trial course that was identified as "Thai language and literature," but which she intended as a combination of "*oprom*" and "*sueksa*," reflecting her lifelong interest in combining the upbringing and rearing of children with formal education. She wanted poetry, singing, dancing, and art all to be included in the curriculum, and students would be expected to participate in their own education instead of spending all their time in lecture halls trying to remember enough of their instructors' words to parrot them back at exam time.

If such ideas seemed to echo beliefs she had held for decades, there were also discernible echoes from the Phibun era, when she worked within the National Institute of Culture. While Boonlua had not been comfortable with the anti-monarchical aspects of that era or the growing

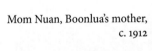

Lan Kunchon, Chao Phraya
Thewet, Boonlua's father, c. 1920

Mom Nuan, Boonlua's mother,
c. 1912

Boonlua, *center front*, with her father, Chao Phraya Thewet, and eight of her sisters. Wang Khlong Toei, 1921

Wang Ban Mo,
the family residence

Portrait of Boonlua
as a young lady

Boonlua's sister Buppha
(Dokmai Sot) at home at Ban Mo

Boonlua, *back row second right*, and other graduates of the
Convent of the Holy Infant Jesus in Penang, 1928

Boonlua, *center front*, with classmates at the Faculty of Arts, Chulalongkorn University

Boonlua's graduation from Chulalongkorn University, 1938 (Boonlua is at back right.)

During her student days at
Chulalongkorn

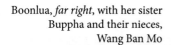

Boonlua, *far right*, with her sister
Buppha and their nieces,
Wang Ban Mo

Boonlua, *right*, with her Filipina
roommate in Minnesota, c. 1949

At an education conference
in New Zealand, 1958

Dancing the *ramwong* with a colleague
at Bang Saen Teachers College

Dr. Chom Debyasuvarn and
Boonlua shortly after their
marriage, Bangkok, 1959

Speaking at a conference on education, Bangkok, c. 1965

Boonlua, *second left*, as dean of the Faculty of Arts,
Silpakorn University, with her graduating students, 1969

Dr. Chom and Boonlua in the garden of their home,
Bangkok, 1969

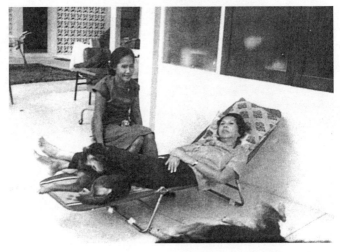

Reclining on her chaise longue, with Professor Mayuree Sukwiwat, 1975

alliance with Japan, she had agreed with Phibun and Luang Wichit Wathakan that the Thai historical and cultural heritage should comprise a significant part of education, not only for children and university students, but also in adult education.[22]

Her students at Thammasat were pleased and surprised to find that studying Thai was not boring at all. At the end of the year, as she planned new activities for the coming semester, she was stunned and hurt to receive a letter informing her that her services would no longer be needed since a "regular professor" had been found.

> It was disappointing to have spent so much time gathering materials for teaching [this course], although I could surely use them elsewhere. I suppose I should think it honor enough . . . to have been asked for my assistance, even though it was subsequently decided that they did not need it (or perhaps they just wanted to get rid of me).[23]

There it was again, the old fear. Despite all, she rated her overall experience at Thammasat University as one of her successes—at least with the students, if not with "certain people" in the administration who were never named. The students' enthusiasm was all the proof she needed that her ideas about education were valid.

In April and May of 1965, during a teacher training mission in Chiang Mai, she began to feel unusually tired, and a month later she also began to experience swelling in different parts of her body. She was diagnosed with an inability to digest protein and was hospitalized for several weeks. Gradually, the symptoms abated and she returned to various consulting projects. Despite some setbacks, it was during the 1960s that Boonlua claimed she made gratifying strides in one aspect of her Buddhist practice: contentment with her life, and acceptance.

> The period during which I worked at the ministry in no fixed position was on the whole a happy time. I had no disagreements with anyone, and felt responsible for no one. When I went to meetings, my only duty was to clarify complex matters. And I taught myself many things, especially, to be content with what I have. I worked with people I

liked and knew well, mainly my old colleagues from the Education Inspection Unit.[24]

She also achieved a victory over a phobia.

Over those seven years, I cured myself of *the disease of not being able to look at palm trees and beaches* by occasionally going [to work in locations near the sea] with the education inspectors. Because the work absorbed my attention, I was able to get used to being near the sea gradually. I also studied the subject of mental health and considered how to improve my own condition.[25]

Boonlua's version of the self-cure for the phobia she so frankly describes ignores two important factors. First, her single most gratifying work experience had been as a director with the Education Inspection Unit, where her colleagues had treated her with both respect and affection. A critical aspect of the seven-year "cure" for the phobia that followed her unhappy tenure at Bang Saen Teachers College, on the beach and amidst palm trees, was the constant presence and support of the "family" of education inspectors that had never abandoned her. Her old colleagues were delighted when she left Bang Saen and made it plain that they looked forward to enjoying her company for the rest of their lives.

Another factor in the cure for the disease of not being able to look at palm trees and beaches was the realization, in the 1960s, of Boonlua's childhood dream of writing and publishing fiction. Her first published novel, *Western Daughter-in-Law*, was completed at home in Bangkok while she recuperated from the teachers college experience, and published in 1962 to generally favorable reviews. Also during that period of recuperation she wrote her first short story, which was much admired, approximately translated as "The Charm of the Cooking Spoon" (*Sane plai chawak*), a Thai phrase referring to the accomplishments of a good wife.[26] She began her second novel, the highly praised *Thutiyawiset* (the title is the name of a government decoration) during her recovery from the "protein deficiency" illness in 1965, and it was published in 1966.[27]

While she was recovering during 1965, she also took the opportunity to accompany Dr. Chom on some of his upcountry travels for the Ministry of Public Health. This was the first time Boonlua and Chom enjoyed an extended time of travel together, and following one of these trips Boonlua talked quite frankly about her marriage, and also about the value of her friendships with Westerners (*farang*). The quotation that follows was her answer to the question posed by Professor Herbert P. Phillips, "How does it feel to live in at least three different worlds—your family, your profession, and [among] the *farang* you know?"

I feel—I don't know. The reason I married my husband is because I thought that it was extraordinary the way he could understand me. And so I sort of—I get some *dependence* on him. So then when he is with me I feel all right, but when he is not with me, I feel like a . . . I . . . I feel that I'm not a real person. I feel like—I don't know—it's very strange. In fact, I feel more at home among *farang*, with *farang* people, than with Thai people. I sort of let myself go. Meet *farang* friends, you know. I don't have to be careful about this and about that all the time. And the happiest time of my life was in the States.

What do you mean about having to be careful?

Well, when you talk to any Thai people you have to be careful all the time, I mean I—you know, I have to be careful not to make them feel stupid, or I have to be careful not to make them feel inferior, or I have to be careful not to make them feel that I am crazy.[28]

This is a rare glimpse of life as experienced by a Thai with a Western education. One's "*farang*" personality worked well abroad and also with Westerners in Thailand, but the same behavior might not endear oneself to one's family or to other Thais. In Boonlua's case, her elder brother and head of the family, Phraya Thewet, had remained in Thailand. He had to deal not only with his Westernized sisters, but also to endure the frequent remarks of friends to the effect that the Kunchon family had "ruined its women" by over-educating them. This kind of remark would not be made today.[29]

It is interesting that Boonlua professed to taking great care "not to make [Thais] feel that I am crazy," something that would never occur to her when speaking with Westerners. The following recollection by Boonlua's friend, Ted Plaister, is revealing.

> I received a telephone call from [Boonlua] and the text of the message went something like this: "Ted, this is Boonlua and I want to eat chicken." (There was no hello, no prefatory remarks, just the statement concerning her desire to eat chicken.) I had other plans for lunch, but I quickly set these aside. . . . The reason she wanted to eat chicken and to eat that chicken with a "farang" was that she had just spent a considerable amount of time with a group from the Ministry of Education and she was, in her words, "tired of all their bureaucratic talk." She wanted to switch languages, cultures, and all that went with it.[30]

Some Thais asserted that Boonlua was not "a real Thai," but really a *farang*, due to her lengthy education under the convent nuns, her Western professors at Chulalongkorn University, and her two years at the University of Minnesota. This did not surprise her; all Thais who had substantially Western educations were criticized in this way at some time or other. A Thai man who once worked as her assistant made these remarks:

> Achan Boonlua always reminded me of my "[European] auntie." My uncle had studied in Europe, and he married a woman there who came back to Thailand with him and made up her mind that she was not going to live as an "outsider" for the rest of her life—she was going to make herself into a Thai. And she became more Thai than the Thai themselves! She spoke Thai and ate only Thai food, and she worked very hard at being Thai.
>
> Achan Boonlua did not really have any Thai education until she went to Chulalongkorn University. She was an "expert" in Thai literature because she made herself into one. She always talked about absorbing all this Thai literature from her family, but think about this:

In fact, she went to the nuns when she was four, and the children were not even allowed to speak Thai in the missionary schools. When she was eleven years old, she went away to Penang and she was there for years—she wasn't hearing all the old Thai stories all the time, like those of us who stayed in Thailand. I did not study abroad, and I was exposed to the Thai classical works constantly. In my family, we read and sang all the time. She had to study those works like a foreigner, and I know how hard she worked not to show that, not to let people know. I was just the right assistant for her and she was always asking me questions.[31]

Although there probably is a kernel of truth in this man's remarks, I was unable to find anyone who would or could corroborate his opinion that Boonlua "had to study [Thai literature] like a foreigner." It is possible that he bore some resentment toward Thais who were able to rise to positions that were not available to him, partly because he lacked a foreign education. Yet I felt certain, as he spoke, that he held Boonlua in high regard and felt great sympathy for this proud, aristocratic woman.

It was during upcountry journeys with Dr. Chom during 1965, far from Bangkok and the bureaucracy, that Boonlua began to write *Thutiyawiset*, the novel she first planned around the life and career of Phibun Songkhram, "Marshal Phibun," as she always referred to him (never "Field Marshal"), the man who had had such a momentous impact upon Thailand and also upon her own life. But after a few weeks, she found herself thinking more and more about his wife, Than Phuying La-iat.[32] She thought about the subject of power: what it does to the lives of men who crave it, and finally achieve it, and to their wives; and she thought also about how women achieve and use power within the Thai social structure. Gradually, *Thutiyawiset* began to take shape, and the "novel about Marshal Phibun" became the story of Than Phuying La-iat. It focused on the complex and critical role of women in Thai society, a subject that would be the theme of a very different book— her 1972 utopian novel *Land of Women (Suratnari)* about a kingdom ruled by women.

There was another important factor besides sufficient time that propelled Boonlua into her belated fiction writing career in the 1960s. When she began *Western Daughter-in-Law*, her sister Buppha, the novelist Dokmai Sot, was already living in India with her husband, Dr. Sukij Nimmanhemin. For many years, Buppha had been too physically frail and, more important, too depressed to complete a novel. In 1963, the year after Boonlua's first novel was published, Buppha died of congestive heart failure. Boonlua always denied that she had postponed her own fiction writing career because of her sister's fame and the inevitable comparisons that would be made.

> When I was young, I simply saw no reason for my taking up writing, because Buppha and I saw most of the same things, we had the same experiences, and we saw things more or less in the same light. And I just didn't feel like writing . . . *corollary* novels. And so I sort of forgot it for a time and went into education.[33]

But these remarks are belied by several facts about the sisters' lives. Buppha and Boonlua had not seen most of the same things nor had the same experiences. Buppha had lived in the Grand Palace for several years during her childhood, had been too frail as an adolescent to be sent to Penang, and spent almost her entire adult life living at Wang Ban Mo. She had taught French for a few months at Rajini School but didn't like it and returned home for good. Like Boonlua, she always claimed that she longed for a home of her own but she never really got one, even when she married Dr. Sukij.[34] The sisters had never "seen things in the same light," and the novels they wrote were anything but "corollary."

By 1968, Boonlua had achieved contentment, a reasonable measure of fame, and, to a greater extent than ever before, the respect of her family. They were proud of the warm reception *Thutiyawiset* had received from critics and readers alike. Ironically, it was now that what she called the last great "failure" of her life would occur, although it might be more accurately described as her last great bad decision.

RETURN TO ACADEMIA: THE LAST FAILURE

In 1968, M.L. Pin Malakul asked Boonlua to found the Faculty of Arts at a new campus of Silpakorn University to be built on the grounds of Sanam Chand Palace, some thirty miles from Bangkok in Nakhon Pathom. King Vajiravudh had commissioned a number of British colonial-style and Tudor structures there during the early 1920s, but the whole compound had fallen into disrepair in the intervening years. It seemed the perfect location for the kind of university M.L. Pin had long dreamed of building, an experimental institution that would incorporate features of the British education system he fondly remembered, particularly the tutorial relationship between professors and students and the establishment of colleges within the larger institution of the university. In the end, M.L. Pin would not be able to effect such innovations, and the structure of the university would be much like that of other Thai universities. But it was a dream worth pursuing and the opportunity to be part of this venture was one that Boonlua found irresistible.

> At that time I was happy writing light fiction. I thought that if I could make a career of it, without doubt I should be happier still. But my relatives and friends were thrilled to hear that I would be the dean of the Faculty of Arts on the new Silpakorn campus. Some of them were thrilled even though they had no idea of what I would be doing. In the end, I did not hear the news that I would be dean from [M.L. Pin], but from one of my friends who said that he had told her![35]

Boonlua was promised that the ground rules at the new university would be very different from those that had caused her such pain during the year at Bang Saen Teachers College. The original, prestigious Silpakorn University in Bangkok, often called "The Fine Arts University" in English, is located near the Grand Palace. The Nakhon Pathom campus would be an extension of that institution and therefore would share its prestige. It would not suffer the neglect that was the usual fate of an ordinary provincial college. Boonlua would not be responsible for student affairs *per se*, as she had been at Bang Saen College in addition to all of her other duties. She was promised that she would be responsible only for faculty, curricula, and research activities.

She thought that M.L. Pin's plan for the new university was intriguing, but the truly tempting aspect of the offer was the opportunity to establish and implement the kind of curriculum for the teaching of Thai language and literature that she had been pressing upon the ministry for decades. Her own teaching style had always been innovative, incorporating singing and dancing with the teaching of language and literature, and she had been given (or had demanded and taken) considerable liberties in this regard, but she had never been given the chance to put her ideas into practice on a wider stage until now.

Boonlua decided against appointing a committee to develop curricula for the Faculty of Fine Arts, on the grounds that such committees always ended up filled with people in high positions—people who were least able to devote the amount of time required to develop superior curricula. Or this was the explanation she gave for taking the task entirely upon herself. She began by going to British, French, and American agencies in Bangkok for ideas. She obtained curricula from twenty small American colleges and studied them closely for ideas that would be useful in the Thai setting. She went to the British Council to consult with friends with whom she had worked on a number of programs for the teaching of English in Thailand, and with their assistance she was able to recruit teachers from London, people who had experience in teaching English as a foreign language and were eager for the chance to live in Thailand for a year or two.

She sent her future instructors of French and German (Thais who had studied in France and Germany) to the Alliance Française and the German Cultural Institute for advice and ideas on curricula and teaching methods. As for the teaching of Thai language and literature, she thought that she would be able to rely on some old friends. In her memoirs, she alludes to problems with the Thai teaching staff, "which I shall explain later," but this explanation never materialized. However much they may have admired Boonlua, the old friends with experience teaching Thai literature were used to their ways of teaching over many years. From the beginning some faculty members were suspicious and uneasy about the new curricula, but Boonlua either did not think of this, or she assumed that all would be well once she had explained her ideas to them. She always thought that people would agree with her once they understood what she was talking about.

One of her first acts in organizing the Thai literature teaching program illustrates both the creativity of her ideas and the fatal flaws in her decision-making process. She recruited Wibha Kongkanan, a young literature professor who had received a master's degree from an American university a few years earlier and had been teaching English at a college in Bangkok since then. She had no experience in teaching Thai literature, but Boonlua convinced her that that would be an advantage, since she would not be burdened with an allegiance to old ways of teaching. (Professor Wibha later completed a PhD at the School for Oriental and African Studies in London, writing a dissertation on early twentieth-century Thai novels.) As for the fact that the other people who would be teaching with her were almost all several years older, Boonlua pointed out that the people with the newest ideas were often younger, and that this would not prove to be a problem. Unfortunately, it immediately proved to be a problem. Professor Wibha recalled her first meeting with the famous professor whose first novels she had read but whom she had never met.

> I was called to a meeting. I had no idea why, or who would be there, or that I would be offered a job at the new university. I couldn't believe that I was sitting at the same table with Mom Luang Boonlua. I had read her novels and I was absolutely in awe. Here she was right in front of me, talking and laughing and smoking her cigarettes and not like anybody else I had ever met. She had heard about me, and she thought I would be the right person for the job.[36]

At that time, Thai "literature" as a subject of study in university was confined to pre-modern literature *only*. Modern fiction was scarcely considered worth studying and was therefore taught, in Boonlua's opinion, even more execrably than were the classics. In a literary debate, she caused an audience to dissolve into laughter by announcing that if she ever learned that any of her own fiction was going to be taught in Thai schools, she would make her own placard and march on the Ministry of Education in protest.[37]

The study of classical literature had deteriorated into the study of vocabulary since the classic works were written in language so archaic that the students could not possibly understand it. Typically, literature students spent all their time being drilled in the most famous passages, which they learned to recite, and they were taught exactly how to appreciate each line of each passage of each work. There was no discussion, and the idea of a "seminar" in which students are responsible for analyzing what they had read was unheard of. This was what Boonlua sometimes scathingly referred to as the "Chulalongkorn University way" of teaching Thai literature.

Boonlua believed that for students between the ages of seventeen and twenty-one, modern literature was far easier to appreciate than classical poetry. Therefore, while the Thai literature curriculum for freshmen and sophomores would include traditional, poetic works, the emphasis would be placed squarely on twentieth-century modern short stories and novels. Moreover, students would be taught to approach all literary works, whether composed forty or four hundred years ago, from the vantage point of a modern sensibility, to think about and discuss characterization, plot, narrative style, and so on. Finally, they would be considering traditional and contemporary works in a comparative way, looking at the methods and objectives of Thai writers over the centuries—up to and including *this* century. In 1968, such ideas about the teaching of literature would have been innovative in quite a few universities in the United States or England, but in Thailand they were shocking. For most of the people who would be teaching Thai literature in Boonlua's new Faculty of Arts, this unprecedented blending of old and new, of *wannakhadi* and *wannakam*—classical literature and modern fiction—was incomprehensible, if not scandalous. In fact, the term *wannakhadi* had been coined by King Vajiravudh only in 1913, and he had intended it to refer to *all* literary works, old or new; but over the years the term had come to be reserved for works that reflected the strict poetic traditions of pre-modern Siam. Defenders of the distinction claimed that it was merely a way to classify works by era, a claim that was undermined when, in 1952, Prince Phittayalongkorn published *Sam krung*, a work composed in classical poetic form. It was promptly dubbed *wannakhadi*, while his contemporaries' works in modern prose continued to be relegated to the status of *wannakam*. Boonlua correctly interpreted this semantic feud as a matter of high culture versus popular culture. And who better to negotiate between these camps than herself?

The new curriculum emphasized four skills: reading, writing, speaking, and listening. Four teachers were to teach four classes each; and in their freshman year, Faculty of Arts students would study four writers: three contemporary writers (M.R. Kukrit Pramoj, Ajin Banjapan, and Kritsna Asokesin) and a fourth writer from the end of the eighteenth and the beginning of the nineteenth century, a court lady named Khun Suwan. Prince Damrong Rajananuphap, a brother of King Chulalongkorn who was a historian and statesman and whose opinions on literature were held in high esteem, had flatly stated that Khun Suwan was mad—on the basis of her satires of life at court full of witty double entendres. During the late 1960s a few young feminist scholars were reexamining her work, finding genius instead of madness in her ribald imagination and brilliant use of language. Boonlua thought that Khun Suwan's work would be perfect for her purposes.

The juxtaposition of Khun Suwan and three contemporary writers was completely incomprehensible to the Thai literature faculty. Boonlua patiently explained that their goal would be to teach students that Thai literature could be studied comparatively and in its totality. It would be so much more interesting than studying it as everyone had been forced to study it in the past!

Boonlua expected her old friends to be thrilled about her exciting new ideas and was oblivious to the fact that instead of being thrilled, they felt threatened, and they were justifiably frightened of having to teach ideas they could barely understand themselves. Moreover, not all of the ideas she was suggesting seemed suitable for teaching young people. One of the tasks of a literature professor was the judicious paring of famous works, removing or ignoring anything that young people should not be reading about or thinking about.

CLEAR WATER, PURE HEARTS

When the university opened its doors, the biggest problems were not theoretical, concerning what and how to teach, but quite literally concrete. Only one building had been completed and so it had to serve all functions. The entire university community—students, Thai faculty, and the English language instructors who had been acquired via the British Council—was housed in that solitary structure, and they had to teach and study in it as well. Boonlua might be dean of the Faculty of Arts, but she had to share her bedroom with the duplicating machine, which was in use constantly because so many of the new teaching materials were homemade.

After a few months, the Faculty of Arts moved into its own building, one so poorly designed that Boonlua wrote, "To my knowledge no one has ever stepped forward to take the credit for designing it. There was no cross ventilation in any of the rooms, and it was so hot that you could ripen fruit in the corners."[38]

The British instructors were appalled by their living and teaching conditions and felt that they had been vastly misled by the British Council as to the realities of life in Thailand, which was not a tropical paradise. Even commuting to Bangkok to enjoy weekends with modern conveniences was a chore because of interminable delays in completing a new bridge between Bangkok and Nakhon Pathom. It was a painful situation for Boonlua, who had to act as liaison between her friends at the British Council, people at the university, and the disgruntled English instructors. They soon left and were replaced by volunteers who had no teaching experience.

Many members of the faculty were unhappy, and the support staff was unhappy as well. Traditionally, each faculty member at a Thai university reported to one superior, but the new lines of authority were much more complicated. The faculty soon fragmented into cliques, and faculty-staff relations became strained. By all accounts, students comprised the most satisfied group on campus, as immortalized in the very popular novel *Clear Water, Pure Hearts* (*Nam Sai Chai Ching*). It was written by "V.

Vinicchaykul," the pen name of Khunying Vinita Diteeyont, who was a young assistant professor during that first unforgettable year.

In Khunying Vinita's novelized version of events, students and professors lived as one big family, keeping each other's spirits up through the worst of times. During the day, everyone learned together; in the evenings, they gathered to sing folk and popular songs and talk into the night. Khunying Vinita recalled that "Achan Boonlua was the best boss I ever had and a very understanding person—I never heard a cross word from her."[39]

Reports concerning Boonlua's brief tenure at Silpakorn University are strikingly at odds. One former colleague claimed that by 1968, Boonlua's teaching ability was so compromised by age, illness, and depression that some students complained they couldn't understand her at all. In fact, she was suffering from high blood pressure and exhaustion, and was taking Valium to calm her "nerve disease." Yet, I was unable to find a single student from this time who mentioned any difficulty in understanding her. The general impression I received was that while the students were aware of her physical frailty, her teaching was nevertheless exciting, demanding, and unlike any educational experience they had ever had, or ever would have.

The award-winning children's book author Panpimon Gajasuta, who writes under the pen name "Doy Ding," recalled Boonlua's unusual teaching style, and the truly profound influence Boonlua had on her career and her life.

> Achan Boonlua interviewed everybody who was applying to the Faculty of Arts. My relatives and friends talked about whether they should tell Achan ahead of time that I am short, and finally they decided not to. Achan had a rule that every student in the Faculty of Arts had to dance and sing. I climbed up onto the chair in her office. She just looked at me for a few moments and then smiled and said, "Well, you can *sing*, can't you?" And I said, "Of *course* I can sing!"

Panpimon is a very small achondroplastic dwarf. Her cousin, a friend of mine who arranged our meeting, did not mention this fact before our meeting. She did describe Panpimon as "short" (*tia*). I said, "Well, I'm very short myself." She replied, "Yes—well, she is shorter than you." She did not use the actual term for a dwarf (*khon khrae*) because it literally means "stunted" or "undeveloped," and thus is avoided. Panpimon also referred to herself as *tia*. It is usual for Thais to avoid mentioning physical differences or limitations, although not because of shame or discomfort. It is because ideally, one is supposed to encounter each person objectively, accepting him or her without surprise. On the other hand, Thai will often ask questions of the individual who is "different" that a Western person probably would not ask. When I asked Panpimon about her family, which includes several dwarfs, she was very open and forthcoming.

Up to the time I entered the university, my friends had always carried me around, because walking a distance is so difficult for me. Achan stopped that. She said I would no longer be carried around like a baby because I was a grown-up woman. I had to walk when I was in the building. But she compromised on the matter of longer trips around campus; my friends could pull me along in a wagon.

In her class we always sat in a circle, and we were divided into teams. One team would be responsible for talking about the characters in whatever work we were reading, another team would be responsible for talking about the plot, and so on. You would not dare to come to Achan's class unprepared because there was no way you could get away with it.

Achan Boonlua was so different from the other professors. She failed some people who were studying to be teachers. She would say, "And what kind of teacher would you be if I passed you anyway?" On the first day of class she told us, "If you want to get a B in this class, just write down everything I've told you on the exam. But if you expect to get an A, you must write your own ideas." No other professor would say such a thing.

Achan Boonlua gave me confidence in myself. Maybe I would still have been a writer, but I think I would have been a *failed* writer. (Laughter) Achan helped me to find my voice, and to find the kind of writing that would suit me.[40]

Although her students were happy, by the middle of the second year Boonlua felt overwhelmed by administrative problems and by the inability or unwillingness of most instructors in the Faculty of Arts to adopt her ideas for the teaching of Thai literature. If the round-table approach that she and her students loved was anathema to most Thai language and literature professors, they were even more uncomfortable with the idea of "seminars" in which students were encouraged to analyze and criticize the treasured literary heritage of the nation. Seminars were for professors, not for students. Behind her back, these professors at last managed to suspend the literature curriculum that meant so much to her and replace it with a more traditional approach. This experience, never directly mentioned in her autobiography, was a crushing defeat. She was the dean of the Faculty of Arts!

Boonlua was tired of the fray and literally sick to death of fighting the battles. Wibha Kongkanan, the young professor she had recruited to help launch her revolutionary Thai literature program, recalled:

Sometimes she would call me and ask me to take her for a ride in my car. Achan Boonlua didn't drive, you know. I would pick her up and we would drive out into the countryside. She liked me to drive to the end of a road and park the car. She especially liked to watch the sun set over the fields, and sometimes she would talk, but often we would simply sit in the silence until she said, "All right, let's go back now."[41]

Boonlua held on until the end of the year, and then asked to resign from the civil service slightly before normal retirement at the age of sixty.

I did not feel that I should jeopardize my health again and began to think that the university should seek someone who was really suitable for this position as soon as possible. It would be better not only for me, but also for the university. Before the close of the 1970 academic year, I went on medical leave, suffering from [exhaustion] and a serious bladder infection, which used up my entire month's sick leave. I then requested early retirement. This request had to go all the way to the prime minister himself [Field Marshal Thanom Kittikachorn], who also was the titular head of the university. . . . He called me in and asked me to explain my health situation and my request for early retirement. . . . I told the prime minister that this position . . . required a person who was strong and could lead, and that I was simply too weak, tired, ill, and old to do a proper job of it. I told him that I could go on and on, giving him many details about the situation at the university, but I would rather spare him, and I trusted him to believe that I was not the right person for the job. When he saw that I was in earnest, he granted my request. On August 1, 1970, I retired from the civil service.

There may be some who will think that I was a coward, and that it is an ordinary thing, after all, to have problems during the first year or so of a new enterprise. I agree. But is one a coward to recognize one's inability to solve a problem—or a realist? And was it not better for me to fail, if failure it was, rather than causing [the university] to fail because of my shortcomings?

With every succeeding illness, not only my physical health declined (which may have been natural enough for my age), but the powers of my mind declined, too. My memory became very bad. I was sure that the only sensible thing to do was to conserve the physical and mental energies that remained to me, expending them on more suitable activities.[42]

Boonlua may well have felt that her physical and also her mental condition were failing. But a year after retirement, she would write the lengthy and complicated novel *Land of Women.*

Some have questioned the role Boonlua's increasing use of drugs, especially Valium, played during the last, sad year at Nakhon Pathom. She was taking a combination of medications for high blood pressure, bladder infections, and pains in her stomach and back. One of Dr. Chom's younger relatives told me in 1996 that she feared Boonlua had become dependent upon Valium during that period of her life, and that it may have been responsible for the confusion and memory loss that others noticed and that she complained of herself. Perhaps also it caused the tremor in her hands that made it almost impossible for her to write, and even, at times, to type.[43] In any event, although her health could never be described as robust, after she retired in 1970 it improved steadily.

At home in her study, she began to write the first notes for her autobiography, *Successes and Failures*. She reflected upon the founding of educational institutions. Teachers were more important than curricula, she wrote. If a university was to be founded in the provinces, the planning should be essentially "military": there must be reserves for everything, and contingency plans. Few people had suffered more for the lack of both.

Campus construction was very important; no one who had had to work in it would ever forget the catastrophe of a building so poorly designed that one could ripen fruit in the corners. She quoted Prince Damrong, who once said that administrators should be chosen for two qualities: first, endurance, and second, maturity. If qualified people cannot be found in sufficient numbers, then the whole plan should be delayed until they have been found. Much better objectives should be set for hiring people to found universities, administer them, and teach in them.

It is impossible to avoid concluding that certain people would be recognized in the following remarks.

[We] must get over the idea that people who have studied in England for many years are therefore guaranteed to be competent in their field. Another sad misunderstanding concerns people with a PhD—not all of them are natural teachers and very few are good at teaching beginners. Finally, we must face the fact that our [high school] students are not prepared for university work—regardless of whether the teaching methods in our universities are old or new.[44]

The last chapter of *Successes and Failures* is a plea for the complete re-thinking of higher education in Thailand, the final draft of the ideas she had long espoused, supplemented by her most recent, painful experiences at the new Nakhon Pathom campus of Silpakorn University.

It is now thought desirable to found new universities in the provinces as well as in Bangkok, but the former are starved until the latter have been given all that they need and want. In the provincial universities, both professors and students are set adrift and must fend for themselves.[45]

Boonlua also made a plea for greatly increased awareness of adolescent psychology on the part of teachers and administrators. Adults tend to forget their own feelings and mental state during adolescence, she wrote, preferring to remember only the happy times and the successes. Moreover, contemporary adolescents are far more influenced by the globalized Western culture than they themselves ever were. This results in unprecedented problems that require unprecedented approaches. For example, in the past all teachers in Thailand assumed the right to be treated with exaggerated respect, but in the contemporary world it is necessary even for teachers and professors to *earn* the respect of students. Finally, she urged the government to use the wisdom and ideas of people with "hands-on" experience when founding new universities rather than leaving the most important decisions to people with PhDs and many years of foreign education but little or no practical experience.

In part because of Boonlua's spoken and written urgings on this subject, over the following decade great strides were made in changing the pattern of "Bangkok first," at least in regard to higher education. By the close of the twentieth century, although Thammasat and Chulalongkorn Universities in Bangkok remained the most prestigious schools in the kingdom, the universities at Chiang Mai in the north and Khon Kaen in the northeast, and the five campuses of Prince of Songkhla University in the south, were well-funded and respected institutions.

After 1970, Boonlua was at last able to live, write, and travel on a schedule entirely of her own choosing. The 1970s might have been the most peaceful decade of Boonlua's life, had it been a peaceful decade for the nation. For the remaining twelve years of her life she would be productive in her writing, surrounded by good friends, comfortable with her family, and secure in the loving companionship of Dr. Chom.

8

THE USES OF FICTION

Boonlua had dreamed of writing fiction all her life, but she could not bear the idea that her own stories would be compared unfavorably with the famous novels written by Dokmai Sot—her sister Buppha. One of several benefits of waiting until midlife to begin writing fiction was that by the age of fifty-one, she brought decades of life experience to the task. All of the Dokmai Sot novels had been written when the author was a single young woman living in her father's house. Although she was limited in experience of the world at large, she was observant, astute about human nature, and able to faithfully represent the lives and conversations of the people among whom she lived. Her readers liked to compare her to Jane Austen, who modestly described her own novels as little bits of ivory on which she worked with a fine brush. The comparison is apt.

Boonlua's fiction was very different from her sister's. While she too focused on families and relationships, like Dokmai Sot and virtually every other Thai novelist, most of her fictional characters were engaged in careers, as she had been. They thought and talked about the great events of their times and pondered the direction of Thai society.

By the time Boonlua's first novel, *Western Daughter-in-Law (Saphai maem)*, appeared in 1962, Buppha had not written anything for several years. She was obsessed by writing a novel that would reveal the full villainy of Field Marshal Phibun Songkhram. It was to be Buppha's masterpiece, but only a few notes and letters provide evidence of such a project. She occasionally wrote and published a short story, but by the late 1950s she was a sick, depressed, and remorseful woman who inspired sympathy and worry on the part of all who knew and cared for her. By 1960, Boonlua's old envy had been eclipsed by her compassion for the sister who was now only the sad shadow of a famous novelist.

Despite Buppha's poor health over many years, friends and family were shocked by her death in India in 1963. They were also shocked by Boonlua's reaction. She had always rather liked telling the story of her mother's death and the cremation ceremony, of how her father held her in his arms to observe her mother's body being consumed by flames. It was a shocking story, one that she insisted she only told to demonstrate her father's very good attitude toward the acceptance of death. But her response to her sister's death calls into question her later construction of that event, especially concerning the famous cremation.

Boonlua became highly agitated as she thought about her sister's cremation in India, obsessed with an image of Buppha exposed on an open funeral pyre beside the Ganges, a frightful and ugly scene—nothing like the actual, ordinary event that took place at a crematorium in New Delhi.[1] She had envied her sister for so many years and in so many ways. When they were girls, Boonlua recalled that "Buppha was always clean and tidy, and of course she was dressed beautifully. I thought she was the ultimate 'palace lady.' Her shining hair was combed meticulously, her face looked so smooth and soft, and she wore embroidered slippers." And then Buppha grew up, began to write, and soon rose to the top of the Thai literary tree, where she remained even after she no longer produced new novels and where she remains to this day.

Boonlua had resisted putting her own work before the public eye, certain that Buppha would read the inevitable remarks about her inability to live up to her sister as a writer. And now, she would never read them, and Boonlua would never see her again. How cruel a lesson it was for a woman who had spent a lifetime devoted to the central

Buddhist teaching that in our desires—and our resentments—lie the seeds of our inevitable suffering.

> "No one thought of my Aunt Boonlua as a writer," one of her great-nieces reflected. "It was my Aunt Buppha, Dokmai Sot, who was the writer, and Boonlua was the teacher of literature, the one who worked in the government and was on committees and traveled abroad."[2]

Although her great-niece was correct, decades after Boonlua's death the best of her novels are considered outstanding not only as works of Thai literature but also as social history. She would be enormously pleased at this, for she had hoped as much. She once remarked, "I don't know if I would call my novels *literature*—I just write down what I'm thinking about." This was a fair assessment. Fortunately, the things she thought about were thought-provoking and important. She believed that the most sensible and useful basis for developing Thai society was a synthesis of Buddhist and Western/Judaeo-Christian approaches to social justice. She believed in progressive, "Western" ideas such as universal education, a social safety net beyond the largesse of temple charity, and equal opportunity for people of all backgrounds and ethnic identities. She believed that such ideas were not in conflict with traditional Thai Buddhist ideals; on the contrary, they were in perfect alignment with them. This point of view permeates all of her fiction.

OVERVIEW OF THE NOVELS

A brief description of Boonlua's five novels, in the order of their publication, will elucidate some of her beliefs and concerns. This will be followed by a more thorough description of the two most important novels: *Thutiyawiset* (1968), which followed the lives of one Thai woman and her family and friends, from the overthrow of the absolute monarchy through the ensuing changes in governance and social organization; and *Land of Women (Suratnari,* 1972), a "Gulliver's Travels" kind of fantasy set in the future. To date, none of Boonlua's novels has ever been translated and published in English. All translations of excerpts that follow are my own, including those from *Thutiyawiset*.

Western Daughter-in-Law (*Saphai maem*, 1962)

The characters and the events in this novel of the years before and during World War II, which have been discussed in chapter 5, were largely based upon Boonlua's relatives and people she knew well, and most of the action takes place at a home reminiscent of her own family home, though far less exalted. Before World War II, a young man in the Kunchon family who had studied military science in Germany brought his German bride home to Wang Ban Mo. He was strongly pro-German, proud of his Nazi uniform, and often wore it to practice drill routines outside the compound, on Atsadang Road. In the novel, however, the fictional Western daughter-in-law is from England, reflecting the sympathies of Boonlua and nearly all members of her family.

Although the presenting subject of this novel is the difficulty of cross-cultural marriage, its chief focus is the Thai experience of World War II and the alliance with the Japanese. Boonlua took full advantage of the sanctuary traditionally accorded the storyteller in Thailand (and elsewhere in Southeast Asia) to reveal her thoughts about the strong official ties between Thailand and Japan during the late 1930s, a subject that was seldom talked or written about at the time she wrote the novel (or since), but Boonlua wrote frankly about the enthusiasm of Thai leaders for these strong ties—at least until the Japanese invaded in 1941. She also wrote about the Phibun Songkhram regime's campaign during the war years to interpret and refashion Thai culture, a campaign about which she knew a great deal for she had played an active role.

Boonlua used this opportunity to share her observations of family life in the West and to explain the difficult adjustments a Westerner marrying into a Thai family would have to make—or might be unable to make. As for the Thai family trying to adjust to a *maem* in its midst, she demonstrates how the desire to appear *siwilai* in the eyes of the young Western bride leads the family in the novel to do things they would never have done if the daughter-in-law were Thai. For example, after their friends warn them that a *maem* will never agree to live in the same house as her in-laws, they build a separate house for the young couple that they cannot really afford. Misunderstandings abound, just as they had in real life when the beautiful young German woman came to live at Wang Ban Mo. Kunchon family members told me that when the real *saphai maem*, the German bride, first came to Wang Ban Mo, she could be heard walking around upstairs while Boonlua's brother Phraya Thewet, now the family patriarch, was in the room directly beneath her. "We could hear her footsteps up there, her feet above his head, which Phraya Thewet and some other people in the family thought was terribly rude." In Thai culture, the head is sacred and the foot is base; one never points one's foot at another person and the foot of a junior person must never be higher than the head of a senior person.

The depiction of the Thai and foreign characters in this novel is remarkably even-handed. Boonlua presents them as equally eager to do and say the right thing, and equally likely to do and say just the opposite.

Thutiyawiset (1968)

This outstanding novel will be discussed in detail below. The title is the name of a decoration awarded to the wives of politically prominent men. *Thutiyawiset* was by far the most popular of Boonlua's novels and the most critically acclaimed. The main female character, Cha-on, is clearly based on Than Phuying La-iat, the wife of Field Marshal Phibun Songkhram, but the personalities of the fictional Cha-on and Than Phuying are very different. La-iat was prominently involved in the cultural and social initiatives of her husband's administration, while the fictional Cha-on is a modest and traditional wife who is concerned only with her home, husband, and children.

A Perilous Fall into Love (*Tok lum tok rong dai dai ko di*, 1969)

My translation of this title is necessarily descriptive, not literal; in Thai, the title is the first line of an old Thai saying composed in the form of poetry called *klong*. An approximate translation of the saying is, "You may fall ten times into a hole in the ground or between the planks of a footbridge and be unhurt; but fall into love only once and you may be stabbed to the heart and fatally wounded."

Apparently, parts of this novel were written much earlier, and it was completed and readied for serialization to take advantage of the success of *Thutiyawiset*. It is far less skillfully composed and more like a traditional Thai romance novel than any of her other works. A relatively poor young woman who is the distant relative and adopted daughter of a wealthy family falls in love with one of the sons in the family, thus providing all elements of the formulaic plots of 1920s and 1930s novels written by and for women. Ironically, Boonlua had excoriated such novels in one of her own public lectures.

> [Such novels] include a heroine with good social status—the daughter of a Phraya, for example—who falls in love with a poor young man. Her parents insist that she break if off and marry someone of whom they approve. The poor young man, devastated and despairing, escapes his misery by going off to work in a far province. Or it might be the other way around: the young man is the son of a Phraya, and falls in love with a poor (but always virtuous) girl, and they are separated by one circumstance or another. If it is the young man whose status is superior, the story ends happily. But if the young woman is in the socially superior position, the ending will be sad. The authors of these novels focused entirely on *romantic love*; we rarely learn anything about how Thais lived at the time the action supposedly takes place, such as the kind of food people eat, the clothing they wear . . . or what they have to pay for a pair of socks.[3]

Boonlua told friends that the plot was based on an incident that occurred in a distant branch of the Kunchon family, but it seems more likely that it was a composite of several incidents in her immediate family. It was not unusual in large, elite families for cousins and even half-siblings to become romantically involved. Like the Kunchon family itself, the novel has a huge cast of characters—a feature of her novels that irritated many readers. Perhaps the difficulty readers would have in keeping track of the dozens of cousins, aunts, great-uncles, and collateral relatives that populated her fiction simply did not occur to her; a family tree of the kind that preceded the text in some densely populated Victorian novels would have helped readers follow *A Perilous Fall* and some of her other novels, but she never included one.

Land of Women (*Suratnari*, 1972)

Suratnari, which is discussed in some detail below, is the name Boonlua invented for a utopian kingdom in which women rule and men's opportunities are limited. It is the novel about which readers and critics were most sharply divided and most frustrated. It has never been popular, but in recent years it has undergone a reevaluation, with literary scholars and others insisting that it was too far ahead of its time for most readers. In fact, they claim that it is one of the most important Thai novels of the twentieth century in its examination of the place of men and women in Thai society, the nature of ideal governance, and the problem of environmental degradation caused by industrial development—an unaccustomed subject for fiction in 1972.

Dr. Luk Thung (1973)

This is the story of a marriage between a young woman from an elite Bangkok family and a brilliant young economist from a middle-class rural background. A *luk thung* is literally a "child of the fields," and the popular music called "*dontri luk thung*" is Thai country music. When they meet in New Zealand, where both are working temporarily, Luk Kaeo has a university education but is working as a secretary to an older relative—typical for educated young ladies of the time; Krit has a PhD in economics from the United States and is doing research for the Thai government.

When I began reading the novel, I assumed that something of Boonlua's and Dr. Chom's at least superficially similar situation would be reflected in its plot. Boonlua was the child of a *chao phraya*, and Dr. Chom grew up beyond Bangkok and once had done public health research in New Zealand. The gap in their social origins is very similar to that of Luk Kaeo and Krit. However, these fictional characters are nothing like Boonlua and Dr. Chom, who were happily married by all accounts, motivated by the idea of service to the nation, and loyal to the civil service despite its problems—qualities that the fictional characters lack completely. Krit abandons his government position to make money in private industry, an idea that is encouraged by his mistress but deplored by Luk Kaeo, an old-fashioned idealist, who tells him:

> A debt like yours [his government scholarship] cannot be repaid by money! Where does this debt come from? From your relatives, your very own brothers and sisters, from the farmers who worked and [paid their taxes to] the government, to be given to people like you to go study abroad. They don't want the money back, Krit—they want the work you are now able to do in payment of that loan.[4]

The ideas are initially interesting, but the characters are simply vehicles for the author's opinions and the dialogue consists of an exchange of lectures. It may be that following her experience founding the Faculty of Arts at the new Silpakorn University campus at Nakhon Pathom, she wrote the novel as something of a personal exercise: the characters endlessly debate whether it is worthwhile to devote one's lives to public service even if one must suffer personally in order to do so, a subject that weighed heavily upon her at the time.

The remainder of this chapter will focus upon Boonlua's two outstanding novels, *Thutiyawiset* and *Land of Women*. Despite great differences, each clearly demonstrates the three characteristics of traditional Thai storytelling: they edify, they entertain, and they make use of the sanctuary of storytelling in order to reveal ideas, opinions, and feelings that would have been criticized if presented as anything but fiction.

THUTIYAWISET

Some years after the publication of this novel, Boonlua had said, "When I began writing this book, I thought that I would base my main character on Field Marshal Phibun." The fact is, such a novel had been the great dream of her sister. "But as I began to write, I realized that men with great power have no dimensions—they have only power. And for that reason, they are just not very interesting. I finally decided that I should write about his wife—because really, *she* was the interesting one."[5] Yet, once Boonlua began writing the novel in earnest, the real Than Phuying La-iat, an outgoing and tireless woman who was very active in her husband's administration, was set aside, and the very different character of Cha-on began to take shape.

Like many of her titles, *Thutiyawiset* is ironic and ambiguous. Boonlua loved irony and ambiguity, and she loved to play with the Thai language. The decoration, the *thutiyawiset*, is an honor. But when the words are separated, each is significant in its own way. *Thutiya* alone means "secondary," while *wiset* means "highly skilled/magical"; both are examples of elegant Thai speech (they are Sanskrit words), not ordinary language. Cha-on is always secondary (*thutiya*) to her husband in terms of education, worldly abilities, accomplishments, and power. Yet, as the story progresses, it becomes clear that if Withun's sharp intellect, social skills, and charisma carry him to power, Cha-on is a far more admirable and loveable person. She is "magical" (*wiset*) in her beauty, goodness, and kindness—a "magical" woman whom other women like, trust, and respect, and with whom men easily fall in love. Of course, their love is not reciprocated by the loyal wife.

There is still another layer of meaning in the title: the *thutiyawiset*, the decoration itself, is visible evidence of Cha-on's worldly success—although only as a reflection of the accomplishments of her husband—but it is, like all honors and awards, ephemeral and finally meaningless. It cannot protect Cha-on from the calamities of human life or from the essential truths of Buddhist teachings.

From the first page to the last, *Thutiyawiset* is suffused with Buddhist ideals and ideas. That which one loves and desires, whether the object of that attachment is another human being, material wealth, or political power, inevitably leads one to sorrow. True contentment can only be achieved when one learns to accept all of life's events, whether joyful or tragic, with equanimity. Contentment is a worthier goal than happiness, because "happiness" (*suk*) implies the fulfillment of some wish, or desire—the ironic and inevitable path to unhappiness (*thuk*). There is but one way to escape: through reflection upon the wisdom of the Buddha.

The Plot of *Thutiyawiset*

The novel begins during the early 1920s in a village in Phetchaburi province, where Boonlua and her family had lived in the years preceding the 1932 overthrow of the absolute monarchy. Cha-on, a good-hearted and intelligent young woman, is the daughter of the head of a famous troupe of musicians. No great occasion in the province can commence until the sounds of their instruments begin to fill the air. Her mother is happy as a traditional wife and mother and can imagine no other life for her daughter. There are two other children in the family: a son, Choe, and another daughter, Cha-em. Cha-on is Boonlua's ideal of the true "*phu di*," literally "the good human being," aside from considerations of social class. As her life unfolds, she also will come to represent most people's idea of a *phu di*—a member of the elite—by virtue of her husband's success.

Cha-on is the favorite student of Protestant American women who teach at the nearby missionary school. Why would Boonlua choose to put her character in such a school? Than Phuying La-iat Phibun Songkhram was teaching at a missionary school when she met her husband, albeit in Phitsanulok, not in Phetchaburi. This may suggest that

Boonlua originally meant her character's personality and achievements to follow those of Than Phuying La-iat more closely than they did, as the writing went on and the character of Cha-on began to speak for herself.

Women are a great influence in the young Cha-on's life, although she does not take their advice. One of them is Khun Kamyan, an aristocratic neighbor who had been the consort of a king in her youth. Khun Kamyan's three nieces—Khun Taeo, Khun Paeo, and Khun Chaeo— are Cha-on's best friends. When Cha-on is about to graduate from the missionary school, her teachers ask her to stay on and teach there. But Khun Kamyan has another idea; she wants Cha-on to go to university in Bangkok and offers to provide financial support. Her parents are not pleased. They see no reason why their daughter should not teach at the local school and continue to live at home until her inevitable marriage to a suitable man. Despite their respect for Khun Kamyan, they cannot imagine sending a daughter off to Bangkok. The debate over Cha-on's future is underway when Withun comes into her life.

Withun is one of two young army officers who appear at Cha-on's home late one afternoon, asking to see her father about hiring his troupe of musicians for an official reception. He comes from a modest background. The other young officer, his military academy friend Kroen, comes from an old, aristocratic family, and he is related to Cha-on's mentor, Khun Kamyan.

Cha-on, who had returned home from school just before their arrival, has changed into a *phasin*, a length of cloth that can be worn as a skirt or pulled up and knotted above the breasts as a bathing garment. She is splashing about in the pond beside the house when she and Withun first see each other.[6]

Cha-on swam back and forth, pretending not to notice two young men in uniform. But soon, one of them walked to the edge of the pond, and spoke in a loud voice. "Is this the house of Muen Chamnan?" [Cha-on's father]

Cha-on had to raise her head, look up and meet his eyes, and at that moment she felt as though lightning had touched her, and she shuddered from the top of her head to her toes.

> The gaze of the young man who stood at the edge of the pond was
> sharp, but also sweet. He seemed to be looking directly into her heart.
> He was graceful, and his uniform fitted him smoothly. Even after he
> had asked his question, his eyes stayed fastened to hers.[7]

Withun proposes marriage not long after their first meeting, and
the infatuated Cha-on promptly abandons the idea of furthering her
education. Her parents are delighted and relieved, and her only regret
is that she must disappoint Khun Kamyan. She goes off to Bangkok to
buy her wedding trousseau and stays with her friend Khun Chaeo, who
is studying at a college there. Cha-on is startled to find that her friend's
life is quite appealing—Khun Chaeo is shockingly independent, making
her own decisions about everything. This, then, is the life Cha-on had
so easily rejected! But the feeling fades as she thinks about her wedding.
While she is in Bangkok, Withun visits her family and their friends in
Phetchaburi, and meets Khun Chaeo's brother, Khun On. The two men
are nearly the same age, but they stand on opposite sides of a great social
divide: Withun is an alarmingly ambitious commoner, a *phrai,* as Khun
Chaeo's well-born brother realizes the moment he meets Withun's frankly
appraising glance. They immediately dislike and distrust one another.

The military traditionally has been an institution through which Thai
men from humble backgrounds can move up in society, and Withun
is the ultimate example of that path to social prominence.[8] He has set
aside his deep-seated resentment of the "old *phu di*" to cultivate Kroen,
the friend who accompanies him to Cha-on's family home on the day
they meet. He does so mindfully because Kroen reads English, so he
has a grasp of politics and history that Withun lacks, and he is willing to
help Withun acquire these things. Unlike Khun Chaeo's brother Khun
On, the easy-going Kroen is not offended by Withun and even agrees
to help him win Cha-on's hand by interceding on his behalf with her
family and with Khun Kamyan.

Withun and Cha-on marry and embark upon the peripatetic life
of a military family. She devotes herself to raising their children, and
gradually the ties to her old friends weaken. Withun joins the Promoters
in 1932, takes an active part in the overthrow of the absolute monarchy,

and swiftly rises to a position of power. Later, he makes a great deal of money by investing in the black market during World War II.[9] Cha-on grows curious about her husband's career and also his investments, and she is interested in the political changes he has helped to bring about. But when she attempts to discuss these things with him, he reacts with anger, warning her that men go to other women when they become tired of talkative and inquisitive wives; henceforth, Cha-on keeps her questions to herself.

While posted near the Burmese border, Withun meets and falls in love with a beautiful, British-educated Burmese princess, Chao Kong Fa. (The term "Chao" identifies her as a princess; her name is "Kong Fa.") Withun is fascinated by and impressed with the opinions of this woman who is his social superior—and better educated. When she wants to discuss politics and other "intellectual" matters with him, he is flattered and gladly agrees. When Cha-on learns about the affair and makes discreet inquiries about Chao Kong Fa, she bitterly reflects that her husband's lover has certain qualities she had chosen not to develop in herself—beginning with her decision to turn down a university education in order to become his wife and the mother of his children.

Withun's friend Kroen and Cha-on's friend Khun Chaeo are briefly engaged during their twenties, and they remain friends after the engagement is canceled, for reasons that are revealed near the novel's end. He marries a woman who will have no role in this story and who dies young, leaving Kroen with two children.

Kroen becomes a general, like Withun, but unlike Withun he never achieves (or wishes for) a position of great power. Khun Chaeo, after finishing her education, works for a while as a teacher in the provinces and then opens a successful restaurant in Bangkok. Sometime during the late 1930s, she tells Cha-on that her father had strongly supported her own university education.

> "Father said that with the change of government [i.e., the overthrow of the absolute monarchy], women had better learn to do something by which they could support themselves. We can never know what the future will be like. . . . As for me, now that they have

committed *demok-krasi-krasoe*,[10] I suppose that I could work for the government—I could be a civil servant—although I used to say that I would starve to death before I would go to work for [this] government, after the way they treated civil servants from the former regime. It was terrible!"[11]

After another coup d'état, Withun is promoted to the position of deputy prime minister and Cha-on's life changes dramatically.[12] It is when her husband attains this high office that she receives the *thutiyawiset* decoration, and the topsy-turvy nature of post-1932 Thai society is made glaring when Khun Chaeo, with royal ancestors, is hired to cater the reception that follows the award ceremony. She stays discreetly in the background and Cha-on must seek her out. Even more puzzling, Cha-on's own brother, Choe, who is now a doctor, also keeps his distance from her. Dr. Choe is a political liberal who had wanted to see democracy in Thailand—but not, he emphasizes, the "guided" democracy that Withun and his friends had created. The people she most loves seem to have disappeared from her life—and when she does see them, they behave strangely.

In mid-life, Cha-on takes stock of her life. She loves her children and she loves her husband despite his infidelity. She is wealthy and socially prominent. In fact, she has everything that she was brought up to think any woman could expect (fidelity was not a realistic expectation), but the truth is that she is sad and lonely.

As they grow older, the friendship between General Kroen and Khun Chaeo becomes closer, and one day he comes to her in great distress seeking her advice upon a very serious matter. Some of Withun's political enemies have asked him to assassinate his old friend. Kroen has long been disappointed in Withun and disapproves of him in many ways, but he is horrified at their request. Never would he commit such an act or be a party to it.

There can be little doubt that this scene, an invitation to an assassination, and Kroen and Khun Chaeo's reaction to it, reflect the Kunchon family's own view of violent recriminations against those who had trespassed against the extended family of the monarchy. Although some family members were involved in the Boworadet Rebellion in 1933, most took the *phu di* high road, turning the other Buddhist cheek to those whom they felt had harmed them.

At the height of her husband's power, Cha-on is unhappy and confused, and then her life is overturned altogether. Alone in the residence one night, she hears noises downstairs. She descends the stairs quietly in the dark, and hears Withun talking with a woman. She stands motionless behind a door, listening to their easy conversation and laughter. She is devastated as she hears Chao Kong Fa comment admiringly on the way the residence was furnished, as if Withun had been the decorator. If the long-ago afternoon at the pond at her father's home had been the high point of her life, this moment is the low point: Withun respects her so little that he has brought his mistress into their home, assuming that Cha-on is asleep above them. After a while, Withun and the woman leave together.

Cha-on returns to her bedroom but cannot sleep. Soon, she again hears noises downstairs. She hears her eldest son outside the front door of the residence arguing with someone whose voice she recognizes— it is the husband of a woman with whom he has been having an affair. She hears a gunshot and runs down the stairs to find that the man has shot and killed her son. A house guard then rushes forward with his gun drawn and kills her son's murderer.

Withun does not return until daybreak. When Cha-on sees the look of fear and grief on his face, she assumes that it is because of their son's murder, but she is wrong. He tells her that he must flee the country at once, because a plot he had engineered to seize power from the prime minister (of which she had known nothing) has been discovered. Kroen, having learned that Withun was about to be arrested, had rushed to warn him and is now waiting in a boat on the bank of the Chao Phraya River to help him escape to Penang. He rushes off again, with scarcely a word about their son.

In one night, within a few hours, Cha-on has been crushed. Her beloved son is dead, her husband has fled after betraying his superior, and she has no one to turn to but her oldest friends. They no longer keep their distance, but come to her at once, eager to protect and defend her. A few days later, she receives a letter from Withun in which he tells her that she must raise money and send it to him. She should sell the antique necklace he gave her on the day she received the *thutiyawiset*. He tells her where to meet a rich buyer who has agreed to purchase it. She takes the necklace to the place Withun has described and finds herself face to face with Chao Kong Fa.

A few months later, Cha-on receives a telegram from Penang, from Kroen. Withun has been shot by an assassin. He is still alive but not expected to recover and she must come at once.[13] To her horror, she learns that the assassin was Khun On, her dear friend Khun Chaeo's brother, acting in retaliation for years of personal insults and for what he considers to be the much greater insult to the entire Thai nation: a false democracy, a dictatorship that Withun and his cronies created instead of the egalitarian society they had promised. Cha-on arrives at her husband's bedside shortly before his death. Her misery is perfected when, after Withun dies, Chao Kong Fa enters the room, rushes to the bedside, and sorrowfully kisses her dead lover good-bye.

Cha-on returns to Thailand and slowly rebuilds her life. Her friends help her gain access to Withun's remaining assets, and she will now be able to live a comfortable if not extravagant life. She is only thirty-eight years old, but both she and her friends consider her to be middle-aged—the generation of grandmothers. Kroen comes to visit, confesses that he has always loved her, and tells her how painful it has been for him to see Cha-on live through the consequences of her decision to marry Withun. It was for her sake alone that he had rescued the ambitious and selfish Withun and organized the flight to Penang. Cha-on thanks him, but tells him that there is no future in a relationship between them. Shortly thereafter, Kroen's son marries Cha-on's daughter, Cha-lo, so that even though Kroen and Cha-on will never marry, they will be members of one family as long as they live.

Some months after this meeting, Kroen asks Khun Chaeo to marry him—as he had done decades before. At the end of the novel, it seems likely that the marriage between them will take place at last. Cha-on finds refuge in her Buddhist faith, and finally is able to forgive both Withun and Chao Kong Fa. She realizes that all she has suffered is the result of her own desires, which she had either invited into her life or failed to resist. There was no other possible outcome for her. As the Buddha had taught:

> By oneself is evil done
> By oneself defiled
> By oneself it's left undone
> By self alone one is purified
> Purity, impurity on oneself depend
> No one can purify another.[14]

Female Characters in *Thutiyawiset*

Cha-on

Cha-on, "the girl in the pond," as her husband will always think of her, is the ideal traditional Thai heroine: small, pretty, gentle, and obedient. When she meets Withun, she is fully aware of the fact that immediately she is sexually attracted to him. In this respect, she is strikingly different from the heroines of earlier Thai fiction, who are obsessed only with the trappings of romance and marriage. While there are no sexually explicit scenes in *Thutiyawiset* or in any other mainstream Thai fiction until the 1990s, sexual fascination and its results are major elements in *Thutiyawiset*.[15]

> All her life, when anyone mentioned a chik tree [chik trees surrounded the pond]—if a foreigner, for example, asked her if chik trees grew in Thailand, while she was politely telling the person that chik trees did indeed grow here and describing their lovely flowers, she would begin to tremble, as she had trembled on that day so long ago. (17)

It is difficult to imagine one of Dokmai Sot's heroines trembling while describing a chik tree because of the power of erotic memories. It has often been asserted that Boonlua's fiction was all about the intellect while Dokmai Sot's novels were about human emotions; but it was Boonlua who described and explored women's emotions and gave younger women writers the courage to reveal female sexuality in stories about ordinary, respectable women.[16]

Khunying Vinita Diteeyont, (pen name V. Vinicchayakul), novelist and literature professor, writes:

> Women surely fell in love in all the old romances. Love and marriage were their goals, and they saved themselves for one man. But this love they felt was ideal, "love for the sake of love," and had nothing to do with sexual desire. Good women in hundreds after hundreds of novels never felt a scintilla of sexual desire. . . . At the very most, the woman would feel "impressed" (*prathapchai*) with the man's disposition and personality. And no "good" female character could be presented as a woman who was conscious of sexual desire; hundreds upon hundreds of these [bad] women all failed to find success in life. . . . for they had committed the monstrous sin of sexual desire.[17]

Khun Kamyan

This wise aristocratic woman teaches Cha-on many skills that are described as "the work of daughters" (*ngan luk phuying*), such as making delectable Thai sweets and arranging flowers. But she is fairly well educated herself, interested in many things beyond making sweets and arranging flowers, and she is disappointed when she fails to convince Cha-on to go on with her education. She is the aunt of Cha-on's great friend Khun Chaeo, and of her sisters Khun Taeo and Khun Paeo. They live and attend school in Bangkok but spend their holidays in Phetchaburi with their intelligent and loving aunt.

The character of Khun Kamyan is clearly based upon Queen Lakshmi, who was briefly married to King Vajiravudh (Rama VI); the marriage was annulled, and she retired to private life.[18] A friend of Boonlua, Queen Lakshmi was an authority on classical dance drama and was sometimes invited to speak to Boonlua's literature classes. On at least one occasion, she loaned costumes from her own collection to be worn in a student theatrical production.

Taeo, Paeo, and Chaeo: Three Sisters Who Seem Familiar

Boonlua clearly enjoyed drawing the characters of Cha-on's three best childhood friends. The oldest of the three sisters, Khun Taeo, is quiet and efficient; the middle sister, Khun Paeo, is a good storyteller; and Khun Chaeo, the youngest and Cha-on's best friend, is smart, amusing, and outspoken, qualities that earn her the reputation of being "too much like a boy." Anyone who knew Boonlua's family saw at once that Khun Taeo was an affectionate representation of her quiet and efficient older sister Chalaem, who never married yet became the matriarch of the family; Khun Paeo, the good storyteller, was Buppha; and Khun Chaeo was Boonlua herself, outspoken and competent and therefore "like a boy." One of the interesting revelations in *Thutiyawiset* is the rare glimpse it provides into the life of the Kunchon family.

> Khun Taeo, the eldest sister [Chalaem], was not much of a talker. She would sit and attend to whatever task she had begun for a very long time, uttering no more than two or three sentences to anyone. She was good-hearted, loving, and helpful, everyone's "little servant," and never spoke crossly. Khun Paeo [Buppha] was the prettiest; she was also the most observant of the three and she told the best stories. Khun Chaeo [Boonlua] was pretty in Cha-on's eyes, but if Cha-on ever said so, everyone would disagree—and then add, "But—she is so amusing!" Khun Kamyan's maid, Pa Jan, once said that Khun Chaeo was too badly behaved to be beautiful. "So naughty. . . . How can she be pretty?" (30)

Upper-class women who were familiar with Wang Ban Mo and the ladies who resided there loved the "in joke" of the sisters Taeo, Paeo and Chaeo. It is interesting that this detail is almost always ignored in essays on Boonlua's writing, not to mention the fact that the story is based upon the lives of Field Marshal Phibun Songkhram and Than Phuying La-iat, a fact of which no Thai reader could be unaware. Instead, the focus is invariably the believability and the attractiveness of her characters, and how her female characters reflect the problems and dilemmas faced by women in modern Thai society *in general*, but never in particular.

What a writer could say in fiction might not be acceptable in an essay, journal article, or lecture.

Khun Chaeo

Khun Chaeo, Cha-on's best friend, is the strongest female character in the novel and the character through whom the author tends to speak. Like Boonlua, she is an educated woman from a royally connected family who chooses to work for a living. She is down to earth, straightforward, independent, and has the courage to do things that society doesn't expect women to do. She represents what I think of as the "authentic non-ideal Thai woman" in Thai fiction, a character that is always popular with readers.

When her family experiences financial problems following her father's death, Khun Chaeo goes to work as a teacher in the provinces. She then returns to Bangkok to become a businesswoman, opening a successful restaurant and hiring the old family retainers who have fallen upon hard times since 1932. She considers herself to be an accurate observer of the old and the young, the rich and the poor, the traditional and the new elites, because her life experiences, like Boonlua's, have placed her in close proximity to people at many social levels. Boonlua often remarked that she had been "the only woman to come 'out of our house,'" which was not a figure of speech but a factual statement. Even Buppha, who became a famous writer, never left home until she married. This is exactly what both Boonlua and Khun Chaeo did: leave the family home to participate in the life of the society at large and make contributions to it.

The reader learns, late in the novel, that the reason Khun Chaeo had ended her engagement to Kroen when she was a young woman was that although she loved him, she knew that he did not really love her and suspected that he was in love with someone else whom he could not marry. Her pride had prevented her from entering marriage as a second-choice bride. When she discovers, years later, that it was Cha-on whom Kroen really loved, the news is hurtful, but she does not let it affect her relationship with either friend. A surprise at the novel's end is Kroen's second proposal to Khun Chaeo. He tells her that she has been the truest friend of his life. He loves and respects her more than he can say. Khun

Chaeo decides that their lifelong friendship and the proven character and decency of this man, are a better predictor of a good marriage than the romantic feelings she had hoped he would feel for her when she was young. The reader should note two things about Kroen and Chaeo: first, by the time they decide to marry, their own generation are nearly all grandparents looking back at lives full of turbulent events and trying times; second, they are only about forty years old.

Chao Kong Fa

The Burmese princess with a British education may be Cha-on's nemesis, but she is not a villainess. In the scene at Withun's deathbed, Chao Kong Fa is revealed as just another human being whose desires have led to suffering. She is the bearer of several of Boonlua's messages about male-female relations in Thai society. She fascinates Withun because she is, intellectually, always ahead of him. Also, she is a princess, far above him in Southeast Asian society. He is amazed and flattered that she has fallen in love with him and will do anything to impress her. When she tells him that she despises rich men who have many young lovers, because *any* rich man can have all the young lovers he wants, Withun gives up his other mistresses. But in the end, despite her beauty, education, and high social status, that is all she can ever be to him—a mistress, a "minor wife."

When Kroen meets Chao Kong Fa in Penang after Withun has been shot (it is the first time he has met her, although she has been Withun's mistress for years), he thinks to himself that she is not as beautiful as Cha-on, but she is a woman whom no man could look at without interest. Chao Kong Fa does not see Withun in the final moments of his life; that is Cha-on's sole right, as Kroen explains to her. They are seated in the parlor of the residence.

> "When [Withun] came to Penang, it was you he sent for, not his major wife. She felt very wronged by that, you know."
>
> "Yes, but what are the rights of a minor wife? When the man is with her, hidden away, he does not call his major wife to announce their whereabouts. But when he knows he is going to die, his first wife is

the one he wants at his bedside—he wants to be with her, he wants to die with his major wife and his children around him."

Kroen looked into her eyes and saw the tears well up and spill down her cheeks. He looked away, feeling so exceedingly weary with the world that he had to close his eyes and rest his head against the back of the chair. (678–79)

In some ways, Chao Kong Fa's situation is more pitiable than Cha-on's. This resolutely modern woman nostalgically recalls an aspect of traditional polygamy that now seems compassionate by comparison with her experience at Withun's deathbed. "In my father's day," she tells Kroen bitterly, "when a man lay dying, all his wives and children surrounded him together."

With official monogamy (Phibun's own decree for the modern era, if not his practice), only a man's official wife had the right to this final intimacy. For Chao Kong Fa, in some ways the most "modern" woman in the book, her experience of Withun's death is—as written by Boonlua—ironic and ambiguous.

Male Characters in *Thutiyawiset*

Withun
Field Marshal Phibun Songkhram, the model for this character, was not only ambitious but idealistic. Many Thais, especially those who were high-born, despised his plans for a modern Thailand that he and his colleagues believed could and should replace the old Siam. Boonlua remarked that "men who have power have no dimensions," and she gave few if any dimensions to the character of Withun. Buppha had longed to write a novel that would show Phibun as a villain; but Boonlua decided on a more disingenuous tactic: she wrote a character who was ambitious and attractive, but finally rather ordinary.

Although he envies and despises members of the old aristocracy, Withun cultivates Kroen as a friend because he is willing to share so many things that Withun lacks.[19] He is attracted to Cha-on because she is beautiful and will be an asset to him in this regard—a successful man must have a beautiful wife—and because she is docile and will follow and obey him. Several years after their marriage, when she wants to share other aspects of his life besides their children and home, he is annoyed.

Withun's failures all are the result of his own desires and attachments—to his career, to power, to the possession of beautiful and interesting women, and to the admiration of others. He gains them all, he loses them all, and then he dies, far from home.

Although the two real individuals who inspired Boonlua to write *Thutiyawiset* were Field Marshal Phibun Songkhram and Than Phuying La-iat, the fictional characters themselves are very unlike their historical predecessors. It is not a biography masquerading as a novel, but a novel about two people who represent the love of power and the power of love.

Kroen

Kroen is Boonlua's ideal Thai man: well-born, well educated, intelligent, not as attractive as Withun, but honorable, understanding, and kind. Boonlua often criticized other writers, including her sister Buppha, for creating male characters who were too good to be true. But there is something different about Kroen, compared to other "ideal men" in Thai literature: his most important character traits have their foundation in Buddhist practice. Kroen passes the ultimate (Buddhist) test of character by loving Cha-on without having to possess her.

It is Kroen who shows Cha-on at the end of the story how pointless it is for her to blame anyone for her unhappiness. He helps her to become a better Buddhist, to forgive Withun and Chao Kong Fa, and to find contentment. Kroen is not a romantically ideal hero; he is a Buddhist spiritual hero.

Decorations

In the first few pages of the novel, Chao-on is sitting at her dressing table preparing herself for the great event at which the *thutiyawiset* will be affixed to the shoulder of her beautiful silk garment.

Soon, flashbacks will take the reader to the day Cha-on first met Withun. But at first, descriptions of jewelry and clothing dominate, as Cha-on dresses for the grand reception. This opening is bewildering until one understands why Boonlua had chosen to begin Cha-on's story with descriptions of jewelry and clothing. Traditionally, the richness and colors of the fabrics in which a Thai woman is able to dress her body as well as the quality of her jewelry have been considered integral components of her beauty rather than additions to it. The person, the body of Cha-on upon which necklaces, bracelets, earrings, and various other baubles are draped, clasped, wrapped, and pinned, seems to have no more life or importance than a mannequin.

The jewels signify everything that the world may know of a woman whose husband's career has carried her to the pinnacle of social prominence, while the tiny woman beneath the jewels (we are often reminded that she is tiny) remains known only to herself and to a small number of true friends from childhood.

At last sufficiently bedecked and bejeweled to go to the ball, Cha-on sits beside her husband in the back of the limousine. He stares out the window, but as the limo races through the dark streets of Bangkok, she stares at him. Throughout the novel, images of Withun's strikingly handsome face and strong male body, always as seen through Cha-on's eyes, convey the magnetic and impressive qualities of male power. Cha-on watches her husband with a brooding intensity. If the "male gaze" was a significant element in the never-to-be-forgotten meeting at the pond, in this novel Boonlua explores the female gaze, almost unknown in Thai fiction up to that time:

> She watched Withun. He had turned away from her and was looking out the window. . . . She marveled at how graceful his body remained. She could not resist a feeling of pride in that body. More than a few foreigners had said, "Among all the Thai leaders, there is no one as elegant or as charming as General Withun." Some of them had said that to her! And age had only improved his looks. His hair remained black, and although he was nearly fifty, things that made other men

show their age seemed not to affect him at all. The years became him; he grew wiser, his mind was quicker than ever, he was more shrewd in his understanding of people.

Cha-on continued to look at her husband with pride. The image of a handsome man of middle age faded, and the image of the young officer he had been twenty years before replaced it. She remembered that first moment . . . the moment that, for her, would never fade. (8–9)

Relatives and friends also notice how the couple see each other.

Soon after Cha-on and Withun had left the residence on that evening, her sister Cha-em had turned to her husband and asked, "Did you see the way he looked at her?" He replied, with scarcely disguised contempt, "Cha-em, he was not looking at her—he was looking at the jewels he had bought her." (45)

Something else is reflected in this scene and other scenes in which Cha-on ponders her feelings for her husband. General Withun was nothing at all like Boonlua's own husband, Dr. Chom. But if General Withun was well-served by advancing years, the real Dr. Chom was also. Pictures of him taken at the time of his marriage to Boonlua show a dapper, handsome, athletic man with a charming smile. Boonlua may have been ill or recuperating much of the time, but Dr. Chom, the picture of good health, never missed his daily tennis game. If he brought many things into Boonlua's life, one of the most important was vitality, along with a cheerful sensuality. Women liked Dr. Chom, he liked them, and he adored Boonlua. She liked manly men, and for all of her sincere promotion of women's rights, she admired male strength and male power. The fact that she married near the age of fifty and had a strong and "unfeminine" personality tended to make people think of her as capable only of a platonic and intellectual relationship with a man, but that was not so.

The Uses—and the Limits—of Power

Two of the important subjects in *Thutiyawiset* are the acquisition and uses of power in Thai society, and the function of the class system before and after the great events of 1932. Although the character of Khun Chaeo typically speaks for Boonlua, in some scenes she sounds even more like Boonlua's sister Buppha, who was unrelenting and vocal in her contempt for the new power elite. Here, Khun Chaeo gives her opinion of changes in manners since the overthrow of the absolute monarchy.

> "I think it is very funny that I always used to hate seeing the old royal civil servants lined up sitting on the floor or crouching on the stairs. We would invite them to sit on chairs, but they would always refuse. And have things really changed? When you go to an official reception, you see people almost crawling toward the new leaders, just as they used to crawl toward the princes. But today, it is all so embarrassing because people don't know if what they are doing is right, or wrong. I say, Thailand today is the land of the embarrassed!" (216)

Withun may seize power and exercise it, but he lacks many things that traditionally signaled a position of power. For example, when Khun Chaeo is called upon to cater the reception on the night Cha-on receives the decoration, she is assisted by a retinue of servants whose families have been attached to her family for generations. Such accoutrements of power cannot be bought or ordered into existence; Withun has subordinates, but he does not have a "retinue" of this kind and he never will. He may be able to buy his wife antique jewelry but when she wears it in public, those who know where it came from, who know who had to sell it to remain solvent, exchange contemptuous glances.

Boonlua makes extensive use of language in exploring issues of power and class. A range of pronouns are used in Thai speech, depending upon the social levels of the people who are conversing. When Cha-on and Withun rise in society, some of their old friends find it difficult to talk to them. Khun Taeo, for example, the oldest of the three sisters who are so like Chalaem, Buppha, and Boonlua, finds it difficult to talk to

Cha-on in her new status because Cha-on used to be in the lower social position and now it is unclear how she should be addressed by an old friend—a friend of the old, "real," upper class.

> "When I talk to her, I feel so awkward. I always called her simply 'Cha-on,' because she was younger. Shall I now call her '*than*' [a respectful second-person pronoun]? Perhaps that would please her— but perhaps it would not please her at all. I don't know, so *perhaps it is best to keep my distance*." (419)

There is a great deal of unapologetic, cheerful snobbery in *Thutiyawiset*. By the time she began writing it, Boonlua had worked with the post-1932 power elite for nearly forty years. In her memoir, *Successes and Failures*, she had reflected ruefully that, "as the daughter of a *chao phraya*," she did not have to work in this ungrateful bureaucracy at all and was only doing so out of a sense of duty. But in *Thutiyawiset*, protected by the sanction accorded to fiction, it appears that Boonlua could let Khun Chaeo say a few things that she herself had wanted to say for a long, long time.

When Cha-on's second child has just been born, she receives a letter from Khun Chaeo mentioning the difficulties some of her relatives have faced since the "change in the form of government"—as it is invariably called. Khun Chaeo's own father, in despair at what he perceives to be unforgivable insults to the monarchy, not to mention the end of his way of life, has become an alcoholic. Cha-on remembers him fondly and deeply pities him, but is happy when the letter ends on a cheerful note. Khun Chaeo's language shows that she does not share her sister's discomfort at the reversal of their situations.

> . . . Know that Auntie Chaeo sends a kiss to Cha-lo [Cha-on's daughter]. And I do not know what your new little fellow's face looks like, but I know that when I see it I will want to kiss it, so I send a kiss to him also. I miss you, I miss you, I miss you . . . You are probably thinking, 'Chaeo is mad!' Are you not thinking that, Cha-on?
>
> Missing you again,
Chaeo (197)

Cha-on reads the letter over and over, weeping first because she feels sorry for Khun Chaeo's family, and then weeping again with laughter at her friend's last, endearing words. Withun comes into the room and sees her at her dressing table, smiling and crying. While she washes her face, combs her hair, and regains her composure, he reads Khun Chaeo's letter. He is annoyed.

"Cha-on, you mustn't believe everything these aristocrats say."

"Aristocrats? Who do you mean?"

"Your Khun Chaeo and Khun Taeo! They are the old aristocracy. You ought to read some history."

"And if I do believe what they say, Khun Withun, what will happen?"

Withun held her face in his hands and kissed her cheek. "My darling little wife. Well now, let me think what will happen if you believe them. To begin with, you will be as unhappy as they are. These days, you see, it is their turn to suffer, and it is owing to their own insatiable greed. . . . Their ancestors lived very comfortably—far too comfortably. . . ." (198)

The foregoing passage is a good example of the limitations of translation. In the English translation, the information conveyed at the surface of this exchange illustrates Withun's attitude toward Cha-on's elite friends. But it is through sheer *language*, in the original Thai, that Boonlua makes a strongly critical statement about the traditional relationship between the husband and wife. Withun is a new leader, a Promoter of the new regime; he casually advises his wife to read history. Yet, his words and his attitude in this conversation are shown to be startlingly old-fashioned. He speaks to her as if she were a child, and she accepts this, looking to her *phi* (a term that means "elder brother" but is also commonly used by wives speaking to their husbands) for wisdom, guidance, and explanations of the world about her.

In contrast, the conversations between the upper-class Khun Chaeo and General Kroen tell the reader immediately, through the language with which they address each other, that they see each other as equals. At the end of the novel, when Khun Chaeo accepts his proposal of marriage, the reader knows that they will never have the kind of "man and girl" relationship Cha-on and Withun had for twenty years. Withun may speak for modernization and progress and a new way of life, but he conducts his own family life as his great-grandfather might have, while Khun Chaeo and General Kroen, who represent the old order, have by far the more "modern" relationship. In fact, their relationship is very like that of Boonlua and Dr. Chom: an equitable partnership between educated equals.[20]

LAND OF WOMEN

Boonlua began writing *Land of Women*, her utopian fantasy about a land in which women govern and are superior to men in all things, in March 1971, seven months after her official retirement from government service, while on a driving trip through southern Thailand. Once she had begun writing, she scarcely left her typewriter, writing the last of its 812 pages only three months later, on June 9, 1971, at her home in Thonburi.[21] It was a phenomenal achievement and a completely bewildering one to nearly everyone who read it. Between June and December of that year, the novel was published in installments in *Satri san,* a popular and respected woman's magazine that published women's writing for decades. The general reaction to it may be summed up in the reaction of Neon Snidwongse, emeritus professor of history at Chulalongkorn, University, who knew Boonlua well, was a good friend, and would have liked to have had something more positive to say: "I didn't understand it at all. I didn't know what she meant by it, or what she was trying to do."[22] This reaction was echoed by many of Boonlua's colleagues and friends, but the popular reaction was much worse. Readers found it baffling, incomprehensible, and, worst of all, boring.

For years, she had told friends that one day she might write a Thai novel modeled on *Gulliver's Travels*, which she had enjoyed reading as a girl at the convent school in Penang. However, what finally moved her to begin work on *Land of Women* was an episode that occurred in the life of one of her friends, a young female English professor whom

Boonlua mentored and liked very much. It was an unusual although not unheard-of event: the young professor's husband, an executive in a large corporation, had arrived home from work one evening and announced that he was never going to go back. He said that that afternoon he had realized, while sitting at his desk, that he did not like working. He would rather stay home with the children and occupy himself with his numerous hobbies and interests. The wife, who enjoyed her academic career, was surprised but agreed to his decision. Fortunately the family would be able to live without the husband's income; henceforth, he stayed at home, while his wife continued to teach, write, and travel to conferences all over the world. This couple's decision made a great impression on Boonlua, and at last she brought her imagination to bear on the subject of what Thai society might be like if all the husbands stayed at home with the children while the wives took charge of supporting families and running the nation. After that, *Gulliver's Travels* was forgotten.

Boonlua began her utopian novel with two complementary objectives: first, she would tell an entertaining and unmistakably Southeast Asian story in which shipwrecked men find themselves in a strange and exotic kingdom. Second, the novel would be edifying: readers would learn how Thai society could be improved, building on the strengths of the Siamese past combined with the best of modern ideas on such matters as gender equality and wise use of technology. She was less than successful with the first objective; hardly anyone was entertained by *Land of Women*. It was, however, definitely edifying, and it was revealing: in its 841 pages, Boonlua revealed a lifetime of reflections on relationships between Thai men and women, as well as her deepest fears and highest hopes for her nation, which at that time was closely allied with US objectives in mainland Southeast Asia, including a devastating war, and enmeshed in a domestic project of economic development that she was finding ever less attractive and more worrisome.

The very title of the novel irked readers before they ever began to read it. It is difficult to translate *surat*. It is usually translated as "state/land" although there is no such Thai word as *surat* meaning land as Boonlua spelled it. As she spelled it, the term means supreme happiness, and there is no question that Boonlua fully intended the ambiguity. The word *nari* is an elegant term for "a lady of moral excellence." Both *surat* and *nari* are of Sanskrit origin. It was the kind of word play she loved, and it is easy to imagine her happily toiling over her typewriter (often, in the back seat of the car while Dr. Chom drove her to a meeting or to visit a friend), enjoying her word games. However, a reader without a very advanced education could not appreciate the games at all—a fact that was apparently of little interest to her. In keeping with its peculiar title, the novel was filled with many other Sanskrit terms—or, even worse, made-up, Sanskrit-suggested words. Most readers could not relate to the novel's language or to most of the characters, with the exception of the character of Luang Praphap, a kindly, wise, old Thai man who was reminiscent of the kindly, wise, old uncle in her novel *Western Daughter-in-Law*.

As Boonlua wrote *Land of Women*, her opinions and emotions flooded the manuscript, and I suspect that the final result, in terms of both length and content, exceeded her original intentions. In the year she began writing it, following the exhausting year at Silpakorn University in Nakhon Pathom, she was at last truly "retired," free to think and write as she pleased, sparing no individual and no institution. If, as some of her colleagues suggested, one of the important purposes of the memoir she would write two years later, in 1974, was "payback," explaining her side of the various conflicts in which she had become embroiled during her career, this novel also had its "payback" aspects. In *Land of Women*, capable women become ministers of state and rectors of universities—not just directors of units or founders of university faculties, as Boonlua had been. The women of Thai-Surat did not have to "assist and support." They were capable of leading, and so they were leaders.

The Plot of *Land of Women*

On a voyage from Sumatra, Indonesia, to Penang, Malaysia, a ship capsizes in a storm, and four male survivors in a lifeboat float to the shore of an unknown island. Two of the men are Thai (Luang Praphap, who is old, and Mick, who is young);[23] the third is American (Lambert) and the fourth is Chinese (Wan).

When two natives of the island appear on the beach, apparently on their way to a fishing expedition, Mick is confused by their appearance; he cannot tell if they are male or female because of their similar dress and grooming. He learns from them that slightly more than a century ago some Siamese people had migrated to this island and had mixed with the native islanders (vaguely identified as "Polynesians.") Although the title of the novel is *Suratnari*, within the novel the island is officially known as "Suwanratanathawip" (literally, "heavenly jewel continent"),[24] and referred to in conversation as "Thai-Surat" or just "Surat," to differentiate it from "Thai-Siam," the original home of its newer inhabitants, and the home of Mick and Luang Praphap. It was a culturally curious society, having retained its major social and religious traditions from the time before the mid-nineteenth century when the Siamese showed up: female supremacy and worship of the gods of rain and the ocean. To this, Buddhism and some features of Thai monarchy had been added.

At a welcoming dinner for the shipwrecked men, they meet a woman named Vishu, director of civil engineering, and Vishu's male wife, Sorawan,[25] who also is her cousin (marriage between first cousins is common in Thai-Surat as in Thai-Siam).[26] Mick is immediately attracted to the married Vishu, and she finds the stranger from Thai-Siam fascinating because he is so unlike the men of her own country, who are very easy to get along with, and very boring. But then, that is what one would expect of a wife.

Mick and Luang Praphap travel throughout Thai-Surat, marveling at the natural beauty and highly developed culture of the kingdom. At one point, Mick becomes the lover of Princess Napasmani,[27] a politically powerful woman who has a number of other male lovers as well as a male wife, Pintupawa. Even though Mick has an affair with the princess, he remains most attracted to Vishu, who is intelligent and virtuous, and who resists his advances not because she does not reciprocate his feelings but because, unlike Princess Napasmani, she chooses to be faithful to her spouse. All women in Thai-Surat, whether married or not, have the freedom to be sexually adventurous, but not all of them take advantage of this freedom.

At the end of the novel, the four men decide to make their way back to Thai-Siam. In the final pages, Mick tells the reader that four years have passed since his return from that strange island kingdom. He has married, fathered a son, and looks to the future with the determination to make the best of what is good in his life and to work for the betterment of his homeland.

For all of her support of wider opportunities and greater rights for women, Boonlua believed in the complementarity of male and female roles: she never suggested that this might be a better world without men. She did hold an essentialist view of male and female characteristics. The better examples of "civilized" women in her utopia employ their wisdom and social skills instead of using physical force. She also strongly supports the rights of mothers, asserting that women are by nature more loving and attentive toward their children. Men can be encouraged to develop these qualities but they do not come naturally. Nevertheless, in a truly "civilized" society, men and women would be equally concerned for their offspring.

> A society in which women love their children is no improvement over the society of forest creatures. [Only] a society in which men love their children as much as women do may be considered truly civilized.[28]

Female Characters in *Land of Women*

Vishu

This is the leading female character, a well-educated woman whose family represents "lesser royalty" in Thai-Surat. As a young woman, on the advice of relatives she had studied engineering instead of medicine, which had been her first choice. Vishu is quite like Boonlua, not only in terms of social class but by virtue of the fact that Boonlua always claimed to have majored in education on the advice of relatives, rather than becoming a writer, her first choice of a career—although just as often, she explained majoring in education on the basis of her sister Buppha's successful writing career and the desire to do something else. After studying "abroad" (no details provided), Vishu had returned to Thai-Surat and gone to work for the government, building rural roads so that national development would reach beyond the capital city—just as Boonlua had gone out to work in the provinces of Thailand with the education inspectors, so that rural educational standards might one day equal those in Bangkok. Like Boonlua, Vishu did not want to see her country change too rapidly in ways that would corrupt its spirit.

> I do not want anyone to say that we people of Surat are a nation that cannot strive and succeed as other nations do. We have customs that are unlike those of other nations. We do not need to be like nations that have more power, but whose people are not happier than ours. If we are diligent, we will study [and master] agriculture, and our nation will be happier than any other. We do not want power in the world. We do not want to be like other nations. What we want is contentment. (176)

Vishu does not love her male wife, Sorawan, in a romantic way, but in a way that involves feelings of protectiveness and responsibility for his welfare. Sorawan is soft, pliant, and rather weak. (Although the character of Vishu is like Boonlua, the character of Sorawan is clearly not based on Dr. Chom but—perhaps—on her young friend's husband who had decided to stay home instead of going to work every day.) Vishu encourages him to find things to do with his abundant spare time. After she urges him to run for the position of mayor of the capital city (a position to which few of the male wives aspire), he does so, but has no real enthusiasm for it. In fact, Vishu is very like the male heroes in the idealistic novels previously written by Boonlua, her sister Buppha, and many other Thai female (and some male) writers.[29] Free to have lovers and minor wives, the ideal husband/hero nevertheless chooses fidelity. This interpretation of "good male character" is clearly borrowed from the Western novels of the Victorian and Edwardian eras, because none of the Thai men of her father's generation, whom Boonlua greatly admired, had been monogamous.[30]

Princess Napasmani

The princess is a highly intelligent, dramatically beautiful woman, wealthier and more powerful than Vishu in Suratian political life. Always interested in attractive young men, she seduces Mick. Although he is easily seduced, he does not love her. When she discovers this fact, she is enraged, and Mick finds her anger frightening. Princess Napasmani's pleasant official male wife, Pintupawa, accepts his spouse's love affairs as the normal behavior of women, whom one cannot expect to be faithful, and he never complains.

Princess Napasmani's unsavory career and love life recall the adventures of any number of powerful Thai men whom Boonlua had known, worked with, and reported to during her years in government.

Male Characters in *Land of Women*

Mick

Mick, the narrator, is a young, often moody Thai man who is cynical but also idealistic. Infatuated with Vishu, at the end of the story he tries to convince her to go home to Thai-Siam with him. The one option that she might consider is for Mick to remain in Surat and become her minor (male) wife, but this he cannot bring himself to do. Vishu cannot understand why Mick will not even consider living "as normal men do." After all, if being her minor wife is the only way he can be with her, why would he not consider it?

Sorawan

Sorawan, the good (male) wife of Vishu, is a soft, dependent man who needs to be protected by his (female) husband in all ways. He is like both the ideal heroines of Thai fiction and some of the weaker men Boonlua had known all her life. When he realizes that Vishu and Mick are attracted to each other, he is heartbroken. He begins to follow Vishu everywhere and beg for more attention. In despair, he decides to be ordained as a Buddhist monk for a while, in order to separate himself from his painful existence. Oddly enough, although women control everything in Suratian society, the monkhood is only for men. Perhaps Boonlua felt that providing Surat with a female Sangha, a most volatile subject in Thailand, would push the sanctuary of storytelling beyond its limits. It is also possible that her devout traditional Thai Buddhism may have precluded the very idea.

Wacharen

Wacharen is the (male) wife of another influential, wise, powerful woman, Sumalaya. Their family is the political rival of Vishu's family, although both support the current government. His main interest is in forwarding the cause of the Surat Men's Association. Thus, he is the counterpart of a female leader of the nascent Thai feminist movement. He believes that all of the nation's problems are the result of the fact that women hold all of the power and all of the important positions. He finds a gemstone mine and tries to make a business of it, but he fails because he is not good enough at business—he is, after all, only a man and thus by nature not competent in such matters. All in all, this is not a character who is presented as interesting or treated with much respect. His appearance seems *pro forma*, as if a "men's movement" must somehow be worked in.

Luang Praphap

This wise, elderly Thai man is a very important character in the novel because he carries Boonlua's messages about social, economic, and environmental problems in contemporary Thailand, including threats to the natural environment from national development efforts. He earns respect from everyone because of his knowledge and his age. He chastises Mick for his "adulterous" relationship with Princess Napasmani—she is married, even if he is not. The Luang Praphap character may well have been modeled on Phya Anuman Rajadhon, the self-educated cultural historian who wrote widely on many Thai subjects during the first half of the twentieth century. Boonlua knew and admired him, and had taken classes with him at Chulalongkorn University when she was young.[31]

Pintupawa

This man is the (male) wife of Princess Napasmani. He is an intelligent, happy-go-lucky fellow, a nature lover who leads a happy and contented life, and ignores the extramarital affairs of his princess-husband. This character is quite like many of the women Boonlua had known all her life, women who had never expected to be the sole object of their husband's attention, were bothered very little or not at all by his inevitable infidelities, and not only found happiness in other areas of life but loved and tolerated their husbands in a simple and comfortable way. Although Boonlua knew that she could never live as they did, she apparently admired and perhaps envied these women. She thought and meditated a good deal on the Buddha's teaching that one ought to "find happiness in that which one has" (*mi khwam suk nai sing thi mi yu*), a goal that was inspiring in theory but so elusive in practice.

Gender, Sexuality, and Power in Thai-Surat and Thai-Siam

Throughout *Land of Women*, we see that most of the women in the country are dignified, responsible, and hard-working. Most of the men are weak and competent only in matters pertaining to the household.

The two most important aspects of female power in Thai-Surat are land ownership and exclusive access to high public office. The women get their own way not through force but through persuasion; this behavior is *not* the opposite of the behavior of women in Thailand but an extension and perfection of it. In general, the women of Thai-Surat possess the best qualities of Thai women and also of Thai men. If this sounds confusing, it is. On one occasion, Mick tries to describe the women of Thai-Siam to his friends in Thai-Surat, then wonders if he has got it right:

> "Our women in Thailand," I explained, "are quite as capable as men and have all the same rights. Yet, most are content to be what we call the 'hind legs of the elephant.'" But after I had said those words, I was not certain whether I had got that right, or not. . . . (77)

Thai-Surat women like Napasmani can have any man they want. Some prefer *farang* men, and they too are available. Lambert, Mick's American friend, remarks ruefully upon this situation.[32]

> "I asked them about night life . . . and do you know what they said? That Suratian women go out and find men to have sex with! I said, 'Well then, how do I find one to have sex with me?' They just laughed— and criticized the whole American nation for not understanding anything. They said that in Surat, men can't call women—we have to wait for them to call us. And then, the women ask, 'How much? What's your price?' This is rather bad, you know. Men here have so little money of their own that they are forced to 'ask a good price!' I met a very rich woman who favors *farang* men, but she laughed at me and said that I was too old to be attractive, and sent me off to find her a younger Thai man. And this rich woman had some very peculiar desires, I can tell you—we talked for a long time before I even understood what she was talking about!" Lambert shook his head dispiritedly. (95–96)

The men of Surat, economically disadvantaged and valued only as sexual partners or housekeepers, "have to ask a good price." But poor Lambert cannot even ask a good price because he is too old for the tastes of those like the rich woman with her (never described) "very peculiar desires." Rich married women of Surat who are old and unattractive, the visitors learn, do not go out to bars to find men. They depend upon their major male wife to provide them with younger and thus more attractive males.

Boonlua had strong feelings about male and female responsibility for children born out of wedlock (or, in the traditional Thai family, born to women whose sexual partner refused to recognize or support them or their child). All of the onus for such births fell on the woman, none on the man. The subject of abortion, generally taboo or treated vaguely in Thai fiction, was faced head-on in *Land of Women*. Vishu makes the following remarks, during a public address:

No woman of Surat has to find an evil doctor to take the infant from her belly and then go to die herself [of complications of the abortion] at a hospital. Or die without anyone ever knowing the truth of what happened. We give birth to all of our children, and we raise all of our children. (174–75)

For Thai women readers who admired *Land of Women*, this speech about abortion, which in Thailand was illegal, common, and dangerous, was the best thing in the novel. Both Wibha Kongkanan and Duangjai Chumphol quote it in its entirety in their essays on Boonlua's fiction, and offer the hope that Thai-Siam might follow the example of Thai-Surat in removing the stigma from pregnancy outside of marriage, thus saving women's lives.[33] The important issue for Thai women at the time the novel was written was not the legal right to terminate a pregnancy, but the right of a single woman to give birth to a child without being stigmatized or dying at the hand of an abortionist rather than risking her reputation, or her family's notions of honor.

In Thai-Surat, Boonlua reverses the roles of men and women— but she then disapproves of the women who take advantage of their freedom. Vishu is free to have lovers, but she does not do so because of her moral standards. Princess Napasmani takes full advantage of her right to have sex with any man who appeals to her—but she is not one of the "approved" characters. All in all, Boonlua extols sexual exclusivity in marriage on the grounds that it is morally correct—whether it is "natural" or not. She makes the point that it would be no improvement over Thai-Siamese society to simply reverse the custom, giving multiple sexual partners to females instead of to males.

Some of the marriage customs she invented for the citizens of Thai-Surat reflect Boonlua's own experiences. Advanced age is no barrier to marriage in Thai-Surat, nor is wealth or the lack of it. It matters not at all which spouse is older or younger, richer or poorer. When children are born, the child will take the surname of whichever parent is better known—which suggests that Boonlua had given some thought to how unfair it would have been, had she married Dr. Chom during her child-bearing years and not been allowed to pass on the Kunchon name.

Naturally, Suratian daughters were favored over sons, as illustrated in the following gleeful description of a typical Thai-Surat family on an outing, a complete reversal of typical family behavior in Thai-Siam.

> When the Suratians go out as a family, the woman leads. Her manner bespeaks her role as leader. One can see that she is clever and wise. . . . The sons are pushed back a bit, they walk behind, while the daughters stride forward to walk with the head of the family, where they belong. Some of these heads of families carry small children in their arms, but when they tire, they give them to the older boys to hold. (373)

Some of the men of Surat had been sent abroad to be educated, but when they returned their spouses regretted their lack of foresight, for the foreign-educated Suratian men tried to resist the authority of women, and sometimes even started unseemly arguments. Suratian women defused this situation by treating their behavior as a joke, just as men in Thai-Siam, Boonlua's readers well knew, joked about unseemly aspirations on the part of wives. Often, they were blamed on *"wimin lip,"* the Thai version of "women's lib(eration)," a term that was familiar the world over in 1972 when the novel was published. Japanese writers, too, were making fun of "umansu-ribu." The Suratian women had thought this problem through, and had come up with an innovative plan to deal with foreign-educated, disaffected men: they trained them to become environmentalists.

National Development and the American Connection

During the 1960s and 1970s in Thailand, the concept of "development," *kan phatthana*, was promoted as the golden key to the nation's future. Industrial development, rural development, educational development all were sacred goals.

An environmental movement was just beginning, as Thais noticed rivers becoming thick, black, and foul-smelling; air was befouled not only by the effluvia of industry but by a huge increase in the numbers of trucks, cars, and motorcycles on the roads. Fear about the declining quality of the environment was exemplified in a poignant 1970 essay entitled "The Chao Phrayaa River Is on the Verge of Dying," by M.R. Kukrit Pramoj, publisher of *Siam Rath* and that newspaper's most popular columnist.[34]

> It will not be long before [the Chao Phrayaa River] will surely breathe his last, and then begin to rot, stink, and become offensive. . . . If the Chao Phrayaa were a human being, he would be the longest serving *Chao Phrayaa* in the history of the royal service, and he would be the oldest witness to the chronicle of events that comprise the history of the Thai nation. . . . The Chao Phrayaa River has been in royal service since the reign of King Uthong [the founder of the Ayutthayan dynasty, in 1350]. . . . But the life of the Chao Phrayaa River is now coming to a close . . . because his children and grandchildren and their descendants have betrayed him. Not only do they refuse to take decent care of him. They even pour into him all kinds of deadly organisms and filth that make it impossible for him to maintain his life any longer.[35]

This essay is not written from the vantage point of "the people," looking up the economic ladder at capitalist perpetrators of pollution. For the most part, that aspect of the environmental movement in Thailand would develop later. Kukrit's essay is written from the vantage point of the old elite, looking down with contempt upon middle-class, capitalist despoilers of the Thai natural heritage (mainly Chinese or Western, though he does not explicitly say so), heedless of the cost to society at large or to the nation's future. Boonlua's view of the destruction of the environment, which she sees as one of the bitter fruits of national development, represents the same elite perspective. In addition, she displays great concern over the growing materialism of Thai society and the obsessive Thai interest in how the nation is perceived by the powerful Western nations. How it may be perceived by other Asian nations is never addressed.

In *Land of Women*, Boonlua provides an answer to Thailand's contemporary problems that involves a return to vaguely described elements of a gracious past—enhanced by universal education, vaccines, and good rural highways; but it is not an entirely logical construct. In Thai-Surat, Vishu's major responsibility is the rural expansion of highways, a goal that would seem to contradict her support for old-fashioned methods of agriculture that do not produce very much, and also her contradictory support for an essentially "locavore" philosophy of subsistence on local products, to use the contemporary term. What, then, are these super highways for? Boonlua makes it plain that life in Thai-Siam was more pleasant in the agrarian past, but never considers how that past might have been experienced by the agrarian majority. The assumption is that rural people are by nature content with what they have and would wish for nothing more—if only they had more and better health care, and a guaranteed sixth-grade education.

Boonlua's ideas about an optimal program of economic development are expressed partly through Vishu, and partly through the elderly Thai shipwreck survivor, Luang Praphap. He expounds upon the old values of Thai-Siam and despairs of its present predicament during a conversation with Vishu and Mick.

> VISHU: "[What others may say about us in Thai-Surat] is never a reason to change anything in our own country. Whatever we do, we do because we consider it to be beneficial. As for what others may think, that is of no importance whatsoever."

> MICK: "You could never live in Siam . . . because the fear of being looked down on by foreign nations is the only motivation anyone has for changing anything." (190)

Luang Praphap is embarrassed by Mick's words, and hastens to tell Vishu that Mick is young and does not understand Thai-Siam as well as he thinks he does—in fact, he insists, Thais often have acted without regard to the possible reactions of foreigners.

> Khun Luang laughed to conceal his discomfiture at the bluntness of Mick's remarks and said, "Young men are like this, you see. But

truthfully we do a great many things [in Thai-Siam] without thinking of whether *farang*—or any other people—would do likewise." And then he led the conversation firmly into another direction, discussing the Thai belief in ghosts . . . and many other matters. (487)

Luang Praphap's most affecting speeches have to do with the nature of an optimal political and economic system for Thai-Siam. He is referred to in this passage as "Khun Luang," a polite form of reference.

"Allow me to contribute the opinion of an old man, if you will," Khun Luang said. "I say that our Asian nations are far too eager in grasping at foreign money with which to improve themselves. I admit that improvements are necessary. But knowing how to use that money— that is the important thing. Citizens ought to use things produced in their own country; and they ought to be thrifty, aware of the limits of what they have; and a nation's industries ought to produce things for their own people's convenience. And we ought not to encourage the sheer pursuit of *money*—wanting more, the more we have." (375)

Boonlua always returned to the importance of being content with what one has, being steadfast in the face of either triumph or calamity, of following the Middle Path in all things: these objectives of Buddhist practice represent the personal goals of Luang Praphap and of the author who created him.

A View of the Americans

The portrayal of the United States and of American people in *Suratnari* is generally ambivalent, sometimes frankly critical, and occasionally hilarious. Rather strangely, Thai-Surat has a sizeable expatriate community, just as Thai-Siam has. Mick admires some of the American men, but he does not much care for the American women he meets. Boonlua's many American friends might have been surprised to see how their countrymen are portrayed in this novel, had it been translated into English. Here, Mick encounters some American women at the swimming pool of a private club (very possibly, an institutional avatar of the Royal Bangkok Sports Club):

> I felt anxious around those American women and offended by their behavior. Their bold speech, the hard sound of their voices, their graceless manners. They did not carry themselves with the dignity of Suratian women, and they dressed with no idea of elegance—their clothes looked straight from a factory. Some [of them came toward us] from the swimming pool with wet hair, and water dripping down their cheeks. They held their bathing caps in one hand, and swung them in a vulgar way. (74)

One of Mick's ruminations upon the relationships between Thai-Surat, Britain, and the United States ends with this remarkable summation:

> The Americans helped the Suratians after the war. At first, the Suratians liked the Americans better than the other *farang*, who had subjugated people and created colonies. But when the Americans began to come as *advisors*, and to engage in trade, the Suratians realized that they were not as well-mannered as the British. . . . McMane [an American] [agreed] that the Americans might be a bit too straightforward, and lack subtlety, especially concerning the matter of [Suratian] men having fewer rights than the women. [The Americans] had boldly announced that the Suratian custom whereby men have fewer rights than women was "unnatural. " But in time, the Americans learned to behave with greater caution, and some of them came to quite like Surat . . . When Khun Luang and I arrived [on the island of] Surat, the Suratians still saw America as a nation in which the level of culture was not yet very high. (553)

Although it is never made sufficiently clear how the leaders of Surat make it all work, we are told that moral suasion and excellent behavior on the part of the educated female elite are the things that do make it work. The government of Thai-Surat operates very much like a successful convent school governed by competent nuns—wise women who always know what to do.

Land of Women ends with several questions for the reader, rather than with the neatly satisfying kind of ending Thai fiction readers were used to. Mick, back at home in Thailand, asks Luang Praphap, "What are we mortals to do in this confusing world?"

> [Luang Praphap] said that there is only one path for every human being, whether we are born during an era of good, or evil. Or whether our personal life flourishes, or we dwell in darkness. We must decide what is *good* in our life, what is *good* in our nation. And then try with all our might to promote that good. For one day, the good will flower, flourish, and spread. He told me that this is all we human beings can do. (804)

The Angle of Observation

During the turbulent 1970s, most young political activists, writers, and critics considered Boonlua to be a survivor of a bygone era. They respected her, and some who had been her students even loved her, but doubted that she could understand modern Thai society as they did. *Land of Women* made little or no impression on them; it seemed to be little more than a confusing, elitist literary riff. Besides, it was heavy going, with all the strange language.

Boonlua was at this time deeply concerned about aspects of national policy that she considered dangerous and shortsighted, such as the devastation of the nation's natural resources in the name of "development" (which was seen as a tangential issue, of little or no interest to political progressives), a concern that has proven to be justified. Her critics thought that she had lived too long to understand human beings as they had come to be; she believed that they had not lived long enough to understand that human beings were now as they had ever been and would remain.

In 1973, one year after the publication of *Land of Women*, Thailand would face its biggest political crisis since World War II. Seething discontent among university students and many other Thais that had been developing since the mid-1960s would suddenly explode. Widespread protests against the military dictatorship headed by Generals Thanom Kittikachorn and Praphat Charusathien would end in bloodshed and terror, and in October of 1973, the military government that had seemed invincible would fall overnight.

Boonlua would not be directly involved in these political events. But she would be active in the intellectual life of the nation during the 1970s, playing a role very like the role she had given to the character of Luang Praphap in *Land of Women*: a wise elder, attempting to impart hard-won wisdom to impatient youth.

9

ANOTHER KIND OF REVOLUTION

The 1970s in Thailand were filled with political strife and social turbulence. If it was a violent decade, it was also a decade of idealism and courage. A passionate political movement, initiated and led by university students, resulted in the fall of the military-dominated government in 1973. This unexpected and overwhelming event was followed by three years of open political participation and freedom of expression. But in 1976, the tide turned once again. On October 6, a combined force of police and right-wing militias killed and injured a great number of people. Many were jailed, or fled into exile, and power was once again in the hands of a repressive and authoritarian government.

Boonlua was deeply involved in the social discourse of the decade, largely because literature became a central issue in contentious ongoing public discussions. Although there was no doubt that her loyalties would always remain with the monarchy and the Thai cultural past, she was remarkably clever in assessing the cultural present, and in challenging ideologues on both the left and the right.

As the decade began, Boonlua had just retired and was looking forward to writing, teaching an occasional literature course, and frequently repairing to the chaise longue in her garden to read books and sip tea while her favorite dogs snoozed around her. She and Dr. Chom were proud of the house they had built on the Thonburi side of the Chao Phraya River and enjoyed welcoming their many relatives and friends.

HONORED BY HIS MAJESTY THE KING

Whatever might happen in the years to follow, for Boonlua the 1970s began wonderfully. On May 5, 1971, she was awarded the Chula Chom Klao medal for outstanding service to the nation by King Bhumibol Adulyadej, at Dusit Palace.[1] She recalled every small and homely detail of her preparation for this event in *Successes and Failures*, which generally is meager in terms of personal revelations.

> [Dr. Chom] and I drove to Ban Mo. My sister [Chalaem] was getting one of her own outfits ready for me to wear, and I had to try it on so that she could alter it. The blouse fit well enough but the *pha nueng* (silk traditional skirt) did not fit because my sister had become quite thin. She had to call her seamstress to make the waist bigger. I was very worried about the matter of shoes. I had no shoes I could wear with my sister's outfit. And I have rather odd feet and never can find shoes that fit properly. The next morning I took a pair of old shoes to my shoemaker, hoping that he could do something with them to make them go with the clothing. On the way, I saw some shoes made of a smooth golden leather that I thought would be perfect, but when I tried them on they were impossible. The man at the shoe store said that he thought his brother had a similar pair, at his own store nearby, and perhaps they would fit. He called him on the telephone, his brother sent a boy with the shoes, and they fit perfectly! But I did wonder how they would feel later, through all the standing and walking I would have to do.
>
> Besides the problem of shoes, I have a chronic ailment that requires me to eat very small amounts of food frequently, and the time at which I was scheduled to appear at the palace coincided with one of my mealtimes. Also, the doctor had advised me to go to the bathroom frequently, and I was rather at a loss as to how I should manage that.

On the day of the ceremony, we went to Dusit Palace. I was carrying my shoulder bag with my little flask [of water] in it, and one of my relatives hurried up to carry the bag for me, so that I wouldn't look untidy.[2] And, thanks to the grace of His Majesty the King, everything went perfectly. On that day, my ailing old body did not trouble me at all. Not even my knees hurt.

It was the best day of my life.[3]

BOONLUA BECOMES A LEGEND

Teaching literature and mentoring students continued to be rewarding. Upon a first meeting with the now legendary professor, most of the students were understandably intimidated—her eccentricities were famous—but they soon came to find her endearing, as in the recollection of Chitlada Suwattikul, her student in a 1971 course at Chulalongkorn University.

The first day of our class, while we were talking, all of a sudden the door opened and a lady in her early sixties slowly walked into the room. We stopped talking immediately, but we smiled at each other because, besides the thick scarf she wore around her neck, Achan Boonlua also wore a brown hat, the kind that beggars wear. She greeted us softly and asked us to set our chairs in a circle, and she began a discussion about what we had read for that first day. As that first class went on, we felt her personality. We looked at her unique clothing, and we were shocked that she smoked cigarettes while she was teaching. To this day, my friends and I who were in that class are impressed by the independence she showed as a professor. Later on, when I got my first job, she gave me good advice. She said, "Chitlada, remember that there will always be problems in any job. Make up your mind to minimize the big problems and to avoid making small problems into big ones."[4]

Chitlada could scarcely imagine the depth of experience upon which Achan Boonlua's cautions were based.

CHANGES IN THE NATIONAL POLITICAL SCRIPT

After the overthrow of the absolute monarchy in 1932 and despite several coups d'etat, each followed by a new constitution, the basic political script had stayed curiously the same. Political scientist Kamol Somvichien explains the socialization that made this script acceptable and enduring:

> Thais accept the fact that there are two categories of people: the powerful and the powerless, the important and the unimportant, the older and the younger. . . . The Thai social system has managed to survive by relying on this principle of inequality. Thais' deep understanding of the truth about power relationships and their lack of national ideology contribute to a flexible value system, features of which can easily be adapted to the changing environment and made relevant to where the power is located or who possesses it.[5]

This was precisely the point Boonlua had made when assessing public behavior during the Phibun administrations, during which she observed Thais behaving toward contemporary generals, field marshals, and far less exalted government officials with the same subservience and caution they once had shown toward people like her father, a *mom rachawong* and a *chao phraya* under the absolute monarchy.

Until the late 1960s, university students had been more concerned with university politics than with national politics. For example, during 1969 and 1970 Chulalongkorn University students reacted with outrage to the under-the-table sale of university land for the development of a new shopping center with handsome rewards for facilitators at the university. At the same time, Thammasat University students organized a referendum to promote their own choice for a new rector: the incorruptible Dr. Puey Ungphakorn, dean of the Faculty of Economics and also governor of the Bank of Thailand.[6] The students were successful in both cases, as well as stunned and hardly able to believe in these testaments to their own influence. From these local beginnings, a national student movement rapidly gathered momentum, at first in Bangkok and finally nationwide. The government paid little attention to this trend because it was expected that university students, who were considered by their elders to be children in most respects, were naturally idealistic and might even behave rashly on occasion. Inevitably, they would mature and get over it. The events of the following three years would prove that this belief was no longer valid.

In 1968, a constitution had finally been promulgated, after more than a decade of delay and unapologetic stalling. But in 1971, the military summarily abrogated the constitution and dissolved the legislature in the interests of "law and order," outraging the students and many other citizens. Still, there were no widespread, overt protests. It was what political scientist Prudhisan Jambala called a period of searching

> ... for identity, purpose, and strategy.... The NSCT [National Student Center of Thailand] pursued fairly traditional activities such as fund-raising for flood victims and organizing television programmes saluting the King. Analyses in internal *ad hoc* publications and such liberal intellectual journals as *Sangkomsart Paritat (Social Science Review)* covered a number of topics.... includ[ing] ... bureaucratic domination of the polity, the undesirability of military dictatorship, the unjust nature of Thailand's economic and legal systems, the domination of the Third World by the United States, genocide in Indo-China, and the obtrusive American presence in Thailand.[7]

In hindsight, it may seem odd that such publications did not alarm the conservative, military-dominated government. But Thai university students had never before organized themselves to demand significant political change and no one expected them to do so now. In any case, very few men in high positions in the military or the civilian bureaucracy were reading the *Social Science Review*, or even wasting the time of junior staff members to do so.

THE RISE OF THE *SAM THORARAT*, THE THREE TYRANTS

By 1971, another military figure had become prominent besides Field Marshal Thanom Kittikachorn, the prime minister, and Field Marshal Praphat Charusathien, the deputy prime minister. This was PM Thanom's son, Colonel Narong Kittikachorn, who was married to Praphat's daughter. Narong became the head of the Committee to Suppress Elements Detrimental to Society and, in the eyes of the students, he was more despicable than either his father or his father-in-law. His attitude toward the university students was one of simple contempt; they were beneath his notice. In the students' eyes, these three men were a triune symbol of all that was worst in contemporary Thai society. Political scientists David L. Morell and Chai-anan Samudavanija, in *Political Conflict in Thailand: Reform, Reaction, Revolution*, describe the great popularity of a satirical folk song of 1972, "My Father Is Not the Prime Minister" (*Pho phi mai dai pen nayok*), sung by a humble country boy with no prospects of riches or power through family connections:[8]

> My father is not the prime minister
> the inheritance I got is
> all gone
> the old 57,000 baht I used to have . . .
> all gone
> I hoped to go back home, to marry you, but that plan
> is stopped, postponed, no date set, and your love is
> all gone too.
> My father is not the prime minister,
> and so my heart must break.
> The fortune teller says my future is beautiful
> next year I'll be a millionaire
> but you still flee from me because
> my father is not the prime minister . . .
> he still works at the district office
> and my older uncle at the municipal office
> and my younger uncle is a big volunteer at the temple

and my sister is a sixth-grade bureaucrat
but you aren't glad to see me anymore . . .[9]

This song represented one classic Thai response to the realities of the social system: if you can't do anything else about it, you can make fun of it.

In 1972, for the first time in memory with the exception of the war years, people in Bangkok stood in queues to buy rice and Japanese goods were pushing native products out of the marketplace. The NSCT, under the leadership of Thammasat University engineering student Thirayut Boonmee, called for a boycott of Japanese goods. It was a very shrewd move. Instead of attacking their own government, the students garnered public support with their demonstration of patriotism and nationalist fervor, invading popular Bangkok shopping centers and pleading with shoppers to buy Thai goods, not Japanese.[10] In September 1973, they demanded a new constitution, and their effrontery was ignored. On October 6, a group of thirteen students and professors distributed leaflets near the Democracy Monument in downtown Bangkok. This time, the protestors were not ignored; they were arrested by the police, who promptly announced that they had uncovered a communist plot to overthrow the administration. But the public, skeptical after decades of hearing vague charges of communist ties or intentions leveled against any and all pro-democracy, pro-civil rights, anti-dictatorship, and anti-military activists, were scornful of the charges.

On October 13, 1973, four hundred thousand Thai citizens, not only university students but thousands of disaffected Thais of all ages and backgrounds, filled the area around Thammasat University, and together they marched to the Democracy Monument carrying flags and pictures of the king and queen.[11]

SIP-SI TULA: OCTOBER 14, 1973

The next day, October 14, riot police attacked the unarmed demonstrators, and before the day was over approximately one hundred people had been killed and many hundreds injured. One unforgettable image of that day was an open truck that moved slowly down the center of Ratchadamnoen Avenue carrying Buddhist monks who stood serenely and silently in the back of the truck, a profound symbol of nonviolent protest. They formed a sacred wall between demonstrators and police, who dared not fire. Another unforgettable image was Colonel Narong Kittikachorn in a helicopter firing down on the demonstrators.

Prime Minister Thanom finally had no choice but to resign as prime minister, but he retained the position of supreme commander of the armed forces. He announced that insurgents and terrorists had infiltrated the demonstrations necessitating an all-out attack, a statement that further inflamed the populace. He was quickly losing support among the military, and General Krit Sivara, commander in chief of the army, publicly disassociated himself from Thanom, Praphat, and Narong.

King Bhumibol intervened, ordering "the three tyrants" (*sam thorarat*), as the students had named them, to leave the country. Soon after, he appointed Sanya Thammasak as prime minister, a highly-respected and apolitical judge who also was a member of the Privy Council, the king's supreme advisory group. This appointment was acceptable to all factions. General Krit remained the highest-ranking military officer in the kingdom.

The students emerged from "*Sip-si tula*"—October 14—in a state of shock and bewilderment. Had they really brought down the government? And now, what would they do? For Thais who experienced the drama, tragedy, and ultimate triumph of those days, the words *Sip-si tula* would forever symbolize the realization of the victory of right against incalculable odds. No one could question that their planning, determination, and bravery had disgraced the three tyrants and brought down their government.

In the wake of *Sip-si tula*, politically liberal and progressive Thais believed that they had changed their nation forever and that henceforth "the people" would determine their own future. Many of them were enthusiastic about socialism and communism but not particularly knowledgeable about the details of these ideologies, much less the results of their implementation in other countries. They translated the works of Che Guevara and other famous political radicals into Thai and revived out-of-print works by Thai political dissidents of the 1950s, such as Chit Phumisak, a radical progressive scholar and political activist who was assassinated in 1965.[12] They were willing and eager to carry their politics and their philosophy to their brothers and sisters in poor rural areas, ready to abandon their university careers (and the plans their middle-class families had for them) to work toward the higher purpose of a radically and permanently reformed polity. On the level of popular culture, they wrote anti-establishment folk songs and impassioned political poetry and short stories, danced to the Doors and the Rolling Stones, grew their hair long and dressed in modified versions of Western hippie garb. This is not to imply that they were not serious about their beliefs, for they were deadly earnest, courageous, and willing to take great personal risks. However, it would not be long before their appearance, their pronouncements, and their behavior would begin to work against them with the majority of Thais, to whom a dignified, mature, and "successful" appearance was reassuring and appealing. On many levels and in many ways, the new progressives, whether they were students or not, did not seem like real leaders or even like people who could become real leaders in ten or fifteen years.

The students had gained the power to effect social change but they failed to consider two critical factors: first, the effects of radical politics in action—including incessant demonstrations and strikes—on their overall support by a public that equated public order with national security and also with personal safety; and second, the fact that General Krit Sivara was quietly and steadily reorganizing the military power base with his supporters in key positions.

POST-VICTORY REALITIES

In retrospect, it is clear that after October 1973 General Krit and his faction, not the students, held the real power. On the surface, the NSCT appeared to be in control, for most of their demands were being met by the civilian government of the appointed prime minister, Sanya

Thammasak. General Krit and his followers were happy to let the NSCT go on attacking the three tyrants and their remaining supporters in absentia, and calling hundreds of strikes, while strategic positions in the armed forces and the police department were methodically and quietly being filled with military personnel who were acceptable to students and the general public.[13]

For three years, the NSCT organized and operated a nationwide Democracy Propagation Program suggested by Prime Minister Sanya, who believed that a major cause of the failure of democracy in Thailand to date had been lack of political education. General Krit and his military colleagues had their own reasons for officially supporting this program: it sent hundreds, and finally thousands, of student activists into rural areas around the nation—and out of the streets of Bangkok. Initially, some three hundred students were trained to take the message of democracy and the rights and responsibilities of all citizens to remote rural areas and to a few urban slums.

Thai author Sri Daoruang described her first encounter with her husband, editor and writer Suchat Sawatsri, when he was a recently graduated propagator of democracy on a visit to the factory in which she then worked. If anyone truly represented "the people," it was Sri Daoruang, who had grown up very poor on the edge of the impoverished Northeast, in Phitsanulok. From her early teens, she worked at many humble jobs. She was a household servant in Bangkok and toiled in a glass factory that would become famous as the result of her prize-winning short story, "One Drop of Glass."

> In those days [1973–76], professors [this appellation could be extended to anyone who had earned an M.A. or even a B.A.] and journalists went around to the factories, teaching workers. They would ask if you liked to read, and if you said you did, they would give you books. When Khun Suchat talked, he talked—you know—like a person who reads books, not like ordinary people talk. But he sat right down on the cement floor with everybody. I thought he was strange.[14]

In 1974, an additional three thousand activists were trained. Some of the students did remarkable work but most of them had never been outside of Bangkok, except for family vacations to the mountains or the seashore—no one would choose to visit the frequently drought-savaged rice-farming villages of the Northeast—and they understood virtually nothing about rural life or rural people. Most of the villagers, on the other hand, could make little of the students' earnest ramblings on the subjects of power to the people, the Indochina War, the CIA, the KGB, and a host of other issues that were of immense importance to the students and of no interest to farmers. Despite all, for the first time in these urban university students' lives they saw what life was like for the majority of Thai citizens, and a remarkable farmers' movement began to take shape, in great measure the result of the students' sincere efforts. Tragically, some who worked the hardest in this movement, themselves farmers and their supporters, would be killed during 1975 and 1976 by official and vigilante assassins.[15]

AUGUST 1974: A MOMENTOUS DEBATE

After October 1973, university students and younger faculty members who were so inclined were free to devote their energies to attacking the canon of classical Thai literature as a feudal tool—a means of keeping the populace drugged with the jasmine-scented opiate of tales about royalty and celestial beings. In August 1974, Boonlua was invited to participate in a debate entitled, "Traditional Literature and Contemporary Social Values," moderated by Professor Direk Kulasirisawat. The other participants were the activist, writer, and editor Suchat Sawatsri and Cholthira (Satyawadhna) Kladyu, a young lecturer in Thai literature at Chulalongkorn University who had recently caused a storm with her psychoanalytical analysis of the beloved epic poem, *Khun Chang Khun Phaen*. She also had questioned the motives behind the composition of the *Traiphum Phra Ruang*, a cosmological text from the Sukhothai period that had long been revered as the first work of Thai literature. Her research occasioned considerable disapproval and bitterness from older professors and many other educated people. For Thais, the old works of literature, whether religious texts like *Traiphum Phra Ruang* or dance dramas such as the *Ramakian*, always had been appreciated as *sing saksit*, "sacred/holy things," and were to be approached only with humility and all due respect. That a young junior professor should have the impertinence to think of questioning, evaluating, or criticizing these works was unthinkable. The fierce debate over the political and social character of the *Traiphum Phra Ruang* is described in a 1995 essay by Soren Ivarsson.[16]

> Following the [political] upheaval in 1973, Thailand experienced a turbulent period in which the radical literature of the [twentieth century, recent] past was "rediscovered" and new analyses of Thailand's history and classical literature were initiated.[17] The heretofore unquestioned trinity nation-king-religion was subject to critical studies in which the nationalistic and royalist mythology was challenged. In that context Traiphum Phra Ruang played a special role because of the justification of royal power and social injustice in this text.[18]

The decision on the part of the debate organizers to invite the conservative *mom luang*, Professor Boonlua, descendant of King Phra Phuttaloetla, to debate Cholthira, leading denouncer of classical Thai literature, and Suchat, leading political radical, may seem strange. Perhaps they were hoping for fireworks; and if that was the case, they were not disappointed—although the fireworks they got were probably not the fireworks they expected. The transcript that survives this debate includes Direk's introduction and some of Boonlua's remarks. Direk's cautious and convoluted introduction to the debate demonstrates a strongly traditional determination not to offend anyone whom one ought not to offend.

> By former/old literature [*wannakam doem*], we shall mean prose or poetry that has been extolled as excellent and is therefore considered to be "literature" [*wannakhadi*]. The term *doem* [former or original] is very difficult to define, but we may say that at any rate it pre-dates the change in the form of government in 1932. As for the term "values" [*kha niyom*] in contemporary society, in general we are referring to

the feelings and opinions [*khwam rusuek nuek-khit*] of people [i.e., the social and political activists, students, and others] in the contemporary era toward this *wannakhadi* of a former time, and the extent to which they either agree or disagree with it. We have raised this issue for discussion because literature, like art, is characterized by the good and the bad, the beautiful and the obscene. We have the art of the palace [*rachasamnak*], of the bourgeoisie [*kadumphi*], and of the masses [*muanchon*]. By the same token, we have a literature of the palace and the aristocracy [*klum sakdina*], of the capitalists [*nai thun*], and a literature of—or for—the people [both "masses" and "people" are identified here but not distinguished]. But when we use the phrase "of the people, for the people," we must ask to what degree this is or has been so, when it has occurred, in which era, and so forth—but in any event, the important matter which we are here to consider is whether the literature of the past was composed in order to drug the masses [*mom mao prachachon*], as in the term "opiate of the masses," and prevent free thought; or whether this literature had a [positive] part in the building of the Thai nation. . . .

Our situation today is so different from how it was prior to 1932 that if the people who were alive then could be here, they would scarcely be able to believe how far we have come. We have confusing and chaotic events in our nation all the time: strikes, drought, floods, polluted waters, polluted air, fraud, and farmers protesting the conditions of their lives to their representatives in Parliament. We could never have imagined or dreamed all the events that have occurred. . . .

[Some say that] the literature of an era that extolled one class while condemning or vilifying or hurting another should no longer be taught, or it should be taught on a selective basis. It is also said that the traditional Thai literature is irrelevant to the people because it is filled with old vocabulary that is understood today by hardly anyone [i.e., it is understood only by people of the elite/educated class] and it is not written in the language of the people. This is an argument that we have seen recently advanced in China, where people have asserted, for example, that Confucianism does not fit the civilization or the culture [*watthanatham*] newly created by the Chinese people.[19]

There is an important linguistic aspect of this debate that is apparent in the last line of the quotation above. Direk, in his reference to the Chinese Cultural Revolution, has at his disposal only the word coined by Prince Wan Waithayakon during the first Phibun Songkhram government, to convey the Western concept of "culture": *watthanatham*. It is ironic that throughout the debate, the participants—whatever their political stance—have no choice but to communicate their ideas through relatively new words devised during the twentieth century by members of the Thai elite, using Sanskrit for the purpose of expressing Western concepts in Thai. It is a circumstance that curiously undermines the role of "the people" [*prachachon*], very few of whom would be able to participate in such debates—and therefore must rely upon university students and their professors to speak for them.

Professor Direk goes on, clearly distressed at the prospect that all of the "former" Thai literature might be considered inappropriate to the demands of the current era, and finally becoming impassioned in defense of the literature he has studied, taught, and loved all his life.

> Those of us who are scholars of literature or simply concerned about classical Thai literature wish to ask, can it be true that this literature is harmful? And if so, to what extent? Is it all evil, this literature of ours? What are the good elements in it? And then there is the question, is not our literature the very outline of our Thai culture? Is not our literature the repository of our finest language [*khrueang klan-kron kan chai phasa thai,* literally, "a sieve for language use,"]? . . . It is said [now, by some] that in the old literature women are there only as sexual beings, as commodities [*phuea kamarom thang nan pen sinkha thang nan*], wives by the hundreds and ten thousands and hundred thousands. Does this old literature fail to praise women entirely? Does it tell of no brave deeds by women?[20]

The next passage of the transcript belongs to Boonlua, and here we see the depth of her understanding of the Thai educational system, her frustration over the way Thai literature had generally been taught, and her astute perceptions of contemporary Thai society. If the young activists had expected to vanquish the old guard in the person of Professor Boonlua, they soon realized that this was not going to happen and that perhaps they were rather out of their depth. She had not been speaking for two minutes before the room had erupted in laughter, which continued throughout her remarks.

> Honored guests, were I to speak concerning all of the subjects that Khun Direk has suggested, I fear that you would never be able to go home. . . . I might begin with the fragment that has to do with the issue of what ought to be taught. Recently I went to a meeting of students, some of whom asked me why we ought to study literature at all. "My friends and I read *Khun Chang Khun Phaen*," one young man said. . . . "We got one point for remembering that Khun Chang was bald and one point for remembering that Khun Phaen was handsome." Well, I say, if that's the way literature is being taught, we may as well get rid of it altogether. And I quite agree with Khun Suchat about the teaching of the *Ramakian* as a story about angels [*thewada*] and giants [*yak*], with the angels fighting on the side of righteousness, the giants on the side of evil. My students generally prefer the giants. And when I ask them to choose their favorite hero on the side of righteousness, they don't want any of them. They claim that the god Siva just likes people to flatter him and gives away magical powers recklessly. . . . As for Prince Rama, oh dear, he can't seem to do anything right, can he? I am quite amazed at Khun Suchat's contention that the *Ramakian* extols the ruling class. In fact, the ruling class is good for nothing at all in the *Ramakian*. . . . Prince Rama himself is consumed with jealousy and has a shocking inferiority complex. [*khihueng . . . pom doi thi sut loei*]. . . . As for the ruling class as portrayed in *Khun Chang Khun Phaen*, can anyone who reads it say that it shows *good* rule? I say, we're awfully lucky not to have such a king ourselves!
>
> Then, there is the matter of *how* we teach literature. Of course, no matter how we teach it, if we're going to do away with the "old" literature, unfortunately we will have to throw out Nai Angkhan Kalyanapongse along with it, for no one will understand him.[21]. . . If we would have literature valued, probably we ought not to teach

it in school at all, since most of the teachers ruin it completely. For example, consider the poem *Lilit Phra Lo*.[22] It is about the loss of what is beautiful and cherished, about loss that is unexpected and total. A beloved son is taken from his family in a moment. . . . a beloved king is taken from his people. Loss is a natural component of life and it is the essence of this poem. . . . *Lilit Phra Lo* is taught in the schools. But what sort of questions are on the tests? "Are the main female characters virtuous or not?" Utterly beside the point! Feminine virtue is beside the point! The beauty of this poem and feminine virtue have nothing to do with each other. We all like jasmine garlands and we all like grilled fish on rice. But when you put the one next to the other, the flower garland is ruined by the smell of the fish, and the taste of the fish is ruined by the smell of the flowers. Allow me to say something about *values*. I am quite confused by the use of the word *values* [*kha niyom*], these days. For example, some people will tell you that Khun Suchat obviously has new values because he has a beard and a mustache, but beards and mustaches are not *values*—they are *fashions*. Values and fashions . . . not at all the same thing. Young men must dress in a certain way today if they wish to be "*the*" [rhymes with the English word *day*].[23] . . . But I do not see any new *values* in this era. I see only old values in a new society. And what is this new society? Look at it—unstable, lacking law and discipline, toppling as if it were riddled with termites. I do not know what we are to do. What are our values now? Alienation, anxiety, and desolation. [*khwam wawe wawun klumchai*].

I would also like to talk about this term *sakdina*, which everyone is talking about all the time.[24] Those things that cause us anxiety today are not caused by *sakdina*, which has not existed for a very long time. Anyway, if anyone is going to complain about *sakdina*, it had better be the women, because all the Thai men were granted *sakdina* and the women never got any![25]

One (unidentified) member of the audience, also a literature professor, comments on the poor teaching of literature, agreeing with Boonlua and suggesting that one of the works under discussion should be taught to students not only in terms of characters and plot, but in terms of its message about the uses of power in society. Boonlua agrees, now unmistakably speaking from the perspective of her age, stage, and class.

> One thing that we Thai do not understand at all is how to contest power. . . . We praise people who have been able to amass power and hold onto it. But power is not a good thing *for ordinary people*. Buddhism teaches us that power ruins the man who has not the intellect to make use of it. We have talked earlier about the teaching of literature. In the *Ramakian*, Siva has power but not always the wisdom to use it properly. Nonthok cajoles him, whines to have a magic finger, and Siva foolishly grants the request, which leads to mischief.[26] Why don't we use this story to teach students about the *responsibility* that ought to accompany power? I have not seen anyone teaching that.
>
> Now, this would be a truly new value for Thai society, don't you think? The *responsible* use of power! And that ought to include students. Students in groups have power. People who write pamphlets have power. And they should use it responsibly. I don't see anyone teaching this, either.
>
> You see, if you want to have democracy, you must have self-control. And if you want to engender new values in a democratic society, you must have discipline.[27]

Boonlua was completely familiar and comfortable with examples of human virtue, folly, and hubris in the classics of Thai literature. For half a century the Thai education system had provided all citizens with fragments of classical literature that had been misrepresented and censored, taught to students only after they had been scoured for traces of bawdiness or eroticism—a scouring that Boonlua despised. Weak, inept rulers were never taught as weak or inept. Very few people had ever thought about the management and censorship of their national literature unless they had been students of Professor Boonlua. Everyone in the audience for this debate would understand allusions such as the story of Siva granting the magic finger to Nonthok and the evil that ensued. He was a small-minded and stupid creature, and giving power to such a creature did no one any good. Let the audience interpret that allusion as they would, or could.

How did the younger radical members of the audience interpret the performance of this elderly, very sharp, and surprisingly hilarious woman? According to one literature professor,

> I believe that they saw Boonlua as a *sakdina seri niyom*, which is to say, a "liberal aristocrat." They never saw her as their enemy. She thought that they knew far too little about their own culture and about the realities of Thai society, and that was their most serious failing. After the terrible events of 1976 she said to me, "If only poor Anut had come to me. [Anut Aphapirom, a radical journalist who fled into exile in 1976.] We should have talked. He would have understood Thai society better." That assumption may not reflect Anut's probable reactions to advice from Boonlua, but she felt sincerely sorry about what happened to Anut and to some of the others who went to the jungle or to prison. And Anut himself later told me, "Our intentions exceeded our knowledge [*rao mi khwam wang di koen kwa khwam rap ru*]." Boonlua was actually quite understanding [of the radical activists]. She was not a "rightist," but she said from the beginning that she *knew* the leaders [of the student movement] were communists. We laughed at her when she said that in 1973, but later on some of the people she had told me were communists confessed to me that yes, they *had* been members of the communist party at the time she said they were. I was so surprised. It was the *pattern* that she had noticed, you see—the *pattern* of their behavior, not just their words, that had made her quite sure they were communists.[28]

Boonlua disagreed with people on the left, but also with people on the right, about politics and about literature during and after the three years of open political activity. Many people of her class blamed Chit Phumisak, who had been assassinated a decade before, insisting that he had made radicals of Thai youth through his Marxist writings, but Boonlua would have none of that, as she made plain in a 1977 interview.

Students became left-wing radicals not because of Chit Phumisak but because of conditions in the nation. We had not had a constitution for over ten years. And young people saw a lot of bad behavior on the part of leaders. It is natural for young men and women to be idealistic, and when they come across ideas that feed their idealism, they adopt them. Social egalitarianism, disregard for rank and privilege, paying attention to the multitudes, whom they call the masses—these are all ideals that are very attractive to the young. The left offered them such ideals. They didn't become leftists and activists because of anything they read by Chit Phumisak or anyone else but *because of what they saw with their own eyes.*[29]

By the time this was written in 1977, everyone was asking the question: what, exactly, had motivated the students and other leftists whose actions led to the collapse of an entrenched government in 1973—and more interesting, why had they failed?

OCTOBER 1976: DEFEAT, DESPAIR, AND DEATH

In March of 1976, the NSCT staged a massive anti-American rally on Ratchadamnoen Avenue in downtown Bangkok, with an "Anti-US Imperialists Exhibition" at Thammasat University that extended to the nearby National Museum and the National Theater. The mood in the country, and especially in Bangkok, was markedly different from the mood of October 1973. Most people could understand workers uniting to demand fair treatment, but they were tired of constant, annoying, disruptive strikes, some of them over seemingly trivial issues. They were not interested in the Anti-US Imperialists Exhibition. By now, several right-wing militias had gained large followings, both in Bangkok and in the provinces.[30]

Three of these organizations were most prominent. The first, the Red Gaurs, was comprised mainly of urban vocational students who supported and worked with university students in 1973 but soon came to resent them, and the fabric of the movement quickly frayed along class lines. The second, Nawaphon, was a privately funded, middle-class movement centered in the provincial bureaucracy and business community. The third was the Village Scouts, formed by a police colonel in the Northeast. It was comprised of young rural members, funded by the Border Patrol Police; it also received royal patronage and interest.[31]

Members of the Red Gaurs threw a grenade and two plastic bombs into the Thammasat University crowd attending the Anti-US Imperialists Exhibition in March. No police action was taken against them. On the contrary, the sight of Red Gaurs and other vigilantes being transported from place to place by police vehicles, and armed with police weapons, was becoming commonplace.

A song composed by an army officer was played daily on some radio stations throughout 1975 and 1976. It was called "*Nak phaendin*" (*nak*, "heavy"; *phaendin*, "earth/homeland"), and it strongly implied that the weight of the left-wing activists was one that the land of the Thai could do without. The dark mood and sinister implications of this song are in stark contrast with "My Father Is Not the Prime Minister," the good-natured country song that had been popular during the heady days of student protests only a few years before. That was a love song with a political cast, but there was no love to be found in this song:

> There are those who use the name Thai,
> and their appearance is Thai,
> and they live on the land, from the land;
> but in their hearts they would destroy it.
> Selling themselves, selling their nation,
> insulting and demeaning the Thai race,
> they depend upon Thailand,
> gain sustenance from it,
> yet hate their countrymen.
> They are a weight upon the face of the earth,
> scum on the face of Thailand.[32]

An intriguing aspect of the song is that a listener who did not know the composer and the intentions of the song could, theoretically, imagine either left-wing or right-wing sympathizers as the loathsome weight, the scum on the face of Thailand. After all, had not military leaders "sold their country" prior to 1973 to the high-bidding United States? But listeners knew exactly who the writer of the song was talking about, and it had a pernicious effect on the April 1976 elections, which became the most violent in modern Thai history.

Grenades were thrown into crowds listening to Socialist and other leftist candidates, and the secretary general of the Socialist Party, Dr. Boonsanong Punyodhayana, who had earned a PhD from Cornell University not long before, was assassinated in his own driveway. A coalition government was finally elected, with M.R. Seni Pramoj, who had led the government briefly following World War II, as prime minister. He named General Krit Sivara as minister of defense. Only two days later, General Krit entered the hospital with symptoms of heart disease, and the nation was stunned when he died on April 23, 1976.

In July, in the midst of the tumultuous 1976 election, Boonlua wrote a cynical and sad letter to her old American friend, Larry Smith.

> Bangkok is now a very exciting place. The counter-comm[unist] activities are in full swing. If it had not been for the very real seriousness of the situation, I might feel like joining the comm[unists] just for the sake of being contradictory, which is my real nature. It's pathetic to see how some people are frightened, and pathetic to see how some people can't realize the seriousness and just "feel sanuk" [amused, entertained]. The only mature person is the poor king, but it's extremely difficult [for him] to keep on in the face of so many semi-fools and semi-pundits around him. Maybe pseudo is a better word than semi; but pseudo-fool is, maybe, too new a concept. Actually it's what most of us are. We're seldom quite foolish or quite wise. Maybe we're pseudo everything. I'm sorry to say that amid all the excitement of demonstrations and plastic bomb throwing, shooting and kidnapping, I'm bored. It seems like I've lived through all this in my former life or something. . . .
>
> By the way, those who are interested in language and culture might like to know that most of the counter-comm[unist] propaganda is

done in verse, and this was very much in evidence during the week preceding the departure of American troops on 20 July. Both left and right abused each other in verse, some of it quite good. . . . It was very Thai, I'm proud to say. But I like best the angry protest of someone from a nearby province. "Why don't [the communists] want us to have a king? After all the vultures have their king-vulture (a Thai idiom for the leader of the group, which the Thai regard as good animals as they feed only on dead bodies and do not kill) and the bees and ants have their queens. Are we to be even worse [i.e., less] than these animals?" I [picture] our queen laying really numerous eggs . . ."[33]

By August of 1976, Field Marshals Thanom and Praphat and Colonel Narong were planning their return. Praphat flew to Bangkok and arranged an audience with the king, but the visit proved somewhat premature and he was forced to return immediately to his home in Taiwan.[34]

Thanom was more astute in planning his return. He arrived in Bangkok on September 19 and used a consummately Thai strategy that would allow him to remain safely in the country: he went directly from the airplane to Wat Bowornivet, a royal monastery, and was ordained as a Buddhist monk. The NSCT students and other political activists were furious when the king and queen indicated that they would do nothing to stand in the way of Thanom's new, expediently pious identity. The monarchy's fundamental and declared interest was then, and has remained, the stability of the nation, the social system, and the dynasty.

Frightened Thais began for the first time to think that the future of the Chakri dynasty might really be threatened, the way things were going. This was certainly the message the king was receiving from many of those whose advice he trusted most, counselors whose affiliations ranged from ISOC [Internal Security Operations Command] to the Siam Commercial Bank. He neither requested nor received opinions from student reform leaders.[35] If the monarchy did not actively support the vicious right-wing attacks that would erupt with fury on October 6, 1976, it did nothing to prevent or control them.

Violence began escalating when two student activists were lynched in Nakhon Pathom province, after being arrested for distributing anti-Thanom posters. When evidence of direct police involvement was found, in retaliation the police office was bombed. On October 5, students staged a mock hanging at Thammasat University to keep attention focused on their fallen comrades. Some observers reported that the makeup was purposefully applied to the effigy to make it resemble Crown Prince Vajiralongkorn—to this day, people disagree on whether that was true or was only a rumor spread by vigilantes in order to gain public support for a serious move against the students. In any event, the rumor of an act of *lèse majesté* spread rapidly, and several right-wing groups coalesced to redress this "final insult" to their nation and king. On the evening of October 5, thousands of vigilantes flocked to Sanam Luang, a large grassy area near Thammasat University and the Grand Palace which has always been used for royal ceremonies, especially royal cremations.

By the morning of October 6, 1976, the vigilantes had been joined by hundreds of armed police and several Border Patrol Police units. The mob stormed the campus. The carnage was horrific, far worse than in 1973. Some students were burned alive, others were lynched and hung from trees, or shot trying to flee. Hundreds were wounded and it is unknown how many died. The official government estimate was forty-six, an implausibly low number.[36] Some three thousand students and other left-wing activists and their supporters were arrested. Not one vigilante was ever charged with responsibility for any of the incidents occurring on that day.

A NEW REACTIONARY GOVERNMENT

On October 9, military leaders announced the appointment of Thanin Kraivichien, a civilian, as the new prime minister. An arch anti-communist and former Supreme Court justice who was close to the queen, Thanin was determined to end the bloodshed and return

Thailand to a state of law and order. In 1997, a Thai writer who asked not to be identified made these remarks to me about Thanin Kraivichien.

> Thanin is remembered by many people as an evil man (*khon chua*). But Thanin was not an evil man. He was honest and well-meaning. Oh yes, he was a great anti-communist, and he really believed that the monarchy was going to be destroyed and the country ruined unless these communists—they were all communists to him— could be destroyed first. Unfortunately, he could not be flexible, and he was not a good decision maker at all.

Thousands of students, socialists, communists, and activists of every stripe continued to be arrested. Some fled to join the Communist Party in remote areas of Thailand and Laos, some went into hiding in or near Bangkok and the other larger cities, and a few escaped or were spirited away to foreign countries.

In March of 1977, Boonlua wrote again to her friend Larry Smith.

> Personally, I am in the midst of some rather grave emotional disturbance. No other coup or revolution has done this to me. . . . The Prime Minister [Thanin Kraivichien] is a good man, but I cannot stand a "good" man. I'd prefer a cunning bandit any time. I'd [have served] under Huey Long if I had lived in Louisiana. This government is tearing down, or wearing away is a better word, the monarchy, with all its good "naive" intentions. If the present king had not been "somebody" in his own right, I really don't know what is going to happen to him within the next two years. I think he is one [of] the few who know what is being done to him and the institution he represents. He couldn't have lived in Switzerland for nothing, and been his father's son as well. I don't know how he is keeping himself. I have stopped [listening to anything, or reading anything], except about animals. . . .[37]

The following October, Thanin's reactionary government was replaced by a more conciliatory and flexible administration headed by General Kriangsak Chomanan, who had the foresight and the courage to make a great political decision. In 1978, he offered amnesty to all dissidents who were in jail, in hiding, out in the countryside with the communists, or living abroad. They were told, through a variety of means of communication, to go back to finish their university studies (most had been students), or find a job. By now, most of them were sad, homesick, and eager to return home, if they could be sure of their safety. They were completely disillusioned with the communists to whom they had fled, who had turned out to be nothing resembling their imaginings. They wanted to believe General Kriangsak, and they were not betrayed.

Today the majority of the political exiles of that period are pragmatic, non-aggressive members of Thai society, like their parents and grandparents before them. Many are disheartened by the continuance of "guided democracy" and feel that it really is no democracy at all. But they have resigned themselves to the world as it is, though it is far from the world they dreamed of. That they have become so is a circumstance not universally admired by some who believe that the intransigence of conservative administrations ever since is partially the result of the exiles' acceptance of General Kriangsak's deal. Yet, the only progressive "extremists" who dare to speak their mind on this or other sensitive issues risk arrest and imprisonment.

Among those who fled to join the communists after October 6, 1976, was Anut Aphapirom, whom Boonlua wished had consulted with her before his dreams ended so disastrously. He returned to journalism but not to radical politics; today, he works for a Bangkok publishing house. Another returnee was Cholthira Kladyu, Boonlua's young Marxist colleague at Chulalongkorn University, whom many people had considered during the heady days of the mid-1970s to be "the country's top contemporary literary critic and authority on Thai literature."[38] Professor Cholthira, who in 1974 had debated Boonlua on the value of classical literature in the contemporary era (dubious, in her view then), returned to Bangkok and became a prominent academic author, teacher, and activist. Suchat Sawatsri, who also participated in that debate, has continued to work as an editor, writer, and most recently as an artist. He has struggled, to a degree unmatched by most of his former comrades, to hold onto the dreams of *Sip-si tula*.[39] His wife, the one-time factory worker who found him "strange" when he met her during his days as a political educator of the masses, has become one of Thailand's iconic contemporary writers and has traveled to Japan and Sweden for readings of her work.[40]

There are some poignant and interesting memoirs of this period written by people who suffered and survived imprisonment or exile, but none of them has been translated into English.[41]

Boonlua had lived through yet another period of uncertainty and crisis, and she had witnessed sickening violence in the streets of Bangkok at a level far exceeding anything that had previously occurred in her lifetime. In 1976, Thais were killing their countrymen with unprecedented malice and cruelty under the flag of "patriotism."

A factor that is sometimes overlooked in assessing the events of 1976 is the end of the war in Vietnam, Cambodia, and Laos. By 1975, communist governments had triumphed and were in power in those nations. People were risking their lives swimming the Mekong River from Laos to Thailand every day and night, and coming by land over the Cambodian border if they could. Thailand was filling up with refugees and building camps to hold and feed them. The news coming from Laos and Cambodia about the behavior of the communists, once they had come to power, was terrifying. Thais might not have wanted a return to a right-wing military dictatorship—but even less did they want to share the plight of their neighbors, who were suffering under brutal communist leaders. How could such things happen in Buddhist nations? Did those horrors have anything to do with the ideas that Thai socialists and other political progressives had insisted would make society so much better?

Soon after Thanin Kraivichien became prime minister, he appointed Pinyo Sathorn, another staunch anti-communist conservative, as minister of education. Pinyo's first act was to call for a complete overhaul of the public school curricula, including—and especially—university curricula: never again, Pinyo declared, would Thai universities be allowed to become hotbeds of communism. Once again, Boonlua found herself involved in an educational effort to teach patriotism cloaked in the garment of Thai culture. Now, the foundation of all education was to reflect an unwavering focus on "nation, religion, king," pro-monarchy and anti-communist, pro-stability and anti-individualism. Indeed, "individualism" was now criticized as a Western concept that Thailand could do without. No one appeared to see the irony of the disposal of respect for individual liberties and freedom of expression in Thailand, and simultaneously, in its neighboring communist nations.

BOONLUA THE PRAGMATIST

The teaching of modern Thai literature was seriously affected by the policies of the Thanin administration. Of course, "Cholthira-style" explorations of literature from a Marxist perspective were not to be thought of. Literature professors knew that this would be the case, and they were prepared for it. However, since the death of Sarit in 1963, they had become used to a fairly relaxed government attitude toward the readings they assigned their students. This state of affairs ended abruptly in November of 1976, when they were given a list of poets and writers whose work had been judged by the new government to be unwholesome, seditious, or harmful to national security. These writers must be expunged from course lists. Seeing Chit Phumisak's name on the list was no surprise, but everyone was stunned to find that the list included most of the best poets and writers of the past two decades. The banning of their work left the modern literature curriculum in a shambles—and there was nothing that anyone could do about it, or so it seemed.

Achan Boonlua took the news with an equanimity that surprised her colleagues and friends. But when she explained her ideas for devising a new, politically correct curriculum, the reason for her calm demeanor became very clear. The younger professors were shocked and delighted by Achan's deviousness. They had always thought of her as a liberal traditionalist, which she was. What they had not understood was that she held extremists at each end of the political spectrum equally in contempt. She had no intention of ignoring good writers because their work did not suit Pinyo's politics, and she would not ignore them. What was needed was imagination and finesse. "Look at it this way," she told a young professor who was considering resigning rather than contributing to the revised curriculum. "They are asking *us* to design the curriculum. *Think*, dear . . . Would you rather have it designed by *them*? We should be very, very quiet."

In the first year of Boonlua's teaching career, M.L. Pin Malakul had given her numerous suggestions on how to teach her first class. She had not paid much attention to him then and had never followed anyone else's suggestions about teaching in the intervening fifty years. In her classroom she had always done exactly as she pleased, wherever she was teaching and whatever the political situation in the nation might be. In 1976, it never occurred to her to behave any differently, and she was amused to find her young colleagues so guileless and so lacking in imagination. In a letter written during this period, Boonlua confides her feelings about teaching, literature, and patriotism in the late 1970s.

> As we [literature professors] work, we keep telling one another, "Never mind, if they throw everything we do overboard, we should be glad we have worked together." Patriotism really gets me down, but I am not spreading the infection. Young people come and pay me false compliments (sincere, on their part) that I have a lot of courage. In reality I just tell myself that it really doesn't matter one way or the other.[42]

A professor who was teaching modern Thai literature in 1976 recalled Boonlua's clever solution to a curriculum crisis that was typical of the times.

> I came in to the university one day to learn that M.R. Nimit Mongkol's utopian novel, *Muang nimit*, had been crossed off my reading list because he was a "communist." What nonsense. I was irate, and went flying into Achan's office. She calmed me down and went with me to see our department head.

Achan looked guilelessly at our boss and said, "But Nimit is a Mom Rachawong [great-grandson of a king]—so how could he possibly be a communist?" And believe it or not, our department head actually agreed with her —"No, *he could hardly be a communist if he is a Mom Rachawong!*"[43]

Another professor was ordered to take the work of admired poet and fiction writer Sathian Chantimathorn off a course reading list. Sathian was then somewhere "in the jungle." The professor solved the problem herself in a way that delighted Boonlua when she heard about it. On the first day of the term the course readers were passed out, still featuring one of Sathian's most famous poems, and the professor said, "Oh dear, I am afraid that one of the poems in your reader is forbidden—so I must ask you all to take out your pencils and cross it out."

In 1978, Praphatson Sewikul, a fiction writer and also a diplomat in the Ministry of Foreign Affairs, wrote a novel in the form of a memoir about a group of friends who had shared the dangerous and thrilling events of October 1973. Boonlua greatly admired this novel, which was entitled *Time in a Bottle* (*Wela nai khuat kaeo*), complete with a Thai translation of Jim Croce's song, "Time in a Bottle" as the preface.[44] It became a tremendous bestseller, appealing to the nostalgia of those who had taken part in the protests and demonstrations. But it was equally popular with students who had been too young to have a part in *Sip-si tula*, but were inspired by a time that seemed to have been filled with brave deeds and heroic friendships, when mere students were larger than life, and life was far more interesting and meaningful than it had since become.

Although many Thais were deeply distressed by the ugliness and violence that had occurred in October 1976, most were agreeable about the return to a conservative government. Many were fearful of a communist attack from Thailand's western border, and some were simply relieved to see the end of a turbulent, confusing three years of "politics." Most Thais chose to face current realities with the attitude conveyed by the term *plong tok*; literally, *plong* is to "put down" or "let down," and *tok* means "to fall, to drop, to slip." The deeper and more contradictory meaning of the two words in combination is to be disillusioned; not take to heart; take philosophically.[45] It was one of Boonlua's favorite expressions, this concept firmly grounded in the Buddha's teaching: terrible things happen, nothing lasts, everyone knows it, and we would do well to get used to it. I also heard the expression from a professor of political science who had gone to identify the bodies of several of his students on the day after October 6, 1976, so that their parents would not have to do it.

> I will never forget what happened and what I was forced to see, and I will never be as I was before that day. When I think now of what I want in life, what I want most is to sit by the sea and watch my children play in the sand. Call it a failure of my ideals, or cowardice, or say that I just *plong tok*, I accept it and then I walk away, or call it whatever you like.[46]

By the end of 1978, life in Bangkok was at least peaceful. But Boonlua continued to feel depressed and fearful, as she confided in a letter to Mayuree Sukwiwat, a young professor whom she had mentored and of whom she was very fond. At the time, Professor Mayuree was teaching at the University of Hawaii, accompanied by her husband and children.

> My dearest Mayuree,
>
> Today I have time to write a letter to you, although someone else is typing for me, because I am unwell. I have many tasks to complete, but I cannot work. . . . Yesterday I was sick all day, and I cannot describe exactly what was wrong. I felt afraid, and I shook. But I have no idea what I was afraid of. As for [the political situation here], I don't know whether things are better, or worse than ever. If you read the newspapers, it seems that everything in the whole world is worse than ever. There is only news of madmen and evildoers killing each other without cause. . . . We're to have another election next April. I tremble as I wonder what extent of madness we will have to witness. . . . But I have not given up hope entirely. I hope that, at the least, the

situation doesn't get any worse. As for the communists [in neighboring countries], they seem to fear nothing. . . .

I don't have any sense of fun about anything, lately. Yet—this is so surprising—when I began this letter I felt thoroughly despondent, and now that I am almost finished, I feel much better. However, I have run out of things to talk about and so will close, sending much love to the Sukwiwat family: father, mother, and children.[47]

Although Boonlua felt weak, weary, and sick at heart when she wrote this letter to Mayuree, the remaining six years of her life would be good years. She would look back upon her work and her accomplishments with satisfaction. She enjoyed her time with Dr. Chom, both at home and on some wonderful trips abroad. She met often with her many friends, and they would laugh together as they lunched at their favorite restaurants and talked about books, politics, people, and life, and her mischievous sense of humor seemed to grow only sharper. After all of the crises and problems of her life, all the successes and all the failures, she had become a very wise and respected woman, and she knew it.

IO

A CIVILIZED WOMAN

During the last decade of Boonlua's life, she was surrounded by people who loved her just as she was, fulfilling the primary dream of her childhood. In the public sphere, she had lived and worked according to her own beliefs, and despite many setbacks she had become a respected, even iconic, figure in Thai society. She was a prolific writer and popular speaker, and the publication of her collected essays, interviews, and lectures launched the field of modern Thai literary criticism.

Before Boonlua began to examine her nation's literature from an analytical perspective, very few Thais had been recognized as authorities on the subject, and the opinions and pronouncements of those who were so recognized had gone unquestioned. Chief among them was Prince Damrong Rajanuphap (1862–1943), a son of King Mongkut and half-brother of King Chulalongkorn who is generally recognized as the founding father of Thai literary historiography.[1] As director of the National Library, he and his staff worked tirelessly to collect all the manuscripts of classical Thai literature that could be found. Like his ancestors in the first and second reigns of the Chakri dynasty (1782–1809, 1809–24) who re-created the kingdom's literature from memory after the Burmese destruction of Ayutthaya, Prince Damrong was determined to protect and preserve the Thai literary heritage. The threat during his era came not from Burma but from Western collectors eager to buy original texts and carry them off to England, the United States, and elsewhere. He was deeply concerned with keeping the Thai literary heritage at home and also with interpreting that heritage. Because of his intelligence, energy, and high position in society, his interpretations were accepted with gratitude and respect and never challenged until the mid-twentieth century.

In 1952, Phluang Na Nakhon published *Thai Literature for Students* (*Wannakhadi thai samrap naksueksa*), and in 1959, Phra Worawetphisit published *Thai Literature (Wannakhadi thai)*. Both works are in the Prince Damrong tradition and neither contains a single example, or even a single mention, of a modern novel or short story. Texts in this tradition were the standard when Boonlua began teaching literature during the late 1930s and when she began writing her ground-breaking essays thirty years later.

If modern Thai literature had been dismissed by the experts as a small and inferior shadow of Western fiction, the only person who explored Thai literature from another perspective than that of Prince Damrong, Pluang Na Nakhon, or Phra Worawetphisit was purposefully ignored: Chit Phumisak. Chit is mainly remembered as a political radical and posthumously honored hero of the student activists during the 1973–76 period. But when he was a student at Chulalongkorn University during the 1950s, he first made a name for himself as an excellent student of comparative linguistics. He wrote meticulous, lengthy essays and books on the relationship between Thai, Lao, and Khom (pre-modern Cambodian/Khmer) that are still available, although only in Thai.

When he was still a student, Chit was fascinated by scholars of the aristocracy and wanted to know them; he called upon Prince Dhani Niwat, Prince Wan Waithayakon, and Prince Damrong's daughter, Princess Poon Pismai Diskul.[2] Chit's father was a low-level bureaucrat, a clerk who had been stationed in various places in Thailand and also in Cambodia, and his mother was a seamstress. Few young Thais of his background, whether matriculating at the nation's top university or not, would have had the courage to pay calls on princes. But Chit was looking for a mentor, and he believed that even though he was still a

university student his reputation as a first-rate scholar would—*should*—
lead to such a relationship. Although he did not find the Thai mentor
he hoped for, eventually he found a sympathetic friend and advisor in
Professor William J. Gedney, a distinguished American linguist who
lived in Thailand for some years and was noted for his expertise in Thai
language and classical literature.

Chit gradually developed a theory of classic Thai literary works as
"products of a corrupt and oppressive aristocratic ruling class, the history
of Thai literature being that of an exploitation of the common people."
He later refined his Marxist interpretation of Thai political and literary
history in jail, where he had plenty of time and few distractions. He also
was obsessed with what he saw as the "incurable sexual obsessions" of
the ruling class—for which he could find plenty of "evidence" in classical
Thai literature.[3]

Boonlua's perspective on Thai literature was all her own. Predictably,
she respected Prince Damrong. Her father and Prince Narit had known
him well, and all three men shared essentially the same views on the
subject. But that did not mean that she would agree with all of his
opinions. She campaigned tirelessly for the teaching of Thai literature as
an integrated subject from the earliest school years through secondary
schools and universities, including folk tales, classical poetry, and
drama—and modern fiction and poetry. The first published collection
of her critical essays and various other writings, *The Turning Point of
Thai Literature (Hua liao khong wannakhadi thai)* appeared in 1973; a
second collection, *Analysis of Thai Literature (Wikhro rot wannakhadi
thai)* was published in 1974.[4] In 1986, four years after her death, a third
collection of her essays, lectures, and transcripts of debates appeared,
entitled *Lens on Literature (Waen wannakam).*

Boonlua was even-handed in what she saw as a lack of intellectual
vigor, creativity, and sheer knowledge on both the conservative right and
the radical left. She did not embrace any particular theories of literary
analysis and never considered herself a true scholar. She wrote, "The
only hitch [in writing essays about literature] is that I can never make
a paper scholarly enough. I was not born a scholar. I am a 'writer' and,
I think, a teacher."[5]

She wanted to write for people who were interested in literature but didn't want to read a textbook. And, she had a well-known distaste for academic pomposity, demonstrated in an incident recalled by Richard A. Via, in *Merit Fulfilled* (*Bun bamphen*):

> At a conference at the East-West Center in 1978, the delegates were seated alphabetically in the circular, U.N. style arrangement. This put Boonlua up front in perhaps the second seat. This was hardly the place for one who wanted to see everything that was taking place, much less for one who had to have a cigarette every now and again. She lasted until the first paper was over and then she moved to the back near me in the U,V,W section.
>
> It was perhaps the second day, after we had listened to many learned papers presented by outstanding people, and one of the participants was giving a rather scholarly rebuttal or response to the previous speaker. Boonlua's hand shot up in the air, dropping ashes without concern, and her clear voice rang out. "Mr. Chairman, Mr. Chairman! Would you please ask the learned gentleman from Great Britain to repeat what he just said in simple words so a poor old Thai lady can understand him."
>
> It was what the conference needed, and everyone became aware that there was a "presence" present.[6]

The Turning Point of Thai Literature was the first inclusive work on Thai literature ever written. The essays were written late in Boonlua's career and represent decades of thinking about the issues that she addresses.

> [Boonlua] turned to literary history late in her career, but what she did produce was epoch-making . . . [*The Turning Point*] deals with the rise of modern Thai literature towards the turn of the century and takes the reader up to the late 1960's. For the first time, the novel as a literary genre receives an objective, scholarly treatment.[7]

Boonlua could quote long passages of the classic poem *Lilit Phra Lo* from memory, just to make a small point, before veering off suddenly to refer to one of the contemporary Thai novelists, or to Ernest Hemingway, or to actor David Niven's memoir, *Bring on the Empty Horses*, which she thought was very well written and funny. Such behavior was very disconcerting to the old literary guard—and thrilling to her students. Professor Mattani Rutnin was one of the small group of female professors who surrounded Boonlua during the 1970s.

> Our *mom luang* was a "Ms. Know-it-all": literature, languages, traditions, culture, philosophy, religions, worldly knowledge—you name it. She combined them all: Chaucer, Shakespeare, Sunthorn Phu [poet], Prince Narit, Ernest Hemingway, Suwanee Sukhontha [novelist], Angkhan Kalyanapongse [contemporary poet] . . . and the Beatles! . . . She was like a bridge to link the old and the new eras, and Thai and *farang* [literature and culture].[8]

Boonlua begins *The Turning Point* with a startling assertion for one who was generally assumed to be a monarchist: that modern literary criticism had been hindered in its development because of the traditional strong link between literature and the monarchy. Kings not only composed literature themselves, but also supported literary endeavors at court centuries before ordinary people could read. All written works, including poetry and dance dramas, were created in the Royal Court and often attributed to the king himself (whether or not he had composed the work), and then bestowed upon the public. How could anyone analyze the literary efforts of the king?

Modern writers, and for that matter modern readers, were created by the rise of newspapers and journals, particularly after 1932. They published not only news and features about various subjects and persons, but also works of fiction. Boonlua points out that this was hardly a Thai phenomenon; instead, it mirrored the British custom of the past many decades. The works of Charles Dickens and Thomas Hardy had been serialized in British newspapers, just as Dokmai Sot and Kulap Saipradit were serialized in Thai papers. If news reporting is essential for an educated public, she wrote, "novels are the journals in which the society's emotions are recorded."[9]

Boonlua analyzes the best Thai novels of the late 1920s and early 1930s, including the Dokmai Sot novels of her sister Buppha, which were not only excellent in terms of style, characterization, and ideas, but also in displaying the lives of at least the upper level of Thai society during the 1930s faithfully and in detail. Her highest praise, in every era, has been for stories that describe recognizable Thai people and depict everyday life while meeting "Western standards" of fiction.[10]

One of the interesting questions Boonlua raises in *The Turning Point* concerns the relative quality and quantity of literature in pre-modern Siam and in the twentieth century. Long ago, when all literature had to be composed and copied by hand, the elite wrote for the elite. Even if commoners could read, the method of production made the "products" very costly. The output was small, the quality high. But in modern times, the situation is reversed: the expansion of basic literacy has produced a large audience of minimally educated readers, encouraging a growing number of writers who might not have great talent, but who are competent enough to provide a constant supply of "products."

Boonlua gives considerable weight to the importance of entertainment in both classical Thai works and modern Thai fiction. Thais have never been impressed, she points out, with tragedy alone. They expect comic relief as a balance; they like stories that are *sanuk*—fun. She enthusiastically praises a 1963 novel by Kanchana Nakanan entitled *Village Headman Li and [His Wife] Ma (Phuyai Li kap nang Ma)*, a humorous, earthy, and poignant story about a village man who receives a university degree in agriculture, then returns to his village to share his knowledge and ideas. After its very popular serialization, Boonlua wrote the introduction to the published book.

> What is most important in this novel, and most unusual, is the author's brilliant display of the *Thai* sense of humor. There have been some who criticized the character of Phuyai Li as a character from a dream. They say that there is no one really like him. But if they would [ever leave Bangkok] and travel in the villages, they would meet many men like Phuyai Li, although they might not all have PhDs in agriculture, as he does. . . . One of the features of *Phuyai Li* that is most important

is the fact that the story is character driven, which is rare in Thai fiction. Phuyai Li, his wife, and neighbors seem very real to us, and everything that happens in the novel happens because they are the people they are.[11]

Boonlua also praises the novelist Suwanee Sukhontha (the pen name of Suwanee Sukhonthieng), who became very popular during the late 1960s for the unprecedented realism with which she depicted women's lives. But Boonlua chooses to focus on other aspects of Suwanee's writing.

Suwanee is recognized for creating complex and realistic characters. But I think it is the fineness of her language that is most extraordinary. Suwanee is an artist in her word choices and in her use of idiomatic Thai speech.[12]

Boonlua is also generous in her support for Krisna Asokesin (the pen name of Sukanya Cholasueks), whose entertaining novels focus upon self-centered, social-climbing, educated urban women. Krisna's many readers knew such women—or at least were familiar with the type. Some of the characters in these novels are outrageous or highly amusing, yet Krisna's novels, like Boonlua's, are firmly grounded in Buddhist teachings. Characters who choose to ignore them, who are grasping, selfish, ambitious, or sexually immoral, suffer the consequences—often in ways that do not reflect the certainty of karmic retribution in this or future lives as much as the certainty of "an eye for an eye" before the end of the last chapter.

Boonlua was an early and strong promoter of Botan (the pen name of Supa Sirising), who wrote one of the most famous, popular, and controversial novels of the twentieth century at the age of twenty-one while she was completing her master's degree in Thai literature at Chulalongkorn University. *Letters from Thailand* (*Chotmai chak mueang thai*) was a largely autobiographical novel. The protagonist is a Chinese man named Tan Suang U, a composite of the author's father and uncle, who arrives in Thailand in 1946 and writes one hundred letters to his mother back in China over the next twenty years. There never had been a Thai novel entirely concerned with an urban Chinese family, much less one that so candidly portrayed family life—regardless of the ethnic origin of the family. Botan has a wonderful ear for ordinary conversation, and readers were amazed at the vigor with which her completely believable characters ridiculed, criticized, envied, despised, but ultimately loved the people in their family. Some critics and readers found the book vulgar and disturbing, but Boonlua adored it. She wrote that it opened up a world to her that she had not known at all. It was everything she admired in fiction: it was well written, poignant, funny, true to life, and emotionally powerful—and she learned so much from it.

The Turning Point exemplifies the lively, non-scholarly style of Boonlua's literary criticism. She attempts to present authors, eras, and issues in a more or less chronological way, but she cannot control her spontaneity. It reflects her teaching style—swooping from subject to subject, era to era, writer to writer—even language to language. For example, she includes the first stanza of Dylan Thomas's poem "Vision and Prayer," which she had translated into Thai to use in her classes, in order to demonstrate the relationship of content and form. I am including both the original stanza and Boonlua's excellent translation, for those who read Thai.

Who
Are you
Who is born
in the next room
So loud to my own
That I can hear the womb
Opening and the dark run
Over the ghost and the dropped son
Behind the wall thin as a wren's bone?
In the birth bloody room unknown
To the burn and turn of time
And the heart print of man
Bows no baptism
But dark alone
Blessing on
The wild
Child

ใคร
คือเจ้า
ซึ่งเกิดมา
ณ ห้องต่อนี้
เสียงลั่นหูเรา
กระทั่งได้ยินเสียงครรภ์
ค่อยเปิดและมีเงาดำไล่
ข้ามเจ้าภูตและเจ้าลูกหล่น
เบื้องหลังผนังบางดุจกระดูกนากระทำ
ในห้องคลอดเคลือบเลือดมิรู้ถึง
ความร้อนและความล่วงเวลา
และถึงดวงใจแห่งมนุษย์
ปราศจากพิธีกรรม
แต่โดยโดดเดี่ยว
จงเป็นสุขเจ้า
ผู้พิสดาร
เทอญ[13]

Boonlua ends *The Turning Point* with what she calls *rampan wannakam*: *rampan* means "to pour out one's heart," in this case, about literature (*wannakam*).

It is far more difficult to do research about things Thai in Thailand than it is to do research in the West. This is because we have thrown away too much, have been too little interested in collecting what has been written or preserving our historical documents in an orderly way for the convenience of future researchers. Writers have lost their original manuscripts. Publishers neglect to print the year in which a book is published. Often they print a statement explaining the reason for publishing the work but neglect to note how many editions have been published before the present one. And the greatest vexation of all for the researcher: misprints and errors, with which those of us who concern ourselves with literature are all too familiar. . . . Before I close this lengthy essay, I wish to remark upon the idea that there is nothing worth serious study in modern fiction. . . . If our knowledge of human beings is based only upon the people we know, how narrow will be our understanding of humanity. . . . And if our knowledge of human beings is based only upon works of psychology and sociology, we shall have little idea of the complexity of personality. [The former] works address the mind, but the heart is not engaged in the search for understanding as it is when we read fiction and poetry that are the products of a creative mind. . . . When we read the work of a truly good fiction writer, we experience the pain of disappointment, the loss of love, the pleasure of words well used, the artistry of excellent narrative. We are improved by good fiction writing. And whether or not it gives us the "truth" of human life, well-written fiction deepens our understanding of the truth of human emotions.[14]

Boonlua was never able to work out all of the contradictions in her opinions concerning either Thai or Western literature. She would claim that Thai literature was more concerned with aesthetic considerations and with "feelings," while Western literature was more concerned with "philosophy" and information—but then, in the next essay she might make quite opposite assertions. She would state that her opinion of any book, including fiction, would always depend upon whether she learned something new from it or not. Then she would do a turnabout and declare, "We cannot forget that the most important thing [in literature] is aesthetic pleasure."[15] She fretted about both the aesthetic and the technical quality of Thai fiction and swung between defending didacticism and extolling flights of imagination. Her highest praise for a novel or a short story was that it approached "Western standards." In her memoir, *Successes and Failures*, she took Western fiction, and especially Western theater, to task for what she considered to be a false sophistication and a misuse of aesthetics.

The *farang* are so very fond of philosophizing in the theater. . . . But the [contemporary] productions that are extolled as the best of their kind seem rather flat to us. . . . We are quite aware, from Buddhist teaching, of the impermanence of all things. We have *always* known that nothing in life is reliable, that there is nothing to which one may cling with certainty, and that human beings are capable of unwholesome desires, coarseness and fineness, and so on and on.

The *farang* playwrights seem to be just discovering these things. This is why I prefer to go to the ballet, which does not insist that the audience plumb the philosophical depths."[16]

Boonlua believed that the performative oral tradition had in some ways been more sophisticated than the written literature that followed. I do not know that Boonlua ever read Kenneth Burke's book *Counter-Statement*, with its discussion of the psychology of form versus the psychology of information; she may well have done so, given her remarks on the role of form in drama. Burke states that the former is the "creation of an appetite in the mind of the [audience or reader], and the adequate satisfying of that appetite."[17] It respects and maintains a focus on the emotional rather than the intellectual experience of the audience. But art in the twentieth century, he claims, includes increasing amounts of sheer information. That Boonlua recognized the difference between the psychology of form and the psychology of information is evident in her criticism of the performance of a scene from the *Ramayana* that she saw in Indonesia sometime during the 1970s. The scene was performed twice: first, in traditional style; the second time, in a modernized version. This dual performance might be *avant-garde*, but that was never enough for Boonlua, and she was not at all impressed with the second, modernized version.

During the [traditional] Javanese performance I was fascinated by the exquisite movements of hands and feet, and the music. I felt that the portrayal of [supernatural monkey characters] Palee and Sukreep, and the angel, and Prince Rama were all artistically wonderful and fine, in the eastern way. That is, the characters of Palee and Sukreep were presented *as monkeys*. Prince Rama was entirely the young warrior prince, and the angel was worthy of her place in heaven.[18]

On the contrary,

the dancing [in the modern version of the scene] went to great lengths to show that human beings are like animals, which is nothing new for people of the East, who are Buddhists, like myself. But they were unable to show how a monkey behaves differently from a human being, in terms of sexual activity. This is different from the traditional characterization of Sukreep, who approached the celestial maiden in the manner of a monkey, not that of a man.[19]

Boonlua was not shocked by the modern performance; she was dismayed and disappointed. The new, overtly sexy Sukreep was a bore, and was no match for the traditional portrayal of this character, which provides the audience not only with art, but with food for the imagination. She might be a purist about theatrical performances of the classics, but she had nothing against the portrayal of sex in theater or in fiction—providing that it was done with art. When an American professor asked her how she explained to students why Thai classical poetry is so full of sex, she replied, "I tell them that it is because Thai poets are people who have sex!"[20] R. J. Owens, who often met with Boonlua during the 1960s when he was at the British Council in Bangkok, recalls:

[She] came in to the British Council for "a coffee and a cool-off," as she called it, and told me that she had been lecturing to a group of students on classical Thai literature. "I don't know what to do with them," she said sadly. "They are so innocent and inexperienced and unimaginative. Thai literature is sophisticated, ironic, [and] earthy. . . ." "Imagine," she said, beginning to heave with laughter, "an old woman like me having to explain indirectly to these youngsters what the stories are all about! What's wrong with the youth of today that they are so ignorant! I don't know who was more embarrassed, they or I."[21]

In traditional Thai stories, depictions of sexual desire and activity are presented with elaborate, subtle nature images: flowers and butterflies, lightning and rain, and so on—all of which provide a pleasurable aesthetic/erotic experience that audiences anticipate and expect. For example, in "The Tale of Prince Samuttakote," the prince and his lover meet:

Precious stones on the bed; fragrances spread;
Perfume from the splendid lady;
And he was long uncertain.

He knew surely a god created this
For wondrous-love-making,
Just as a heart would wish.
. . . .
His stomach covered her circular one;
Breasts bumped together;
On top he squeezed the glorious flower.[22]

Boonlua, like most Thais, dismissed graphic descriptions of sex in contemporary fiction as evidence of a lack of skill and imagination on the part of the writer. When Erica Jong's *Fear of Flying* was published in 1978, Boonlua told a friend, "We've had sex in our literature for five hundred years. Should we be impressed with Miss Jong?"[23] The glory of erotic writing, for Boonlua, lay in the skill and subtlety with which the writer suggests all the senses: hearing, smell, touch, sight, and taste. The traditional Thai audience for poetry and for the classical dance drama expects a subtle sensual feast.

The Turning Point appeared while Thai literary radicalism was in full flower. The timing was unfortunate for a message of inclusiveness and integration, of respect for all genres written in all eras. Her delight in juxtaposing "Chaucer, Shakespeare . . . Sunthorn Phu . . . Prince Narit . . . and the Beatles," as Professor Mattani Rutnin had put it, was out of step with both camps of the early 1970s: the unyielding conservative elitists, and the earnest political radicals. Yet, it was Boonlua who would prove to be the most astute interpreter of her nation's literary past, and predictor of its literary future.

DISCOVERING MOM LUANG BOONLUA

During the last decade of her life, Boonlua joined only the committees that were interesting to her, worked only with the people she admired, and socialized only with the friends she loved. I was fortunate in being able to interview many of these friends.

Abigail Stewart, in her essay "Towards a Feminist Strategy for Studying Women's Lives," cautions the biographer:

> The women whose lives we study are unlikely to have more stable or monolithic identities than we do, but the effort to "tell a good story" and to summarize and define a person pushes us to represent them as unified persons and personalities. This effort to organize and structure the different voices and selves must be understood as an effort to control—literally to impose an order or unity on what is in fact multiple and even disorderly.[24]

If the biographer is susceptible to the temptation to impose "unity" on his or her subject, the friends and relatives of that subject are at least as interested in doing so. Most of the people I interviewed stated outright that they hoped I would present Boonlua to the world as a "unified" person. They tended to bridle at the suggestion that she was "complicated," which I had not realized Thais consider to be a pejorative term when applied to a person. I never suggested it again, after an interview conducted in English with an old friend of Boonlua who said, "No, she was not at all *complicated*—she was *happy*." Those who loved her looked forward to a biography of Boonlua the devoted, brilliant teacher; the founder of modern Thai literary criticism; the witty observer of society; the wise and kindly friend. Her detractors, on the other hand, wanted me to see how she "really" was: Boonlua the spoiled child; the arrogant aristocrat; the neurotic hypochondriac; the so-called Thai literary scholar who didn't really know as much about Thai literature as she wanted people to think.

I was very fortunate to discover what Boonlua herself thought about the task of the biographer. She praised Somphop Chantaraprapha for his biography of her sister Buppha. Somphop's depiction of his subject is sympathetic and heart-rending. He shows us a beautiful, talented, deeply flawed, pitiable, and very "complicated" woman. That Boonlua praised such a work—a work about her own sister—made it quite clear that she did not share the majority Thai view that the only proper task of the biographer is the celebration of the subject and the protection of his or her reputation. Nor did she share the almost universal opinion that one should never speak or write of the people in one's family in any way that could be construed as criticism—and never mention such things as depression, drug dependence, unhappiness, or any of the numerous problems and sad situations that filled Buppha Kunchon Nimmanhemin's life.

Unquestionably, the person who most celebrated Boonlua and all her works was Dr. Chom, her devoted husband and companion, who recalled their last years together in *Merit Fulfilled (Bun bamphen)*:

> After we both were retired, we were happy. Boonlua had a teaching job here and a meeting there, and I never tired of driving her everywhere, carrying all the bags and being her mailman, too, so that her *farang* friends teased her, asking how much she paid me.
>
> The only time she ever showed anger at me was when I ad libbed some lines in a play reading with some of our friends, because she thought it was a very undisciplined thing to do and she hated undisciplined behavior. I never did that again!
>
> We had very similar tastes in drama and music, and she taught me to sing some traditional Thai songs. We usually thought and felt the same things, as if we had telepathy. I learned a lot from her. I have always been curious about the subjects of language and history, and she could always answer my questions. Unlike me, she had an excellent memory and she was very good at telling funny stories. People always gathered around to listen to her.
>
> When she got upset at work, she wouldn't talk with her superiors or her peers about what was bothering her. If she had learned to talk out her frustrations, she would have been more successful, I think. There were times when I almost went to her supervisor to explain

what she was upset about, but that would have been too interfering a thing to do. When she had problems in her family, I just listened and sometimes offered advice, but I never interfered.

She was a strange wife in that she never asked about money—how much I made or what I spent. Yet, she would ask if I had any debts, and if I did she would offer some money of her own to reduce the interest or pay it off, although she earned a much smaller pension than I did and made only a little money from her writing.

Boonlua was very religious and wouldn't even spray DDT around our house so that the ants and cockroaches would stay away, much less spray the poison directly on them.[25] She convinced me to say prayers every night before bedtime, which we did together.

She really hated liars and tried not to lie herself. If she couldn't avoid saying something that might cause a problem, she would be silent.

When we traveled, she always tried to see people from whom she could learn something new. She would say, "We are spending a lot of money on this trip, so we should use the opportunity to learn everything we can." And she would buy a lot of books while we were abroad. One of my duties at home was buying plastic book covers to protect her beloved books and putting them on properly.

She had bad luck with her health. She was sick all the time with kidney problems, allergies, her inability to digest protein, and she was always going to the doctor. I was a doctor, but my field was public health, so I was really not much help. Once when she had diarrhea and I prescribed something, she got worse, and I had to take her to the hospital, and the doctor there, who was one of my own former students, sternly told me not to do that again—if she was sick, I should bring her to see him. Her worst problem was her high blood pressure, especially when she was under stress. I took a blood pressure monitor along on our trips abroad, and she usually had more stable blood pressure then because she was relaxed and enjoying herself. But even though she was ill so much, she worked harder and faster than most healthy people because she planned her schedule so well.

I was healthy and played sports all the time, but she worried about my health anyway. She was terrified that I might die before her and she would be lonely. Like other old couples, we knew that one of us was going to die before too long, but Boonlua just couldn't resign herself to this fact. She often said, "Khun Mo, please don't die first and leave me—let me go first."

If I may summarize what I see as Boonlua's "successes and failures," I would say that first, she had a husband who was her best friend and life mate, and we had the same thoughts and tastes, and good communication and understanding. She was not disappointed by me. Before I started seeing her, I hung around clubs playing billiards all night long. I stopped this when she asked me to. But about some things I was stubborn because of my self-confidence. For instance, I continued to drive at night, which she didn't like at all because she was afraid I would have an accident.

She was happiest after she stopped working for the government and had more time with her family and doing the work she liked best—writing.

She didn't feel inferior to anyone by having a husband like me, because I had worked hard on my way to a high position and had not done any shameful things. We went out together without embarrassment, and I got along well with all of her friends and students.[26]

Nearly all of Boonlua's female friends were younger than she and successful in their careers. Most were professors of language or literature, some were bureaucrats in the Ministry of Education, and a few were fiction writers. A small group that called itself the "*phuak thoet thoeng*" was particularly dear to her.[27] The word *phuak* means "group," and the term *thoet thoeng* describes a procession of Buddhist lay persons taking gifts to a revered monk. Boonlua's young friends adopted the name with tongue in cheek after they had come to her house on one birthday, dancing and singing as they entered the house bearing gifts. Thereafter, the *thoet thoeng* group invited Boonlua and Dr. Chom to a birthday party every year, usually in a private room at a hotel restaurant. Nitaya Masavisut's contribution to *Merit Fulfilled* was a description of this group.

We gave her just the kind of practical gifts you give to a monk: soap, toothbrush, toothpaste, towels, detergent, toilet paper, tea, coffee, Ovaltine, and body lotions. And every year, she would let us know, in a casual way, what kind of container she wanted the gifts to be presented in. For example, a few weeks before the day, she would say, "You know, this year my good *wicker basket* has been ruined," or, "My *plastic bucket* got broken." And then we would know what she wanted us to put her gifts in that year. We would also give her one "good" gift, such as her favorite soap—Christian Dior.

The atmosphere in our group was just like that in a classroom, but in this class you could eat and talk while the teacher listened. Often, the "students" would fight to talk over each other and the "teacher" would wave her hand in protest: "Listen, let me talk too!" If nobody listened to her, she would say, "Does anyone in this group ever listen?"

She thought it very rude the way we all talked over one another, and sometimes she got quite upset about it. But we never improved.[28]

In Thai society, the nature of the relationship between people is immediately conveyed by the pronouns they use for themselves and for the person to whom they are speaking. Boonlua referred to herself as *khru* (teacher) and called her younger friends by their names or nicknames. Although she referred to herself as *khru,* her young friends always used the more respectful *achan* (professor) when speaking to her or when talking about her. The following literal translation of a passage from Professor Nitaya's recollections of the *thoet thoeng* group demonstrates the psychological nuances of Thai conversation that are completely lost when they are translated into English. It would have been unthinkable to refer to Boonlua as "she." It is for this reason that every reference is to *achan*—professor.

Our conversations with Achan were not exclusively "fun" [*sanuk sanan hehakan*]. Even though every time we met we began with *rueang manosare* [small talk], to use Achan's expression, because Achan often was weary from wherever Achan had just been, from whatever Achan had been doing, and would say, "Today, let us speak only of *rueang manosare*, but this would continue for only a little while and then one of us would put some question or other that was on our minds to Achan, for to us Achan was a *phu rop ru* [a person of wide-ranging knowledge], and no matter what we asked, Achan would have an answer to give us. Achan's answer was not always precisely to the point, and Achan would ramble on; it was up to us to search for our answer within the text of Achan's response. Achan's answers to our questions often were sharp, strange, and new to us. . . .

Sometimes Achan's point of view was greatly at odds with ours. Or, vice versa. We would claim that Achan's view was out of fashion [*choei*] or out of date [*la samai*]. We would giggle among ourselves behind Achan's back. But when some time had passed, as often as not we would decide that Achan had been right. . . .

What was more important to us at the memorable lunches we shared than the food for our bodies, or even the food for our minds, was the food for our hearts that we received from Achan. When Phi Wanpen [*phi* means "elder sibling"] suffered her terrible event [a car accident in which Wanpen was injured and her husband and child were killed], Achan rushed to the hospital although at that time Achan was not well herself. The moment Wanpen saw Achan's face, she said, "*Achan, nu tham bun. . .* Achan, I have made merit . . ." [implying, "Why has this happened to me, when I have been a pious person?"].

Achan immediately stopped Wanpen from saying anymore, and said, "Wanpen, *wibak* [suffering in this life resulting from one's actions in previous lives] is too difficult for us to understand or explain." Before she left Wanpen's room, Achan said, "Wanpen, *khru pai la* [I am leaving now] . . . *don't nurse your suffering for too long*": I do not know to what extent Wanpen was affected by Achan's words, but to us she became the "*Iron Lady*" who could contend with anything in life and emerge gracefully victorious. [Note: these phrases in italics are in English in the original Thai text, indicating that Boonlua chose to used the English phrases, which have no exact Thai equivalent.][29]

For Boonlua and her relatives and friends who had been educated abroad, English words and terms often laced their Thai conversations, as in the passage above, and sometimes they conversed in English altogether. The following recollection is from Boonlua's grand-niece, M.L. Pattaratorn Chirapravat.

> I grew up at Wang Ban Mo, and so I spent a lot of time with my elderly aunties, whom I called Chuat Lua, Chuat Buppha, and Chuat Chalaem (*chuat* means great-grandmother or great aunt). We kids didn't know any English, and when the aunties wanted to say something they didn't want us to know about, they simply switched into English. Or French—Chuat Buppha and Chuat Chalaem spoke better French than English, really. My grandmother [Mom Anuwong] can't write Thai at all. She went to the convent in Penang when she was only seven and stayed there until she graduated at seventeen. She writes letters to me in English and she signs her name in Thai; and as far as I know, writing her name is the extent of her Thai writing ability.[30]

To one extent or another, Boonlua, her sisters, and her friends were bilingual and bicultural. If a familiar concept could not be expressed in one language, they would express it in another. "Don't nurse your suffering too long" is a familiar idea for Buddhists, but these particular English words expressed exactly what Boonlua felt and meant, and so she slipped out of Thai into English for six words, and then slipped back into Thai.

As Dr. Chom indicated in his recollections of their life together, some of Boonlua's happiest memories were of travels abroad. Friends and relatives with whom they stayed have vivid memories of their visits. Pariyachart (English nickname "Pris") Chaiyarat Bear, the daughter of one of Boonlua's oldest friends, Prachum Chaiyarat, remembers one visit.[31]

> I went to the Los Angeles airport to pick up Auntie Boonlua. I waited and waited, and everyone else was off the plane, and I thought she must have missed the flight. And suddenly there she was, and I thought, "*Oh, my God! She looks like a bag lady!*" She was all bundled up, with that old woolen cap on her head, and one of those cardigan

sweaters she always wore, and she was wearing bedroom slippers and carrying her special pillow and a little blanket, and some bags with books and things sticking out of them. There was a flight attendant on either side of her, carrying more stuff, and Dr. Chom, bringing up the rear with more bags.[32]

Pris's husband, Dr. Michael Bear, remembered breakfast the next morning:

> At that time we lived in a Hawaiian-style house on Lido Isle in Newport Beach. It was summertime and Boonlua and Chom came to the dining table swaddled in sweaters and wool mufflers, wearing knitted ski caps and some sort of thick booties on their feet. Our small son David was barefoot in shorts and a tank top. Later, David came to me and asked, "Dad, why does Auntie Boonlua have a whole suitcase full of rags?" The "rags" turned out to be an assortment of small blankets that Dr. Chom would roll up and place around her every night so that she could sleep comfortably. As far as I could tell, he slept on the narrow edge of the bed. He also placed one of the "rags" on the floor next to her side of the bed so that when she got up her feet wouldn't touch the bare floor.[33]

As the week of their visit to Newport Beach wore on, Boonlua made a discovery that caused some friction between her host and hostess. According to Pris Bear in the previous interview,

> It began when Auntie Boonlua discovered the senior citizen discount at the Sizzler Restaurant, and she became sort of obsessed with it. Whenever we were going to go out for a meal, she wanted to go to Sizzler's so that she could use her senior citizen discount. My husband wanted to take them out for California-style food and seafood and so on, and he absolutely couldn't stand it. He had no intention of going to Sizzler's for dinner. Between the rags and the coats and mufflers at breakfast and the Sizzler obsession, it was a memorable visit.

Who was the real Boonlua, especially in her later years? Was she the wise and beloved "Achan" who guided the women of the *thoet thoeng* group through times of joy and tragedy? Or the eccentric old lady who slept surrounded by "rags" and was obsessed with using her senior citizen discount at Sizzler's? Another view of Boonlua was expressed by Revadee Crabbe, a younger relative of Dr. Chom who lived with the couple and acted as Boonlua's secretary. In the following translated excerpt from a letter, Revadee shows yet another view of Boonlua in her life at home—both her own home and Wang Ban Mo, which she visited every week. Revadee refers to Dr. Chom as "Phi Mo," a familiar yet respectful blend of "elder brother" and "doctor," and to Boonlua as "Khun Phi," a respectful yet intimate form of address for an older female relative.

Khun Phi was kind to everyone, and she never raised her voice at us. There were three of us girls in the house, all in our early twenties: me, Pom (Revadee's nickname); Phi Mo's daughter Nim; and Ang, Phi Mo's younger sister by another of his father's wives. Khun Phi was fair to us all, and loving. She taught us girls to be honest and to take responsibility for ourselves. Once, we told her that we suspected the cook of keeping some of the market money for herself. Instead of suggesting that we might be wrong (which turned out to be the case), Khun Phi gave the three of us the same amount of money she usually gave the cook and made us go to the market and buy food with it— and we learned our lesson!

Khun Phi loved Phi Mo very much. It wasn't just a marriage of convenience, as you say some people have hinted to you. Khun Phi loved Phi Mo as a woman loves a man, and he both loved and respected her very much. When I was a little girl, I was sick and had to come to Bangkok to stay in the hospital, and then for a while I lived with Phi Mo. He was already divorced from his first wife then, and I remember that he had girlfriends, and he seemed to like them all a lot. But after he married Khun Phi, he was faithful to her. We girls thought of her as the perfect "stepmother." Once, when one of us was heartbroken because of a romance that didn't work out and too sad to eat, Khun Phi was very worried and feared that the girl would make herself ill. Khun Phi comforted her and even slept in her bedroom until she felt better, and of course she could easily have made someone else go and sleep in there.

When I came to live with them, Phi Mo told me that Khun Phi suffered from nerves and that I was to assist her personally, and with her work. It so happened that I, too, worked at the Education Inspection Unit, where Khun Phi used to work—she in a much higher position, of course—which made it all quite convenient. As for Khun Phi's health, about which you asked, it is true that she was usually sick. And I worried about the pills she took. She took a lot of them. It was my job to count them out and give them to her every day. I worried that she took too many Valium and that it might have caused some of her problems, like dizziness.[34]

Most Sundays, Khun Phi would go to Wang Ban Mo to play cards with her relatives and get her hair done.[35] If she stayed home, she would relax on her plastic reclining lawn chair. If her hands bothered her too much to type, she would dictate and I would type. Every so often, she would get up and walk around and around in the garden, for exercise.

Khun Phi was kind to all of the servants. She taught us that when we bought anything for the family, like *khanom* [snacks, especially sweets], we had to buy some for the servants as well, because Khun Phi said that when they saw others eating something interesting and delicious looking, of course they would like to have some too. She taught us never to call the servants *khon chai* (the usual term; literally, "one who is used"). She made us call them *luk chang* [ironically, the literal meaning of this term is "hired children" but in common usage it means "employee"]. If we all went to the seashore, the servants went along with us, and Khun Phi made us do everything for ourselves so that the servants could enjoy themselves at the seashore too.[36]

Revadee, like everyone else who knew Boonlua, spoke of the role of illness in her life. But there was one aspect of her continuing ill health that did not seem to occur to anyone: its enormous usefulness.

THE USES OF ILLNESS

As an adolescent at the convent school in Penang, Boonlua had spent a good deal of time immersed in her schoolwork and in novels while she was confined to the infirmary, due either to illness or to the menstrual problems that kept her bedridden for a week each month. As an adult, even when she was ill for weeks or months at a time, her notebooks and her typewriter were always beside her. Whether at home or at work, she would interrupt her activities three or four times a day to rest in her reclining lawn chair. She would work for ten minutes, rest for fifteen, and go back to writing again, throughout the day and sometimes until late at night.

Illness provided the conditions under which she could fully relax and enjoy both companionship and sympathy. When she married Dr. Chom, for the first time in her life she had the opportunity to enjoy these things without the excuse of illness, but by then the pattern was firmly established, and Dr. Chom was happy to care for her in sickness and in health.

Boonlua's literary output during the last fifteen years of her life would have been impressive for a healthy person, much more so for a woman who was an intermittent invalid confined to a chaise longue in the garden. Her sister Buppha also had suffered from a number of chronic illnesses, but the details and the effects of these illnesses were quite different. Buppha had no other "job" to go to when she was not writing. She taught French briefly when she was quite young, but until her marriage only a few years before her death in India, she stayed at home with her sisters and other relatives, with occasional visits to friends or relatives who lived elsewhere.

Buppha's novels frequently deal with the themes of illness and death. One of her most interesting and affecting characters, Khunying Saisawat in the novel *People of Quality* (*Phu di*), slowly dies of tuberculosis.[37] It is a powerful portrayal of the corrosive effects of illness on the body and also on the human spirit. Buppha had kept vigil at the deathbeds of several women in the family who died of this disease. Death from tuberculosis, which for a time was considered a melodramatic trope in too many early twentieth-century novels, was nothing of the kind. These authors were using some of the most traumatic and grievous events of their own lives, the slow and inexorable loss of loved ones to a "wasting disease" that destroyed its victims cruelly and slowly and left those who mourned them exhausted in every way.

Many people believed that both Buppha and Boonlua were hypochondriacs mainly because they were unmarried. If only they had married, went the gossip, they would not have been sick all their lives. One of Boonlua's friends remarked, "Oh, a lot of people thought that way—especially men. They felt that there was nothing wrong with a sickly woman that . . . you know . . . 'having a man' wouldn't cure. It was quite disgusting."

In this regard, there is a curious passage in Somphop Chantaraprapha's *Life and Work of Dokmai Sot*, about the day of Buppha's wedding to Dr. Sukij Nimmanhemin, in San Francisco in 1954.

> In the evening they went to the hotel, and her new husband took Buppha's many vials of pills out of her suitcase and dumped the contents down the drain of the sink in the bathroom, saying, "You won't be needing these any more."[38]

On the contrary, Dr. Sukij was soon disabused of any such notions about the therapeutic effects of the marital relationship. By the time they returned to Bangkok, Buppha had so many vials of medication with her that she was again using a separate suitcase for them, and she was so weak when they arrived at the airport that she had to be helped into the car—by Dr. Sukij's ex-wife and her servants, who had come to meet the returning bride and groom. It was not an auspicious beginning to the marriage.[39]

Unlike Buppha, who blamed her poor health for her inability to write for the last fifteen years of her life, Boonlua was always able, sick or well, to accomplish the goals that were important to her. She was recuperating from a serious illness when she wrote *Thutiyawiset*, yet she never missed submitting a chapter to the magazine *Satri San*, in which it was first serialized. If she was too ill to sit at her desk, or too dizzy, or her back hurt, or her legs felt numb, she reclined on the lawn chair with her portable typewriter on her lap. If she was too weak to type, or if the "nervous condition" in her hand was more vexing than usual, Revadee or another assistant (or even, on occasion, Dr. Chom) typed for her. Despite all, she finished *Thutiyawiset* in a year—all 775 pages of it. She told me herself that she had composed long passages of that novel sitting in the back seat of her car with her small typewriter on her lap, while her driver navigated traffic jams caused by road building projects during that year. *Land of Women* was completed when she was ten years older, certainly not in better health, and it is over 800 pages long.

Illness, whatever the mysterious and ultimately unknowable balance of its physiological and psychological roots may have been, must be considered a form of agency in Boonlua's life. Unquestionably, she would have preferred to live in good health. Nevertheless, it was not health but illnesses, ailments, syndromes, and puzzling conditions that gave her the time, peace, and solitude in which to think and to write, and they provided a good deal of "found time" that enabled her to realize her dream of being a novelist.

On January 19, 1982, Boonlua wrote to her friend Larry Smith:

> I am glad to tell you that it looks, if God is willing, that I will be alive and well at least for two years. Both my husband and I went and had a general check-up and none of my major organs show any signs of serious effects. . . . [During a recent trip to Japan,] Kamakura was disappointing. I am surprised the Japanese allowed such a historic place to be so commercialized and full of bad taste, when they are so clever everywhere else. . . . The guide at the top of the mountain at Hakone was good in her own way, very efficient, but like all guides she muddled up Buddhism. . . . I must have over used my strength, because the next day my blood pressure rose rather frighteningly and I had to keep in bed. . . . I am not surprised anymore why all the Japanese tourists make straight for Pattaya as soon as they arrive in Thailand. It's because their own beaches are black like they are strewn with bits of charcoal. It's the volcanic material that is blown from everywhere. . . . Anyway, it was a lot of fun while we were in Japan.

Boonlua was in good spirits, spilling over with observations and opinions about the places she had visited and what she had learned. But the blood pressure that rose "frighteningly" was a bad sign.

On May 2, 1982, Boonlua again wrote to Larry Smith:

> I got back from Singapore a few days ago. I went to attend the seminar on Interlanguage Transfer Processes in Multilingual Societies. I enjoyed myself very much because I had the opportunity of meeting several old friends and made a few new ones. I was not disappointed because I attend international seminars to learn about the world, and not just to obtain information. . . . If you look carefully, you will certainly find that all meetings, esp. international, always have some message for you, since human nature is more or less alike anywhere. Of course, at my age I don't expect to learn too many new things.

About two weeks later, Mattani Rutnin called upon Boonlua.

> A few days before Achan left us, I had a premonition. I hurried to see her, to talk about video-taping an interview in which she would talk about Thai literature and society, and we could keep that interview for students. Also, I wanted to ask permission to produce *Thutiyawiset* as a television movie and *Suratnari* [*Land of Women*] as a stage play.

> Achan said, "Hurry, do it soon, because Teacher doesn't have much time—I am utterly weary." That day, she took me out to lunch. . . . That was truly a special time for me, for Achan kindly fed me: food for the body, for the mind, for the heart. . . . our last meal together, teacher and student.[40]

As in Nitaya Masavisut's memories of the *thoet thoeng* group, Mattani, also a member of the group, uses the image of the teacher as a mother bird feeding the students' bodies, minds, and hearts.

On June 3, 1982, Dr. Chom had to travel to Ratchaburi province on business. Boonlua was particularly nervous about this trip because a friend of his, a fellow physician who had graduated from medical school with him, had just been killed in a car accident. Upon his return that evening, Dr. Chom would be going to Wat Trithotsathep to pay his respects to that friend.

When he returned from Ratchaburi at about three thirty in the afternoon, Boonlua was greatly relieved. He called a few friends about going to the temple, but all of them had prior plans and they asked Chom to go in their stead and contribute to the cremation expenses in their names. As he did every day, at five o'clock Chom went to play tennis at the nearby Siriraj Hospital tennis courts. He returned at six, bathed, and hurried through dinner. Although Wat Trithotsathep was only a twenty-minute drive from home, Boonlua insisted that one of the boys in the house accompany him because she hated it when he drove after dark. He protested that the boy should stay home and do his homework instead. He finally drove off to the temple alone, and when the ceremony ended he decided to drop in at the home of his younger sister, who lived nearby.

THE DEATH OF MOM LUANG BOONLUA

Dr. Chom returned home shortly after nine o'clock to find Boonlua lying on the bedroom floor, in the arms of a servant. He saw that she was paralyzed on her left side and knew that she had suffered a stroke on the right side of her brain. She could still speak, although her words were slurred, and she was able to hold his hand firmly. No one knew when the stroke had occurred because she had asked the cook to take her dinner up to the air-conditioned bedroom and she had dined alone.

Earlier, several people in the house had thought they heard someone softly call out, "Tua! Tua!" Chom's nephew, Tua, was living with them at the time. Shortly after that, a servant went up to the bedroom to see if she had finished her dinner and found her lying across a stack of newspapers next to the electric bell switch she used to call the servants. She was conscious and refused to allow anyone to call Dr. Chom, for fear that he would be so upset that he would have an accident on the way home. Dr. Chom later remarked that Boonlua, who never denied being superstitious, was probably terrified at the coincidence of his friend's death in an auto accident, and the fact that Chom was at the prayer ceremony for this man when she had the stroke. He gave her a sedative and called an ambulance. Her blood pressure was 240/110. She lost consciousness during the drive to Siriraj Hospital, and although the doctors there did all they could, she remained in a coma.

Boonlua died at 2:40 a.m. on June 7, 1982, after four days in the Intensive Care Unit of Siriraj Hospital. On that evening, M.L. Jirayu Nopawong, former dean of the Faculty of Arts at Chulalongkorn University and a member of the Privy Council (the king's senior advisors) came to the hospital and was the first person to pour sacred water over her hand. Boonlua had arranged some time before to donate her body to the Medical School at Siriraj Hospital, and that was done. Dr. Chom liked to show people the photograph of himself with the four medical students who received this honor, and point out that they all got excellent grades based upon their work.

Her memorial volume contains the charter for the M.L. Boonlua Debyasuvarn Fund, established and funded by friends, relatives, and devoted former students. Its purpose is the continuation of Boonlua's work through the recognition and support of young people doing outstanding research and writing in the fields of education, literature, literary criticism, and the performing arts. The foundation is located at Chulalongkorn University and is administered by a committee of five to nine people.

A ROYALLY SPONSORED CREMATION CEREMONY

Boonlua's cremation ceremony took place two years after her death at Wat Makutkasatriyaram, a royal temple, on June 7, 1984. Typically, the higher the rank of the individual the longer the period of time that elapses between death and cremation. Her Royal Highness Princess Maha Chakri Sirindhorn, the third child and second daughter of King Bhumibol and Queen Sirikit, presided over the ceremony. This was especially fitting and no doubt would have pleased Boonlua very much, for Princess Sirindhorn, then twenty-nine years old, had a great interest in literature. In the years to come she would become a prolific writer of prose, poetry, essays, and memoir, and would translate Chinese fiction and poetry into Thai.

Every Thai Buddhist is taught from childhood that the basic facts of life are "birth, old age, suffering, death." It is customary for close relatives to bathe the body of the departed; friends come to participate in the water-pouring ceremony. The cremation ceremony is usually followed by a cheerful party, especially if the individual has died after a long life. Traditionally, it was a far more serious matter to miss a friend's cremation than his or her wedding. The cremation is the last chance a person has to show respect or love, or to express regret for any difficulties in the relationship. If the cremation takes place at a temple with a conventional crematorium, one by one the friends and relatives file by the open door, gently tossing candles and flowers into the fire while they say their farewells. They may silently apologize for any word or deed by which they may have offended and ask for forgiveness. Theravada Buddhists believe that only after cremation can the person's current life be considered irrevocably finished. But even cremations leave something, and people often request bone fragments and are comforted by having them. One of Boonlua's friends told me about asking a special favor from Dr. Chom.

> Before the cremation, I asked Dr. Chom if I might have one of Achan's finger bones, and he kindly arranged for one to be given to me. She was such a wonderful writer. To me, her hands were the essence of Boonlua as a writer. I feel comforted and inspired, having that little finger bone with me always. I did wonder, later, if the bone was from her right hand, the one she wrote with, or her left hand—but then I decided that it doesn't matter.[41]

Boonlua's old friend Professor Chetana Nagavajara had his own thoughts about her cremation ceremony.

Those who attended the royally sponsored cremation on 7 June 1984 knew the full extent of Achan Boonlua's contributions: her generosity was unequalled, even to the extent of donating her body to the Siriraj Medical School. When the time came for the ceremony, there was little left to cremate, because Achan Boonlua had given all of herself away.[42]

Professor Chetana expressed surprise when I told him that I was thinking of writing this biography. "If you want to write a biography of a Thai, why have you chosen to write about Boonlua? She was such a *farang!*" He said these words in jest, laughing and then adding, "We worked together for years, you know—and God, how I miss our fights!"

Boonlua drew upon a lavish and supremely eclectic supply of cultural elements from East and West, synthesized them, and created an identity that she explained and sometimes defended as essentially Thai. "My father taught me to speak my own mind" was the rejoinder to those who maintained that Thai ladies, unlike some Western women, were careful never to offend by their remarks. Her father had sometimes spoken unpleasant truths even to King Chulalongkorn, she maintained, because that is what a loyal subject must do. She did not bother to go into the matter of gender considerations and was more concerned with how a *phu di*, a person of quality, would behave in a given situation than with how an ideal Thai woman might behave.

She was never prudish and could be contemptuous of those who were. She said things that other ladies of her class would never think of saying, and she relished the shocked reactions that her remarks sometimes produced. Early in her teaching career, when female colleagues at the Mater Dei School expressed dismay at her decision to use folk music in a student production—"so crude"—Boonlua let them know that their knowledge of Thai theater was paper thin, and that earthy folk songs and tales were the heart of the original Thai theater. They needed to get out of Bangkok, she said, and open their eyes and ears to "Thai culture."

Professor Chetana was not alone in stressing the *farang* aspects of Boonlua's personality. This was a significant issue in the lives of all Western-educated Thais and other Southeast Asians of the early twentieth century who were educated in Western schools and universities, especially those who were sent abroad for many years and then returned home to live the rest of their lives in the country of their birth. They had to create their own identity, as their contemporaries who had stayed in Thailand would never have to do. Their experience was not at all like that of contemporary Thai students who study abroad, flying home from New York, London, or Sydney during winter or summer breaks if they can afford to do so, and who are in almost constant electronic touch with family and friends at home in Thailand. Until at least the 1950s, Thais who went abroad to study stayed there until they had earned their final degree. The experience of the Thai world and the Western world were sequential for them, never parallel, never simultaneous.

Several older Thais who lived the "sequential" version of Thai ethnicity and Western education have told me that their parents sent them Thai books while they were abroad, and many letters, which of course were written in Thai—treasures that they have kept with them throughout their life. For Boonlua, no Thai books arrived by ship, no letters from her mother or father. Nothing was more precious to her than the memories of the father who had cheerfully acknowledged her as his favorite and beloved child, his prodigy and *duang chai*, "heart." He, at least, had loved and approved of her. Her love for Thai language, literature, culture, and history was in some measure an homage to him.

Boonlua's Western education began with Bible stories and proceeded to Shakespeare, Sir Walter Scott, Jane Austen, and Charles Dickens. From then on, her taste in Western literature was eclectic, and her library included such diverse residents as Colette, Virginia Woolf, Agatha Christie, Simone de Beauvoir, Erica Jong, Eudora Welty, Sidney Sheldon, and Philip Roth—and all of their books were protected in the neat covers the Sisters had taught her to make.

The love of shocking people, of making outrageous statements, was hardly a result of her education in the convent schools. She possessed a natural contrariness and the mischievousness that had charmed her father and Prince Narit when she was a small prodigy. This contrariness was one of the reasons, she said, why "my older brothers and sisters couldn't stand me."

I met Boonlua only once, in 1981. Through mutual friends, she had invited me to join her for lunch. She wanted to talk about my recent English translation of Botan's *Letters from Thailand*, the prize-winning novel about three decades in the life of a Chinese merchant family in Bangkok.

I went to her office at Chulalongkorn University, and we took a taxi to a popular and busy restaurant. She praised my translation. I demurred and talked about its flaws, she disagreed and said that what she liked best was that I was a writer, not "just a person looking up the words in a dictionary." We agreed that we liked translations by writers. And then she asked, "Do you know why the rich Chinese businessmen have so many young mistresses?" I tried to think of a reasonable response. She grinned, not waiting for a reply, and said, "It is because they are impotent. (Pause) They're married to their work. All of their energy and their passion goes to the business, they work all the time, and there's nothing left. They think that another pretty young girl will solve the problem."

I knew very little about Boonlua when I met her, only that she taught literature and had written some novels. I did realize that she must have been thinking up this interesting remark about the Chinese businessmen before I arrived at her office and enjoyed thinking about how I might react. Finally I said, "I would never have thought of that." Then I pulled a pen and a notebook from my handbag and made a note of her remark. I did not look around to see what the people seated around us in the restaurant might be making of our conversation—which they could hardly avoid hearing—and neither did she.

THE END OF THE JOURNEY

Boonlua was a deeply religious person, a Theravada Buddhist who also believed wholeheartedly in the reality and the power of the spirit world. The Roman Catholicism that permeated the fabric of everyday life in the convent schools had little or no effect on her belief system. She had prayed to Jesus to enter her heart, as one of the Sisters in Penang had earnestly advised, nothing had happened, and she had given it up. But the ghost tales she had heard as a child stayed with her throughout her life. I have never encountered a Thai who was told ghost stories as a child and was able to completely overcome these fears as an adult. It is interesting that Chao Phraya Thewet himself hated ghost stories and insisted to his children that dead people are just bodies, no different from a dead pig or ox, and that spirits do not rise up from dead bodies to harm the living. I do not know how he came by this eminently rational point of view. Perhaps he really did fear ghosts and he blamed the ghost stories of his own childhood for those fears. Despite his strong disapproval, his children would not give up frightening each other after dark with tales of malign spirits and grisly violence, and so they lived with the consequences.

Boonlua's friend Khunying Ambhorn Meesook summed up her thoughts on Boonlua with the words, "I have always wondered—why was she the way she was? So outspoken, so unwilling to compromise." Boonlua herself always answered questions of this kind by saying that she knew she was unusual for a Thai woman, and the reason was that she had an essentially "male" intelligence due to the fact that she had been "raised by men." The truth, however, is that while Boonlua was *indulged* by her father and his friend Prince Narit, she was *raised* by women—first, by her mother, stepmothers, older sisters, and other female relatives in the household, and then by the nuns of St. Joseph Convent in Bangkok and the Convent of the Holy Infant Jesus in Penang.

Boonlua went into the world and made a career there, which was ground-breaking for the time. But she was not alone among the women in her family in excelling at a profession and finding recognition for her accomplishments. Her sister Buppha also excelled and was recognized in the world beyond home. And in the Kunchon family of that generation, only these two women, among their many siblings, male and female, achieved lasting recognition and fame.

When I began this biography, a friend who was then working on the biography of a British woman of about the same era suggested that I look more closely at Boonlua's relationship with her mother. The relationship with the mother, she said, especially in the case of a female subject, must be examined carefully. I patiently explained that Boonlua had practically no relationship with her mother and looked to her father as her primary role model and primary parent. But as time has passed, I have changed my mind, and I am grateful to my colleague for planting this idea in my mind.

Buppha's mother, Malai, scandalized Thai society by leaving her husband, demanding a bill of divorcement, supporting herself by teaching dancing, and going to live with a foreign man. Less is known about Boonlua's mother, Nuan, who died very young, but the few words Boonlua wrote about her mother in *Successes and Failures* are more significant than they first appear: "My mother was never too ill to reach out and pinch me." Nuan, unlike most of the other women in the household, had insisted that her daughter learn to read when she was only three years old, and was strict to the point of pinching the child whenever she did not learn her lessons, or misbehaved, or "talked back," which was a frequent occurrence. Boonlua was ill most of her life but, like her mother, Boonlua was never too ill to reach out, sometimes "pinching" those whose words or behavior she found wanting.

Both mothers, Malai and Nuan, were intelligent, talented, competitive, and willful—traits that also characterized their daughters. Both daughters chose to pursue professions that in the past had been generally reserved for males: both wrote for publication, and Boonlua was a government official like all of her male ancestors.

Although she insisted that her father was responsible for the resolute way she dealt with the world, the truth is that except for his desire to see all of his children receive a Western education, Chao Phraya was a conservative, old-fashioned man—as was his great friend, Prince Narit. I believe that their piety, the monarchy-centered nature of their patriotism, and their love of the theatrical arts were major bequests to Boonlua's intellectual development. As for the contrary nature she proudly confessed, she may have owed more to her maternal than her paternal inheritance, regardless of the very few years she had with her mother.

Boonlua came onto the playing field of the bureaucracy just after the game had been opened to women. True, she did not win many of the

bureaucratic competitions in which she engaged, but she played a critical
role and prepared the way for other women, just as her mother had
paved the way for her by giving her the gifts of literacy and discipline,
gifts that served her excellently throughout her life.

Boonlua acquired a deep knowledge and understanding of great
and disparate cultures from the great teachers and writers of those
cultures, and then, in her own teaching and writing, she gradually and
purposefully gave it all away, gave all of herself away, and was gone.

> There is no suffering for those who have finished the journey and
> abandoned grief, who have freed themselves on all sides, and thrown
> off all fetters. They depart with their thoughts well-collected, they do
> not delight in an abode. Like swans who have left their lake, they leave
> their house and home.
>
> —*Dhammapada*, 90–93

A CHRONOLOGY OF BOONLUA'S LIFE

1852   Birth of Boonlua's father, Chao Phraya Thewet (Mom Rachawong Lan Kunchon).

1910   King Vajiravudh (1910–25), sixth king of the Chakri dynasty (1782–present) ascends the throne.

1911   December 13: Birth of Mom Luang Boonlua Kunchon, thirty-second child of Chao Phraya Thewet; first and only child of Mom Nuan.

1915   Death of Boonlua's mother, Mom Nuan. Boonlua enters St. Joseph Convent School, Bangkok.

1922   Chao Phraya Thewet dies. Boonlua is sent to the Convent of the Holy Infant Jesus in Penang, where she remains until 1928.

1925   King Vajiravudh dies and is succeeded by his brother, King Prajadhipok (1925–35).

1927   Phraya Thewet, Boonlua's eldest brother, builds the successful Ban Mo movie theater on the grounds of Wang Ban Mo.

1928   Boonlua returns from the convent school in Penang.

1929   Phraya Thewet moves the family to a new residence in Petchaburi.

1930   Boonlua studies at Saint Mary's College, Bangkok, where she also teaches and prepares to enter Chulalongkorn University in the first class admitting women.

1932   The absolute monarchy of Siam is overthrown by the People's Party and replaced by a constitutional monarchy.

1933   Boworadet Rebellion against the 1932 overthrow of the absolute monarchy. Some relatives and friends of Boonlua are imprisoned.

1935   King Prajadhipok abdicates and is succeeded by King Ananda Mahidol (1935–46), a ten-year-old prince residing in Switzerland.

1938   Boonlua graduates from Chulalongkorn University with
          a BA and a teaching certificate, and she begins teaching at
          the elite Rajini Girls' School.
1941   Japan invades Thailand and embarks upon a comparatively
          benign occupation. Allied forces bomb many sites in
          Thailand and a Thai resistance movement is established.
          Thailand formally declares war upon the United States, but
          the declaration is kept unopened in the desk of the Thai
          ambassador to Washington.
1943–45   Boonlua participates in the National Cultural Program
          while teaching, and she briefly moves with her family to a
          safe rural location.
1945   The war ends, Thailand reestablishes ties with Great Britain
          and the United States.
          Pridi Banomyong (regent for the young King Ananda
          Mahidol) declares the 1941 Declaration of War against the
          United States and Great Britain to be null and void.
          Boonlua asks for a leave of absence on the grounds of
          exhaustion, and it is granted.
1946   King Ananda Mahidol dies, succeeded by his brother,
          Bhumibol Adulyadej.
          Boonlua returns to teaching Thai literature at
          Chulalongkorn University.
1948–50   Boonlua enters graduate school at the University of
          Minnesota, earning an MA in education.
1953   Boonlua is appointed director of the Education Inspection
          Unit, responsible for secondary education throughout the
          kingdom.
1950s   Boonlua occupies several positions in the Ministry of
          Education including acting director of admissions at Triam
          Udom school (prep school attached to Chulalongkorn
          University), and principal of a UNESCO-sponsored
          regional program to improve the teaching of English in all
          of Southeast Asia.

1956   Death of Phraya Thewet, Boonlua's eldest brother and head of the family.

1957   Coup d'état by Field Marshal Sarit Thanarat restoring a prominent role for the king and royal family.

1959   Boonlua marries Dr. Chom Debyasuvarn, an epidemiologist in the Ministry of Public Health.

1960   Boonlua is appointed vice rector of a new provincial college at Bang Saen on the Gulf of Thailand; she resigns after one year.

1962   Boonlua publishes her first novel, *Western Daughter-in-Law* (*Saphai maem*), set before and during World War II.

1963   Death of Buppha Kunchon Nimmanhemin, Boonlua's closest sister, a famous novelist writing under the pen name Dokmai Sot (fresh flower), in India, where her husband Dr. Sukij Nimmanhemin served as Thai ambassador.

1968   Boonlua founds the Faculty of Arts at the new campus of Silpakorn University in Nakhon Pathom.
        Publication of Boonlua's novel *Thutiyawiset*, the name of a decoration given to the women of high officials.

1970   Boonlua's retirement from government service for health reasons.

1971   Boonlua is awarded the Chula Chom Klao medal for outstanding service to the nation by King Bhumibol Adulyadej.

1972   Publication of a collection of translated American short stories, *Ruap-ruam rueang san chak saharat America* (Collected American short stories).
        Publication of the novel *Land of Women* (*Suratnari*).

1973   October 14: Protests by students and other political activists, followed by police and military massacre of demonstrators and the fall of the military government.
        Publication of Boonlua's collection of essays on Thai literature, *The Turning Point of Thai Literature* (*Hua liao khong wannakhadi thai*).

1974   Publication of Boonlua's memoir, *Successes and Failures*
             (Khwam samret lae khwam lom laeo).
             Publication of her collected essays on literary criticism,
             Analysis of Thai Literature (Wikhro rot wannakhadi thai).

1976   October 6: Military government regains power, with
             massacres of students and others; survivors are imprisoned
             or flee into exile.

1978   General Kriangsak Chomanan declares amnesty for all
             October 1976 political prisoners, persons in hiding, and
             those in exile.

1982   June 7: Boonlua dies at Siriraj Hospital, four days after
             suffering a heart attack.

1984   June 7: Cremation ceremony at Wat Makutkasatriyaram,
             Bangkok. Her Royal Highness Princess Maha Chakri
             Sirindhorn presides.

KINGS OF THE CHAKRI DYNASTY

The Chakri dynasty was founded in 1782, fifteen years after Ayutthaya, the former capital of the kingdom of Siam, fell to invading Burmese forces in 1767. The appellations "Rama I, Rama II," and so on were instituted and made retroactive to the first five kings of the dynasty by King Vajiravudh (1910–1825), who was educated in England and felt that the names of the Thai kings were too difficult for non-Thais. The full titles are longer, but the shortened versions are given below.

Phra Phutthayotfa (Rama I)
1782–1809

Phra Phutthaloetla (Rama II)
1809–1824

Phra Nangklao (Rama III)
1824–1851

Mongkut (Rama IV)
1851–1868

Chulalongkorn (Rama V)
1868–1910

Vajiravudh (Rama VI)
1910–1925

Prajadhipok (Rama VII)
1925–1935 (abdicated)

Ananda Mahidol (Rama VIII)
1935–1946

Bhumibol Adulyadej (Rama IX)
9 June 1946–

THAI ROYAL TITLES AND ROYALLY CONFERRED TITLES

The King
Phrabat Somdet Phra Chao Yu Hua (crowned king)
Somdet Phra Chao Yu Hua (uncrowned king)

The King's Consorts

Queens
Somdet Phra Borommarachininat (highest honor; a queen with this
    title may act as regent during the king's absence)
Somdet Phra Borommarachini
Somdet Phra Rachini

Other consorts descended from royalty (obsolete)
Somdet Phra Borommaratchathewi
Phra Nangchao Phra Ratchathewi/Phra Nangchao Phra Akkhra
    Ratchathewi
Phra Nang Thoe
Phra Akkhra Chaya Thoe
Phra Ratcha Chaya

Consorts who were born commoners (obsolete)
Chao Chom
Chao Chom Manda (Chao Chom who has borne a child to the king)

Descendants of a King
Royal princes and princesses
Chao Fa (HRH Prince) (HRH Princess)
Phra Ong Chao (HRH Prince) (HRH Princess)

Mom Chao (His/Her Serene Highness)
Mom Ratchawong (M.R.)
Mom Luang (M.L.)

Miscellaneous titles of royal descendants (obsolete)
Mom (royalty)
Prince's wife's title (unless otherwise elevated by the sovereign)
Phra Chaya
Chaya
Mom (wife)

Feudal titles for male commoners (all obsolete since 1932)
Somdet Chao Phraya
Chao Phraya
Phraya
Phra
Luang
Khun
Muean
Phan
Nai
Phrai

Lifetime conferred titles for female commoners (still in use, given to the wife of a high-ranking man, also given to a woman for her own service and contributions to the kingdom)
  Than Phuying (wife of a prime minister)
  Khunying (wife of a high-ranking man, or a woman who has made
    substantial contributions to the kingdom)

PRIME MINISTERS OF THAILAND
1932–1982

1. Phraya Manopakonnitithada (Kot Hutasing)	June 28, 1932–June 20, 1933
2. Phraya Phahonphonphayuhasena (Phot Phahonyothin)	June 21, 1933–September 11, 1938
3. Luang Phibunsongkhram (Plaek Phibunsongkhram)	December 16, 1938–August 1, 1944
4. Khuang Aphaiwong	August 1, 1944–August 31, 1945
5. Thawi Bunyaket	August 31, 1945–September 17, 1945
6. M.R. Seni Pramoj	September 17, 1945–October 15, 1945
7. Khuang Aphaiwong	January 31, 1946–March 24, 1946
8. Pridi Phanomyong	March 24, 1946–August 23, 1946
9. Luang Thamrongnawasawat (Thawan Thamrongnawasawat)	August 23, 1946–November 8, 1947
10. Khuang Aphaiwong	November 10, 1947–April 8, 1948
11. P. Phibunsongkhram	April 8, 1948–September 16, 1957
12. Phot Sarasin	September 21, 1956–December 26, 1957
13. Thanom Kittikachorn	January 1, 1958–October 20, 1958
14. Sarit Thanarat	February 9, 1959–December 8, 1963
15. Thanom Kittikachorn	December 9, 1963–October 14, 1973
16. Sanya Dharmasakti	October 14, 1973–January 21, 1975
17. M.R. Seni Pramoj	February 21, 1975–March 6, 1975
18. M.R. Kukrit Pramoj	March 17, 1975–January 12, 1976
19. M.R. Seni Pramoj	April 21, 1976–October 8, 1976
20. Thanin Kraivichien	October 22, 1976–October 20, 1977
21. Kriangsak Chomanand	November 12, 1977–February 29, 1980
22. Prem Tinsulanonda	March 12, 1980–April 29, 1988

NOTES

1. IN HER FATHER'S HOUSE

1. The Chakri dynasty was founded in 1782 and continues to the present day. See appendix 1 for the names and dates of the Chakri dynasty kings, and appendix 2 for an outline of royal titles used before and after the overthrow of the absolute monarchy in 1932.

2. Costumes that were divided between Western and native influences—above and below, respectively—were common at the time throughout Southeast Asia. For a description and photographs of similar integrations of costume in Indonesia, see Pemberton, *On the Subject of "Java,"* 102–47.

3. There might also be a smaller bed at the foot of the large, royal bed where a woman could sleep.

4. Surnames were officially adopted during the reign of King Vajiravudh (1910–25).

5. *Phi* means elder (sister). Younger friends and relatives referred to Boonlua as "Phi Lua," a shortened and familiar version of her name.

Ayutthaya was the capital of Siam from the fifteenth century until 1767, when it was destroyed by the Burmese. In Boonlua's childhood, the journey there would have taken one day by boat and ox cart.

6. Rukchira Akarasena, interview with author, June 1995. Rukchira was a relative of Boonlua, whose mother, like Boonlua's own mother, died when Rukchira was a young girl. Boonlua always looked after Rukchira, who lived on at Wang Thewet into old age and was provided for in Boonlua's will.

7. In Kumut Chandruang's memoir, *My Boyhood in Siam*, he also tells of his father's disapproval of ghost stories, which had its foundation in the modern, "scientific" view of the world that became fashionable among men of the elite who followed the example of King Mongkut and his son King Chulalongkorn. Kumut's father, who was of the same generation as Chao Phraya Thewet, told his children,

"You should not be afraid of dead people, because they are more than too sick or too weak. They are dead. And the skeletons are not different from fish bones or dead leaves" (68). However, this is not a typical Thai view of the dead, who traditionally are imagined to have great power, especially if they died violently.

8. Boonlua, *Khwam samret lae khwam lom laeo*, (hereafter *Khwam samret* in notes, *Successes and Failures* in text), 9. A significant element in Suntaree's 1990 NIDA study of Thai values, *Psychology of the Thai People*, is its focus on the important role of supernatural and "extra-Buddhist" beliefs in Thai life. These beliefs, she claims, as one result of the research, comprise an element of the religious life of Buddhists that is at least as important as orthodox Buddhist teachings.

9. Mom Rachawong Kukrit Pramoj, born in 1911 like Boonlua, was one of the "Renaissance men" of the twentieth century. He was a banker, newspaper publisher, diplomat, prime minister, and author of many short stories and novels, including *Four Reigns (Si phaendin)*, the most popular novel of the twentieth century.

10. See Wyatt, *Studies*, 185–209. Prince Anu is remembered as a traitor, from the Thai perspective, but celebrated as a hero and martyr by the Lao.

11. For information on the controversy surrounding the succession, see Wyatt, *Thailand: A Short History*, 167, and Keyes, *Thailand: Buddhist Kingdom as Modern Nation-State*, 57, 139. Mongkut did not simply retreat to the safety of the yellow robe. He studied many subjects including English and Latin, wrote essays on Thai Buddhism, engineered far-reaching religious reforms including the foundation of the strict, reformist Thammayut sect, and carried out significant research on Siamese history and art.

12. The body of a member of the royal family, or of a person of very high rank, is folded upright in a fetal position inside a narrow urn, which is then put into an elaborate spired structure called a *monthop*. The *monthop* is not burned; it is reused for future royal cremations. Thai Buddhists at all levels of society are cremated, and the ashes kept by relatives; only Chinese Buddhists and Christians are buried in Thailand.

13. King Taksin was ceremonially executed by General Chakri, his brother, and their followers, who claimed that Taksin's religious fanaticism and increasingly bizarre behavior made him a danger to the kingdom, which was struggling to survive after the Burmese devastation. See Gesick, *Kingship*, for a detailed examination of Taksin's rise, rule, and death, and the subsequent rise of the Chakri dynasty.

14. The top-knot (or tonsure) cutting ceremony is a Brahmanist rather than Buddhist ceremony and was of great importance until modern times. A lengthy description can be found in Plion-Bernier, *Festivals and Ceremonies of Thailand*, and a brief account of a royally sponsored tonsure ceremony is included in Smithies, *Descriptions of Old Siam*.

15. Boonlua, Phillips interviews, 1966.

16. See Jiraporn, "Nationalism," 26–43, for information about the *lakhon* within and beyond the Royal Palace.

17. Buppha married Dr. Sukij Nimmanhemin in 1954. A few years later he was appointed ambassador to India. In 1963, Buppha died of chronic lung and heart disease at the Thai embassy in New Delhi.

18. For example, commoners *pai* (go), but royals *sadet*. Other societies throughout Asia employ similar indicators of rank and status through language.

19. Somphop, *Dokmai Sot*, 28.

20. Boonlua, Phillips interviews, 1966.

21. Ibid.

22. Siphroma, *Autobiography*, 14.

23. Several people who knew her told me that Mom Anuwong was actually very bright and won prizes at school. Nevertheless, in speaking to me she positioned herself as having been "the pretty one," by comparison with Boonlua, "the smart one," declining to mention her own outstanding school performance.

24. Classical dancers must be able to arch their fingers back gracefully. Besides the finger-bending that occurred in dance classes, it was common practice to bend the fingers back as a punishment when a girl disobeyed, which was supposed to improve both her behavior and the beauty of her hands.

25. Mom Anuwong, interview with author, July 1995. She spoke English very well, and in fact was unable to write Thai, except for her name, because she had no education outside of the convent schools. Her marriage to Mom Chao (Prince) Nidhasanatorn Chirapravati was considered a "brilliant match," especially by comparison with Boonlua's marriage at forty-eight to a middle-class physician—a point that Mom Anuwong emphasized: "None of us liked him."

26. The omission is largely a result of the fact that the NIDA study on Thai personality employed a "culture-corrected" conceptual framework based on the work of American social psychologist James Rokeach. Culture corrected or not, it made no provision for the role of aesthetics.

27. *Bun bamphen*, 2.

28. Boonlua, Phillips interviews, 1966.

29. In the most famous and beloved novel of the twentieth century, *Four Reigns*, the main character, Phloi, suffers as a result of the intrigues in her father's polygynous household, as do her siblings. Yet there is never a hint of disapproval of this system on the part of any of the characters. Phloi admires and loves her father, and longs for his approval.

30. Boonlua, Phillips interviews, 1966.

31. Boonlua, *Waen wannakam*, 126. This is a poignant element in the plot of *Phu di*, her sister Dokmai Sot's novel. A dying wife hopes that following her death, her husband will marry the good young woman who lives nearby. Yet, she is consumed with jealousy for the young woman, who would be not only wife to her husband, but mother to her young son. This novel has not been translated from Thai, but the situation I have described appears as an excerpt in Kepner, *The Lioness in Bloom*.

32. Kepner, *Lioness in Bloom*, 125 and 128, italics added. This novel has been translated into English in its entirety by David Smyth. See Siburapa, *Behind the Painting*.

33. Boonlua, *Khwam samret*, 4–5.

34. *Bun bamphen*, 4–5.

35. Boonlua, *Khwam samret*, 10.

36. *Bun bamphen*, 3.

37. Boonlua told several people that while studying the concept of the "mature mind" as a graduate student at the University of Minnesota, as soon as she had grasped the meaning of the term, she immediately thought of Prince Narit.

38. Boonlua, Phillips interviews, 1966.

39. Ibid.

40. Ibid.

41. Ibid.

42. In Thai, *tham*. This might involve any number of acts, including bringing food or supplies to the monks (who cannot handle money themselves), or contributing money for various temple projects.

43. Boonlua, Phillips interviews, 1966.

44. Siphroma, *Autobiography*, 2–3. Phra Wetsandon is believed by Thai to have been the last incarnation of the Buddha prior to his final incarnation as Lord Gautama, when he achieved enlightenment and became the Buddha. In giving away his children, Phra Wetsandon showed that he had overcome all attachments, even to his own children. This story is read over the radio and in temples once each year, and is known as the Mahachat. Thai Buddhists believe that listening to the entire story earns merit.

2. FROM THE PALACE TO THE NUNS

1. Chetana, "Literature in Thai Life," 19.

2. Ibid., 20.

3. Ibid., 21.

4. Ibid., 20.

5. Hudak, *Translation*, 1–3.

6. Thai writers, like writers in neighboring countries, went through several stages in developing modern literature. At first they made (very loose) translations of Western novels and stories. These were more like adaptations or synopses or "condensed books" than true translations; Boonlua's "translation" of *Ivanhoe* is such a work. Gradually, they began to use Western forms to write novels and stories with Thai characters, in Thai settings. One significant way in which the Thai early novels and short stories differ from those produced in Vietnam or Indonesia is that writers in those nations used literature to protest, with varying degrees of subtlety, the domination of their colonial masters. Since loyalty to the Royal Government of Siam was synonymous with virtue, and since very few Thais would have equated the internal hegemony of the absolute monarchy and the Siamese elite with domination by a foreign power, the most politically controversial elements in Thai fiction at that time were relatively mild indictments of class inequities. Novels available in translation that address these themes include Siburapha, *Behind the Painting*, and K. Surangkhanang, *The Prostitute*. Both translations are by David Smyth.

7. Vella, *Chaiyo!*, 3.

8. Chula Chakrabongse, *Lords of Life*, 232; italics added.

9. General Thamasak Senivongse Na Ayutthaya, conversation with author, July 2010.

10. Somphop, *Dokmai Sot*, 30.

11. Knight, *Treasured One*, 46–47.

12. Somphop, *Dokmai Sot*, 28–29.

13. Black was worn only by farmers in Thailand. In the early twentieth century, urban Thais who could afford to do so began to wear "mourning" garments after a death in the family, in imitation of the European custom. Boonlua disapproved of this borrowed practice as an "affectation."

14. Boonlua, *Khwam samret*, 10–11.

15. Ibid., 11. This is one of the first Buddhist teachings a child is taught: *Tham di dai di tham chua dai chua* (Do good, receive good; do evil, receive evil).

16. Boonlua, Phillips interviews, 1966.

17. Ibid.

18. This information appears in the introduction to the complete collected *Lakhon duekdamban* composed by Prince Naritsara-anuwattiwong, in the cremation volume published in honor of Mr. Khatawut Intaratut.

19. Boonlua, conversation with author, 1981.

20. Boonlua, Phillips interviews, 1966.

21. Boonlua, *Khwam samret*, 29–30.

22. See chapter 1 for Mom Anuwong's remarks on their rivalry.

23. Sunetra Khomsiri, interview with author, Bangkok, June 15, 1995. Years later, many of the women who had studied at this convent together continued to meet regularly for lunch in Bangkok or to play cards. According to a great-niece, Boonlua never joined them.

24. Boonlua, *Khwam samret*, 26; italics added.

25. Ibid., 28.

25. Ibid.

27 Ibid., 29.

28. Boonlua, Phillips interviews, 1966.

29. Boonlua, *Khwam samret*, 36.

30. Ibid., 33–34.

3. RETURN AND REVOLUTION

Initial quotation from Boonlua, Phillips interviews, 1966.

1. See Blanche Wiesen Cook, *Eleanor Roosevelt*, vol. 1, chapter 3: "Childhood of Loss and Tears."

2. Ibid., 62.

3. Ibid.

4. Ibid.

5. Information about the Ban Mo theater is taken from Somphop, *Chiwit*, 46–48, and from a number of interviews.

6. In Thai, *phu ko kan [plian plaeng]*, literally, "people who initiate/incite/cause [change]."

7. In Thai, *kan plian plaeng khong rabop kan mueang*.

8. See Chai-anan, "Political History," 1–11; Chai-anan, "State-Identity Creation"; Morell and Chai-anan, *Political Conflict*, chapter 2; Suchit, "Political Institutions and Processes"; Thak, *Despotic Paternalism*, xii–xix; and Thinaphan, "Political Culture".

9. Yos, "Power and Personality," 56.

10. See Barmé, *Luang Wichit Wathakan*, chapter 4; Keyes, *Thailand: Buddhist Kingdom*, 61–66; Thawatt, *Thai Revolution*, 43–96; and Thompson, *Thailand: The New Siam*, 60–61.

11. Despite all, Col. Khap's career prospects would remain bright in the years following 1932 because of his ability to make himself useful to the Promoters as a liaison between the old elite and the new leadership. His role in the following decades will be discussed in chapters 5 and 8 in the context of Boonlua's novel *Thuthiyawiset*.

12. See Batson, *The End of the Absolute Monarchy*, 71–128; and Wyatt, *Thailand*, 234–42.

13. Chula Chakrabongse, *Lords of Life*, 222–23; also see Malcolm Smith, *Physician*, chapter 6, "Polygamy in Siam."

14. Smith, *Physician*, 51–137, focuses on the "queen's side" of the history of the fifth reign. Chulalongkorn's own mother was Princess Rampoei, another of King Mongkut's consorts, and a granddaughter of King Rama III (1824–54). Rama III was the half-brother of King Mongkut (Rama IV, 1851–68), who succeeded him and who was Chulalongkorn's father.

15. Prince Vajirunhis died of kidney disease, a common affliction in the royal family. It has also been suggested that Vajirunhis was infected by the plague and that kidney failure was one complication of his illness. I have not been able to verify whether this rumor, which I have heard from several people, is true. There is no question that the Grand Palace was heavily infested with rats. Lady Siphroma Kridakon, who lived at the palace, recounts in her memoirs that on the evening of King Chulalongkorn's death, "I woke up suddenly because there was a creature biting my big toe, drawing blood. At the same time I heard the noise of rats. There must have been several score of them.... Besides running back and forth along the full length of the building... the rats also uttered the sound 'kook, kook' the whole time. I used to hear grown-ups say that when the rats cried 'kook, kook' a bad thing would happen" (*Autobiography*, 85). Another version of the crown prince's death—that he was deliberately poisoned—is found in Sarasas, *My Country Thailand*, 135. It must be understood that Phra Sarasas held a very dim view of the monarchy, and that he offered no evidence in support of his conjecture.

16. Brailey, *Two Views of Siam*, 39. One possible source of the rumor that Vajirunhis had been poisoned was the general knowledge of the rivalry between the two queens, each of whom promoted her sons for the succession.

17. Walter F. Vella's biography, *Chaiyo! King Vajiravudh and the Development of Thai Nationalism*, remains the chief source of information about this king and his reign available in English. Also see Hunter and Chakrabongse, *Katya and the Prince of Siam*, a biography of Prince Chakrabongse's Russian wife that contains substantial information on life in Siam during King Vajiravudh's reign.

18. This information was confided in interviews during 1995 and 1996 by several knowledgeable informants who asked to remain anonymous.

19. Although Thai society is not entirely without prejudice toward homosexuality, in general, sexual preference is considered to be a private matter and is believed to be the result of an individual's karma, that is, a result of behaviors and events in one's former lives. There is virtually no prejudice against homosexuals who marry, produce children to carry on their family name, and pursue their sexual preferences in a discreet manner.

20. One recently published book on the subject is David Streckfuss, *Truth on Trial in Thailand: Defamation, Treason, and Lèse-Majesté* (London: Routledge, 2011).

21. This suggests that people closest to him were not his closest relatives or princes of very high rank, as most of his father's closest advisors and friends had been. Vajiravudh created his own circle in his own palace.

22. Smith, *Physician*, 114.

23. Sarasas, *My Country Thailand*, 130.

24. See Wyatt, *Thailand*, 54.

25. For detailed information on King Vajiravudh's literary works, see Vella, *Chaiyo!*, chapter 8, "The Past as Model."

26. The social extravagance and theatricality of the Rama VI era are well displayed in M.R. Kukrit Pramoj's *Four Reigns*. The more controversial aspects of the reign are not ignored but are presented in subtle but unmistakable ways. The English translation is by "Tulachandra" (Chiang Mai: Silkworm Books, 199).

27. Barmé, *Luang Wichit Wathakan*, 19; italics added.

28. Ibid., 159.

29. Ibid., 160.

30. In fact, many young elite Thai women (including all of the women in Boonlua's family) had started wearing their hair long some years before, after King Chulalongkorn's trips to Europe in 1897 and 1907. Young Thai males returning from European universities also had an effect on their sisters and future wives in regard to fashion. Finally, there were quite a few European women living in Bangkok from the reign of King Chulalongkorn on, displaying their fashions and coiffures at various social events. Vajiravudh was more responsible for changes in dress than in hairstyles, encouraging women to wear the simple *pha nung*, a straight length of cloth wrapped about the body in a tube-like fashion. Until then, only Lao and Northern Thai women had worn such plain and form-fitting lower garments. Initially, Thai women were alarmed at the idea of the change, but the new fashion quickly caught on, and the *chongkraben* style soon became an artifact of earlier reigns, or a costume to be donned on special occasions. Men continued to wear the *chongkraben* to social functions long after women had ceased to do so.

31. Vella, *Chaiyo!*, 159.

32. Knight, *Treasured One*, 105–6.

33. See Barmé, *Luang Wichit Wathakan*, 27–34; Hamilton, "Rumours"; Kanpirom, *Phrabat somdet phra mongkut klao*; and Vella, *Chaiyo!*, chapter 7.

34. Kanpirom, *Phrabat somdet phra mongkut klao*, 48.

35. Prince Chula Chakrabongse, who wrote *Lords of Life*, one of the first books about the Chakri dynasty written in English, was the son of Prince Chakrabongse, who was a son of King Chulalongkorn and his Russian wife, Ekaterina.

36. See Kanpirom, *Phrabat somdet phra mongkut klao*, 81–85; and Vella, *Chaiyo!*, 193–94.

37. Kanpirom, *Phrabat somdet phra mongkut klao*, 71–73.

38. This paradigm was somewhat altered, temporarily, under the administrations of Field Marshal Phibun Songkhram (1937–45 and 1947–57), when the monarchy's role was much diminished. The political and social dimensions of this era are discussed in chapter 5.

39. Kanpirom, *Phrabat somdet phra mongkut klao*, 65; Vella, *Chaiyo!*, 207–8.

40. Vella, *Chaiyo!*, 130.

41. See Kanpirom, *Phrabat somdet phra mongkut klao*, 239–49; and Vella, *Chaiyo!*, 75–76.

42. Vella, *Chaiyo!*, 75–76.

43. Ibid., 29.

44. Ibid., 32.

45. Boonlua, Phillips interviews, 1966.

46. Anonymous source, April 1997.

47. See Thawatt, *Thai Revolution*, 25–30, for a brief description of the 1912 coup attempt and a comparison with the successful 1932 attempt.

48. Batson, *The End of the Absolute Monarchy*, 16–19.

49. Vella, *Chaiyo!*, 252.

50. Batson, *The End of the Absolute Monarchy*, 17.

51. Ibid., 18.

52. Kanpirom, *Phrabat somdet phra mongkut klao*, 184.

53. Princess Lakshami was the sister of Princess Rudivoravan, who wrote in her autobiography, *The Treasured One*, "Since [my sister] Lakshmi had married Rama VI and was queen of Siam, why was she living in Udorn Palace alone? My father showed no inclination to tell me" (84). The implication, throughout this memoir, is that the king fell in love with another woman, and thus was no longer interested in Princess Lakshami. The fact that she was the second of his consorts, not the first, is never mentioned.

54. Vella, *Chaiyo!*, 158.

55. See Batson, *The End of the Absolute Monarchy*; Landon, *Siam in Transition*, 9–39; Prudhisan, *Nation-building*, 19–23; Thak, *Thai Politics*, 1–35; Thawatt, *Thai Revolution*, 43–104; and Wyatt, *Thailand*, 234–42.

56. Wyatt, *Thailand*, 235.

57. Chula Chakrabongse, *Lords of Life*, 287.

58. Monks are not allowed to eat between midday and the following morning, and the prince suffered from a digestive ailment that was aggravated by these dietary restrictions.

59. Batson, *The End of the Absolute Monarchy*, 43.

60. Chula Chakrabongse, *Lords of Life*, 26.

61. Wyatt, *Thailand*, 235.

62. Batson, *The End of the Absolute Monarchy*, 31.

63. Yos, "Power and Personality," 47.

64. Thak, ed., *Thai Politics*, 5.

65. The Kunchon family's experiences during the week of the coup are detailed in Boonlua's autobiography, *Khwam samret*.

66. "Luang" was his civil service title under the pre-overthrow system. Other common spellings of his appointive name include Phibunsongkram and Phibul Songkram. He is also referred to as "Chomphon Pho," or "Field Marshal P."

67. The novel *Thutiyawiset* is discussed in chapter 8, with translations of passages from the novel.

68. Thawatt, *Thai Revolution*, 30.

69. Kunchon family member, interview with author, July 1995.

70. Thawatt, *Thai Revolution*, 37.

71. "Announcement of the People's Party," in Thak, ed., *Thai Politics*, 4–7.

72. Thawatt, *Thai Revolution*, 38; originally published in *The Bangkok Times*, June 24, 1932.

73. Chula Chakrabongse, *Lords of Life*, 313–14.

74. See "Queen Rambhai's Memoir [of the events of 1932]," in Thak, ed., *Thai Politics*, 8–35. This document also includes communications from Prince Narit and King Prajadhipok.

75. Thawatt, *Thai Revolution*, 41.

76. Ibid., 21.

77. Chai-anan, "*Political History*," 6.

78. Yos, "Power and Personality," 55.

79. Landon, *Siam in Transition*, 23.

80. Thak, ed., *Thai Politics*, 110; italics added.

81. Boonlua, Phillips interviews, 1966.

82. Batson, *The End of the Absolute Monarchy*, 250.

83. Ibid., 252.

84. Prince Mahidol studied medicine in the United States, where his two sons (including the present king, Bhumibol Adulyadej) were born. After his early death, his wife took their sons to Switzerland, where they lived until they reached adulthood

4. THE YEARS OF OPPORTUNITY

1. Boonlua, *Khwam samret*, 42–45.

2. Coincidentally, another man named Tom Johnson, an American, visited Siam in 1926–27. Interested readers may wish to read his observations of the kingdom at that time, including meetings with King Prajadhipok and Queen Rambhai, attending *lakhon* performances, attending the changing of garments of the Emerald Buddha at Wat Phra Kaeo, and so on: www.vermonthistory.org/journal/76/VHS760203_149-180.pdf.

3. Boonlua, *Khwam samret*, 38; italics added.

4. Ibid., 40.

5. Phya Anuman was a famous scholar and writer on Thai cultural and historical subjects. He was born into a Chinese family of modest means and created his own, unique niche in Thai society. Many of his writings, particularly a series of booklets on Thai culture, were translated into English.

6. Boonlua, Phillips interviews, 46.

7. Ladies of the palace, and other elite ladies, dressed in the traditionally appropriate color of the day: Sunday, red; Monday, yellow; Tuesday, pink; Wednesday, green; Thursday, orange; Friday, blue; Saturday, purple.

8. Chulalongkorn classmate, interview with author, July 1995, unnamed here by request of the family. The error about Boonlua's name was so infuriating because, first, the prefix *nang* before a woman's name is only used to refer to a married woman. A single woman would be referred to using the prefix *nang sao*. Second, and much worse, he failed to use her title, *mom luang*, which in fact would have taken precedence over and negated the need to use either *nang* or *nang sao*. One could speculate that the individual reading the names had been "set up" by students wishing to play a practical joke on Mom Luang Boonlua, whose regard for her family connections was well known.

9. Khunying Ambhorn Meesook was given her title by His Majesty King Bhumibol Adulyadej for her substantial service to the kingdom. Her long and distinguished career included many high government positions including that of Human Rights Commissioner.

10. Ambhorn Meesook, conversation with author, Bangkok, July 20, 1995.

11. Boonlua, Phillips interviews, 45.

12. Sulloway, *Born to Rebel*, 22.

13. Ibid., 21.

14. Ibid., 95.

15. Boonlua, Phillips interviews, 5.

16. The word I have translated as "heart" is *chit chai*. This word may be compared, depending upon the context, to the English words "spirit," "mind," "state of mind," and "heart."

17. Boonlua, Phillips interviews, 13.

18. There was some latitude. A suitor's family might be quite willing to compromise on the matter of a woman's age if her social status was very high and her family wealthy. This was the case in the novel, *Beyond the Painting*, by Sriburapha, which is set in the 1930s. The heroine is thirty-five, when her father arranges her marriage to his friend, an old man of fifty-five.

19. The bride, a beautiful young German woman, appears in a family photograph standing between Boonlua's sisters Chalaem and Buppha in front of the main building of Wang Ban Mo. A character based upon this young woman would appear in Boonlua's novel *Saphai maem* (Western daughter-in-law).

20. Boonlua, *Khwam samret*, 54–55.

21. Former colleague of Boonlua, interview with author, June 1995.

22. Boonlua, *Khwam samret*, 56.

23. The subject of death and illness in novels by both Boonlua and Buppha is discussed in chapter 8.

24. I once attended a royally sponsored cremation ceremony at which several friends and relatives of the deceased (a man of high status in Thai society although not of royal blood) commented that he would have been proud to know how many of his grandchildren would attend his cremation ceremony in their government uniforms.

25. Boonlua, *Khwam samret*, 47–48.

26. Ibid., 48.

27. The women refer to her as "Khun" Boonlua in deference to her rank. "Boonlua" alone would not suffice.

28. Boonlua, *Khwam samret*, 57.

29. For information on this important ceremony of pre-modern times, see Thawatt, *Thai Revolution*, 25, note 23; and Wales, *Siamese State Ceremonies*, 193–98. All government officials, including women who resided and worked in the inner Grand Palace where no men were allowed, were required to drink the Water of Allegiance. This very old Brahmanic ceremony ended with officials drinking the water from small cups. The manner of drinking the water was very important; any observed difficulty in swallowing was considered to be an indication that the individual might be disloyal.

30. Prince Damrong Rajanuphap was a brother of King Chulalongkorn and also one of his closest advisors. He held many important positions, and it would be difficult to overestimate Prince Damrong's influence in matters of foreign policy, education, art, and the writing of Thai history. The Damrong school of Thai history, now criticized by quite a few contemporary scholars, is examined in many works, including essays by Charnvit, "Thai Historiography," and Thongchai, "Changing Landscape."

31. Nidhi, *Chat Thai*, 48–49.

32. Ibid., 50–51.

33. Ibid., 54.

34. Ibid., 55.

35. Boonlua, *Khwam samret*, 63.

36. Ibid., 66.

37. This is an issue that will resonate strongly for those readers who are aware of the political violence that occurred during April and May of 2010. Many members of the "Red Shirt" faction proudly wore shirts emblazoned with the term "*phrai*." They did not identify the people against whom they were demonstrating (the appointed administration currently in power—and indirectly, "royalists") as *phu di*, but as *amat*, an old term designating government officials.

38. Boonlua, *Khwam samret*, 67.

5. CULTURE WARS

1. Thai interest in and admiration of Germany had also been evident before and during World War I. However, King Vajiravudh had been educated in England and mistrusted Germany; moreover, most of the Western advisors who were active in the Thai government at the outbreak of World War I were British.

2. Subhadradis Diskul, in *Uphayobai*, 15. *Nam phrik*, a staple of Thai cuisine, is made by pounding together chili peppers, herbs, and other ingredients.

3. Boonlua, *Khwam samret*, 71.

4. Kukrit, Phillips interviews, 1965.

5. Boonlua, *Khwam samret*, 76.

6. Prince Subhadradis Diskul, in *Uphayobai*, 15. The remark about "Miss University" is a sarcastic one. Instead of being "Miss Thailand" (*Nang sao thai*, a term everyone would know), Boonlua was "Miss University" (*Nang sao mahawitthayalai*), a young woman who might have won academic laurels, but was unlikely to win any beauty contests.

7. Boonlua, *Khwam samret*, 79.

tion。

8. This diagnosis was dropped from the Diagnostic and Statistical Manual (DSM) in 1980. The symptoms of neurasthenia are sometimes compared, during the present era, to symptoms of fibromyalgia, which also seems to be most common among older women and is treated with a variety of modalities.

9. *Foreign Ministry Archives*, Bangkok, File 2 (Second World War), quoted in Thamsook, *Thailand*, 2.

10. Thak, *Thai Politics*, 450–51.

11. This statement appeared in the January 25, 1943, issue of *Malai Sinpo*, an English newspaper published in Kuala Lumpur, quoted in Thamsook, *Thailand*, 8.

12. This excerpt from "The Declaration of War on Great Britain and the United States" appears in *The Royal Gazette*, part 55, January 25, 1942, 558–59. The US government had decided not to ship the airplanes, which were ordered in 1940, for fear that they would fall into the hands of the Japanese, who even then maintained a substantial presence in Thailand. This information is in the cremation volume for Khuang Aphaiwong, the postwar prime minister, quoted in Thamsook, *Thailand*, 8.

13. Crosby, *Siam*, 137.

14. The most complete examination of the life and contributions of Luang Wichit Wathakan is found in Barme, *Luang Wichit Watakan and the Creation of a Thai Identity*.

15. This novel has not been translated in its entirety; excerpts that appear in this work are mine. The character of the Western daughter-in-law was suggested by the German wife of one of Boonlua's male relatives who had a difficult time adjusting to life in Thailand. She also wrote about the war years in the 1968 novel *Thutiyawiset*, her most famous and critically acclaimed work, which is loosely based on the life of Than Phuying La-iat Phibun Songkhram. This novel is discussed in detail in chapter 8.

16. Boonlua, *Saphai maem*, 17–19.

17. Ibid., 19–20.

18. Ibid., 28.

19. Ibid., 78. The remark about "crazy songs" (*phleng bababobo*) is almost certainly a reference to the jingoistic patriotic songs of the times, most of them written by Wichit Wathakan.

20. In *The Royal Gazette*, vol. 59, part 1221, "The Professions Reservations Act, 1942," June 5, 1942.

21. An interesting fact beyond the scope of this biography is that Nazi leaders in Germany decided whose Jewish ancestors would be taken notice of and whose would not; the latter included Himmler and some other high officials in the Nazi government.

22. Thamsook, *Thailand*, v.

23. *Ukigumo* is a fine example of social history in fiction and has been translated into English. It is a story about Japanese people in occupied lands during the war. There is no evidence that the author intended to demean the Vietnamese or to depict them as an inferior people; they are simply "the natives" in her story. French characters in the novel (clearly civilized, even if their civilization is on the wane) have distinct personalities. No Vietnamese character does.

24. Kukrit, *Four Reigns*, 1098.

25. Anonymous source, conversation with author, July 2010.

26. *Khu kam* has not been translated into English (*khu* means pair or couple; *kam* means karma). A film based on the novel but somewhat different in its details was made in 1996 and distributed abroad with English subtitles in 1998. Copies are available from various sources on the Internet and in university libraries under the title *Sunset at Chaophraya*.

27. Boonlua, *Khwam samret*, 81–85.

28. The English language curriculum was never threatened. Japanese language was added to university offerings but European languages remained most important. The Thai would have balked at the suggestion that they be discontinued; moreover, the Japanese expected the English language to be useful in their future dealings with the West.

29. Boonlua, *Saphai maem*, 35–36.

30. Anong Lertrakskul, conversation with author, July 1995, and from conversations with a number of other informants during 1995 and 1996.

31. Thak, *Thai Politics*, 267–58.

32. Barme, *Luang Wichit Wathakan*, 19.

33. Luang Wichit also wrote a great many patriotic plays that were popular with most Thai (although not with some members of the "intelligentsia," including Boonlua's family). They are the focus of Jiraporn Witayasakpan, "Nationalism and the Transformation of Aesthetic Concepts: Theatre in Thailand during the Phibun Period."

34. Thak, *Thai Politics*, 272.

35. Boonlua, Phillips interviews, 15.

36. Whether by design or happenstance, the first article in the first newly named issue was in German. There was no Thai translation, as had been customary when articles in French or German were published. Some people believe that this was a message meant for the Japanese: no one should assume that educated Thai could only appreciate scholarly articles when they were translated into the "vernacular."

37. Thailand was briefly renamed Siam in 1945, following the war; the name "Thailand" was soon reinstated, however, probably because "Siam" was by then connected with absolute monarchy and pre-democratic government. However, the Siam Society kept its name.

38. Prince Wan, "Thai Culture," 135.

39. Ibid., 136.

40. For information on both the *rathaniyom* and the *wiratham*, see Barme, *Luang Wichit Wathakan*, chapter 6.

41. Prince Wan, "Thai Culture," 138.

42. Described as the "National Code of Bravery" in Kobkua, *Thailand's Durable Premier*, 124–25; in Thai, *wiratham*. The term is not exactly synonymous with "National Code of Bravery." *Wira* means "hero," and *tham* means "doctrine" or "law" but is also used in other ways. It is noteworthy that while several compounds with the prefix *wira* may be found in contemporary Thai dictionaries, such as *wirachon*, "heroic people," the term *wiratham* does not appear.

43. Prince Wan, "Thai Culture," 143.

44. Thamsook, *Thailand*, 24–25.

45. Boonlua, *Khwam samret*, 83.

46. Ibid., 83.

47. Ibid., 88.

48. These were pageants, not religious ceremonies. Thai Buddhists typically make merit on the morning of their wedding day by giving food to monks. But no monks are involved in the wedding ceremony itself, which takes place later in the day and is a family and community event, not a religious one. At a Thai wedding, the couple is considered married after the water-pouring ceremony. The man and woman kneel beside each other, facing a small table on which a small bowl has been set. They place their hands, palms together, over the bowl. A blessed white string is tied between the groom's head and the bride's. Guests pour water from a decorated conch shell over the couple's hands into the bowl as a blessing. Senior and honored guests will drip a bit of the water over the couple's heads. Legal marriage is quite separate, and is a matter of registering the marriage at a district office.

49. Boonlua, *Khwam samret*, 86.

50. Ibid., 86.

51. Ibid., 82.

52. Ibid., 94, italics added.

53. Boonlua, *Saphai maem*, 178.

54. Rukchira Akarasena, interview with author, Bangkok, June 1995.

55. Somphop, *Dokmai Sot*, 56–57.

56. From an interview conducted in 1981 by Suchat Sawatsri, originally published in the literary magazine *Lok nangsue*, in honor of Boonlua's seventieth birthday.

57. Stowe, *Siam Becomes Thailand*, 258–335.

58. It is commonly thought that Seni kept the declaration locked in his desk throughout the war. Stowe contends that Seni did in fact deliver it, but announced as he did so that he would ignore it because he did not believe that it represented the wishes of the Thai people. (*Siam Becomes Thailand*, 260.) Colonel Kap again became a personal advisor to Phibun when he returned to power in 1947. It is a noteworthy example of Thai flexibility in responding to political exigencies, reflecting Suntaree Komin's contention that underlying all Thai political behavior, "It is always the 'person' and the 'situation' over 'principles' and 'system.'" (Suntaree, *Psychology*, 201).

59. Stowe, *Siam Becomes Thailand*, 260, 270, 274.

60. Boonlua, *Saphai maem*, 82.

61. Although Pridi Banomyong had headed the resistance within Thailand, he had done so as a government official and so was tainted by the Japanese connection. Also, Pridi had always been the most "left-wing" of the original group of coup promoters in 1932; it was his National Economic Plan that had led to the Anti-Communist Act of 1933. But Pridi's "communism," like Phibun's "fascism," was indelibly "Thai." See Morell and Morell, "Open Politics," for a discussion of the character of Pridi's "Marxism."

62. Wright, *Balancing Act*, 155–56.

63. Boonlua, *Khwam samret*, 88–89.

6. LIFE AT MID-CENTURY

1. This book is discussed in chapter 8, with translated excerpts.

2. Like many Thai, Phraya Thewet feared postwar retaliation by the British and perhaps the French as well. However, according to family members, he sought the advice of his brother Colonel Kap, who had been an important figure in the resistance and who convinced him that the United States would not only refrain from retaliation but could also be counted upon to work on Thailand's behalf with the other Allies.

3. Thonburi is a large city across the Chao Phraya River from Bangkok. It was the capital of Siam after the fall of Ayutthaya, from 1767 to 1782.

4. Wright, *Balancing Act*, 151.

5. A summary of the Free Thai movement (focusing on Pridi's role) is included in Vichitvong, *Pridi Banomyong*, 177–203; also see Puey Ungphakorn's memoir, "Temporary Soldiers," in *Puey Ungphakorn: A Siamese for All Seasons*.

6. Likhit, *Demi Democracy*, 126.

7. The most complete view of events during the year following the war, from Pridi's vantage point, is found in Vichitvong, *Pridi Banomyong*, 222–50.

8. Fineman, *A Special Relationship*, 73–75; 262–63.

9. Pridi was the third man to serve as prime minister after the war's end. Khuang Aphaiwongse had succeeded Phibun in 1944 and occupied the office until August 1945; Thawi Bunyaket served from August to September of 1945; and M.R. Seni Pramoj served from September of 1945 to January of 1946. Likhit classifies these men, in addition to Admiral Thamrongnavasawat (August 1946–November 1947) as "liberals." Khuang again served as prime minister from November 1947 to April 1948, when Field Marshal Phibun Songkhram returned to power (Likhit, *Demi Democracy*, 127).

10. Wright, *Balancing Act*, 162.

11. Kruger, *The Devil's Discus*, 89.

12. Kukrit, *Four Reigns*, 1254–55.

13. Members of the royal family do not use *rachasap* in speaking to others; it is for "speaking up," and by definition they are always "speaking down." Using *rachasap* shows respect and reverence.

14. Alexander MacDonald, *Bangkok Editor* (New York: Macmillian, 1949), 53; quoted in Wright, *Balancing Act*, 351, note 71. MacDonald's memoir contains a great deal of information about Ananda Mahidol; very little is available in Thai. Wright states that Pridi and Alexander MacDonald, an O.S.S. officer assigned to Bangkok after the war and also editor of the *Bangkok Post*, escorted King Ananda to one of the formerly secret guerrilla bases at Sriracha, a district on the southeastern gulf coast. Ananda was reportedly thrilled by the mock battle that the *Seri Thai* (Free Thai, the resistance) staged for his amusement, using the carbines, machine guns, and light mortars provided by the US military during the war. After the demonstration Ananda asked to try his hand at firing some of the fancy weaponry and spent nearly an hour at target practice, "wincing with anticipation of each charge" (Wright, *Balancing Act*, 164).

15. Two anonymous informants told me, in 1995 and in 1996, that England's Lord Mountbatten, having been informed of the truth, went to Bangkok after the king's death and implored the royal family to make the true events public, insisting that the new young King Bhumibol would otherwise have to bear not only the sad memory of his beloved brother's death but also the weight of the knowledge that injustice had been done following the death. The king's advisors, however, felt that such an acknowledgment would be impossible, and that it was better simply to go on. Henceforth, discussion of the entire event was forbidden on the (always tacit but well understood) grounds that any mention of it would be both disrespectful and hurtful to King Bhumibol.

16. Two of the accused, Chit Singhasenee and Busaya Patamasarin, were pages for the royal chamber; the third, Chaleo Patoomros (spellings of these names are as they appear in Vichitvong), had formerly been a royal personal secretary. None had a motive to kill the king. "At Chit Singhasenee's cremation on February 12, 1978, twenty-four years after his execution, his children [who apparently had ceased

to hope that their father's name would be officially cleared] published a book in memory of their father which contained the following account: 'After father's death, the prime minister (Field Marshal Pibul-Songgram) instructed his secretary to offer his assistance to our family for the education of the children. We discussed it within the family and finally decided to accept the offer as a token of evidence that even the government then was convinced of father's innocence'" (Vichitvong, *Pridi Banomyong*, 270).

17. Fineman, *A Special Relationship*, 21.

18. Wright, *Balancing Act*, 171 ff.

19. Ibid., 172.

20. Vichitvong, *Pridi Banomyong*, 251.

21. Somphop, *Dokmai Sot*, 60–61.

22. Boonlua, *Khwam samret*, 99.

23. *Khun Chang Khun Phaen* is the great national epic of Thailand, completed in the eighteenth century. An English translation was published in 2010 by Silkworm Books, Chiang Mai, Thailand.

24. This lady was (briefly) one of King Vajiravudh's consorts. Boonlua used her as the basis for a character in her novel, *Thutiyawiset*, which is described in chapter 8.

25. Aristocrats who attended the plays King Vajiravudh wrote and produced were scandalized at the idea of their king, much less his fiancée, or queen, performing on stage.

26. Supicha Sonakul, interview with author, July 15, 1995.

27. *Uphayobai* is also the name of a memorial volume produced at Chulalongkorn University after Boonlua's death.

28. Student, in *Uphayobai*, 34–35.

29. Mattani Rutnin, in *Uphayobai*, 34.

30. In one of Boonlua's best-known short stories, "The Charm of the Cooking Spoon" (*Sane plai chawak*), a friend of the heroine is going abroad for an MA at the age of forty. Boonlua's portrayal of this pitiable old maid, who only floats through the heroine's thoughts and is never seen, is a sly parody of Thai attitudes toward unmarried educated women. See Phillips, *Modern Thai Literature*, 152–88.

31. Before World War II, most Thais who studied abroad, particularly those from the elite class, preferred to study in England. After the war, because of the strong economic and diplomatic ties with the United States and the tempting number of scholarships available from universities there, the United States became the most popular destination, especially for graduate school. Nevertheless, Thais who could afford to send their children wherever they liked still preferred England; a not insignificant reason was their wish that their children learn to speak English with a British, rather than an American, accent.

32. The "degree disease" and its effects on the Thai bureaucracy during this period are discussed in Riggs, *Thailand*, 341–42; and Suntaree, *Psychology*, 226–30.

33. Boonlua, *Khwam samret*, 102.

34. Morell and Chai-anan, "Open Politics", 20.

35. Which is to say, to learn to accept both the good and bad events of life with equanimity, the Buddhist virtue of *upekkha*.

36. Boonlua, *Khwam samret*, 104–5.

37. Ibid., 117.

38. Ibid., 116.

39. This raises the intriguing question of whether Boonlua might have suffered from various allergies, a possibility suggested to me by an American physician who knew her. The vague, flu-like symptoms Boonlua complained of all her life could have been the result of undiagnosed and untreated allergies to certain substances common to the Bangkok environment, but not present (or less present) in the United States and Europe. Except for the stressful year she spent in Bang Saen (1959–60), and another, similarly stressful year in Nakhon Pathom (1968–69), Boonlua usually enjoyed better health in rural areas of Thailand than in Bangkok. Of course, the fact that she enjoyed traveling in rural areas and found her welcome there gratifying should not be underestimated.

40. Boonlua, Phillips interviews, 15.

41. Pattaratorn Chirapravat, interview with author, December 22, 1997.

42. See Suntaree, *Psychology*, 197–207, for a discussion of Thai "flexibility and adjustment orientation": "It is the ability of balancing ego [including the notion of 'face'], power, and situations that counts, not ideology, nor even law and order. . . ." (197).

43. Boonlua, *Khwam samret*, 108.

44. Ambhorn Meesook, interview with author, Bangkok, July 25, 1995. Khunying Ambhorn, who made great contributions to the Thai education system, and held several high-level positions in government, was a lifelong friend and frequently a working colleague of Boonlua.

45. Ibid., 120–21.

46. Ibid., 129.

47. Ibid., 130.

48. Ibid., 156.

49. Ibid., 132–35.

50. Ibid., 137.

51. Ibid., 142.

52. Ibid., 144–45.

53. Suntaree, *Psychology*, 162–63; italics added.

54. Michael Smithies, in *Bun bamphen*, 73.

55. Morell and Chai-anan, *Political Conflict*, 18–19, italics added.

56. Ambhorn Meesook, conversation with author, July 25, 1995.

57. Boonlua, *Khwam samret*, 165. "We cannot *not* tell His Majesty, in Thai, is expressed as *mai krap thun mai dai*. The verb "to tell" must be expressed in *rachasap*, so that Boonlua's phrase would be literally translated as, "We may not *not* prostrate ourselves and speak to the king." In other words, one must have the courage to speak to the king as to any man—but one must do so while crouched on the floor in a position of obeisance.

58. Doris Gold Wibunsin, in *Bun bamphen*, 73.

59. For contrasting views of Sarit's character and career, see Kokbua, *Thailand's Durable Premier*; Morell and Chai-anan, *Political Conflict*; and Sulak, "The Crisis of Siamese Identity." The complexities of Sarit's character are most fully explored in Thak, *Thailand: The Politics of Despotic Paternalism*, more than half of which is devoted to Sarit's career and the political details of the 1957–63 period.

60.   For a succinct description of Sarit's vision of "'Thai-style democracy," see Likhit, *Demi Democracy*, 159–66. "Sarit's view was that the Thai-style democracy should be a system characterised by a strong Executive wielding greater political power than the Legislative. Sarit also viewed political parties as unsuitable for Thailand. . . . Sarit believed that government was the esoteric affair of kings and the elite. The only thing that mattered was for the ruling elite to be righteous and moral. Putting the belief into practice, Sarit held that the prime minister had to have absolute power but it had to be power which was based on righteousness. In the Thai society, this would correspond to a father who was charged with the duty to keep the children happy and obedient. Punitive measures would be taken for the child's own good. . . . [This] reasoning is based on . . . the political tradition [of] the patriarchal ruler concept or *pho khun*, "honored father," as the model" (160–61).

61. Morell and Chai-anan, *Political Conflict*, 65–66.

62. Nitaya Masavisut, conversation with author, February 10, 1998.

63. Pin Malakul, in *Bun bamphen*, 32–33, italics added.

7. AN INDEPENDENT WOMAN

1.   All remarks by Dr. Chom Debyasuvarn, unless otherwise noted, are from *Bun bamphen*, Boonlua's cremation volume, 21–31. Contributions to *Bun bamphen* are in English and in untranslated Thai. Translations of all Thai contributions from that volume appearing in this work are mine.

2. Dr. Chom, interview with author, June 19, 1995.

3. Boonlua's relationships with Dr. Chom's first wife and with his daughter, who sometimes lived with Boonlua and Chom, were amicable by all accounts.

4. The intimation is that they fell in love, although Dr. Chom's polite words in Thai were, *rao pho chai sueng kan lae kan* ("we were pleased with each other").

5. A family member, interview with author, 1995.

6. The friend's daughter, interview with author.

7. Anonymous source, interview with author 1995.

8. Nitaya Masavisut, interview with author, Bangkok, August 15, 1995.

9. Remark made during a conversation with several of Boonlua's friends, in July 1995.

10. Boonlua, *Khwam samret*, 171.

11. Ibid., 177–78.

12. Ibid., 180–81.

13. Ibid., 182–84.

14. Boonlua, Phillips interviews, 38–39, italics added.

14. Ibid., 41.

16. Sawatri Suwannasithi, in *Bun bamphen*, 132. Boonlua was not a princess, despite her royal title.

17. Sawatri Suwannasithi and Nitaya Masavisut, in *Bun bamphen*, 132.

18. Michael Smithies, in *Bun bamphen*, 73.

19. Anonymous source, interview with author, July 1995.

20. Ibid.

21. Ted Plaister, in *Bun bamphen*, 75.

22. This is reflected in "Thailand," a forty-one-page document on Thai history and culture that Boonlua wrote for UNESCO in 1962. The tone of this document and its rendering of Thai history and culture are reminiscent of the nationalist rhetoric of the 1930s and early 1940s.

23. Boonlua, *Khwam samret*, 200.

24. Ibid., 204.

25. Italics added. Boonlua specifically describes this as a disease, "*rok hen ton maphrao kap chai hat mai dai*" (Boonlua, *Khwam samret*, 204).

26. "*Sane plai chawak*" is included in Phillips, *Modern Thai Literature*, under the title "The Enchanting Cooking Spoon," 152–88.

27. This novel has been translated into English by Marcel Barang but is not yet published.

28. Boonlua, Phillips interviews, 6.

29. M.L. Pattaratorn Chirapravat (Phraya Thewet's granddaughter), personal communication with author, December 10, 1997. Professor Pattaratorn holds a PhD in art history from Cornell University and has been teaching in American universities for many years. She told me that her Great-aunt Bunluea had predicted, when Pattaratorn was very young, that she would live most of her life abroad in a Western country.

30. Ted Plaister, in *Bun bamphen*, 76.

31. A former assistant to Boonlua, interview with author, June 27, 1995. In fact, while Boonlua was living at home, before she went to Penang at the age of eleven, she was always involved in Thai singing and dancing with her stepmothers and sisters. She was not a boarder at St. Joseph's Convent, but went home every day. She committed these precious experiences to memory, and it is highly improbable that she would have been able to write and direct Thai theatrical performances as a young teacher had this not been the case.

32. "Than Phuying" is an honorific pronoun prefix for the wife of a prime minister.

33. Boonlua, Phillips interviews, 9.

34. After her marriage to Dr. Sukij, Buppha lived in a house at the school where his first wife was headmistress and where he had continued to live after their divorce. This small house was entirely prepared and furnished by the first wife, and Buppha had only a tiny space of her own in which to write, and perhaps even less privacy than she had enjoyed at Wang Ban Mo. By the time Buppha and Dr. Sukij moved to India, she was very ill, and she remained an invalid virtually the entire time she lived in India. Her only writing there consisted of rambling, unhappy letters to relatives and friends at home, in which we see her obsession with the idea of returning to Thailand to build a small house on land of her own, and to live there with some of her close female relatives and friends. Although she often wrote that she pitied poor Dr. Sukij for having to care for her "like a nurse," there was no mention in these letters of how Dr. Sukij could fit into the plans for a home of her own in Thailand. See Somphop, *Dokmai Sot*, chapter 13 (in Thai).

35. Boonlua, *Khwam samret*, 207–8.

36. Wibha Kongkanan, interview with author, July 1, 1995.

37. In a debate entitled "*Wannakam doem kap kha-niyom khong sangkhom patchuban*" (Literature of the past and values of contemporary society). In *Waen wannakam*, 306.

38. Boonlua, *Khwam samret*, 212–13.

39. Vinita Diteeyont, interview with author, Nakhon Pathom, July 5, 1995.

40. Panpimon Gajasuta, interview with author, July 1, 1995.

41. Wibha Kongkanan, interview with author, June 22, 1995.

42. Boonlua, *Khwam samret*, 216–17.

43. In June of 1995, I was accompanied by Boonlua's husband, Dr. Chom, to an interview with an old friend of hers, who commented on her own health problems. Dr. Chom remarked (in Thai), "You should try Valium. It is a very good drug because it is not addictive." When her doctors first prescribed it for Boonlua in the 1960s (in fact, it was widely available as an "over the counter" drug in Thailand), neither they nor Dr. Chom could predict that Valium eventually would be found to have a number of side effects, including confusion and tremor. Dr. Chom had been retired for several years by 1995 and presumably was not aware of these findings. Yet, it is not clear whether Boonlua took enough of the drug, or took it long enough, for these side effects to occur as a result. While the symptoms of her medical condition were well known (including headaches, stomach pains, nervousness, high blood pressure, bladder infections, protein deficiency, and essential tremor), one can only speculate as to the causes of these symptoms and the role of emotional stress on her physical condition.

44. Boonlua, *Khwam samret*, 221.

45. Ibid.

8. THE USES OF FICTION

1. From a conversation with a family member who did not wish to be identified.

2. M.L. Pattaratorn Chiraprawat, personal communication.

3. Boonlua, *Hua liao hua to khong wannakhadi thai* (The turning point of Thai literature), 86. This collection of essays and lectures will be referred to as *Hua liao* in the notes, as *The Turning Point* in the text.

4. *Dr. Luk Thung*, 289.

5. Boonlua, conversation with author, August 1981.

6. This famous scene at the pond, when Cha-on meets Withun, is discussed in my essay, "Dropping the Towel: Images of the Body in Contemporary Thai Women's Writing."

7. Ibid., 159–80.

8. Another avenue of advancement for Thai men of humble origins was the Buddhist Sangha. Boys could be sent to a temple school in a rural area, and the cleverest could advance to higher education in Bangkok. Field Marshal Phibun Songkram advanced through the military; his closest advisor, Wichit Wathakan, had advanced beyond his own rural origins by becoming a monk, going from a rural temple school to a university in Bangkok. Both men then won scholarships to study in France.

9. This is perhaps the most glaring departure from the life of Field Marshal Phibun Songkhram, who pursued power and was dedicated to a reformation of the

Thai social order, but apparently was never motivated by wealth and did not amass a fortune as the result of high political office.

10. Khun Chaeo is making fun of the English word "democracy" and thus reveals her contempt for the new government; the Thai term that was developed for "democracy" is *prachathipatai*, not the transliterated "demok-krasi-krasoe." Pronouncing a foreign term with a Thai accent is a common way of casting aspersions upon the concept involved.

11. *Thutiyawiset*, 183–84. Thai readers understood the implication that she would not serve those who had mistreated members of the old regime—her own relatives—after the overthrow of the absolute monarchy, and particularly after the Boworadet Rebellion of 1933.

12. Withun never becomes prime minister, as Phibun did. To make him prime minister would have complicated the author's task immensely.

13. None of these events reflects the later life of Phibun, who died of natural causes in Japan on June 11, 1964, at the age of sixty-seven. In the years before his death, he spent some time in the Buddhist monkhood in India, and traveled in the United States. After his death, the government allowed his family to bring his ashes home and place them in Wat Phra Sri Mahathat in Bangkok. Wright, *The Balancing Act*, 190.

14. Khantipalo, *Buddhism Explained*, 28.

15. Explicit sexual behavior has been confined to pornography sold "under the counter" and never considered part of "literature." The line between pornography and "literature" seems to be drawn at the use of words for genitals. Stories such as Anchan's prize-winning and ground-breaking "A Pot That Scouring Will Not Save," about a woman married to a brutal man, contains a sexually explicit scene, but specific terms for genitals are avoided. An English translation of this story appears in Kepner, *The Lioness in Bloom*.

16. See Kepner, "Dropping the Towel: Images of the Body in Contemporary Thai Women's Writing."

17. Vinita Diteeyont, "Phaphalak khong phuying," 3.

18. Princess Varnbimol Voravarn, daughter of HRH Prince Naradhip Prapanphong, a son of King Mongkut (1851–68).

19. Boonlua's own brother, M.L. (Colonel) Kap Kunchon, was an army officer of aristocratic origins who was useful to Phibun and served as his military attache in Washington, DC (see chapter 5). However, several people I interviewed emphasized that Colonel Kap was far from the moral hero that Boonlua created in the character of Kroen and was not trusted by Phibun, the Japanese, or the Allies when he volunteered to take a role in the resistance. The only mention of Colonel Kap in Boonlua's autobiography is an anecdote about his frightened reaction to the 1932 coup d'état, when he was a young officer. *Khwam samret*, 16.

20. Dr. Chom was not Boonlua's social equal, to the (elite) Thai way of thinking; however, he was educated, witty, and possessed of naturally "courtly" manners.

21. This information follows the last paragraph of the novel.

22. Neon Snidwongse, personal communication to author, February 27, 1998.

23. "Luang" is a royal civil service title from the days of the absolute monarchy; "Mick" is a typical modern Thai nickname. Thus, these two characters represent traditional Siam and contemporary Thailand. Boonlua named the "Mick" character after the young son of a friend, literature professor Nitaya Masavisut. Boonlua often surprised her friends by naming her characters after them or their children.

24. The word "Suwanratanathawip" may be dismantled as follows: *suwan* (heaven, a heaven), *ratana* (jewel, superior/supreme object), and *thawip* (continent).

25. The linguistic elements from which this name is fashioned imply "politeness" and "soft behavior," desirable wifely attributes in Thai-Siam.

26. Boonlua invented new Thai words for the concepts of male and female, and for female husband and male wife, from Sanskrit and Pali. Thais in the literary world have suggested that the difficulty for average readers in understanding these linguistic references had a negative effect on the book's success, although the same features of the book were much enjoyed by educated readers.

27. The name implies "lightning," a traditional symbol for unexpected sexual passion in classical Thai literature.

28. *Suratnari*, 250.

29. The most outstanding example of such a male in a novel by a male writer is the character of Khun Prem, the husband of the heroine Phloi, in Kukrit Pramoj's *Four Reigns*. Although when he marries Phloi, he already has fathered an infant son by a servant in his household (whom the author has allowed to run away and never reappear), after marriage Khun Prem never strays, even when, in middle age, Phloi tells him that if it will make him happy, she will not mind if he takes a minor wife.

30. A possible exception to this would be Prince Narit, who was married and widowed three times. He seems to have been the only person to upbraid his friend Chao Phraya Thewet for his numerous romantic companions.

31. See chapter 4.

32. Lambert and Mick employ an odd combination of old-fashioned first- and second-person Thai and Chinese pronouns, providing a linguistic kaleidoscope in keeping with the novel's overall kaleidoscopic presentation of cultures and customs.

33. Because rebirth as a human being is generally considered to be extremely difficult by Thai Buddhists, conception within the body of a human female is seen as a great victory, and the woman who has an abortion turns that victory to defeat. There is a "pro-choice" faction within the feminist Buddhist movement; its adherents argue that, according to certain Buddhist teachings, the fetus immediately after

conception has not yet received the new soul and it is, as the character Miw asserts in Boonlua's unfinished *Sit* (Rights in Three-Quarters of a Century), merely a "lump of jelly." This (minority) view is somewhat like the official Roman Catholic view until the late nineteenth century that the fetus gained personhood only with "quickening" (movement perceptible to the pregnant woman), at about the beginning of the second trimester.

34. An English translation of this essay, with an introduction to it, is included in Phillips, *Modern Thai Literature*, 269–76.

35. Ibid., 273–74.

9. ANOTHER KIND OF REVOLUTION

1. While the presentation of medals to outstanding citizens by the king and sometimes by the queen is a long-standing tradition, after the rise of Field Marshal Sarit in 1957 the number of royally bestowed medals and related ceremonies increased noticeably. The Chula Chom Klao medal (named for the "second king" during the reign of King Mongkut, a position that was discontinued during the reign of his son King Chulalongkorn), was awarded to Boonlua for her service to the nation in education, literature, and the arts. Other medals are awarded to women because of their husband's position (for example, the *thutiyawiset*), or in recognition of their own intellectual or philanthropic contributions to Thai society.

2. The implication is that the relatives not only dressed her properly but were determined that she would not go to receive her decoration from the king carrying her usual notorious assortment of bags and other paraphernalia. Traditionally, a lady did not carry her own things; younger female relatives or servants carried them for her and handed them to her as needed.

3. Boonlua, *Khwam samret*, 241–42.

4. Chitlada Suwattikul, in *Bun bamphen*, 118–22.

5. Kamon Somvichien, in Morell and Chai-anan, *Political Conflict*, 22–23.

6. Morell and Chai-anan, *Political Conflict*, 141–43; also, Prudhisan Jambala, "Interest and Pressure Groups."

7. Prudhisan, "Interest and Pressure Groups," 138.

8. Morell and Chai-anan, *Political Conflict*, 146.

9. "My Father Is Not the Prime Minister," song by country singer Dang Danthong, the stage name of Bangkok-born Sumit Jarakan. Excerpt of my translation of the original Thai version, available on numerous Internet websites. The song (in Thai) may be heard on YouTube: http://www.youtube.com/watch?v=BlDicc9Bqik.

10. Prudhisan, "Interest and Pressure Groups," 138–39; Morell and Chai-anan, *Political Conflict*, 143–44.

11. Morell and Chai-anan, *Political Conflict*, 147. While it is true that students marched in front carrying the pictures of the king and queen, at this point the movement had been joined by many Thais who were politically middle-of the-road.

12. See Reynolds, *Thai Radical Discourse*, a translation of Chit's major work, prefaced by a brief biography.

13. Morell and Chai-anan, *Political Conflict*, 148–49.

14. Sri Daoruang, interview with Wan Pen, 1993, quoted in Kepner, *Married to the Demon King*, 3.

15. Morell and Chai-anan, *Political Conflict*, 153–54, 205–34. See also Haberkorn, *Revolution Interrupted*.

16. Ivarsson, "The Study of *Traiphum Phra Ruang*: Some Considerations," 56–86. The *Traiphum Phra Ruang* is also discussed in Chontira, *Wannakhadi khong puangchon*, 1974 (in Thai). Somewhat later, other scholars, particularly Professor Piriya Krairiksh, a Silpakorn University archaeologist, also began questioning the authenticity of the equally revered Ramkhamhaeng Inscription, which had long been accepted as a description of Thai society and culture during the thirteenth century C.E., the Sukhothai era. These scholars speculated that perhaps neither of these treasured national symbols were products of the thirteenth century; rather, they might have been created by King Mongkut during the mid-nineteenth century to prove to Europeans that Siam was a venerable state, and to suggest that the kingdoms of Sukhothai, Ayutthaya, Thonburi, and Bangkok represented successive capitals of one kingdom.

17. The "radical literature of the past" refers to leftist fiction and essays by Thai activists such as Chit Phumisak, whose works composed in the 1950s were reprinted during the early 1970s.

18. Ivarsson, *Traiphum Phra Ruang*, 67.

19. Boonlua, *Waen wannakam*, 265–66.

20. Ibid., 266.

21. The poetry of the contemporary, erudite poet Angkhan, much respected by the radicals, makes lavish use of Sanskrit-based terms and classical allusions.

22. As Boonlua well knew, this poem was a favorite target of the radicals, who insisted that it glorified royalty and denigrated women. Composed during the Ayutthaya period (1350–1767), *Lilit Phra Lo* relates the life and death of Phra Lo, a heroic prince who is loved by two princesses, sisters, from a neighboring kingdom. The trio defy the forces that would separate them and eventually die tragically together. See Bickner, *An Introduction to the Poem "Lilit Phra Law."*

23. The slang term "*the*," in use since the 1970s, means fashionable or "cool" and evolved rather improbably from the English word "taste," which had to be modified to reflect the lack of the *st* consonant cluster in Thai. The final *st* is simply dropped.

24. The issue of *sakdina* was a critical one in the political discourse of the 1970s. The term refers to the pre-1932 system through which people were given societal "dignity marks" by the monarch. David Wilson describes it as "the traditional law of social organization in Thailand . . . designed to structure society as a monolith integrated to serve the state, or more precisely the king. . . . Each man was allotted thereby a degree of dignity and privilege measured quantitatively. Free men obliged to the king or some royal department of the court were registered and received the *sakdina* number 25. With this as a base each official or prince was allotted his *sakdina* grade up the scale. This system was part and parcel of the patron-client relationship by which Thai society was traditionally integrated. . . . Traditional Thai social structure thus emphasized a consciousness of status rather than class . . . insofar as institutions made up of legal and nonhereditary relationships of right and obligation and vertically organized social groups had a genuine vitality, *[which] worked against the development of class consciousness.*" See Wilson, *Politics in Thailand*, 50–51, italics added. Also see Riggs, *Thailand*, 243–44.

Leftists, especially Marxists, interpret *sakdina* in a very different way. The foremost source of information on this interpretation is found in Craig Reynolds's brief biography and translation of Chit Phumisak's political treatise, *The Real Face of Thai Feudalism*. Chit interpreted and translated the concept of *sakdina* as "feudalism," a definition that Boonlua and many other Thai intellectuals considered to be completely inaccurate. This hero of the political activists of the 1970s (assassinated in 1965) wrote that "Sakdina literally means 'power' [*sak*] in controlling the 'fields' [*na*], and if we expand on this meaning to clarify the term we can say that sakdina means power over the land which was the crucial factor in agriculture, and agriculture in that age was the principal livelihood of the People. . . . According to economic science, 'land' is considered one of the factors in production (means of production). . . . [B]efore the capitalist age when the machine emerged as a tool for making a living, the principal tool human beings had to make their living was land. . . . If we compare [the Thai system] with the capitalist system, those with a great deal of land correspond to the big capitalists who have many factories and much of the commerce in their clutches. This is the group which enjoys happiness and wealth *and has merit* [*bun*]. Those with no land at all. . . . are forced to sell their labor and hire themselves out in order to sustain themselves day by day according to '*the merit and misfortunes of sentient beings*'" (Reynolds, *Thai Radical Discourse*, 45–46), italics added. The language of Chit's treatise combined traditional Thai ideas such as "merit" and the "misfortunes of sentient beings" with Marxist philosophy and terminology.

25. Boonlua, *Waen wannakam*, 297–303.

26. In the *Ramakian*, Nonthok is a humble guard before the higher gates of heaven. Everyone who passes him knocks him on the head, which he bitterly resents. When Siva grants him a magic finger, he gleefully points it at all those he thinks have wronged him, and they fall dead.

27. Boonlua, *Waen wannakam*, 308–10. It is interesting that this is precisely the kind of argument used nearly forty years later in criticizing the "red-shirt" challenge to the elite class and to the sitting government in April and May 2010, which led to serious rioting, an armed response by the government, and deaths on both sides.

28. Anonymous source, personal communication, 1998.

29. From the profile, "A Writer of Books: M.L. Boonlua Debyasuvarn," by "Supawan" (pseud.), in *Siam Rath*, November 23, 1977, 9, italics added. (In Thai.)

30. The right-wing organizations of this period are described in Morell and Chai-anan, *Political Conflict*, chapter 9.

31. Prudhisan, "Interest and Pressure Groups," 51; and Morell and Chai-anan, *Political Conflict*, 242–43.

32. Morell and Chai-anan, *Political Conflict*, 235.

33. Letter to Larry Smith, July 25, 1976.

34. It was generally believed that the royal family favored Thanom, who was dignified, gracious, of good family, and possessed respectable social skills, compared with the bumptious, rotund, and vulgar Praphat, who was the favorite of the caricaturists.

35. Morell and Chai-anan, *Political Conflict*, 271.

36. Ibid., 275.

37. Letter to Larry Smith, March 1, 1977. King Bhumibol was born in Boston, Massachusetts, grew up and was educated in Switzerland, and never lived in Thailand until shortly before he became king. The reference to the king as "somebody" (quotation marks are Boonlua's) implies that he is not only a descendant of kings, but also that he is a superior person regardless of his position.

38. Morell and Chai-anan, *Political Conflict*, 301.

39. Suchat was a founding editor of *Writer* magazine, the October 1997 issue of which features a haunting portrait of Che Guevara on its cover, above the words, *Che: Yang mi chiwit yu rue* (Che: Does He Still Live?). The lead article in this issue is, *Che Kuwara: Khon klahan tamnan* (Che Guevara: Brave Man of History). Curiously, the word used here to mean history, *tamnan*, is usually translated as "chronicle" or legend" and refers to a narrative of ancient times, often unsubstantiated, that begins with the birth of the Buddha.

40. See Sidaoru'ang, *A Drop of Glass*, and Kepner, *Married to the Demon King*. The latter work focuses upon Sri Daoruang's six short stories based upon characters in the *Ramakian* but set in contemporary Bangkok.

41. Among the most interesting are the memoirs of Seksan Prasertkul and Chiranan Pitpreecha. *The Moonhunter*, a scripted film based upon their experiences, may be available at some university libraries.

42. Letter to Larry Smith, March 1, 1977.

43. Former colleague of Boonlua, interview with author, May 1998.

44. An English translation of this novel by Marcel Barang is available through this website: www.thaifiction.com/book_show.php.

45. Tianchai Iamworamate, *New Thai-English Dictionary*, 1989, 588.

46. These remarks from an anonymous source are represented to the best of my memory.

47. Letter to Mayuree Sukwiwat, November 26, 1978.

10. A CIVILIZED WOMAN

1. Prince Damrong lived in exile in Penang, Malaya, after 1932; he was allowed to return to Thailand in 1942 and died the following year in Bangkok.

2. Reynolds, *Thai Radical Discourse*, 20–21.

3. See Chetana, *Comparative Literature*, 54–55.

4. A literal translation of the title is "The flavor(s) of Thai literature."

5. Letter to Larry Smith, March 1, 1977.

6. Richard Via, in *Bun bamphen*, 78.

7. Chetana, *Comparative Literature*, 55.

8. Mattani Rutnin, in *Bun bamphen*, 144–45.

9. Boonlua, *Hua liao*, 81.

10. Ibid., 91.

11. Ibid., 111.

12. Ibid., 114.

13. Ibid., 151.

14. Ibid., 155.

15. Boonlua, *Waen wannakam*, 110.

16. Boonlua, *Khwam samret*, 21.

17. Kenneth Burke, *Counter-Statement*, 31.

18. Boonlua, *Khwam samret*, 22.

19. Ibid.

20. In *Bun bamphen*, 76.

21. Ibid., 80.

22. Excerpt from Thomas John Hudak, trans., *The Tale of Prince Samuttakote*.

23. Wanpen Chantirawirot, conversation with author, July 1995.

24. Stewart, "Toward a Feminist Strategy," 29–30.

25. DDT spray was the usual defense against insects at that time in Bangkok. A householder could request a visit from a city-owned DDT-spraying truck on the afternoon before a lawn party. Shortly before the truck arrived, neighbors would be warned by a loudspeaker to close their doors and shutters against the clouds of poison.

26. Dr. Chom, in *Bun bamphen*, 21–31.

27. The *thoet thoeng* group included Nitaya Masavisut, Mayuree Sukwiwat, Mattani Rutnin, Nisa Chenakun, Sawittri Suwannasathit, Wanpen Chantarawirot, and Wibha Chulachat, professors of Thai and/or English literature—plus one honorary member, Dr. Chom.

28. Nitaya Masavisut, in *Bun bamphen*, 125–30.

29. Ibid., 129–30.

30. M.L. Pattaratorn Chirapravati, interview with author, December 1997.

31. Chinda and Prachum Chaiyarat were attorneys; Chinda acted as Boonlua's personal attorney in sorting out the complicated affair of the Kunchon family inheritance, and Prachum was Boonlua's lifelong friend.

32. Pris Chaiyarat Bear, conversation with author, August 2009. Words in italics were spoken in English.

33. D. Michael Bear, conversation with author, July 2010.

34. When I followed up on this information, Revadee told me that she gave Boonlua a white Valium pill once a day, with her other medications for high blood pressure and various ailments. A white Valium pill contains only 2.5 mg of medication, the lowest dosage available. According to the physicians I contacted, it was unlikely that Boonlua would suffer significant side effects. However, if she took additional Valium during the day, besides the dosage meted out to her by Revadee, it could have caused the dizziness and forgetfulness of which she complained. I had questioned whether the hand tremor that so disturbed her might be the result of long-term Valium use, but the same doctors agreed that age-related "benign familial tremor" was a more likely cause.

35. There was a private beauty parlor on the grounds of Wang Ban Mo where the women of the family had their hair done at least once a week.

36. Revadee Crabbe, letter to author, September 17, 1997.

37. An excerpt from this novel directly concerning Khunying Saisawat's illness appears in Kepner, *The Lioness in Bloom*, 68–83.

38. Somphop, *Dokmai Sot*, 82.

39. Ibid., 85.

40 Mattani Rutnin, in *Bun bamphen*, 145.

41. Anonymous friend, conversation with author, July 5, 1996.

42. Chetana, *Comparative Literature from a Thai Perspective*.

BIBLIOGRAPHY

WORKS IN ENGLISH

Adas, Michael. "From Avoidance to Confrontation: Peasant Protest in Precolonial Southeast Asia." In *Colonialism and Culture*, edited by Nicholas B. Dirks, 89–126. Ann Arbor, MI: University of Michigan Press, 2001.

Akin Rabibhadana. *The Organization of Thai Society during the Early Bangkok Period, 1782–1873*. Data Paper 74. Ithaca, NY: Southeast Asia Program, Department of Asian Studies, 1969.

Alagappa, Muthiah, ed. *Political Legitimacy in Southeast Asia: The Quest for Moral Authority*. Stanford, CA: Stanford University Press, 1995.

Amara Pongsapich, ed. *Traditional and Changing Thai World View*. Bangkok: Chulalongkorn University Social Research Institute, 1998.

Amranand, Ping, and Pimsai Svasti. *Siamese Memoirs: The Life and Times of Pimsai Svasti*. Bangkok: Amulet Production, 2011.

Anchan (pen name of Anchalee Vivathanachai). "A Pot That Scouring Will Not Save" [*Mo thi khut mai ok*]. In *The Lioness in Bloom*, by Susan F. Kepner, 172–204. Berkeley: University of California Press, 1996.

Anderson, Benedict R. O'G. "Studies of the Thai State: The State of Thai Studies." In *The Study of Thailand: Analyses of Knowledge, Approaches, and Prospects in Anthropology, Art History, Economics, History and Political Science*, edited by Eliezer B. Ayal, 193–247. Papers in International Studies, Southeast Asian Series, no. 54. Athens: Ohio University, Center for International Studies, 1979.

Anderson, Benedict R. O'G., and Ruchira Mendiones. *In the Mirror: Literature and Politics in Siam in the American Era*. Bangkok: Duang Kamol, 1985.

Anuman Rajadhon (pen name Sathirakoses). *Life and Ritual in Old Siam: Three Studies of Thai Life and Customs.* Translated and edited by William J. Gedney. New Haven, CT: Hraf Press, 1961.

_____. *Looking Back: Book One.* Bangkok: Chulalongkorn University Press, 1992.

Apichart Chinwanno. "Thailand's Search for Protection: The Making of the Alliance with the United States, 1947–1954." PhD diss., Oxford University, 1985.

Baker, Chris, and Pasuk Phongpaichit. *A History of Thailand.* Cambridge: Cambridge University Press, 2005.

_____. *The Tale of Khun Chang Khun Phaen.* Chiang Mai: Silkworm Books, 2010.

Barmé, Scot. *Luang Wichit Wathakan and the Creation of a Thai Identity.* Singapore: Institute of Southeast Asian Studies, 1993.

Bartkowski, Frances. *Feminist Utopias.* Lincoln, NB: University of Nebraska Press, 1989.

Batson, Benjamin A. *The End of the Absolute Monarchy in Siam.* Asian Studies Association of Australia Southeast Asia Publications Series, no. 10. Singapore: Oxford University Press, 1984.

Bickner, Robert J. *An Introduction to the Poem "Lilit Phra Law" (The Story of King Law),* Monograph no. 25. DeKalb, IL: Northern Illinois University Center for Southeast Asian Studies, 1991.

Bofman, Theodora Helene. *The Poetics of the Ramakian.* Monograph Series on Southeast Asia, Special Report no. 21. DeKalb, IL: Northern Illinois University Center for Southeast Asian Studies, 1984.

Botan (pen name of Supa Sirising). *Letters from Thailand* [*Chotmai chak mueang thai*]. Translated by Susan F. Kepner. Chiang Mai: Silkworm Books, 2002.

Bowen, John R. "The Forms Culture Takes: A State-of-the-Field Essay on the Anthropology of Southeast Asia." *Journal of Asian Studies* 54, no. 4: 1047–78.

Brailey, Nigel. *Two Views of Siam on the Eve of the Chakri Reformation.* Whiting Bay, Arran, Scotland: Kiscadale Publications, 1989.

Buddhadasa Bhikkhu. *Handbook for Mankind.* Unidentified translator. Bangkok: Buddhadasa Foundation, 1988.

Bunnag, Tej, and Michael Smithies, eds. *In Memoriam: Phya Anuman Rajadhon.* Bangkok: Siam Society, 1970.

Burgan, Mary. *Illness, Gender and Writing: The Case of Katherine Mansfield.* Baltimore and London: Johns Hopkins University Press, 1994.

Burke, Kenneth. *Counter-Statement.* Berkeley: University of California Press, 1968 [reprint]. First published 1931.

_____. *Language as Symbolic Action: Essays on Life, Literature, and Method.* Berkeley: University of California Press, 1966.

Casey, Edward S. "Imagining and Remembering." *Review of Metaphysics* 31, no. 2 (December 1977): 187–209.

Chai Podhisita. "Buddhism and Thai World View." In Amara Pongsapich, ed., *Traditional and Changing Thai World View*, 25–53.

Chai-anan Samudavanija. "The Bureaucracy." In Somsakdi, *Government and Politics*, 75–109.

_____. "Political History." In Somsakdi, *Government and Politics*, 1–40.

_____. "State-Identity Creation, State-Building and Civil Society." In Craig Reynolds, *National Identity*, 59–86.

Charnvit Kasetsiri. "Thai Historiography from Ancient Times to the Modern Period." In *Perceptions of the Past in Southeast Asia*, edited by Anthony Reid and David Marr, 156–70. Singapore: Heinemann Educational Books (Asia), 1979.

Chati Kobjitti. *The Judgement [Kham phiphaksa]*. Translated by Laurie Maund. Bangkok: Laurie Maund, 1983. Distributed in Thailand by Thammasat University Book Store.

Chatsumarn Kabilsingh. *Thai Women in Buddhism*. Berkeley: Parallax Press, 1991.

Chetana Nagavajara. *Comparative Literature from a Thai Perspective: Collected Articles 1978–1992*. Bangkok: Chulalongkorn University Press, 1996.

_____. "Literature in Thai Life: Reflections of a Native." Paper delivered at the Fifth International Conference on Thai Studies, School of Oriental and African Studies, University of London, July 1993.

_____. "Parody as Translation: A Thai Case Study." In *Translation East and West: A Cross-Cultural Approach*. Literary Studies East and West, vol. 5. Honolulu: East-West Center, 1992. Distributed by the University of Hawaii Press.

Chula Chakrabongse (Prince). *Lords of Life: The Paternal Monarchy of Bangkok, 1782–1932*. New York: Taplinger Publishing Co., 1960.

Cook, Blanche Wiesen. *Eleanor Roosevelt, Volume One: 1884–1933*. New York: Penguin Books, 1993.

Crosby, Josiah. *Siam: The Crossroads*. London: Hollis and Carter, 1945.

Direk Jayanama. *Thailand and World War II*. Chiang Mai: Silkworm Books, 2008.

Dirks, Nicholas B. *Colonialism and Culture*. Ann Arbor: University of Michigan Press, 1992.

Dokmai Sot. (pen name of Buppha Kunchon Nimmanhemin.) *A Secret Past [Kam kao]*. Translated by Ted Strehlow. Ithaca, NY: Southeast Asia Publications, Cornell University, 1992.

Durrenberger, E. Paul, ed. *State Power and Culture in Thailand*. Monograph 44. New Haven, CT: Yale University Southeast Asia Studies, 1996.

Fineman, Daniel. A *Special Relationship: The United States and Military Government in Thailand, 1947–1958*. Honolulu: University of Hawai'i Press, 1997.

Franz, Carol E. and Abigail J. Stewart. *Women Creating Lives: Identities, Resilience, and Resistance*. Boulder, CO: Westview Press, 1994.

Gedney, William J. "Siamese Verse Forms in Historical Perspective." In *Selected Papers on Comparative Tai Studies*, edited by Robert J. Bickner, John Hartmann, Thomas John Hudak, and Patcharin Peyasantiwong, 489–544. Michigan Papers on South and Southeast Asia, no. 29. Ann Arbor, MI: University of Michigan, Center for South and Southeast Asian Studies, 1988.

Gesick, Lorraine. *Kingship and Political Integration in Traditional Siam, 1767–1824*. PhD dissertation, Cornell University, 1976.

_____."The Rise and Fall of King Taksin: A Drama of Buddhist Kingship." In *Centers, Symbols, and Hierarchies: Essays on the Classical States of Southeast Asia*, edited by Lorraine Gesick, 87–105. Monograph Series no. 26. New Haven, CT: Yale University Southeast Asia Studies, 1983.

Gluck, Sherna Berger, and Daphne Patai, eds. *Women's Words: The Feminist Practice of Oral History*. New York and London: Routledge, 1991.

Gordon, Linda. "The Struggle for Reproductive Freedom: Three Stages of Feminism." In *Capitalist Patriarchy and the Case for Socialist Feminism*, edited by Zillah R. Eisenstein. 107–36. New York: Monthly Review Press, 1979.

Gross, Rita. *Buddhism after Patriarchy*. Albany, NY: State University of New York Press, 1993.

Guenther, Herbert V. *Buddhist Philosophy in Theory and Practice*. Boulder, CO and London: Shambhala, 1976.

Haberkorn, Tyrell. *Revolution Interrupted: Farmers, Students, Law, and Violence in Northern Thailand*. Chiang Mai: Silkworm Books, 2011.

Hamilton, Annette. "Rumours, Foul Calumnies and the Safety of the State: Mass Media and National Identity in Thailand." In Craig Reynolds, *National Identity*, 277–307.

Hanks, Jane. "A Rural Thai Village's View of Human Character." *Volume in honor of the eightieth birthday of His Highness Prince Dhaninivat Kromamun Bidyalabh Bidhyakorn*. Bangkok: The Siam Society, 1965.

_____. "Thai Character and Its Development." Unpublished draft, June 1959; used by permission of the author.

Hanks, Lucien. "Merit and Power in the Thai Social Order." *American Anthropologist* 64, no. 6 (1962): 1247–61.

_____."The Thai Social Order as Entourage and Circle." In Skinner et al., eds., *Change and Persistence in Thai Society*, 197–218.

Harrison, Rachel, trans. See Sidaoru'ang.

Havelock, Ellis. *The Muse Learns to Write: Reflections on Orality and Literacy from Antiquity to the Present*. New Haven, CT: Yale University Press, 1986.

Hayashi Fumiko. *Floating Clouds* [*Ukigumo*]. Translated by Y. Koitabashi. Tokyo: Information Publishers, 1957.

Heilbrun, Carolyn G. *Writing a Woman's Life*. New York: Ballantine Books, 1988.

Hudak, Thomas John. "Spelling Reforms of Field Marshall Pibulsongkram." *Crossroads* 3, no. 1 (1986): 123–33.

————, trans. *The Tale of Prince Samuttakote: A Buddhist Epic from Thailand*. Research in International Studies, Southeast Asia Series no. 90. Athens, OH: Ohio University Press, 1993.

Hunter, Eileen, and Narisa Chakrabongse. *Katya and the Prince of Siam*. Bangkok: River Books, 1994. Distributed by APA Publications (Thailand).

Ivarsson, Soren. "The Study of *Traiphum Phra Ruang*: Some Considerations." In *Thai Literary Traditions*, edited by Manas Chitkasem, 56–86. Bangkok: Chulalongkorn University Press, 1995.

Jiraporn Witayasakpan. "Nationalism and the Transformation of Aesthetic Concepts: Theatre in Thailand during the Phibun Period." PhD dissertation, Cornell University, 1992.

Jones, Daniel, ed. *The Poems of Dylan Thomas*. New York: New Directions, 1971.

Jottrand, Mr., and Mrs. Emile. *In Siam: The Diary of a Legal Adviser of King Chulalongkorn's Government*. Translated and with an introduction by Walter E. J. Tips. Bangkok: White Lotus, 1996.

Kabilsingh. See Chatsumarn Kabilsingh.

Kampoon Boontawee. *A Child of the Northeast* [*Luk Isan*]. Translated by Susan F. Kepner. Bangkok: Pouysian Publisher, 117/275 Soi 9/5 Banbuathong Bangrakpattana, Nonthaburi 11110, Thailand, n.d. (c. 2000).

Kartini, Raden Adjeng. *Letters of a Javanese Princess*. Translated by Agnes Louise Symmers. Kuala Lumpur: Oxford University Press, 1976.

Kepner, Susan F., trans. *A Child of the Northeast*. See Kampoon Boontawee.

————. "Dropping the Towel: Images of the Body in Contemporary Thai Women's Writing." In *Transnational Asia Pacific: Gender, Culture, and the Public Sphere*, edited by Shirley Geok-lin Lim, Larry E. Smith, and Wimal Dissanayake, 159–80. Urbana, IL: University of Illinois Press, 1999.

————, trans. "The Letter She Never Received." (Translation of a Thai short story by Sri Daoruang.) In *Tracks*, edited by Olivia Sears, Spring 1995 edition of *Two Lines: The Stanford Translation Journal*. Stanford, CA: Stanford University, 1995.

_____, trans. *Letters from Thailand*. See Botan.

_____. *The Lioness in Bloom*. Berkeley: University of California Press, 1996.

_____. *Married to the Demon King: Sri Dao Ruang's Tales of the Demon Folk*. Chiang Mai: Silkworm Books, 2004. Distributed by the University of Washington Press.

Keyes, Charles F. *Thailand: Buddhist Kingdom as Modern Nation-State*. Boulder, CO: Westview Press, 1987.

Khantipalo Bhikkhu. *Buddhism Explained*. Bangkok: Jareuk Publications, 1989 [reprint].

Kirsch, A. Thomas. "Text and Context: Buddhist Sex Roles/Culture of Gender Revisited." *American Ethnologist* 12, no. 2 (1985): 302–20.

Knight, Ruth Adams. *The Treasured One: The Story of Rudivoravan Princess of Siam*. New York: E. P. Dutton, 1957.

Kobkua Suwannathat-Pian. *Thailand's Durable Premier: Phibun through Three Decades, 1932–1957*. Kuala Lumpur: Oxford University Press, 1995.

Kruger, Rayne. *The Devil's Discus*. London: Cassell, 1964.

Kukrit Pramoj. *Four Reigns* [*Si phaendin*]. Translation by Tulachandra. Bangkok: Siam Rath, 1988.

Kumut, Chandruang. *My Boyhood in Siam*. New York: Frederick A. Praeger, 1969. Originally published by The John Day Company, 1938.

Landon, Kenneth Perry. *Siam in Transition: A Brief Survey of Cultural Trends in the Five Years since the Revolution of 1932*. Shanghai: Kelly and Walsh, 1939. Distributed by the University of Chicago Press.

Likhit Dhiravegin. *Demi Democracy: The Evolution of the Thai Political System*. Singapore: Times Academic Press, 1992.

Lowenthal, David. *The Past is a Foreign Country*. Cambridge: Cambridge University Press, 1993 [reprint].

Manas Chitkasem, ed. *Thai Literary Traditions*. Bangkok: Chulalongkorn University Press, 1995.

Montgomery, John D. *The Politics of Foreign Aid: American Experience in Southeast Asia*. New York: Praeger, 1962.

Morell, David, and Chai-anan Samudavanija. *Political Conflict in Thailand: Reform, Reaction, Revolution*. Cambridge, MA: Oelgeschlager, Gunn and Hain, 1981.

Morell, David, and Susan Morell. "The Impermanence of Society: Marxism, Buddhism and the Political Philosophy of Thailand's Pridi Banomyong." *Southeast Asia* 2 (Fall 1972): 4.

_____. "Open Politics in Thailand: The Costs of Political Conflict." *Pacific Community* 8, no. 2 (1977): 327–39.

Morris, Pam. *Literature and Feminism*. Oxford: Blackwell Publishers, 1993.

Muscat, Robert J. *Thailand and the United States: Development, Security, and Foreign Aid*. New York: Columbia University Press, 1990.

Navavan Bandhumedha. "Thai Views of Man as a Social Being." In Amara Pongsapich, ed., *Traditional and Changing Thai World View*, 86–109.

Neher, Arlene Becker. "Prelude to Alliance: The Expansion of American Economic Interest in Thailand during the 1940s." PhD dissertation, Northern Illinois University, 1980.

_____. Review of *Thailand's Durable Premier: Phibun through Three Decades, 1932–1957* by Kobkua Suwannathat-Pian. *Journal of Asian Studies* 55 (November 1996): 4.

Nitaya Masavisut. "Kindling the Literary Flame: Then and Now." In Manas Chitkasem, ed., *Thai Literary Traditions*, 1–28.

Ong, Aihwa, and Michael G. Peletz, eds. *Betwitching Women, Pious Men: Gender and Body Politics in Southeast Asia*. Berkeley: University of California Press, 1995.

Payuttho, P. A. *Dependent Origination: The Buddhist Law of Conditionality*. Translated by Bruce Evans. Bangkok: Buddhadhamma Foundation, 1994.

Pemberton, John. *On the Subject of "Java."* Ithaca, NY: Cornell University Press, 1994.

Phillips, Herbert P. *Modern Thai Literature: An Ethnographic Interpretation*. Honolulu: University of Hawaii Press, 1987.

_____. Taped interviews with M.L. Boonlua Debyasuvarn. Bangkok, 1966.

_____. Taped interviews with M.R. Kukrit Pramoj. Bangkok. 1966.

_____. Taped interviews with Sulak Sivaraksa. Bangkok, 1966.

Piker, Steven. *The Psychological Study of Theravada Societies*. Vol. 8, Contributions to Asian Studies, Canadian Association of South Asian Studies. Leiden: E. J. Brill, 1975.

Pimsai Svasti and Ping Amranand. *Siamese Memoirs: The Life and Times of Pimsai Svasti*. Bangkok: Asia Books, 2011.

Plion-Bernier, Raymond. *Festivals and Ceremonies of Thailand*. Translated by J. E. Soulier. Self-published, n.d.

Prudhisan Jumbala. "Interest and Pressure Groups." In Somsakdi, *Government and Politics*, 110–67.

_____. *Nation-building and Democratization in Thailand: A Political History*. Bangkok: Chulalongkorn University Social Research Institute, 1992.

_____. "Toward a Theory of Group Formation in Thai Society and Pressure Groups in Thailand after the October 1973 Uprising." *Asian Survey* 14, no. 6 (1974): 530–45.

Puey Ungphakorn. *Puey Ungphakorn: A Siamese for all Seasons*. Bangkok: Komol Keemthong Foundation, 1981.

Race, Jeffrey. "Thailand in 1974: A New Constitution. *"Asian Survey* 15, no. 2 (1975): 157–65.

Rahula, Walpola. *What the Buddha Taught*. New York: Grove Weidenfeld, 1974.

Ray, Jayanta K., Thawee Bunyaketu, and Seni Pramoj. *Portraits of Thai Politics*. New Delhi: Orient Longman,

Reid, Anthony, and David Marr, eds. *Perceptions of the Past in Southeast Asia*. Singapore: Heinemann Educational Books (Asia), 1979.

Reynolds, Craig. "The Case of K.S.R. Kulap: A Challenge to Royal Historical Writing in Late Nineteenth Century Thailand." *Journal of the Siam Society* 61, no. 2 (1973): 63–90.

———, ed. *National Identity and Its Defenders: Thailand, 1939–1989*. Chiang Mai, Thailand: Silkworm Books, 1991.

———. *Thai Radical Discourse: The Real Face of Thai Feudalism Today*. Ithaca, NY: Cornell University Southeast Asia Research Program, 1987.

Reynolds, Frank E. "Sacral Kingship and National Development: The Case of Thailand." In *Religion and Legitimation of Power in Thailand, Laos, and Burma*, edited by Bardwell Smith, 100–110. Chambersburg, PA: Anima Books, Conococheague Associates, 1978.

Rhiel, Mary, and David Suchoff. *The Seductions of Biography*. New York: Routledge, 1996.

Riggs, Fred Warren. *Thailand: The Modernization of a Bureaucratic Polity*. Honolulu: East-West Center Press, 1966.

Rudivoravan (Princess). See Knight, Ruth Adams.

Russ, Joanna. *To Write Like a Woman: Essays in Feminism and Science Fiction*. Bloomington and Indianapolis, IN: University of Indiana Press, 1995.

Saitip Sukatipan. "Thailand: The Evolution of Legitimacy." In *Political Legitimacy in Southeast Asia: The Quest for Moral Authority*, edited by Alagappa, Muthiah. Stanford, CA: Stanford University Press, 1995.

Sarasas Balakhan (Phra). *My Country Thailand: Its History, Geography, and Civilization*. Bangkok: C. Chakrabandhu, 1942. [Rev. ed. 1956.]

Sathirakoses. See Anuman Rajadhon.

Seni Pramoj and Kukrit Pramoj. *A King of Siam Speaks*. Bangkok: The Siam Society, 1987.

Seni Pramoj. "Political Memoir." In *Portraits of Thai Politics* by Jayanta K. Ray, Thawee Bunyaketu, and Seni Pramoj. New Delhi: Orient Longman, 1972.

Seri Phongphit. *Religion in a Changing Society: Buddhism, Reform and the Role of Monks in Community Development in Thailand*. Hong Kong: Arena Press, 1988.

Shari, M. H., ed. *Culture and Environment in Thailand: Dynamics of a Complex Relationship*. Bangkok: The Siam Society, 1988.

Siburapha (pen name of Kulab Saipradit). *Behind the Painting and Other Stories*. Translated and with an introduction by David Smyth. Singapore: Oxford University Press, 1992.

Sidaoru'ang (Sri Daoruang). *A Drop of Glass and Other Stories [Kaeo yot diao]*. Translated and edited by Rachel Harrison. Bangkok: Duang Kamol, 1994.

Siphroma Kridakon (Lady). *The Autobiography of Lady Siphroma Kridakon*. Translated by Pongsuwan T. Bilmes. Southeast Asia Paper no. 22, Center for Asian and Pacific Studies. Honolulu: University of Hawaii at Manoa, 1982.

Skinner, G. William, Lauriston Sharp, and A. Thomas Kirsch, eds. *Change and Persistence in Thai Society: Essays in Honor of Lauriston Sharp*. Ithaca and London: Cornell University Press, 1975.

Smith, Bardwell L., ed. *Religion and Legitimation of Power in Thailand, Laos, and Burma*. Chambersburg, PA: Anima Books, Conococheague Associates, 1978.

Smith, Malcolm. *A Physician at the Court of Siam*. Kuala Lumpur: Oxford University Press, 1982.

Smithies, Michael. *Descriptions of Old Siam*. Kuala Lumpur: Oxford University Press, 1995.

Smyth, David, trans. *Behind the Painting and Other Stories*. See Siburapha.

————, trans. *The Prostitute*. See Surangkanang,

Somsakdi, Xuto, ed. *Government and Politics of Thailand*. Singapore: Southeast Asia Studies Program, Oxford University Press, 1987.

Spender, Dale, ed. *Feminist Theorists: Three Centuries of Key Women Thinkers*. New York: Pantheon Books, 1983.

Sri Thanonchai, Thailand's Artful Trickster. Bangkok: Naga Books, 1991.

Stanton, Domna C., ed. *The Female Autograph*. Chicago and London: The University of Chicago Press, 1987.

Stewart, Abigail J. "Toward a Feminist Strategy for Studying Women's Lives." In *Women Creating Lives*, edited by Carol E. Franz and Abigail J. Stewart, 11–36. Boulder, CO: Westview Press, 1994.

Strehlow, Ted. See Dokmai Sot.

Stowe, Judith A. *Siam Becomes Thailand: A Story of Intrigue*. Honolulu: University of Hawaii Press, 1991.

Suchit Bunbongkarn. "Political Institutions and Processes." In Somsakdi, *Government and Politics*, 41–74.

Sulak Sivaraksa. *A Buddhist Vision for Renewing Society*. Bangkok: Thai Inter-religious Commission for Development, 1994.

_____. "The Crisis of Siamese Identity." In Craig Reynolds, *National Identity*, 33–48.

Sulloway, Frank J. *Born to Rebel: Birth Order, Family Dynamics, and Revolutionary Genius*. New York: Pantheon Books, 1996.

Suntaree Komin. *Psychology of the Thai People: Values and Behavioral Patterns*. Bangkok: Research Center, National Institute of Development Administration (NIDA), 1990.

Sunthorn Plamintr. *Getting to Know Buddhism*. Bangkok: Buddhadhamma Foundation, 1994.

"Supawaan" (pen name). "A Writer of Books: M.L. Boonlua Debyasuvarn." *Siam Rath*, 23 November 1977, 9.

Surangkanang, K. (pen name of Kanha Kiangsiri). *The Prostitute [Ying khon chua]*. Translated and with an introduction by David Smyth. Singapore: Oxford University Press, 1994.

Suzuki, Tomi. *Narrating the Self: Fictions of Japanese Modernity*. Stanford, CA: Stanford University Press, 1996.

Swearer, Donald. *The Buddhist World of Southeast Asia*. SUNY Series in Religion. Albany, NY: State University of New York Press, 1995.

Thak Chaloemtiarana. *Thailand: The Politics of Despotic Paternalism*. Chiang Mai: Silkworm Books, 2007. First published 1979 by Social Science Association of Thailand.

_____, ed. *Thai Politics: Extracts and Documents 1932–1957*. Bangkok: Social Science Association of Thailand, Thammasat University, 1978.

Thamsook Numnonda. "Phibulsongkram's Thai Nation-Building Programme during the Japanese Military Presence, 1941–1945." *Journal of Southeast Asian Studies* 9, no. 2 (September 1978): 234–47.

_____. *Thailand and the Japanese Presence, 1941–1945*. Singapore: Institute of Southeast Asian Studies, 1977.

Thawatt Mokarapong. *History of the Thai Revolution: A Study in Political Behaviour*. Bangkok: Chalermnit, 1972.

Thinaphan Nakata. "Political Culture: Problems of Development of Democracy." In Somsakdi, *Government and Politics*, 168–95.

_____. *The Problems of Democracy in Thailand: A Study of Political Culture and Socialization of College Students*. Bangkok: Prae Pittaya, 1975.

Thomas, Dylan. See Jones, Daniel.

Thompson, Virginia. *Thailand: The New Siam*. New York: Paragon Book Reprint Corporation, 1967. Originally published in 1941 under the auspices of the Secretariat, Institute of Public Relations, International Research Service.

Thongchai Winichakul. "The Changing Landscape of the Past: New Histories in Thailand Since 1973." *Journal of Southeast Asian Studies* 26, no. 1 (March1995): 99–120.

————. *Siam Mapped: A History of the Geo-Body of a Nation*. Honolulu: University of Hawaii Press, 1994.

Todd, Janet. *Women's Friendship in Literature*. New York: Columbia University Press, 1980.

Trisilpa Bunkhachorn. "The Unfinished Pagoda: An Epistemological Perspective on the Theory of Intertextuality." In *Comparative Literature*, Center for Research in Comparative Literature. Bangkok: Chulalongkorn University, 1993. (This is a Thai-language book, except for this essay and Chetana Nagavajara's essay, "Spatial Concentration and Emotional Intensity: Inspiration from Sartre and Camus in the Works of a Contemporary Thai Novelist" [Chati Kobjitti].)

Vadakarn, Vichitr. *Thailand's Case*. Bangkok: 1941. (Unidentified publisher; published under the auspices of the Thai government.)

Van Praagh, David. *Seni Pramoj, Alone on the Sharp Edge: The Story of M.R. Seni Pramoj and Thailand's Struggle for Democracy*. Bangkok: Editions Duang Kamol, 1989.

Vella, Walter F. *Chaiyo! King Vajiravudh and the Development of Thai Nationalism*. Honolulu: University of Hawaii Press, 1978.

Vichitvong Na Pombhejara. *Pridi Banomyong and the Making of Thailand's Modern History*. Singapore: Institute of Southeast Asian Studies, 1980.

————. *Siam under Rama III: 1824–1851*. Locust Valley, NY: J. J. Augustin (for the Association for Asian Studies), 1957.

Wagner-Martin, Linda. *Telling Women's Lives: The New Biography*. New Brunswick, NJ: Rutgers University Press, 1994.

Wales, H. G. Quaritch. *Siamese State Ceremonies: Their History and Function*. London: H. G. Quaritch, 1931.

Wan Waithayakon (Prince Wan). "Coining Thai Words." In *In Memoriam: Phya Anuman Rajadhon*, edited by Tej Bunnag and Michael Smithies, 33–38. Bangkok: Siam Society, 1970.

————. "Thai Culture. "*Journal of the Thai Research Society*, September 1944, 135–45.

Watakan. See Vadakarn, Vichitr.

Watson, C. W., and Roy Ellen, eds. *Understanding Witchcraft and Sorcery in Southeast Asia*. Honolulu: University of Hawaii Press, 1993.

Wedel, Paul, and Yuangrat Wedel. *Radical Thought, Thai Mind: The Development of Revolutionary Ideas in Thailand*. Bangkok: Assumption Business Administration College, 1987.

Wibha Senanan [Kongkana]. *Genesis of the Thai Novel*. Bangkok: Thai Watana Panich, 1975.

Wijeyewardene, Gehan, and E. C. Chapman, eds. *Patterns and Illusions: Thai History and Thought*. Published by the Richard Davis Fund and the Department of Anthropology, Research School of Pacific Studies, The Australian National University, Canberra, under the auspices of the Institute of Southeast Asian Studies, Singapore, 1993.

Wilson, David A. *Politics in Thailand*. Ithaca, NY: Cornell University Press, 1962.

Wolters, O. W. *History, Culture, and Region in Southeast Asian Perspectives*. Singapore: Institute of Southeast Asian Studies, 1982.

————. "Southeast Asia as a Southeast Asian Field of Study." *Indonesia* 58 (October 1994): 1–17.

Wray, Elizabeth, et al. *Ten Lives of The Buddha: Siamese Temple Painting and Jataka Tales*. New York: Weatherhill, 1996.

Wright, Joseph J. Jr. *The Balancing Act: A History of Modern Thailand*. Oakland, CA: Pacific Rim Press, 1991.

Wyatt, David K. *Studies in Thai History*. Chiang Mai: Silkworm Books, 1994.

————. *Thailand: A Short History*. New Haven: Yale University Press, 1984.

Yos Santasombat. "Power and Personality: An Anthropological Study of the Thai Political Elite." PhD dissertation, University of California, Berkeley, 1985.

WORKS IN THAI

Bun bamphen [Merit fulfilled]. Cremation volume for M.L. Boonlua Kunchon Debyasuvarn. Bangkok: Dansuthakanphim, 1984.

Chai-anan Samudavanija. *Prachathipatai sangkhom niyom kap kan mueang thai* [Democracy, socialism, communism, and Thai politics]. Bangkok: Pitkaness Press, 1976.

Chit Phumisak. *Khwam pen ma khong kham sayam thai lao lae khom lae laksana thang sangkhom khong chawa* [Origins of Siamese, Thai, Lao and Khmer words, and characteristics of Javanese society. Bangkok: Duang Kamol, 1981.

Chontira Kladyu. *Wannakhadi khong puang chon* [Literature of all the people]. Bangkok: Aksorn, 1974.

_____. *Trai phum phra ruang: Lakthan khong udomkan mueang thai* [Traiphum Phra Ruang: The foundation of Thai political ideology]. *Warasan Thammasat* 4, no. 1 (1974): 106–21.

Chulalongkorn, King. *Chotmaihet prakop rueang klai ban* (Letters written far from home). Bangkok: Thammasat University, 1941.

Dokmai Sot (pen name of Buppha Kunchon Nimmanhemin). *Phu di* [People of Quality]. Bangkok: Bannakan, 1973.

_____. *Wannakam chin sut thai* [The last bit of literature]. Bangkok: Prae Pittaya, 1964.

Kanchana Nakana. *Phuyai Li kap nang Ma* [Headman Li and his wife Nang Ma]. Bangkok: Prae Pittaya, 1963. (Excerpts of a film based upon the novel can be accessed at YouTube.com.

Kanpirom Suwannanonda. *Phrabat Somdet Phra Mongkut Klao chao yu hua kap kan sang chat thai.* [King Vajiravudh and his nation-building program]. PhD dissertation, Chulalongkorn University, Bangkok, 1981.

Kukrit Pramoj. *Si phaendin* (Four reigns). Bangkok: Siam Rath, 1988. Originally published in 1953 by Prae Pittaya.

Kusuma Raksamanee. *Si san wannakhadi* (The colors of literature). Bangkok: Siam Publishing, 1991.

Naowarat Pongpaiboon. *Phiang khwam khluean wai* [Mere movement]. In Thai, with English translations. Bangkok: Kiaw Klao, fifth printing 1995.

Naritsaranuwattiwong (Prince Narit). *Bot lakhon duekdamban chabap boribun...* (The complete edition of *lakhon* composed by H.R.H. Prince Naritsaranuwattiwong). Published as the cremation volume for Khatawut Intharathut, n.p., 1986. (Note: A copy of this work is located at the University of California, Berkeley libraries, under "Naritsarānuwattiwong, Prince, son of Mongkut, King of Siam, 1863–1947.")

Nitthi Aeursriwongse. "*Amnat phi-set nai watthanatham thai*" (Special power in Thai culture). *Matichon Sut Saphada*, August 24, 1997.

_____. *Chat thai mueang thai baep rian lae anusawari* [Thai nation, land of the Thai, how students learn, and monuments]. Bangkok: Matichon, 1995.

_____. *Phithikam khong rat lae sangkhom* [Rituals of state and society]. *Matichon Sut Saphada*, August 17, 1997.

_____. *Sao phromachan*. [Young virgin women]. *Matichon Sut Saphada*, August 10, 1997.

Phluang Na Nakhon. *Prawat wannakhadi thai samrap nakrian* [History of Thai literature for students]. Bangkok: Thai Watana Panich, 1980.

Sang Pattanothai. *Khwam nuek nai khrong khang* [Reflections while in prison]. Bangkok: Prasanchaiyasit, 1956.

Silpakorn University Central Library. *Nithat kan chiwit lae ngan satrachan phi-set M.L. Boonlua Debyasuvarn* [Life and work of Adjunct Professor M.L. Boonlua Debyasuvarn]. Brochure published for a four-day memorial program in honor of M.L. Boonlua, 13–17 December 1983. Nakhon Pathom, Thailand: Silpakorn University, December 1983.

Somphop Chantaraprapha. *Chiwit lae ngan khong Dokmai Sot* [The life and work of Dokmaisot]. Bangkok: Bamrungsan, 1986.

Suchat Sawatsri. *"70 pi M.L. Boonlua Debyasuvarn"* [Interview with M.L. Boonlua during her seventieth year]. *Lok nangsue* (World of Books).

Sumalee Wirawong, ed. *Roi kaeo naeo mai khong thai 2417–2453* [The new path of Thai prose fiction,1874–1910]. Bangkok: P.E.N. International Thailand Centre, 1987.

Supawaan (pen name). *"Khon khian nangsue: ML Boonlua Debyasuvarn."* [A writer of books: M.L. Boonlua Debyasuvarn]. *Siam Rath*, 23 November 1977, 9.

Suwanna Kriangkraipetch and Suchitra Chongsathitwattana, eds. *Tho mai nai sai nam: 200 pi wannakhadi wichan thai* [A silk-loom in the river: Two hundred years of Thai literary criticism]. Bangkok: Pachariyasan, n.d. (c. 1985).

Thai National Women's Council. *Rueang satri thai* [About Thai women]. Bangkok: Thai National Women's Council, 1975.

Tianchai Iamworamate. *Pochananukrom thai-angkrit chabap mai* (Thai-English dictionary, new edition) Bangkok: Bamrungsan, 1989.

Vajiravudh, King. *Wenit wanit* [Translation of William Shakespeare's *Merchant of Venice*]. Bangkok: Khlang Witaya, 1970.

Vinita Diteeyont. "Phaphalak khong phuying nai nawaniyai thai nai adit lae patchuban" [Characteristics of women in Thai novels of the past and present]. In *Song thotsawat akson sinlapakon* (Two decades of the Faculty of Arts at Silpakorn University). Bangkok: Homecoming Committee, Faculty of Arts, Silpakorn University, 1987.

Warunee Osatharom. *Kan sueksa nai sangkhom thai 2411–2475* [Education in Thai society 1868–1932]. PhD dissertation, Chulalongkorn University, Bangkok, 1981.

Wibha (Senanan) Kongkanan. "Satri nai botpraphan khong mom luang Boonlua" [Women in the Writing of Mom Luang Boonlua Debyasuvarn]. Lecture presented at the Faculty of Arts, Silpakorn University, Nakhon Pathom, 18 August 1994.

Win Liao-warin. *Prachathipatai bon sen khanan* [Democracy on a parallel]. Bangkok: Dok Ya, 1994.

Worawetphisit (Phra). *Wannakhadi* [Thai literature]. Bangkok: Rare Books Project, Center for Thai Language and Literature, Faculty of Arts, Chulalongkorn University, 1991. Originally published in 1959.

SELECTED WORKS OF M.L. BOONLUA DEBYASUVARN (ANNOTATED)

Chak nueng nai chiwit [One scene in a lifetime]. Bangkok: Bankij, 1977. Collection of short stories.

Dr. luk thung [also known as "Rural doctor"]. Bangkok: Prae Pittaya, 1973. Novel.

"The Enchanting Cooking Spoon." In *Modern Thai Literature: An Ethnographic Interpretation,* by Herbert P. Phillips. Translated by Herbert P. Phillips. Original Thai version in M.L. Boonlua, *Chak nueng nai chiwit.* Short story.

Hua liao khong wannakhadi thai [The turning point of Thai literature]. Bangkok: Thai Watana Panich, 1973. Essays on Thai literature.

Kan aphiprai rueang nawaniyai khong Dokmai Sot [Memorial address on the novels of Dokmai Sot]. Presented in Bangkok at the National Library, February 17, 1971.

Khwam samret lae khwam lom laeo [Successes and failures]. Bangkok: Social Science Association of Thailand, 1973. Memoir.

Khwam-suk khong satri [Women's happiness]. Bangkok: Mental Health Association of Thailand, 1973. Essay.

Nae naeo thang kan sueksa wicha wannakhadi [Path to the study of literature]. Bangkok: Banthit Kan Phim, 1975. Textbook.

Phasa angkrit [English language]. Bangkok: Krom Wichakan, 1962. Textbook for secondary students.

Phasa thai wicha thi thuk luem [Thai language, a subject that has been forgotten]. Bangkok: Educational Inspection Unit of the Ministry of Education, 1975. Essay.

Ruap ruam rueang san chak saharat America [Collected short stories from America]. Bangkok: Sahamitr Kan Phim, 1972. Translations of American short stories.

Rueang khong chang Phlai Mongkhon phu aphap [Story of Phlai Mongkhon the unfortunate elephant]. Bangkok: Aksonsamai, 1971. Story based on a true event, followed by an essay on Thai culture and history related to the story, including information on Boonlua's family.

Sane plai chawak. See under "The Enchanting Cooking Spoon."

Saphai maem [Western daughter-in-law]. Bangkok: Prae Pittaya, 1962. Novel.

Suratnari [Land of women]. Bangkok: Prae Pittaya, 1972. Novel.

Than phu chit charoen [A mature/highly developed man]. Bangkok: Suan Thong Thin, under the auspices of Chulalongkorn University, 1964. Essay on Prince Narit.

Thutiyawiset [the name of a government decoration awarded to the wife of a high-ranking man, or to another woman who has made substantial contributions of her own to the kingdom]. Bangkok: Prae Pittaya, 1968. Novel.

Tok lum tok rong dai-dai ko di [A perilous fall into love. Bangkok: Prae Pittaya, 1969. Novel.

Uphayobai. Nakhon Pathom: Faculty of Arts, Silpakorn University, 1983. Drama written for school performance at Mater Dei School in 1946.

Waen wannakam [Lens on literature]. Bangkok: An Thai, 1986. Essays on Thai literature.

Watthanatham khong khon thi phut phasa angkrit [Cultures of English-speaking peoples]. Bangkok: Ministry of Education, 1973. Essays.

INTERVIEWS BY THE AUTHOR

Khunying Ambhorn Meesook

Anong Lertrakskul

Mom Anuwong Chirapravat na Ayudhya

Bear, Michael D., MD

Chetana Nagavajara

Chom Debyasuvarn, MD

Chusak Pattarakulvanit

Foy-faa Phanuphak

Kanchanee Winicchayakul

Micco, Guy, MD

Nappa Phongphipat

Nitaya Masavisut

Panpimon Gajasuta

Pariyachart Chaiyarat Bear

M.L. Pattaratorn Chirapravat

Ambassador Nid Pibulsonggram

Pibulsonggram, Patricia

Revadee Crabbe

Rukchira Akarasena

San Techakampuch

Siraporn Sangprabha

Sirilak Rangsiklat

Her Royal Highness Maha Chakri Princess Sirindhorn

Smith, Larry
Suchat Sawatsri
Sulak Sivaraksa
Supa Sirising (Botan)
M.R. Supicha Sonakul
Termsak Kritsanamara
Thamsook Numnonda
Thappani Nakhonthap
Thongchai Winichakul
Khunying Vinita Diteeyont
Wanpen Chantarawirot
Warunyubha Sanitwongse na Ayuthya
Wibha Kongkanan
Yupin Chantaracheroensin

INDEX

absolute monarchy, 80–81, 97, 115. *See also* overthrow of absolute monarchy
aesthetics, 18
Ambhorn Meesook, 179, 188, 200, 209, 348, 369n9
American Association of University Women, 171–72, 175–76
Analysis of Thai Literature (Wikhro rot wannadkhadi thai), 317
Ananda Mahidol, King (Rama VIII), 89, 144, 149, 162–67
  death of, 165, 376n15
Anuman Rajadhon, Phya, 96, 216, 272, 369n5
Anut Aphapirom, 300
Anuwong's rebellion, 7
Anuwong Chirapravat na Ayudhya (niece), 54, 107, 177, 334
  childhood competition with Boonlua, 17, 29, 46, 48, 102, 107
  at Convent of the Holy Infant Jesus, 8, 46, 48, 52, 361n23, 361n25

Ban Mo theater, 43–44, 59–61
Bang Saen Teachers College, 191, 201, 203, 205, 209, 220, 225
  Boonlua as vice-rector at, 203–8
Bear, Michael, 334–35
Bear, Pariyachart (Chaiyarat), 334–35
betel chewing, 2, 69, 143, 150
Bhumibol Adulyadej, King, 163, 165, 190, 290, 369
Boonlua (Kunchon) Debyasuvarn
  ancestry and heritage, 7–8
  awarded Chula Chom Klao medal, 284–85
  birth, 1
  Buddhist training and beliefs, 2, 30, 42, 50, 187, 205, 219, 347
  and Buppha, 14–15, 30, 61, 102–5, 224, 238, 270, 339
  career
    Education Inspection Unit, 180–81
    Triam Udom school, 183
    Bang Saen Teachers College, 203
    Thammasat University, 218–19
    Silpakorn University, 225–33

409

Wichit Wathakan, Luang (*cont.*)
   and culture construction, 140,
      145–48
   and relationship with Japan, 131
   and radio plays during World War
      II, 142
Wiratham, Fourteen, 146–48, 374n40,
      374n42
Wong, Mom, 25
Worawetphisit, Phra, 316
World War II, 122, 123–24, 128–32, 137,
      144, 160–61
   and Boonlua, 153, 155
   in *Four Reigns*, 136
   and Japan, 131–32, 135–36, 142
   in *Khu Kam*, 137
   and lost territories, 131–32
   in *Western Daughter-in-Law*, 132,
      134, 152, 156, 240, 249

Yos Santasombat, 62, 80